Against Injustice

T0328814

Traditional theories of justice as formulated by political philosophers, jurists, and economists have all tended to see injustice as simply a breach of justice, a breakdown of the normal order. Amartya Sen's work acts as a corrective to this tradition by arguing that we can recognize patent injustices and come to a reasoned agreement about the need to remedy them, without reference to an explicit theory of justice. *Against Injustice* brings together distinguished academics from a variety of different fields – including economics, law, philosophy, and anthropology – to explore the ideas underlying Sen's critique of traditional approaches to injustice. The centerpiece of the book is the first chapter by Sen, in which he outlines his conception of the relationship between economics, law, and ethics. The rest of book addresses a variety of theoretical and empirical issues that relate to this conception, concluding with a response from Sen to his critics.

REIKO GOTOH is Full Professor in the Graduate School of Core Ethics and Frontier Sciences at Ritsumeikan University, Japan.

PAUL DUMOUCHEL is Full Professor in the Graduate School of Core Ethics and Frontier Sciences at Ritsumeikan University, Japan.

Against Injustice

The New Economics of Amartya Sen

Edited by

Reiko Gotoh

Paul Dumouchel

CAMBRIDGE UNIVERSITY PRESS
Cambridge, New York, Melbourne, Madrid, Cape Town, Singapore,
São Paulo, Delhi, Dubai, Tokyo, Mexico City

Cambridge University Press
The Edinburgh Building, Cambridge CB2 8RU, UK

Published in the United States of America by Cambridge University Press, New York

www.cambridge.org
Information on this title: www.cambridge.org/9780521182614

© Cambridge University Press 2009

First published 2009
First paperback edition 2010

A catalogue record for this publication is available from the British Library

ISBN 978-0-521-89959-8 Hardback
ISBN 978-0-521-18261-4 Paperback

Contents

Figures

Tables

Contributors

ANDREA BRANDOLINI Economist, Department of Structural Economic Analysis, Bank of Italy

JOHN BROOME White's Professor of Moral Philosophy and Fellow of Corpus Christi College, University of Oxford

FLAVIO COMIM Senior Economist, United Nations Development Programme in Brazil

JEAN-LUC DUBOIS Director of Research at IRD (Institut de Recherche sur le Développement) and Researcher at C3ED (Centre d'économie et d'éthique pour le développement), University of Versailles

PAUL DUMOUCHEL Professor of Philosophy, Graduate School of Core Ethics and Frontier Sciences, Ritsumeikan University

REIKO GOTOH Professor of Economic Philosophy, Graduate School of Core Ethics and Frontier Sciences, Ritsumeikan University

MARCEL HÉNAFF Professor of Philosophy and Anthropology, Department of Political Science, University of California, San Diego

MARTHA C. NUSSBAUM Ernst Freund Distinguished Service Professor of Law and Ethics, Law and Philosophy, The University of Chicago

PRASANTA K. PATTANAIK Professor of Economics, University of California, Riverside

PHILIP PETTIT Laurance S. Rockefeller University Professor of Politics and Human Values, Princeton University

AMARTYA SEN Lamont University Professor and Professor of Economics and Philosophy, Harvard University

YONGSHENG XU Professor of Economics, Georgia State University

Acknowledgements

The editors wish to thank all those who helped make this project a success, both the book itself and the 2005 International Conference "Ethics, Economics, and Law: Against Injustice" held at Ritsumeikan University, Kyoto, Japan, on which this volume is based. First we want to thank all the participants in the conference, speakers, chairs, or commentators, in particular Kozo Watanabe, Kotaro Suzumura, Monte Cassim, David Estlund, Enrica Chiappero-Martinetti, Sabina Alkire, Basudeb Chaudhuri, Anantha Duraiappah, as well as discussants Yoshiki Wakamatsu, Noriatsu Matsui, Ko Hasegawa, Koichi Suga, Koichi Tadenuma, Naoki Yoshihara, Makoto Usami, Susumu Morimura, Hitohiko Hirano, Shinichiro Hama, Yuko Kamishima, Noriko Kashiwazaki, Madoka Saito, Kumiko Otsuka, Iwao Hirose. Taku Saito provided substantial help in the revision of the manuscript. Students of the Graduate School of Core Ethics and Frontier Sciences and the Research Staff of Ritsumeikan University gave us indispensable support during the conference itself and the rest of this project. We also want to thank the HDCA (Human Development and Capability Association), in the framework of which the 2005 conference was organized. Finally, we are grateful to JSPS (Japan Society for the Promotion of Science) for grant 16330055 "The Idea of Global Welfare System Based on a Formulation of the Capability Approach" as well as grant 17633003 "International Meeting towards the Capability Conference in Japan" and to Ritsumeikan University for financial support.

Introduction

Reiko Gotoh and Paul Dumouchel

Most injustices occur continuously within the framework of an established polity with an operative system of law, in normal times. Often, it is the very people who are supposed to prevent injustice who, in their official capacity, commit the gravest acts of injustice, without much protest from the citizenry.[1]

Amartya Sen's alternative economics: a new methodology for a theory of justice

"Why then," asks Judith Shklar, "do most philosophers refuse to think about injustice as deeply or as subtly as they do about justice?"[2] Philosophers, she argues, generally construe injustice as a breach of justice, as a breakdown or transgression of the normal order of the world. Therefore, even when they do not agree with Hobbes that "Where there is no common power, there is no law; where no law, no injustice,"[3] they spontaneously think of injustice against the background of a conception of justice, as if injustices were invisible and made no sense outside a shared ideal of justice.

In Amartya Sen's work the expression "against injustice" is inseparable from the idea of "patent injustice" and indicates that the perception of injustice comes first. "Against injustice" as it is understood by Sen constitutes a challenge to most theories of justice. One that says that the recognition of patent injustices is possible without reference to an explicit theory of justice, and that coming to a reasoned agreement about such injustices and the need to remedy them does not presuppose a shared conception of justice. How can this be possible?

Themes and subjects

In *Development as Freedom* (1999) Sen states that "The greatest relevance of the idea of justice lies in the identification of patent injustice,

---

[1] Shklar (1990: 19).   [2] Ibid.: 16.   [3] Hobbes (1994: 78).

on which reasoned agreement is possible, rather than in the derivation of some extant formula for how the world should be precisely run" (Sen 1999: 287).[4] This statement expresses in a condensed form the gist of Sen's stand "against injustice" and of his critique of traditional theories of justice formulated by political philosophers, jurists, and economists (i.e. Rawls, Dworkin, or utilitarianism, or social welfare function approaches). The goal of this volume is to explore the ideas underlying Sen's critique of these traditional methods and to pursue a new road to the idea of justice. Our strategy is, beginning with Sen's original contribution to this volume, to discuss in detail his criticism of the relation between economics, ethics, and laws, and then to work towards a better understanding of "against injustice" with the help of political philosophers and economists who share the spirit of Sen's critique.

In this introduction, we wish, before presenting the various contributions, to re-examine some methodological features of economic thinking in order to analyze both its limits, which Sen points out in his criticism of the law and economics movement, and its merits, on which he builds in his critique of ideal ethical approaches to justice. History has shown that too much as well as too little of the influence of economic thinking distorts the idea of justice. Economic thought crystallized into clear conceptions some dimensions of our daily mode of thinking; however, through that very process it also closed to further reflection and hid from view other aspects of life. Because of this questions arise about which parts of economic thinking an inquiry concerning justice should take on and which it should leave out, and why. These questions in turn lead us to revisit Sen's new perspective on economics, for it provides, we will argue, an alternative methodology to address issues of justice.

In the first chapter of this volume Sen compares and contrasts two types of approaches to the question of justice. Those of the first type, which he rejects and criticizes, he names "transcendental approaches." They aim at finding perfectly just social arrangements, and he associates them with philosophical theories of justice. The second type, "comparative approaches," concentrates on ranking alternative social arrangements (whether an arrangement is "less just" or "more just" than another) and is characteristic of the way questions of justice have been addressed within economics. This simple dichotomy may invite a number of objections, either from philosophers who seek to balance a plurality of values in their attempt at reforming society or from

---

[4] All references to Sen will be given directly in parentheses in the main body of the text.

economists who pursue favored conditions for optimal solutions that might be interpreted as "best" or "most just." Further, the comparative approaches may be accused of weakening the impact of the idea of justice and its ability to induce reforms, as well as of neglecting the difference between different conceptions of justice like fairness or equity. Finally Sen's own conception of "patent" injustice might open him to accusations of "transcendentalism," given that it apparently rests on an ethical judgment free from all justification, something which both economic thinking and philosophy should try to avoid.

In order to respond to these objections and understand better Sen's criticism, it is necessary first to pay attention, precisely, to what his perspective abandons and what it retains from traditional economics. Second, we need to explore the possibility of extending the comparative approach in order to be able to make consistent use of the idea of "patent injustice" within a comparative framework. Once again it is in Sen's economics, in his perspective as a whole, including the capability approach and social choice theory, that we find a sketch of a positive answer. To wit: a social choice procedure that can specify a social evaluation to avoid "patent injustice," or at least which allows us to choose less unjust "patent injustice." This somewhat paradoxical expression means, as we will see in more detail later on, a social state which is "patently unjust," but nonetheless "maximal" given existing economic circumstances.

Merits and pitfalls of economic thinking

According to Sen, one of the fundamental merits of economic thinking in its approach to justice lies in its ability to make comparative evaluations over alternative options. Each option is evaluated as "better than" or "same as" another. When on the basis of such evaluations a complete ordering of all alternatives is possible, the "optimal set" can be defined as the set of alternatives that is at least as good as all others. In such cases, one can be tempted to interpret elements belonging to the optimal set as just and other alternatives as unjust. In partitioning thus the world in two, with the optimal set corresponding to the set of all just alternatives, economics can mimic "transcendental" theories of justice. However, the interest of economic thinking is not in dividing the world in this way. Rather it is in ranking all options in the search for solutions in diverse circumstances, solutions that are relative to the set of feasible social states, which may change depending on economic conditions. This relativity entails that the distance separating any two alternatives belonging to the optimal set, or two alternatives which do not so belong, cannot be assumed to be smaller than the distance between any two alternatives, one of which is an element of the optimal set and the other which is not. In other words, being an element of the optimal set does not reflect a radical difference between alternatives.

Another important characteristic of economic thinking in this context is the assumption of substitutability among plural goods which assumes that different alternatives made up of a plurality of goods in varying proportions, like consumption vectors, can be considered equivalent. Technically a substitution pattern is represented by an "indifference curve." Indifference curves vary according to the amount of each individual good among the plurality of goods. Therefore a lexicographical order of preferences, one that gives complete priority to one specific good, constitutes an exception rather than the rule. It corresponds to a very particular pattern of substitution. These two characteristics taken together distinguish economic thinking from "transcendental approaches," and have the further advantage that they help avoid strong conflicts among individual interests. For example, it might be true that we can never erase scars left from historical injustice, yet it might be possible to mitigate the victims' current agonies by preventing further expansion of social and economic disadvantage through appropriate systems of economic compensation.

Kenneth Arrow (1963) suggested that if individual preferences can be interpreted not only as the expression of individual tastes, but also as individuals' "values on values,"[5] (that is to say as the evaluations individuals give to different values), it should be possible to extend economic thinking to the issues of justice, by replacing consumption vectors by social policies, preferences by normative evaluations, and plural goods by a plurality of ethical values. Given this interpretation, an individual evaluation can allow for substitution between different ethical values and lead to comparative judgments over alternative social policies that embody a plurality of ethical values in different proportions. Indeed, Bergson–Samuelson's type of social welfare functions can be understood as evaluations of a social planner that have precisely these characteristics. They are also known to bring optimal solutions under favorable economic circumstances.

This extension of economic thinking to the field of ethical judgments faces several difficulties, however. The first is that without information similar to market prices, there is no guarantee that individual evaluations can be aggregated in a social evaluation leading to a social optimum satisfying certain reasonable conditions. This is the problem

[5] Arrow (1963: 18).

Arrow addressed and which led to his famous impossibility theorem.[6] Moreover, even if we succeed in constructing a social evaluation leading to a social optimum, for example by introducing an assumption concerning the interpersonal comparison of individual evaluations (Sen 1970: chapter 7, 7*; 1977b), we are still faced with a second type of difficulty. A social optimum brought about through a social evaluation constrained by the feasible choice set does not guarantee that what may be called "the ethical purpose" of the social evaluation will be satisfied. This can be illustrated by economic attempts at operationalizing John Rawls' "difference principle."

Economists decomposed the difference principle into primitive criteria (axioms) to explore its normative characteristics and reformulated it as a Bergson–Samuelson's type of social welfare function in order to investigate its operational performance. It is defined as a lexicographical social welfare function which, under the assumption of ordinal comparability of individuals' utilities, aims at maximizing the utility of the least advantaged in given economic circumstances, which include individual preferences over alternative combinations of income and leisure. Such an operational formulation of the difference principle has the advantage that it can identify social optimums, i.e. alternatives in which the utility of the least advantaged is greater than in any other feasible alternatives in given economic circumstances. It also contributed to making it clear that the difference principle focuses on the least advantaged only under the provision that a priority be given to individuals' freedom to form their preferences relative to their own conceptions of the good.

However, a formulation of this type, which considers all individuals' revealed preferences as formally equal, whatever they may be, and leaves no room for individuals to accept any normative criterion, except self-interest maximization, cannot prevent results which belie "the ethical purpose" of the difference principle, i.e. to realize the right to well-being freedom for all by securing basic well-being for the least advantaged. If we recognize individual freedom, as well as the formal equal treatment of preferences, and rationality as paramount values, we must be satisfied with realized social optimums, whatever they may be. Yet, if our interest is to secure basic well-being freedom for all through focusing on the position of the least advantaged, we should pursue alternative formulations of the difference principle.[7]

---

[6] The conditions introduced by Arrow are: unrestricted domain, weak Pareto principle, non-dictatorship, the independence of irrelevant alternatives. Arrow showed that it was impossible to aggregate individual preference orderings in social order satisfying these conditions (Arrow 1963).

[7] See Gotoh (2006).

The third difficulty facing the extension of economic thinking to ethical issues is that it may be impossible to assume full interpersonal comparability, or, to put it another way, we may be unable to identify the least advantaged in society taken as a whole because of the incommensurability of diverse forms of injustice. We cannot for example easily compare which disadvantage is most serious among the disadvantage derived from having been a victim of the atomic bomb, disadvantage resulting from mental disabilities, or disadvantage caused by an accumulation of personal difficulties. Nor can we easily specify a substitution rate among compensations for different disadvantage groups, e.g. how much compensation for the first disadvantage can be substituted to compensate the second, while keeping social utility as a whole unchanged. When that is the case we cannot achieve a complete ordering determining which social policy is more just. We cannot specify optimal solutions for the whole domain of alternative social policies.

At this point, it is useful to recall Sen's distinction between an "optimal set" and a "maximal set" (Sen 2002a: 160). The former is defined as above, in the same way as it usually is in economics, while the latter is defined as a set of "alternatives which are not known to be worse than any other" (Sen 2002a: 182). If our goal is to describe an ideally just society, then the comparison should include every alternative and lead to an "optimum." However, if it is to avoid "patent injustices" one by one as they arise, we do not need to identify the "optimal set." In what follows, we wish to pursue this alternative approach to justice, but first we must look in greater detail at some of the central difficulties of traditional economics according to Sen's critique.

Sen's critique of traditional economic theory

Traditionally, economists are interested in the welfare of individuals, which can be promoted by transferring goods and services in a society. They build simple models which help to analyze and evaluate the correlated influences of economic activities – production, distribution, and consumption – on the welfare of differently positioned individuals (Sen 1987). Given this, there must be many occasions in economics to address ethically controversial issues. Yet during its history the main concerns of economic theory have been with questions of rationality, such as the *internal consistency* of choices or the *completeness* of evaluations, while ethical considerations that could contradict these rationality requirements have been exported outside economic models. The former condition, internal consistency of choice, requires "inter-menu correspondence," that is to say "relating choices from different subsets to each other" (Sen 2002a: 122), regardless of the situation of choices. This means, for example, that if a person chooses x from the alternative set {x, y, z}, she should also choose x from the set of alternatives {x, y}.[8] Completeness requires that an evaluation compares all pairs of social states and ranks each as better, worse, or indifferent. As long as these conditions of rationality are satisfied, the model is taken to be morally neutral, whatever results it may bring. No ethical consideration that contradicts the rationality conditions can be introduced in the model. Conversely, as long as it does not contradict the conditions of rationality, any ethical consideration whatsoever can be introduced regardless of its plausibility.[9]

Actually, ethical viewpoints can enter the model following two different routes, without engendering any contradiction with the rationality conditions. The first is the informational basis of the domain of the model; the other is the correspondence rule between the domain and the outcome. Take for example the Walrasian rule which describes a free competitive market. Its domain is the non-comparable ordinal utility functions of agencies in each and every market and its informational basis, information concerning these utility functions only. The correspondence rule is the minimum requirement to clean the market: making the exceeded demands weighted by prices zero over all the markets. For a Bergson–Samuelson type of social welfare function, the correspondence rule and the informational basis of the domain can reflect an ethical criterion of distributive justice that implicitly comes from outside the model.[10] Both cases have in common that individual preferences are viewed as given and are similar in that to any other part of the economic environment.

Social choice theory, which originated with Arrow, is epoch making in economic history because it opens a way to make explicit ethical criteria externally imposed on economic models and to examine their plausibility in the light of "the consistency of various value judgments."[11] Arrow's "social welfare function" represents "a procedure for passing from a set of known individual tastes to a pattern of social decision-making."[12] According to Arrow, a Bergson–Samuelson type social

---

[8] Xu and Pattanaik introduce a weaker condition of rationality than this; see their contribution to this volume, p. 199–200.

[9] That is why economic models are indifferent, for example, concerning the normative characteristics of individual preferences. Whether preferences are fully deontological or fully self-centric is irrelevant as long as the rationality conditions are satisfied.

[10] See Samuelson (1983). This was explicitly the case in the formulation of Rawls' difference principle as a Bergson–Samuelson social welfare function analyzed earlier.

[11] Arrow (1963: 5).

[12] Ibid.: 2

welfare function is nothing but a pattern of social decision-making, which distributes resources according to a given ethical criteria.[13] Thus social choice theory paves the way to study the normative character-istics of Bergson–Samuelson-type social welfare functions including measurements of inequality or poverty, such as the Gini coefficient, which were previously considered to be purely descriptive. Further, it allows one to study the normative characteristics of the procedure that specifies a pattern of social decision-making on the basis of individ-ual preferences. However, we must note that Arrow's basic concern is to elaborate a general framework where, as he says, "the distinction between voting and the market mechanism will be disregarded, both being regarded as special cases of the more general category of collect-ive social choice."[14] This indicates that central features of economic thinking including the narrow conception of rationality, *internal consist-ency*, and *completeness* are expected to apply to all issues of social choice, to questions of social policy as well as those of market distribution.

As Sen points out, such an approach excludes all information other than the formal orderings of social states revealed through individuals' preferences, and the formally equal treatment of everyone's preference. It also allows, given a profile of individual preferences, to treat in simi-lar manner any pairwise rankings which have a common form, inde-pendently of the position of individuals or of the nature of the social states involved in those orderings.

Economists other than Sen also doubt the soundness of these assump-tions and of the related requirements concerning rationality. However, they usually focus either on the irrationality or bounded-rationality of agents in their attempts to improve our understanding of individual behavior, and to provide better explanations of how conflicts or coop-eration arise in interactions (Sen 2002a: 29).[15] The specific feature of Sen's inquiry into rationality is to challenge the fundamental require-ments of *internal consistency of choice* and *completeness*.

Ethical considerations, Sen notes, constitute external points of view. They act from outside and constrain choices. They are independent of considerations of the internal consistency of choices with which they sometimes conflict. However, Sen argues, "[w]hat appears to be con-ditions of *internal consistency* are typically the implications of external correspondence with some standard and regular preference ordering (complete and transitive)" (Sen 2002a: 21). An important example of such external correspondence is the internal consistency of choices construed in terms of *self-interest maximization*, something which most economists *prima facie* consider as an actual characteristic of individuals. This phenomenon, Sen argues, can be best understood as the result of a correspondence with a norm of *self-interest maximization* which is imposed over the whole domain of choices. However, and this is the fundamental question, is it not excessive to assume that a unique criterion, whatever it may be, can be applied over the whole domain of choices independently of all and every change in external circumstances? Especially, given that the "internal properties of choice can be far from simple when the reasoning involved in choice incorporates something more complex than mechanically following a given complete ordering, and involves such features as respecting rules, or employing resolutions, or being guided by commitments, or using meta-rankings, or anticipating taste changes, or having endogenous preferences, among many other possibilities" (Sen 2002a: 21).

As mentioned earlier, internal consistency of choice entails inter-menu correspondence.[16] Yet, when an individual recognizes that her choice limits others' possibilities to choose, she may come to change not only her choice but also the criteria of reasoning involved in the choice. For example, a person faced with the set of alternatives (x, y), either taking an apple from the fruit basket (y) or not taking anything (x) decides to act decently and refrains from seizing the last apple. However, if there were two apples in the basket, that is to say from the set of alternatives (x, y, z) she would chose (y) over (x). "The presence of another apple (z) makes one of the two apples decently choosable, but this combination of choices would violate standard consistency conditions ... even though there is nothing particularly 'inconsistent' in this pair of choices (given her values and scruples)" (Sen 2002a: 129).

To this criticism of the standard assumption some may wish to object that if we refine our description of the situation in such a way as to include in the social state itself the factors that lead an individual to a different attitude or criteria of choice, we can expect global internal consistency of choice to be satisfied, given that such a strategy allows us to treat all possible contradictory cases as different social states. Let us explain this briefly with the help of the previous example. First, denote the set of alternatives {x, y} by X and {x, y, z} by Y and suppose there exist extended social states such as (x, X), (x, Y), (y, X), (y, Y), (z, Y) that combine alternative factors and alternative sets. In this way we can distinguish "choosing nothing from a basket where there is only one apple" (x, X) from "choosing nothing from a basket where there are

---

[16] See above, p. 6.

2 apples" (x, Y). This allows us to reinterpret the behavior of the above individual: she prefers (x, X) over (y, X) and (y, Y) to (x, Y). No contradiction is involved if she chooses (x, X) from the set {(x, X), (y, X)} and (y, Y) from the set {(x, X), (y, X), (x, Y), (y, Y), (z, Y)}. It is true that if we can treat all possibly contradictory cases as different social states and if we can compare all extended social states completely, global consistency can be obtained. However, by insisting on global internal consistency one overlooks the important point that Sen's argument seeks to bring out.

An individual faced with serious conflicts among different issues may stop ordering her preferences halfway, leave crucial conflicts untouched, and offer herself a quick justification. Or she may, upon fuller reflection on the meaning of her situation, decide to refrain from further evaluation and simply reduce the weight she gives to self-interest maximization. Moreover, even if at some point a global internal consistency can be established, it may disappear later on as a result of changes in "meta-rankings." That is to say, second-order preferences, preferences over preferences over actual alternatives. Meta-rankings are important in reasoning on the merits of having different types of preferences (or of acting as if one had them) (Sen 1977a; 1982a: 103–4).[17] "A particular morality," Sen says, "can be viewed, not just in terms of the 'most moral' ranking of the set of alternative actions, but as a moral ranking of the ranking of actions" (Sen 1977a; 1982a: 100).

What is at stake here is that of themselves, such "unresolved situations" do not indicate a failure of rationality. According to Sen's usage of that word, rationality is nothing but a discipline of thinking, or systematic use of reason (Sen 2002a: 19), which reflects, as well as revises, an individual's goals, values, strategies, and motivations in view of relevant information. Given this definition of rationality, it is clear that to accept external viewpoints including ethical criteria that might constrain the individual's interest is neither irrational nor outside of the strict requirements of rationality. It is also clear that *incompleteness*, in either individual or social preference, that is to say to abstain from evaluating several pairs of social states, never implies a deficit of rationality. Rather, "systematic guidance to reasoned decisions can come from incomplete orderings that reflect unresolved conflicts" (Sen 2002a: 468); incompleteness suggests the existence of value conflicts which should be seriously taken into account.

---

[17] Sen also notes that meta-ranking "can provide the format for expressing what preferences one would have preferred to have" or "can be used to analyze the conflicts involved in addiction." See also Sen (1982b) and (1982a: Introduction).

However, such a conception of rationality, which accepts incompleteness in evaluations, social and individual, entails giving up the general guarantee of the existence of "optimal" solutions relative to various economic circumstances, including individuals' preferences. This constitutes a great departure from traditional economics and raises many questions. Can we be satisfied with the absence of optimal solutions in some cases? If, as argued earlier, our goal is not to identify an "ideally just society" but to avoid "patent injustice" then the answer may be "Yes." This answer leads to another question: how should we define "patent injustice"? Is it, for example, possible to define patent injustices in a comparative approach by identifying them with social states such that there are no worse alternatives? The answer must be "No." The evaluation "y is worse than x" merely represents a relative judgment. Even if no other alternative is worse than y, we cannot immediately say that y is patently unjust, for the same reason that even if no other alternative is better than x, we cannot immediately say x is "evidently just." To identify a social state as "patent injustice," we need an "external reference," an ethical criterion, distinguished from the criteria that specify the relative comparison itself. Can we introduce without contradiction in a comparative approach an ethical criterion that directly judges if a social state constitutes a "patent injustice" or not? It is now time to examine Sen's alternative framework for economics, going back to our initial theme: how should we approach the idea of justice?

Sen's perspective on alternative economics

Central to an exploration of Sen's alternative framework for economics in relation to the idea of justice is the capability approach, another of his important contributions. This section inquires into an "extended comparative approach" which can introduce the conception of "patent injustice" into traditional comparative approaches, by clarifying the methodological characteristics of the capability approach in the context of social choice procedures.[18]

A social choice procedure is a procedure that specifies social evaluations over alternative social policies on the basis of individual information. It can be formulated as a function that transforms a profile of individual information into a social evaluation, which embodies certain values, or aims, such as respecting democracy, procedural justice, or individual rights. The concrete definition of the social values or

---

[18] The following is based on Gotoh (2007).

aims is given by a set of conditions that are externally imposed on the social choice procedure. This basic framework is essentially the same as Arrow's yet, as will soon be clear, we depart from Arrow and move closer to Sen's idea of a "social welfare functional," which explicitly permits the variety of informational bases that are easily scrutinized, and which allows individual welfare to be interpreted not as an individual evaluation but as an observable individual situation (Sen 1970: 126). Furthermore, it also makes it possible to interpret social evaluation not as a function of an individual element, but of non-individualized information.[19] The social choice procedure we now wish to analyze respects the social aim "against injustice: to secure basic capability for all." That is to say, it aims at ensuring the right of all to well-being freedom in a way that entails going beyond the formal equal treatment of individuals.

According to Sen, *capability* is defined as a set of functionings vectors which are realized by using goods and services. *Basic capability* refers to "a person being able to do certain basic things" (Sen 1980: 367) "e.g. the ability to be well-nourished and well-sheltered, the ability of escaping avoidable morbidity and premature mortality, and so forth" (Sen 1992: 45). When a shortage relative to basic capability for certain individuals is recognized it should be compensated through social policies. It is important to note that what a functionings vector actually achieves depends on the individual's choice (Sen 1985). One of the advantages of the approach in terms of capability is that while it allows at least partial interpersonal comparison, "[t]here is no compulsion to rank the capability sets completely, nor to have a partial order extensive enough for a 'best' capability set to be identified (and chosen)" (Sen 1980: 66). For example, even when we cannot identify the best capability set for society as a whole, we can say the capability of a person *i* who enjoys a decent material standard of living, a sufficient level of social activities, and is able to plan for the future is superior to that of a person *j* who is limited in terms of the last two items, and this can be said independently of these individuals' satisfaction with their own life. In what follows, since our interest is in "the identification of patent injustice, on which reasoned agreement is possible," we focus on "basic capabilities."

---

[19] Sen seems to be opposed not only to a purely subjective model but also to a purely individualistic model in the context of capability comparison: "there is, in none of these cases, the possibility of using one valuation function for one person, another for the second, and then make of the *inter-utility-functional* comparisons in the case of valuation of well-being" (Sen 1985: 57).

Before going any further, let us illustrate our problem to bring out its central difficulties. Suppose that a society disregards the disadvantages that are derived from historical injustice, gives no attention to drawbacks stemming from belonging to certain natural or social categories, and does not take into account hardships that proceed from the accumulation of personal difficulties (i.e. unemployment, disease, accident, etc.). We can probably reasonably agree that these disadvantages constitute "patent injustice" when the burdens they impose relegate individuals below basic capability. We may also agree that individuals who suffer from one or another of these patent injustices are entitled to receive compensation. Suppose next that we now must evaluate alternative social policies in terms of how – in what way or to what extent – we should transfer economic resources to compensate these disadvantaged individuals, while taking into account what is economically feasible as well as other social information. It might then become rather difficult to come to a "reasoned agreement" as to which social policy leads to "patent injustice."

This is first of all because we cannot easily compare disadvantages across different disadvantaged groups. Though there is some agreement as to what constitutes injustice, there is no overarching conception of justice that is shared by all. Second, different conceptions of justice may require different definitions of basic capability for each group, under the common goal of securing basic capability for all. Given this we cannot identify the least advantaged in society taken as a whole, nor define a basic capability that uniformly applies to all disadvantaged groups. Nonetheless, it might be possible to identify the least advantaged within each disadvantaged group, for example, through scrutinizing the particular meaning of each disadvantage. Similarly we could identify the content of basic capability that is most appropriate to the members of each disadvantaged group. If at the theoretical level these two forms of identification are distinct, at the practical level they could be carried out in interrelation, the results of each being revised by those of the other.

Assume then that this is possible and consider next a two-step social choice procedure, which requires social evaluation to be reflexive and transitive, but not necessarily complete, and that respects the social aim "against injustice: to secure basic capability for all." The first step consists of forming local evaluations over alternative social policies. A local evaluation corresponds to a type of disadvantage or particular disadvantaged group (type l-based evaluation) and has the following characteristics. The informational basis or domain of a local evaluation is the capability appraisal of the least advantaged in each disadvantaged group, relative to each and every social policy.[20] We impose the three following conditions on this procedure:

1. A local evaluation should say that x is more just than y, if (a) in social policy x the capability of the least advantaged is at least the same as basic capability and in y it is worse than (or cannot be compared with) basic capability, or (b) in y the capability of the least advantaged is worse than basic capability and in x it cannot be compared with basic capability (Basic Capability Condition). (c) In social policy x the capability of the least advantaged is at least the same as basic capability and in y it cannot be compared with basic capability.
2. A local evaluation should not express any ordering, if in both x and y the capability of the least advantaged is at least the same as basic capability (Refrain Condition).
3. A local evaluation should say that x is at least as just as y if in both social states the capability of the least advantaged is worse than basic capability and if the capability of the least advantaged in x is at least the same as in y (Restricted Monotonicity Condition).

The second step is the process of forming global social evaluations over alternative social policies. The domain or informational basis of this process is made up of two categories of information: one is constituted by the profiles of local evaluations over alternative social policies; the other corresponds to the capability appraisals of all individuals in society relative to each and every social policy. The procedure to form global social evaluations given a local evaluation and the capability appraisals of all individuals is characterized by the two following conditions, each of which relates to one of the two categories in the domain.

1. If there is a type l-based evaluation which says "x is more just than y" and there is no type l-based evaluation which says "y is more just than x," society must say "x is more just than y" (Non-Contradiction Condition).
2. If the capabilities of all individuals in society are better in x than in y, society must say "x is more just than y" (Weak Capability-Based Pareto Condition).[21]

---

[20] We assume that a *capability appraisal* is represented as a binary relation that is reflexive and transitive but not necessarily complete. Considering the plurality of functionings which constitutes an individual capability, incompleteness is generally natural, yet if we regard all pairs as "indifferent," except those where one dominates the other in all functionings, we can achieve completeness.

[21] The difference between this and the usual definition of the Weak Pareto Condition is the index. The latter is defined by utility index.

The Non-Contradiction Condition requires us to give priority to the evaluations of disadvantage groups and to treat them as formally equal relative to each other. Even if the capabilities of all non-disadvantaged individuals become worse in x than y if a local evaluation, that is not contradicted by any other l-type evaluation, evaluates x as more just than y, the social evaluation must also say that x is more just than y. In contrast, the Weak Capability-Based Pareto Condition requires treating formally equally the capability appraisals of all individuals. In consequence, in circumstances where every disadvantage groups refrains from ordering x relative to y, because in both the capabilities of those least advantaged are all at least the same as basic capability, if the capabilities of all individuals are better in x than y, the social evaluation must say x is more just than y.

Gotoh (2007) proved that the Non-Contradiction Condition can specify an incomplete but reflexive and transitive social evaluation if we can assume completeness on local evaluations restricted to the range of social states in which the capabilities of the least advantaged is worse than basic capability.[22] She also demonstrated that the Non-Contradiction Condition and the Weak Capability-Based Pareto Condition are compatible. Therefore, the social choice procedure constituted by the Non-Contradiction Condition and the Weak Capability-Based Pareto Condition can guarantee for any profile of capability appraisals and any profile of local evaluations the existence of "maximal set" in the sense of Sen (2002a),[23] for any subsets of alternative social policies.

The introduction of the notion of *basic capability*, which can be sensitive to the plurality of disadvantages, into a social choice procedure allows a social evaluation to identify certain social policies as "patent injustices." Meanwhile, the comparative approach, which gives an incomplete ordering among alternatives, allows social evaluation to specify "maximal" social policies, that is, policies that no other feasible alternatives dominate, in any economic circumstances. This "extended comparative approach," which combines these two angles, is not expected to identify an "ideally just society," since among social policies in which the capabilities of all least-advantaged individuals are at least the same as basic capability, no criterion other than the Capability-Based Pareto Condition applies, a criterion that becomes inoperative as soon as contestation arises between any two individuals. It can nonetheless help us avoid "patent injustice" or, at least, to choose less unjust "patent injustice," that is to say social

---

[22] See note 20 above.

[23] See also above, p. 6. The maximal set is defined as the set of "alternatives which are not known to be worse than any other."

policies that though they are "patently unjust" are "maximal" according to existing economic circumstances. In view of the incommensurability of many disadvantages and of the many different conceptions of the good which exist in our actual, non-ideal society, it seems best to give up *completeness* in social evaluation. However, we need not in consequence, and should not, give up choosing social policies "against injustice."

Philosophical foundation of the economic theory of Sen

Social welfare functions, whether of the Bergson–Samuelson or Arrow type, that exclude all information apart from revealed preferences of individuals are usually valued because of their inherent fairness and the place they give to individual freedom. They require the formal equal treatment of all and respect individual autonomy of choice. In contrast, as we have just seen, a social choice procedure that pursues the social aim "against injustice: to secure basic capability for all" treats individuals asymmetrically, giving priority to the evaluations of disadvantaged groups over those of other individuals.

This raises at least two questions. First, is this type of social choice procedure in contradiction to fairness or freedom (individual autonomy)?[24] Second, assuming that it is not and that formal equal treatment and individual autonomy are respected, is it possible to come to an agreement on a social choice procedure of this type? Can we avoid serious moral conflicts regarding different types of social choice procedure that embody different social aims and ethical criteria?

Answering these questions requires us to re-examine conceptual issues relative to fairness and freedom, as well as practical issues relating to public values and public reason, all of which will be addressed later on in this volume. At this point, we want to rapidly respond to these difficulties, once again in reference to Sen's work. First, as mentioned earlier, in the light of Sen's definition of rationality, to accept an external criterion that requires one to give at times priority to other people's interests over one's own does not necessarily conflict with individual rationality.[25] This understanding of rationality also suggests an alternative view of individual autonomy. When a person can reason freely in the absence of serious interference or threat, it seems legitimate to claim that the reasoning process through which she formed her choice is autonomous, even if she finally decides to accept certain external constraints on her action.[26] Furthermore, treating the revealed

---

[24] As argued for example by Nozick (1974: chapter 7, especially pages 160–6).
[25] See above, p. 9.
[26] On this, see also Philip Pettit, "Neorepublicanism and Sen's economic, legal, and ethical desiderata," this volume, pp. 55–65.

preferences of various individuals asymmetrically in view of externally imposed criteria can constitute a form of equal treatment in the context of a social choice procedure where these criteria can be publicly scrutinized and are acceptable to all individuals (Sen 1997; 2002b).

These considerations bring us back to the question, mentioned earlier, of the structure of individual preferences or evaluations. As Sen argued, "it is important to distinguish between a person's preferences as they actually are and what he thinks he would accept as a basis of public policy given the preferences of others and given his values on collective choice procedures" (Sen 1970: 66). Guided by this and in an effort to make this claim more concrete, let us illustrate the multilayered preferences an individual could have in the context of the social choice procedure introduced in the previous section.

Suppose a person is reflecting on the type of social evaluation that should form the basis of public policy. First, it seems plausible to assume that she is interested in her own capabilities in alternative social policies. This interest shapes her personal preferences, the domain of which is restricted to her own capability, and here self-interest maximization, a criterion characterized by the formal property of monotonicity, may be expected to rule. We can also plausibly assume that she has other kinds of interests and preferences, for example she is sensitive to the capabilities of different disadvantage groups given different social policies. Her personal preferences are formed according to her own conception of the good. The latter preferences may be formed in view of conceptions of basic capability, taking into account the local evaluations of each disadvantage group. All of which are taken to be shaped and revised through public reasoning and discussions.

On the basis of the several different kinds of preferences she actually has, what type of social evaluation will she form? According to Sen, the process of synthesizing plural preferences is conducted by meta-preference, preferences on preferences, which embody certain normative criteria.[27] Here let us assume that after a full deliberation she adopts the social aim "against injustice: to secure basic capability for all" and understands what the realization of this goal involves. Then we can expect that her meta-preferences will induce her to endorse a social choice procedure similar to the one introduced above, which requires giving priority to non-contradicted l-type evaluations, based on the interests of disadvantaged groups.

We should note in addition that the process of forming an individual social evaluation will have an influence on choices that are considered

---

[27] See above, p. 10 and also the references in note 10.

to belong to her personal sphere, if these actually have social consequences, like her favored work-time–leisure ratio. If, for example, she
agrees that abandoning members of one or another disadvantaged
group below basic capability is patently unjust and predicts, based on
the current economic circumstances, that in order to secure basic capability for all, those who can work should work and provide for others,
she may decide to work more than she otherwise would given that she
personally prefers having more leisure time.

To sum up, the existence of different criteria such as "self-interest
maximization" or "securing basic capability against injustice" can be
a source of internal conflict, especially if an individual applies both
criteria with the same weight to all subsets of alternatives. Yet, if after
sufficient deliberation – both individual and public – an individual can
put appropriate weights on the various criteria, depending on the situations of choice, we can view her very efforts as an exercise in rationality and freedom. The upshot of this is that Sen's challenge to traditional
economic theory implies a challenge to ethical arguments, to our conception of "moral agency," and to epistemological issues relative to the
process of social choice based on individual evaluations. But this first
part of the introduction is already quite long, and at this point we wish
only to indicate where in Sen's work more detailed discussions of these
issues can be found: in his philosophical reflection on non-basic and
non-compulsive judgment (Sen 1967), on non-hierarchical pluralism
(Sen and Williams 1982: 12), on a coherent goal–right system (Sen
1985), on positional objectivity (Sen 1997), on consequential evaluation and practical reason (Sen 2000), on open and closed impartiality
(Sen 2002a), as well as in his contributions to this book.

Against injustice: ethics, economics, and law

Economics, ethics, law, neorepublicanism, and Prajâpati's test

The volume opens with a contribution by Amartya Sen, "Economics,
law, and ethics," that inquires into the complex relationships between
those three disciplines and especially asks: what can they learn from
each other? Interestingly enough, concerning law the focus is rather
on what it has already learned from economics, and which perhaps it
should not have.

Sen's first target is the "law and economics" movement, which to
some extent already constitutes an independent discipline and has led
to a partial institutionalization of the relations between economics and
law. As such this movement provides an important recognition of the

analytical rigor of economics and of its value in tackling complex issues. It is the particular usage of economic theory that the economics and law movement makes that Sen criticizes. "Law and economics," he argues, has taken from economics a shallow understanding of human behavior and rationality and uncritically adopted as its central presupposition a conception of human agents as "simple-minded self-interest maximizers." In consequence, it tries to apply to the understanding of law an excessively rigid and narrow conception of behavior and considers as a fundamental characteristic of human beings what really is only the result of an externally imposed consistency between a given domain of action and a rule of behavior.[28] Sen argues that, on the contrary, economics does not exclude the possibility that a diversity of behavioral principles can guide a person's action at different times. The important question is to understand when and why one principle rather than another applies.

If "law and economics" takes from economic theory an excessively narrow view of human behavior and rationality it must be recognized that economists often adopt an equally restricted understanding of law. For example, law and rights tend to enter economic models only to the extent they influence economic development. Legal measures are thus seen as the servants of economic growth and to be evaluated in relation to the sole advantage, or disadvantage, they can procure in this regard. Such an understanding of law remains blind to the fact that economic development can very well go hand in hand with major transgressions of justice and rights. The relation between law and economics, claims Sen, will only be profitable if it results in broadening the points of view of each; that is to say only if the proponents of each discipline allow this encounter to change not only their conception of the other discipline, but also of their own.

In the second part of his text Sen addresses the relationship between ethics and economics, which has been at the center of so much of his work. The main thrust of his argument concerns the contribution economic thinking can make to our understanding of justice. What economics can learn from moral and political philosophy is, as he reminds us, a topic on which he has extensively written in the past, and his focus this time is on the inverse relation: what can ethics learn from economics.[29] Philosophers often view their task as providing an answer to the question "What is a just society?" Such an approach, according to Sen, leads them to develop "transcendental conceptions of justice" that aim

---

[28] See above in this introduction (p. 9) as well as Sen (1995: 19–35).
[29] For example see Sen (1987).

to provide the blueprint of a perfectly just social arrangement. However, if our goal is to identify patent injustices on which reasoned agreement is possible, a transcendental conception of justice, he argues, is neither sufficient nor necessary, and may even constitute an obstacle.

Insufficiency comes from the fact that in relation to a transcendental point all departures are equally distant. In comparison to a perfectly just social arrangement all failures of justice are equivalent. Yet are there not some injustices that are more patent than others? What philosophical theories of justice need to learn from economics, argues Sen, are the joys and difficulties of comparing. Social choice theory, as was remarked earlier, compares and ranks social states in relation to one another as "less just," "just as just," or "more just." This opens a space in which we can rationally evaluate different situations and judge of their urgency. It also leads to many difficulties and problems to resolve. One is that failures of justice can happen in many disparate spaces and that it is not clear how, for example, transgressions of rights can be compared with economic inequality. Further, when relating such different domains to each other, we can attribute to them different weights and compare them in a variety of ways. Therefore in carrying out such comparisons many choices are to be made and there is much room for discussion. Over the years social choice theory and economics have developed formal tools to address these issues. What is surprising is that philosophers, especially those who, like Rawls, have paid serious interest to economics, have given so little attention to those tools and to the methodological and epistemological issues underlying their development.

Clearly a conception of what is a perfectly just society by itself is insufficient to allow us to compare between different social states. Neither is it necessary. In social choice theory social states are directly compared pairwise, without referring to what Sen calls an "irrelevant" third alternative.[30] If these states can be completely ordered it becomes possible to identify which one is best or most just. However, this "most just" social state cannot be identified as a perfectly just society for it varies in relation to the set of feasible alternatives. It should also be noted that such an optimum is a result, rather than a precondition of the comparison of social states. Many times the ordering will be incomplete because there are in society incommensurable conceptions of justice. Even when such is the case, reasoned decision concerning patent injustice may be possible. It is not necessary to be able to answer the question "What is a just society?" in order to identify situations that need to be remedied or even to able to be order them at least partially.

[30] This volume, p. 51.

The responses of Philip Pettit and Marcel Hénaff may seem excessively conciliatory and in agreement. They dispute neither the diagnostic, nor the conclusion. What they do is to widen the debate by turning to new domains of inquiry. Professor Pettit in "Neorepublicanism and Sen's economic, legal, and ethical desiderata" begins by summarizing Sen's views on economics, ethics, and law into three fundamental desiderata. First, that economics should not be taken to postulate that we simply are self-interest maximizers incapable of commitments to others. Two, that law should not be solely evaluated by its economic payoffs only; and, three, that ethics should not be construed as the search for an ideal model of society in the absence of any comparative yardstick. He then goes on to argue that neorepublicanism as a political theory satisfies these three desiderata (suitably translated to fit this different case). For example, the first requirement becomes the rejection of the "knaves' principle": the idea that institutions should be designed in such a way that they would continue to function properly even if everyone turned out to be a knave. This displacement brings to the fore the fact that Sen's claims, beyond the interrelations between three particular disciplines, refer to fundamental rules of our living together.

A different displacement is to be found in the Vedic text recounted by Professor Hénaff in his commentary of "The Prajâpati test." When Prajâpati, the first human, wanted to distinguish among spirits the demons from the gods, he invited them all to a feast where he served them an abundance of rich and varied food. Some ravenously grabbed for themselves all that they could while others offered food to each other. Prajâpati wisely concluded that the first were demons and the second the gods, whom we should imitate. Humans are not mere seekers of their own interest, though they are also that. They are creatures whose behavior is deeply structured by a need for mutual recognition. This is the need that is expressed by the Vedic gods' "useless" exchange of food in a situation of complete abundance.

The ten following chapters all address different issues that occupy a central place in Professor Sen's work. Chapters 4 and 5, each in its own way, concern the reach of public reason, the extent to which public deliberation is essential in social choice, how it structures our understanding of justice, and determines the options that are available to us. Chapters 6 and 7 address the issue of reciprocity, chapter 8 is on preferences, chapter 9 on the formalization of the concept of rights, chapters 10 and 11 on the measurement of capabilities, and finally chapter 12 is on development. In the last chapter of the book, Professor Sen dialogues with the various contributors and responds to the issues they have raised.

The reach of public reason

In chapter 4, "The power of a democratic public," Philip Pettit focuses on an often neglected dimension of democracy: the role and importance of an active public. A public exists when people have a concern with what their government does that goes beyond the simple consequences that the government's actions may have on their private atomized interests. It results from the coming together in public forums of private conversations concerning the value, advantage, justice, fairness, or interest of proposed and ongoing policies. Such a public, Pettit argues, though it is a difference-making enterprise, a means through which disagreements are voiced, a locus of dissent rather than consensus, necessarily gives rise to two types of commonalities.

The first are participatory commonplaces about titles and rights to participate. The way individuals are included in public conversation entails that should some participants be suddenly silenced or ignored, they can appeal to the requirements of that practice itself to vindicate their position. As long as people participate with one another in public discourse they must be assumed to eschew fraud or force, and we can expect them to recognize each other as equal voices with equal claims. Of course, they may not always live up to those ideals, but these will nonetheless constitute common presuppositions to which it is possible to appeal publicly. Inferential commonplaces constitute the second type of commonalities that all members of a public must be taken to endorse as they come to agree on what counts, and what does not count, as an argument. Arguments and counter-arguments, argues Pettit, can only be advanced on the basis of "unavowed infrastructure of agreements,"[31] which will necessarily constitute shared presuppositions to the debate. In this way the process of discussing opposing positions inevitably generates a common ground that will in time become conscious.

It remains true, however, that a public may be limited to certain members of society only, excluding for example women, or those who are not property owners, as was long the case in most societies. However, once a public is formed, claims Pettit, it becomes difficult to guard its borders. A public normally tends to be porous at its periphery and left to itself will tend to grow and include more and more members of society.

A public exerts power indirectly through electoral and non-electoral means, including popular protest and contestation. This control, rather than determining the specific content of the process of deliberation, constrains its possible issues. The public constitutes a successful regime of challenge and justification when it can take off the government's

[31] This volume, p. 79.

agenda policies that clearly challenge received ideas.[32] It really rules the polity when its shared ideas filter out any unacceptable policy.

Chapter 5 by Martha Nussbaum, "The challenge of gender justice," may be viewed as providing an example of what happens when a public opens up to include members of society that previously were less than full participants. It can also be understood as illustrating the way in which through this process of opening up, both participatory and inferential commonplaces come to change and received ideas are challenged. The focus of her text is the transformation of liberal theories of justice that resulted from taking into account gender-related issues. Professor Nussbaum identifies four topics on which this still ongoing process of transformation has had major influence. First is the criticism of the distinction between a public sphere, where all are equal before the law, and a private domain identified with the family, and characterized by strong affective ties and natural hierarchies. Feminist criticism brought to light the way in which this distinction was grounded in prejudice concerning the "nature" of women and the extent to which it could not resist serious scrutiny. Not only did this distinction exclude women from the public domain, it also gave them unequal property and inheritance rights and shielded criminal behavior, like marital rape and domestic violence, from the eyes of the law. The second locus of change was the realization that "equal treatment" does not necessarily mean similar treatment. Granting equal protection to agents sometimes requires that they be treated asymmetrically, in a way that reflects their unequal power in a given situation. The third area of transformation is the recognition of deformed preferences, of the fact that people's preferences can be ill-formed for many reasons; that they may be, for example, sadistic or vicious, but mainly that the expressed preferences of individuals, rather than their real values, may reflect their accommodation to difficult circumstances or unfair situations of which they are the victims. The last still ongoing area of change concerns a fundamental presupposition of most social contract theories: the myth that all participants in the social contract are fully cooperating members of society over their whole life. Feminist criticism is bringing us to abandon this fallacy, which seriously distorts the choice of political principles and makes provisions for care, as well as respect for those who provide it, less central than they should be.

What is involved in these transformations is more than a simple extension to women of protections that in the past were reserved to men. The progressive inclusion of women and of gender issues into the

<hr>

[32] This volume, p. 85.

public conversation concerning justice led to a profound rethinking of liberal theories of justice that made them more adequate theories of justice, not only for women, but for all. The addition of new participants to our public discussion concerning justice changed both participatory and inferential commonplaces. It brought about a modification of what constitutes a receivable argument and of who may take part in that discussion.

Reciprocity from ceremonial exchange to public assistance

In chapter 6, "Gift, market, and social justice," Marcel Hénaff inquires into the nature of ceremonial gift-giving in traditional societies. Gift, the exchange of presents in traditional societies, has often been understood as an imperfect and primitive form of economic exchange. Ethnologic data, argues Professor Hénaff, clearly show that this cannot be the case. First, ceremonial gifts concern certain goods only, like precious objects or festive food. Second, gift-giving is ritualized, structured by a formal procedure, and public. Giving a gift is something which is done in the presence of others, and it constitutes a means of gaining prestige and of showing one's value. Through ceremonial gift-giving are determined and revealed the social rank of both donor and recipient. Finally, ceremonial gift-giving is mandatory and comprises three distinct but interrelated obligations: to give, to accept, and to reciprocate. What is involved here is different from a simple misunderstanding of the means to economic profit and utility maximization. Ceremonial gift-giving is a radically different type of social phenomena than economic exchange. Its role is not the circulation of goods, but to create and to strengthen social bonds.

As Hénaff reminds us, this aspect of gift-giving, as a means of building trust, has been perceived and analyzed by some modern economists, in particular, for example, Akerlof (1982; 1984) and Camerer (1988). However, both authors understand gift-giving and trust-building as enclosed within market relations, as means to facilitate economic exchanges. They fail in consequence to recognize the specific human need to which ceremonial gift giving responds. Ceremonial gift-giving, argues Hénaff, is a form of reciprocal recognition. It is a political activity. Through the exchange of gifts individuals recognize, measure, and position each other. Its central characteristic is reciprocity: a gift received requires a counter-gift in return. Reciprocity in this sense cannot be reduced to symmetry, complementariness, or simultaneity. On the contrary, the reciprocal process of gifts and counter-gifts constitutes an asymmetric sequence where the action of one agent responds to that of another. This "sequential symmetry" can also be recognized in violence, the exchange of blows. Reciprocity therefore, insists Hénaff, should not be identified with morality, and it should be remembered that ceremonial gift-giving takes place against the background of possible conflict.

In societies like ours which are no longer organized in moieties, lineages, and clans, it is at the level of rights rather than gift-giving that the process of mutual recognition takes place. In this modern institutionalization of the human demand for recognition the reciprocity requirement has been replaced by equal rights. However, recognition is also what is and what has been at stake in demands for social justice, and the awareness of this has been central in Sen's work. As Hénaff reminds us: "what is at stake in capabilities is always the dignity of the agent; higher income, health, education, and gender equality are not ends in themselves but confirmations of each person's humanness."[33] Demands for social justice are not only demands for more material goods, but also, and perhaps essentially, demands for recognition.

Chapter 7, "Justice and public reciprocity," by Reiko Gotoh inquires into the idea of a public assistance system resting on a plurality of evaluations and public reciprocity. Her motivation is based on a recent re-evaluation of current Japanese assistance that led to proposals for reducing support, arguing "that the level of income support (presently) provided by public assistance is too high to maintain individuals' motivation for 'independence'."[34] Using data concerning Japanese single-mother, low-income households and single-mother recipient households, Gotoh argues that this criticism, because it focuses on levels of income and of commodity consumption, fails to recognize the real difference in capabilities between agents. In particular it is blind to the effects of the complementary requirement of Japanese public assistance which, much more than the level of support, reduces agents' "independence." Compliance with this requirement that forces agents to exhaust all their assets before qualifying for help shapes their preferences and constrains the set of options that are later open to them. On the contrary, as she writes, "[i]t is one of the merits of the capability approach to further our understanding of the objective conditions under which an individual chooses a specific bundle of consumption or *functioning* given her own preference and of the reasons why an individual develops his or her preferences."[35]

Based on this motivation, she proposes a two-tier system that comprises, first, reason-based assistance programs, where individuals qualify

[33] This volume, p. 135. [34] This volume, p. 144. [35] This volume, p. 148–9.

for help on the basis of characteristics that are publicly recognized as causing particular hardship, and a second level of general assistance aimed at
compensating lack of resources. Individuals who qualify for both chose
either one or the other. The plurality of evaluation motivating the first
level of assistance reflects the fact that certain characteristics – being for
example a single mother, or being aged, or disabled – negatively influence agents' functionings; they constrain what different persons can do
with identical resources. The second level reflects the fact that below a
certain point resource deprivation qualifies one for help independently
of the reasons or causes of this scarcity of resources.

However, the second layer of assistance, because it offers help to all
those who are in need, independently of the reason why, including for
example their apparent refusal to work, faces two fundamental objections. First, is such a system feasible, for who will work if all can receive
help without any condition? Second, is it fair if some can simply ride
free all their life on the work of others? It is to respond to these objections that Gotoh introduces the idea of public reciprocity. The basic
rule of public assistance as she understands it simply says "If you can
work and afford to provide, do so; if you are in need, receive help and
be well." This rule, inasmuch as it realizes and represents reciprocity,
ensures the goal feasibility of the system. The rule is reciprocal in the
sense that agents are inclined to accept it given that others will likewise
do so. It represents reciprocity to the extent that through this rule reciprocity is realized in society. Finally it ensures the goal reciprocity of
the assistance system in that the second part of the rule, "if you are in
need, receive help," defines the goal of the system, while the first part,
"if you can work and afford to provide do so," expresses its feasibility
condition. The rule implies both a right – to receive help if in need – and
an ethical obligation – to help if you can. However, because public reciprocity, like mutual advantage, is expected to provide reasons for voluntary interactions among individuals, it can be seen as alleviating the
weight of the moral commitment required by the assistance system.

*Concepts and methodology: reasoning with preferences and the
formalization of rights and freedom*

John Broome's contribution, as well as that of Prasanta Pattanaik
and Yongsheng Xu, raises issues related to fundamental conceptual
and methodological presuppositions of social choice. In chapter 8,
"Reasoning with preferences?" John Broome asks whether we can reason with preference? That is to say, is there a rational process through
which an individual can transform her preferences in order to make

them more rational? The underlying worry comes from the fact that economics, rational choice theory, and many disciplines influenced by the models they propose impose rationality conditions, like transitivity, on the preferences sets of agents. However, such requirements make sense only if it is possible for agents to satisfy them. As Professor Sen has often argued, and as Martha Nussbaum reminds us in this volume,[36] often an agent's preferences reflect circumstances that distort them or make them irrational. Given this, is it possible for persons to transform their preferences, and preferences ordering, in such a way that they come to satisfy the rationality conditions required by the theory? Doing that is what reasoning with preferences means. Should it turn out that it is not possible to reason with preferences, it seems that it makes little sense to impose any such rationality conditions.

Professor Broome starts his inquiry by an analysis of reasoning in the case which is most familiar to us, reasoning with beliefs. He distinguishes two different forms of reasoning. First-order reasoning consists in reasoning directly about the content of one's beliefs, while second-order reasoning sets out from a second-order belief about one's first-order belief, for example a rationality requirement like *modus ponens*. Second-order reasoning is about the first-order beliefs one has rather than about their content. Starting from such a requirement, for instance, from "if you believe (1) that it is raining and if you believe (2) that if it is raining the snow will melt, you should believe (3) that the snow will melt," can you actually arrive at the belief that the snow will melt with the help of that second-order belief if it is the case that you already possess the two first relevant beliefs but not the third? [37] Broome argues that you cannot. A belief that rationality requires one to believe X, or says that one should believe X, cannot by itself bring a person to acquire the belief X. One can only acquire such a belief by gaining sufficient evidence about X and/or by directly reasoning about the contents of her beliefs. In this case if you believe it is raining and that if it is raining the snow will melt, then you can acquire the belief that the snow will melt, but this is done by working directly on the content of the two first beliefs rather than as a result of applying the second-order requirement. The reasoning that fulfills the requirement of *modus ponens* is not the result of applying that requirement.

Can we then reason with preferences? Professor Broome argues that to some extent we can. He proposes, first, to distinguish ordinary preferences from broad preferences. The latter correspond more closely to what economists and other theorists mean when they use that term.

[36] This volume, p. 104–6.   [37] This is the same example used by Professor Broome.

Ordinary preferences are more or less what may be called comparative desires. In this sense to prefer *a* to *b* is to desire *a* more than *b*. While in the broad sense an individual is said to prefer *a* to *b* when she is in a mental state where given the choice between *a* or *b* only she would choose *a* over *b*. Broad preferences are broader than ordinary preferences because many other factors than one's desire may enter in a choice. In the case of broad preferences, second-order reasoning may succeed, because such preferences include intentions and out of second-order reasoning one can form new intentions, as the Aristotelian practical syllogism already indicates. While the intention to believe X cannot directly lead to acquiring the belief X, the intention of choosing X normally precedes choosing X. In the case of ordinary preferences we may, argues Broome, resort to first-order reasoning. Yet, as he also argues, both first-order reasoning with ordinary preferences and second-order reasoning with broad preference are very difficult to distinguish from reasoning with belief concerning the betterness of options. It may very well be that what appears to be reasoning with preferences is nothing other than reasoning with a certain class of beliefs. Because the relation of betterness is transitive, the requirement of transitivity of preferences would not reflect anything particular or internal about preference taken as mental states. Rather it would reflect something about the relation of relative goodness between options and indicate a connection between preferences and the external world. This brings us back to a central issue in Professor Sen's work that was mentioned earlier, the claim that what appears as internal consistency in rationality may very well be the result of an external consistency between a domain and the criteria which are applied to it.[38]

Chapter 9, "Conceptions of individual rights and freedom in welfare economics: a re-examination," by Professors Xu and Pattanaik addresses methodological questions related to an issue raised in Sen's opening contribution. As Xu and Pattanaik write, in most welfarist models individual rights, freedom, and fairness enter in the evaluation of social states only "indirectly as instruments affecting the utilities of the individuals involved."[39] Their inquiry surveys recent formalizations that try to capture the independent status of rights and freedom in the assessment of social states. Its goal is to evaluate the formal translation of rights and freedom in models that follow Sen's call to consider rights and freedoms as more than mere instruments for economic growth.

According to them, these formalizations can be divided into two main categories: outcome-based preference-dependent formulations on the

[38] See above, p. 9.   [39] This volume, p. 187.

one hand and action-based preference-free formulations on the other hand. The first are standard in social choice theory, and as their name suggests they focus on the social states that should or should not arise as outcomes in a given situation. These formulations are preference-dependent inasmuch as agents' preferences over the outcomes are indispensable to express an agent's right. Action-based formulations focus, on the other hand, on the actions which an individual may or may not take and on those that others can or cannot choose in return. They are preference-free because in these formulations to specify what it means for an agent to have a right it is not necessary to take into account the agent's motives or preferences. A somewhat similar dichotomy can be applied to the formalization of freedom.

The strategy adopted by Xu and Pattanaik is to evaluate the extent to which these different formalizations conform to our intuitions concerning rights and freedom. In the case of outcome-based preference-dependent formulations their interest centers on Sen's (1986) particular formulation. According to them, Sen's model leads to results that contradict our intuitions concerning individual rights. This, they argue, is because he translates an individual's right as his or her global dominance over two alternative social states x and y, taken to represent outcomes uniquely relevant to that individual's private domain. According to Xu and Pattanaik an individual's rights should, on the contrary, be understood as requiring a person's local rather than global dominance over those alternatives. This difference, they claim, ultimately reflects the place of social rationality in social choice theory and is the reason why social choice theory "does not provide a convenient framework for articulating our intuition about a very broad range of individual rights."[40] This shift of emphasis, from a class of models – for even formulations requiring local dominance only are outcome-based and preference-dependent – to a particular assumption within social choice theory raises an important issue related to reforming outcome-based methodology in line with Sen's critique of rationality and "welfarism." Unfortunately our authors choose not to pursue this issue, turning instead to action-based preference-free formulations.

Measurements

The next two chapters deal with the measurement of capacities and functionings. In "On applying synthetic indices of multidimensional well-being," Andrea Brandolini inquires into the implications and

[40] This volume, p. 200.

requirements of using synthetic multivariate indices of inequality. During the last few years multidimensional conceptions of human well-being have gained a larger audience not only in academic milieus but also among policy-oriented analysts, a development which owes much to the conceptualization put forward in Sen's capability approach. In 1990 the United Nations Development Program adopted in place of the GDP per capita as the measure of progress the Human Development Index that is influenced by that approach. It replaces a single measure by an index that combines income, life expectancy, and educational achievement. Multidimensional views of human well-being reject the exclusive identification of poverty with income deprivation and aim to reflect the multidimensional nature of the mechanisms leading to social exclusion, as well as the interrelation of lower achievements in multiple domains. However intuitively attractive such a view may be it offers, as Brandolini writes, "little guidance on its practical implementation ... The central problem is how to translate intuition into measurement."[41]

Andrea Brandolini's inquiry combines an analytical discussion of central features of multidimensional measurements of well-being with an examination of their application to health and income inequalities in Germany, France, Italy, and the United Kingdom. The analysis may prove difficult for readers who are not familiar with the technicalities of mathematical formalization; however, the effort involved in reading is well rewarded when we arrive at the empirical illustration, which clearly brings to the fore the policy issues at stake behind apparently abstruse technical questions.

Two main conceptual distinctions can be drawn among multidimensional analyses of well-being. One is whether functionings are investigated singly or comprehensively. In the first case indicators are analyzed one by one and no attempt is made at reducing the complexity of the information. The second distinction is among comprehensive approaches, whether multidimensionality is retained or collapsed into a synthetic indicator of well-being. The focus of Brandolini's chapter is on aggregative strategies and more precisely on the construction of synthetic indicators at the individual level, rather than at the country level. Synthetic indices aggregate the measurements of different functionings, and one difficulty concerns the weights which are to be attributed to distinct functionings. These weights reflect the extent to which each is taken to contribute to an individual's overall well-being. Another difficult question is that of the substitutability rate embedded in the

---

[41] This volume, p. 222.

functional form of the synthetic index. It corresponds to the assumed independence of functionings, to the extent to which one can replace another.

The conclusions which emerge from Brandolini's rich analyses can be distributed over different levels. At a purely technical level he draws our attention to the influence of assumptions made in calculation, for example the decision whether to represent income directly or as its logarithmic transform, or the degree of inequality aversion which is assumed in a model. As he notes, such questions are not specific to multidimensional analyses. At a more specific level, the importance of the weighing structure of functionings and their degree of substitutability are proper to multivariate context. These questions, however, cannot be reduced to mere technical difficulties. Weights and degree of substitutability are the expression of implicit value judgments. Therefore he concludes that "[f]ar from being a weakness of multidimensional approaches, the investigation of alternative assumptions is necessary to allow for the presence of different views in the society."[42] At this social level the informative advantage of adopting multidimensional analyses is not only that they give a more complete image of well-being, but also that they include dimensions of a public discussion concerning what constitutes a "life a person would want to have and have reason to value" (Sen 2002a: 5).

The second contribution in the measurement section is quite different. Rather than conceptually and empirically analyzing difficulties related to multidimensional indices, Flavio Comim provides an attempt at directly measuring capabilities. More precisely he presents the findings of an inquiry to measure the capacities enhancement of children as a result of their participation in a music awareness project that was implemented in underprivileged regions of Brazil. Comim's long-term aim is to develop a methodology to evaluate the impact of educational changes on children's capabilities.

The TIM (Música nas Escolas) project is part of Italia Telecom's Corporate Social Responsibility Agenda in Brazil. The program's general aims are to promote interest in music through music lessons and workshops. It targets primary school students in deprived neighborhoods located on the outskirts of large Brazilian cities and was assessed during the second year of its implementation. As Comim argues, programs developed under the aegis of corporate social responsibility "are often implemented for publicity reasons, without monitoring or assessment. The same happens quite often at government level in developing countries." Assessments to improve the efficiency and distributive

---

[42] This volume, p. 247.

impact of such programs are certainly needed. However, the measurement of capabilities remains a challenge, and the translation of normative categories into operative measures has not been fully explored. This chapter provides an attempt in that direction.

One of the interests of the evaluation on which Comim reports in a sense is simply that it was done, that is to say that TIM (Música nas Escolas) was evaluated using the capability approach, rather than resorting, as is too often the case, to opinion polls or economic impact analyses to provide assessment. However, a central difficulty of such an evaluation is to know precisely what one is measuring. Is it the influence of music on children's cognitive and social development understood as capabilities or is it the influence of the program as a whole? What makes the answer to that question difficult is not only that the program was complementary to the music education children already receive, but mainly that the promotion of values such as non-violence and cooperation was an intrinsic part of its strategy of implementation. It is therefore extremely difficult to disentangle the particular contribution of music learning from other aspects of the project.

A central conclusion of this chapter is its argument that "it is possible to measure capabilities (rather than simply functionings) according to their main features, namely, objectivity, multidimensional, counterfactuality and autonomy."[43] There remains, nonetheless, some ambiguity as to the exact scope of this claim. According to Professor Comim, the direct measurement of capabilities is possible in this case because of the particular characteristics of the three dimensions related to cognitive and social development that were chosen for measurement. However, he also warns us that the "choice of dimensions was tailor-made to the objectives of 'Music in Schools' and should not be mechanically extrapolated to other programmes."

Development

In "The search for socially sustainable development" Jean-Luc Dubois argues that development, apart from having to be economically and ecologically sustainable, must also be socially sustainable. The idea of a socially sustainable development is that of a development which guarantees the improvement of well-being capability for all by means of a fair distribution of capabilities within the current generation and ensures an equitable transmission of capabilities to future generations. It is derived from relating Sen's capability approach to the idea of

[43] This volume, p. 273.

sustainable development. The underlying worry is that the social consequences of development cannot and should not, as they usually are, be reduced to poverty alleviation only. Endeavors to lessen poverty, depending on how they are designed and carried out, can weaken social bonds, lead to internal conflicts or irreversible social transformations that may endanger the continuation of the development process and cause more damage to the social fabric than poverty itself. The goal of this exploratory study is to inquire into the methodological and conceptual requirements and implications of social sustainability.

Dubois list three series of components that need to be identified and taken into account in any attempt at determining the social sustainability of a project or policy. First, it is necessary to distinguish the specific type of social issues at stake. Sustainable development has a social dimension and asks, for example, how to ensure education and human development in the long term. "In contrast, 'socially sustainable development' focuses on the effects of education on social behaviour, and on the quality of relationships with other people, as well as on self-esteem, respect and dignity."[44] Second, we must take into account the interrelations between the different dimensions of socially sustainable development, like the effect of employment creation programs on health, education, or family ties. Third, questions concerning the justice of the consequences of development both in the present generation and with the next generation have to be addressed.

Taking into account this new set of issues requires, according to Dubois, methodological developments and implies a conceptual displacement relative to the classical economic approach. At that last level, thinking in terms of socially sustainable development demands at least that we abandon the image of economic agents as simple utility maximizers in favor of a richer conception of persons embedded in social networks and committed to various ethical values and rules of reciprocity; one which can be grounded in an ethic of responsibility centered on the interactions between freedom and responsibility. At the methodological level, Dubois argues that we should focus on positive ethics; that is to say the study of people's actual moral norms and values, as well as the way in which they adjust these to their self-interests and adapt them to changing circumstances. He insists finally on the need to develop instruments to measure the relativity of social choice and identify the moral rules motivating action and illustrates his arguments by examples taken from field studies on developments in Moroccan villages.

[44] This volume, p. 282.

The book ends with a generous response from Professor Sen, where he addresses again some of the issues raised in the book, clarifying his own position through agreement and friendly disagreement.

References

Akerlof, George A. 1982. "Labor Contract as Partial Gift Exchange," *Quarterly Journal of Economics*, **97** (4): 543–69 (repr. in Akerlof, *An Economics Theorist's Book of Tales*, Cambridge University Press, 1984, ch. 8).
1984. "Gift Exchange and Efficiency-Wage Theory," *American Economic Review*, **74** (2): 79–83.
Altham, J. E. J. and Harrison, Ross (eds.) 1995. *World, Mind and Ethics. Essays on the Ethical Philosophy of Bernard Williams*, Cambridge University Press.
Arrow, K. J. 1963. *Social Choice and Individual Values*, 2nd edn., New York: J. Wiley & Sons; originally published 1951.
Arrow, K. J. and Intriligator, M. (eds.) 1986. *Handbook of Mathematical Economics*, vol. III, Amsterdam: North-Holland.
Bergson, A. 1938. "A Reformulation of Certain Aspects of Welfare Economics," *Quarterly Journal of Economics*, **52**: 310–34.
Camerer, Colin F. 1988. "Gifts as Economic Signals and Social Symbols," *American Journal of Sociology*, **94** (Supplement): 180–214.
Gotoh, R. 2006, "Welfare Reform Based on Capability Theory and Public Reciprocity – An Idea of Reformulation of Basic Income," paper presented at the 2006 Annual Meeting of the Human Development and Capability Association, Groningen.
2007. "A Note on Capability Comparison and Social Evaluation," paper for the Oxford Poverty and Human Development Initiative (OPHI), Department of International Development, Queen Elizabeth House, University of Oxford, May 29 –June 1, 2007.
Hobbes, Thomas. 1994. *Leviathan*, in Curley, Edwin (ed.), *Leviathan: With Selected Variants from the Latin Edition of 1668*, Hackett Pub Co Inc.; originally published in 1651 as *Leviathan, or the Matter, Forme, and Power of a Commonwealth, Ecclesiasticall and Civil*.
Kahneman, Daniel, Slovic, Paul, and Tversky, Amos (eds.) 1982. *Judgment under Uncertainty: Heuristics and Biases*, Cambridge University Press.
Nozick, R. 1974. *Anarchy, State and Utopia*. New York: Basic Books.
Rawls, J. 1971. *A Theory of Justice*, Cambridge, MA: Harvard University Press.
Samuelson, P. A. 1983. *Foundations of Economic Analysis*, enlarged edn., Cambridge, MA: Harvard University Press; first published 1947.
Sen, A. K. 1967. "The Nature and Classes of Prescriptive Judgements," *Philosophical Quarterly*, **17**: 46–62.
1970. *Collective Choice and Social Welfare*, San Francisco: Holden-Day.
1977a. "Rational Fools: A Critique of the Behavioural Foundations of Economic Theory," *Philosophy and Public Affairs*, **6**: 317–44.
1977b. "On Weights and Measures: Informational Constraints in Social Welfare Analysis," *Econometrica*, **45** (7): 1539–72.

1980. "Equality of What?" *The Tanner Lectures on Human Values*, vol. I, Salt Lake City: University of Utah Press; (reprinted in Sen 1982a: 353–69).

1982a. *Choice, Welfare and Measurement*, Oxford: Basil Blackwell.

1982b. "Choice, Orderings and Morality," in Sen 1982a: 74–83.

1985. *Commodities and Capabilities*, Amsterdam: North-Holland.

1986. "Social Choice Theory," in Arrow and Intriligator (eds.), pp. 1079–181.

1987. *On Ethics and Economics*, Oxford: Blackwell.

1992. *Inequality Reexamined*, Cambridge, MA: Harvard University Press.

1993. "Positional Objectivity," *Philosophy and Public Affairs*, **22**: 126–45; (reprinted in Sen 2002a: 463–83).

1995. "Is the Idea of a Purely Internal Consistency of Choice Bizarre?" in Altham and Harrison (eds.), pp. 19–35.

1997. *On Economic Inequality*, expanded edn. with a substantial annex by James E. Foster and Amartya K. Sen, Oxford: Clarendon Press.

1999. *Development as Freedom*, New York: Alfred A. Knopf.

2000. "Consequential Evaluation and Practical Reason," *The Journal of Philosophy*, **97** (9): 477–502.

2002a. *Rationality and Freedom*, Cambridge, MA: Harvard University Press.

2002b. "Open and Closed Impartiality," *The Journal of Philosophy*, **99** (9): 445–69.

Sen, A. K. and Williams, B. (eds.) 1982. *Utilitarianism and Beyond*, Cambridge University Press.

Shklar, J. 1990. *The Faces of Injustice*, New Haven: Yale University Press.

Simon, H. 1955. "A Behavioral Model of Rational Choice," *Quarterly Journal of Economics*, **69** (1): 99–118.

Simon, H. 1979. *Models of Thought*, New Haven: Yale University Press.

Part I

1 Economics, law, and ethics

Amartya Sen

Introduction

In this presentation, I shall try to comment on the interrelations of economics, ethics and law. I shall argue that these interconnections are deep and complex, and there are good reasons for us to take satisfaction in the fact that these linkages are now receiving more attention than they did in the past. Indeed, this conference at the famous Ritsumeikan University is itself a significant attempt at constructively investigating the ties between these apparently disparate but strongly interlinked subjects. However, along with that "positive" theme, I want to present a somewhat critical reflection as well, to wit, that these interconnections tend sometimes to be inadequately explored, because they do not go deeply enough into the actual nature of the respective disciplines. If the interconnections have to be given their due weight, it is critically important for us to take each subject in an adequately rich form.

Let me illustrate the dual comments I am trying to make by first considering the relation between the two disciplines of economics and law, and the recent emergence of a new subject called "law and economics." Given their interdependences, we have reason enough to welcome the fact that "law and economics" as a discipline has now become such a standard part of law education in many parts of the world, led by the United States. Economic relations function in a world of human relations that are deeply influenced by the legal framework in operation, and the practice of law, in turn, cannot but take into account the impact of legal decisions on human lives through the economic consequences of these decisions. It can be important in understanding the rationale and reach of legal rules, and it may also offer insight into the way economic systems operate and function. The combination of legal and economic thinking must also have a strong role in helping us to achieve an adequate appreciation of the demands of justice and their extensive practical implications.

It is clear that the general case for a subject like "law and econom-ics" must be strong. The basic idea of combining legal reasoning with economic analysis is very sound. The shortcomings of that integrative approach do not arise from the general pursuit of "law and economics" as a discipline, but specifically from taking some of the special assump-tions of a particularly over-simple kind of economics to be a good rep-resentation of the general discipline of economics itself.

Philosophers, perhaps, do not take economics sufficiently seriously. I shall come to that issue later, but it does certainly look as if legal theorists, in contrast, take some of the most elementary formulations in economics far too seriously. And this can be somewhat distressing since ardent attention is frequently bestowed on a particularly anemic form of economics.

Perhaps the most important source of difficulty lies in the use of what is called "rational choice theory," which, in this interpretation, works on the presumption that people's intellectual horizons are suffi-ciently limited to make them respond to only one kind of motivation for action, to wit, the personal gain that the actor expects from that action. Self-gain is seen as the only operative motivation for conscious human acts. It is hard to think of a motivational assumption that is more devoid of the wealth of human reasoning than the modeling of humanity as simple-minded self-interest maximizers.[1]

More recently, broader interpretations of self-gain have been offered, with some gain in reach, but without any foundational revision of the basic presumption of the complete dominance of self-interest itself. In more inclusive formulations, for example in the richly carved theory developed by Gary Becker,[2] the motivating personal gain can take the form of enjoying (and through that, benefiting from) the effects of that action on the lives of others. This allows human beings to be interested in each other's lives and to take into account the fact that someone else's well-being may influence one's own well-being. This is clearly a move in the right direction, but even in this inclusive formulation, the so-called rational choice theory does not allow human beings to act on the basis of reasons other than self-gain – indirect or direct – from the action that is being considered. There is a failure here to see the distinc-tion between a person's *values and priorities,* on the one hand, and his or her *well-being and personal interests,* on the other. For example, this

---

[1] I have discussed some of the main problems involved in such oversimplification of the motivational basis of behavior in Sen 1973; 1977; 1985; 1997. The first two essays are included in Sen 1982, and the second two in Sen 2002, with further discussions in each collection.

[2] Becker 1996.

over-simple framework does not allow acting on grounds of valuing the lives of others *per se*; the motivation has to be the benefit or enjoyment that the actor himself gets from the lives of others.

"Law and economics": an excessively narrow conception of economics

One of the leading figures in the new discipline of "law and economics," Professor Richard Posner, who is a distinguished American judge in addition to being a leading and innovative legal theorist, has argued that the characterization of the new discipline has followed the lead given by the classical writings of Adam Smith and Jeremy Bentham. He notes that "it was not until the mid-20th century" that "the links between law and economics became an object of serious academic pursuit."[3] Posner also notes that in "many respects, the impact of law and economics has exceeded its planned ambitions." He points out:

One effect of the incorporation of economics into the study of law was to irreversibly transform traditional legal methodology. Legal rules began to be studied as a working system – a clear change from the Langdellian tradition, which had relied almost exclusively on the self-contained framework of case analysis and classification, viewing law as little more than a filing system. Economics provided the analytical rigor necessary for the study of the vast body of legal rules present in a modern legal system.[4]

An economist cannot but be gratified by the constructive role that is given to the discipline of economics by such a leading legal analyst.

However, Posner goes on to note that "despite the powerful analytical reach of economics, it was clear from the outset that the economist's competence in the evaluation of legal issues was limited" (p. x). This sad diagnosis seems plausible enough, but we must also ask whether the lawyer's competence in the evaluation of economic issues might not be similarly limited. Indeed, it appears that the particular economic theories that have been marshaled into the discipline of "law and economics" (and have been very widely used) are sometimes peculiarly constricted and shallow.

This is exactly where the basic assumption of narrowly self-interested behavior, rapidly adopted as the basic norm in the new discipline of "law and economics," requires close scrutiny. Even though that assumption was explicitly rejected by many classical economists, including Adam Smith (whom Posner invokes but not for this point), it has been used

---

[3] This is stated in a joint article with Francesco Parisi: Posner and Parisi 1997: ix.
[4] Posner and Parisi 1997: x.

by many later economists, but typically with some acknowledgement of its limitations (for example, by Knut Wicksell, Francis Edgeworth and Kenneth Arrow). In general, the use of that assumption in economics has tended to be combined, at least in the hands of sophisticated economic theorists, for specific analytical purposes (such as developing a pure model of competitive market economy relying on very simple assumptions). The presumption of exclusively self-interested choice has also come under growing criticism in recent years both from economic methodologists and from theorists influenced by the findings of experimental games.[5]

In contrast, the use of that limiting assumption has a history of quite full-blooded use in "law and economics," not least in the writings of Richard Posner himself. The reliance on a very narrow motivational assumption has had a critically restrictive role in constraining the reach of "law and economics."

The problem with "rational choice theory" does not lie so much in the presumption that people, by and large, behave according to the dictates of reason: that is a sensible enough presumption in most cases. The problem lies, rather, in the assumption made in so-called rational choice theory that the dictates of reason must take the peculiarly restricted form of making everyone act according to their narrowly defined self-interest, with no concern for any other aim, or objective, or principle. As Christine Jolls, Cass Sunstein and Richard Thaler point out in a far-reaching critique, "people care about being treated fairly and want to treat others fairly if those others are themselves behaving fairly."[6] To take economics in the extraordinarily simple form that the so-called rational choice theory presents can hardly do justice to the importance of economic considerations in assessing legal rules and their implications.

Economics, rationality and self-interest

A distinction of some importance is particularly worth clarifying in this context. In the old, narrow version of rational choice theory, it is assumed that no one really worries much about the lives of others, except to the extent that those lives affect their own. But the subject has moved away from that narrow version, and as was mentioned earlier, the more permissive version of rational choice theory, pioneeringly explored in particular by Gary Becker, it is not presumed that a person does not worry about others. They may well love other people, but whatever

[5] See, for example, Rabin 1993.   [6] Jolls, Sunstein and Richard 1998: 1479.

their feelings are towards others is reflected in their *own* welfare, and it is their own welfare that they continue to pursue. That is, they may do nice things to others precisely because they would themselves suffer, given their concern for others, if they neglected these concerns. This idea of sympathetic self-interestedness can be contrasted with what has been called "commitment," which includes the possibility that a person may do things for others even if the person's own welfare were not affected by these actions.[7]

Rational choice theory, in the broader form, does not rule out worrying about others. But as reasons for action each person is ultimately moved only by what influences his or her own welfare, after taking into account the way in which other people's lives may affect any person's own well-being. Even in the broad – more permissive – version of rational choice theory (like that of Gary Becker), it would be irrational to go beyond what can be justified in terms of one's own welfare (no matter how that is determined). It would be incomprehensible in this system, even with the broader version of rational choice theory, to say something like this: "The AIDS epidemic in the world does not affect my own well-being in any way, but given my commitment to a just world, it is still rational for me to do something to fight that epidemic." It would be also difficult to see, through the narrow lenses of rational choice theory, the rationality of sophisticated judgments such as: "The AIDS epidemic touches my life marginally, since I am pained at the thought of so many people suffering from pain and avoidable death, but it is rational for me to do much more than could be justified by the marginal extent to which my own well-being is affected, given my much bigger commitment to helping to build a just world."

As a contrast to this priority of self-interest, we may consider an argument presented by Ragnar Frisch, a great economist and a pioneering econometrician. Frisch argued for the need to take note particularly of the demands of responsibility that people feel towards others. While he illustrated the point with an example from family behavior, the purpose was to draw some lessons for public policy, through what he called the "cooperation between politicians and econometricians." His example was the following:

Assume that my wife and I have had dinner alone as we usually do. For dessert two cakes have been purchased. They are very different, but both are very fine cakes and expensive – according to our standard. My wife hands me the tray and suggests that I help myself. What shall I do? By looking up my own total

---

[7] The distinction and its importance have been extensively discussed in Sen 1977, and also Sen 1982; 2002.

utility function I find that I very much would like to devour one particular one of the two cakes. I will propound that this introspective observation is *completely irrelevant* for the choice problem I face. The really relevant problem is: which one of the two cakes does my wife prefer? If I knew that the case would be easy. I would say "yes please" and take the *other* cake, the one that is her second priority.[8]

Frisch's point is not that in social and economic relations people must invariably behave in such a noble and other-regarding way (that would be too much to expect), but that sometimes people do just that, and it is important to investigate when they would behave in a committed way and when they would not. Economic behavior can take diverse forms, and any integrating effort, like that of "law and economics" (at least in its traditional form), which puts all human conduct within a rigidly self-centered model, must end up missing the richness of the discipline of economics.

As it happens, a similar point to Ragnar Frisch's was made by Adam Smith himself, whom the practitioners of "law and economics" take as a great guru, without being particularly inclined, it would appear, to read his writings. Adam Smith discussed many different ways in which a person's non-self-interested concerns can "enter into the principles of his conduct."[9] He emphasized particularly the role of "public spirit" as well as "generosity," and extensively discussed the need for non-self-interested behavior in many spheres of activities. He was keen also to study the impact of not entirely self-interested conduct on social institutions and on the investigation of legal arrangements that would be useful to have. Adam Smith insisted that while "prudence" is "of all virtues that which is most helpful to the individual," it is frequently the case that "humanity, justice, generosity, and public spirit" could prove to be "the qualities most useful to others."[10] And he also discussed why we do take an interest in how our actions influence other people's lives.

Diversity of behavioral principles is not ruled out by the discipline of economics. What is needed is a better understanding of the contingent dominance of some principles in certain types of cases while other principles have greater influence in other types of cases. It may turn out that in many situations, the assumption that self-interest is the only motive would work just fine (most of us do not worry about our responsibility towards others when we decide whether to have tea or coffee in a restaurant), whereas in other situations it would be critically important to

[8] Frisch 1971.   [9] See Smith 1976a: 190–2; see also Smith 1976b.
[10] Smith 1976a: 189.

bring in other motivations, different objectives and broader principles
of behavior (for example, in determining whether we should shirk our
specified duties in a production process that relies on the cooperation
of all). Economics cannot escape being interested in such questions as:
why are group responsibilities and norm-based behavior powerful in
some economic relations and not at all so in others?

Each discipline must be taken in a sufficiently capacious form

The mistake of taking an arbitrarily narrow view of economics is not
the only way in which the integration of law and economics may be
hindered. Taking an unduly restricted view of law is another. For example, legal developments are constitutive parts of development in general
and cannot be seen only as instruments for economic expansion (as
economic models are often inclined to presume). The realization of the
rights that people legally have has importance of its own. So does, it can
be argued, the rule of law in general.

The case for taking each subject in its capacious form applies, of
course, not only to economics, but also to law. This is worth emphasizing, particularly since there has been a tendency, especially in the literature on economic development, to treat law and legal achievements
entirely in terms of how they serve economic goals, rather than taking
them to be of importance in other ways as well. Legal arrangements
can, of course, be useful for economic accomplishments, but this does
not imply that any integration of economics and law must take law to
be nothing other than a servant of economics – judged only by how it
serves economic goals.

Indeed, the process of economic and social development has many
dimensions, and legal development is part of that many-sided operation
of social change. The soundness of legal development cannot be judged
only in terms of what it does to the growth of GNP (gross national
product), or even in terms of broader economic objectives, such as
removing hunger and economic deprivation and of expanding economic capabilities of people. There are other dimensions with which
legal thinking has rightly been concerned for a very long time. We cannot, for example, plausibly say that the development process has gone
beautifully well – because of economic progress – even though many
people are being arbitrarily executed, many criminals go free while
many perfectly ordinary citizens end up in jail, and so on. If there are
such transgressions of law and justice, then we have to accept that there
is something deeply wrong with the process of development itself.

It is quite apparent from the literature on economic development that economists have often tried to confine their understanding of the relevance of law to some elementary phenomena, for example the role of property rights, ignoring the importance of wider legal and law-related considerations, such as democracy and individual rights, which can be central to the process of economic development and to the practice of economics in general. Indeed, development has a strong association of meanings that make a basic level of legality and judicial attainment a constitutive part of the idea of development, just as economic progress is an integral component of it as well. The notion of development cannot be conceptually delinked from the soundness of legal and judicial fairness.

We have to conclude, therefore, that the marriage between economics and law demands that each of the two disciplines be taken in an adequately capacious form. There is much to be actually gained from viewing economics and law in an integrated way, doing justice to each. The problem with substantial parts of the brand-named product that has come to be called "law and economics" is that, among other simplifications, it takes an unduly narrow view of economics, just as the economic literature on development and progress fall often enough for the temptation of seeing nothing in law other than its instrumental importance – a denuded view of law and jurisprudence. The success of integration of economics and law must depend on taking both economics and law in their full reach, rather than seeing each in an arbitrarily imprisoned form. Combining law and economics has to be a *broadening* exercise, not a *narrowing* one.[11]

Ethics and economics: "transcendental" and comparative approaches to justice

Since I have been concentrating so far on the relation between economics and law, I should now ask: what about ethics? Here again something of the general point I am trying to make would, I believe, be relevant. Ethics and economics can benefit greatly from constructive interactions, and so can law and ethics. Indeed, the multilateral interrelations between economics, law and ethics can be extremely important to pursue in an integrated way. What has to be avoided, again, is shortchanging any of the individual subjects – either economics, or ethics, or law – even as we try to reach out beyond the borders of each individual

---

[11] I have discussed the demands of such integration in my K. C. Basu Memorial Lecture, given at West Bengal National University of Juridical Sciences, in Kolkata on December 20, 2003, under the title "Law, Economics and Social Change."

discipline. Each subject deserves an adequate understanding of its own discipline, even when interdisciplinary boundaries are crossed.

Let me illustrate my point with a rather grand example. The contemporary political philosophy of justice has been much influenced by the outstanding contributions of John Rawls. He certainly has taken economics very seriously, and his classic *A Theory of Justice* (perhaps the most important work on political philosophy in a century) is full of references to economic analyses.[12] But there is one feature of Rawls's "justice as fairness" that draws entirely from philosophical tradition (going back not only to Kant but also to Hobbes), and rather firmly ignores the standard discipline of reasoning in economics.

The point at issue is an underlying "transcendentalism" in the political philosophy of Rawlsian justice, in contrast with the "comparative" framework of social choice and welfare economics – a distinction which Rawls does not seem to take seriously enough. Let me elaborate.[13]

In his "justice as fairness," Rawls takes the principal question to be: what is a just society? Indeed, in most theories of justice in contemporary political philosophy, that question is taken to be central. This is why I am calling it a "transcendental" approach to justice, since it focuses on identifying perfectly just societal arrangements. In contrast, what can be called a "comparative" approach is the standard starting point in economics and in social choice theory. The latter approach concentrates on ranking alternative social arrangements (whether some arrangement is "less just" or "more just" than another), rather than focusing exclusively – or at all – on the identification of a fully just society.[14] The transcendental and comparative approaches are quite distinct, and neither in general subsumes the other.

The transcendental approach to justice is not new (it can be traced at least to Thomas Hobbes), but recent contributions have done much to consolidate the reliance on this approach. In his investigation of "justice as fairness," Rawls explores in depth the nature of an entirely just society seen in the perspective of contractarian fairness.[15] Rawls's investigation begins with identifying the demands of fairness through exploring an imagined "original position" in which the members of the society are ignorant of their respective individual characteristics including their own comprehensive preferences. The principles of justice that

[12] Rawls 1971; 1999.
[13] Since this talk was given at the Ritsumeikan University in 2005, I have tried to carry my complaints to the philosophers, in the form of a paper, Sen 2006. A similar theme was pursued, among others, in my Condorcet Lecture given at the University of Caen, at a meeting of the Social Choice and Welfare Society, June 20–21, 2005.
[14] See for example Sen 1970 and Suzumura 1983.   [15] Rawls 1971; 1993.

emerge in the original position are taken to be impartial because they are chosen by the persons involved under a "veil of ignorance," without knowledge of their individual identities in the society with specific vested interests and particular priorities.

The practical relevance of comparative questions about justice is hard to deny. Investigation of different ways of advancing justice in a society (or in the world), or of reducing manifest injustices that may exist, demands comparative judgments about justice, for which the identification of fully just social arrangements is neither necessary nor sufficient. To illustrate the contrast involved, it may well turn out that in a comparative perspective, the introduction of social policies that eliminate widespread hunger (or remove rampant illiteracy) can be shown to yield an advancement of justice. But the implementation of such policies could still leave the societies involved far away from the transcendental requirements of a fully just society (since transcendence would have other demands regarding equal liberties, distributional equity, and many other requirements that have been explored by Rawls and others). To take another example, instituting a system of health insurance in the United States that does not leave close to 50 million Americans without any guarantee of medical attention at all may be judged to be an enormous advancement of justice, but such an institutional change would not turn the United States into a "just society" (since there would remain a great many other suboptimalities to remedy).

It is a grand partition between the "just" and the "non-just" that a theory of transcendental justice yields. Even after extensive justice-enhancing advancements, we would still be left on the "non-just" side, since an improvement – even a radically important improvement – would not typically take us to a transcendentally "right" or "best" state which cannot have any further improvement. In making public policy, or in working for institutional change, some non-transcendental articulation is clearly needed.

The question that is somewhat puzzling is this. Welfare economics has always been concerned with comparative rather than transcendental questions, no matter whether the subject matter has been policy choice or institutional choice. The theory of justice in ethics, as interpreted by John Rawls among our contemporaries (in line with a long tradition in moral philosophy), is deeply concerned with institutional choice (this is the basic point of Rawlsian theory in moving from "fairness" to "principles of justice" that would lead to the choice of just institutions), and later on (for example, in what Rawls calls "the legislative phase") with policy choice as well. Rawls himself has taken a very serious interest in economics, as have other contemporary moral philosophers. And yet the perspicacity and relevance of the comparative question seem to have been persistently missed in mainstream moral philosophy, including in Rawlsian theory, by the almost exclusive concentration on the transcendental question.

Could economics have been of greater use to moral philosophy if that single-minded concentration were dispensed with in favor of taking a fuller view of the discipline of welfare economics or of social choice theory? It is hard to brush away that question as a silly doubt.

Is a transcendental approach to justice "sufficient" in order to compare social states?

A transcendental approach cannot, on its own, address questions about advancing justice and compare alternative proposals for having a more just society, short of proposing a radical jump to a *perfectly just* world. Indeed, the answers that a transcendental approach to justice gives – or can give – are quite distinct and distant from the type of concerns that engage people in discussions on justice and injustice in the world (for example, iniquities of hunger, illiteracy, torture, arbitrary incarceration, or medical exclusion as particular social features that need remedying), rather than looking only for the full cluster of perfectly just societal arrangements. This is where the comparative framework of welfare economics and social choice has some real advantage.[16]

Nevertheless, important as this elementary contrast is, the formal remoteness of the transcendental approach from functional judgments about justice does not in itself indicate that the transcendental approach cannot be the right approach. Two further questions in particular have to be addressed. First, can it be the case that transcendence is sufficient for yielding much more than what its formal content suggests? In particular, can the answers to transcendental queries take us indirectly to comparative assessments of justice as well (as a kind of "by-product"), in particular through comparisons of "distances" from transcendence at which any particular set of societal arrangements stands? Second, can it be the case that the transcendental question ("what is a just society?") has to be answered, as an essential requirement, for a cogent and well-founded theory of *comparative* justice, which would otherwise be foundationally defective or incomplete? Is a transcendental approach either

---

[16] Similarly in pursuing the important objectives of "independence, responsibility and self-respect" in addition to the requirements of well-being (on which see Reiko Gotoh, "Justice and Public Reciprocity," Chapter 7), the need for a relational "comparative" approach has much more plausibility than can be found in the totalism of a transcendental framework.

sufficient or *necessary* for the institutional choices and policy selections that bind together moral philosophy and welfare economics?

I believe the answer must be in the negative. Consider the issue of sufficiency first. Does a transcendental approach produce, as a by-product, relational conclusions that are ready to be drawn out, so that transcendence may end up giving us a great deal more than its overt form claims? In particular, is the specification of an entirely just society sufficient to give us rankings of departures from justness in terms of comparative "distances" from perfection, so that a transcendental identification might *inter alia* entail comparative grading as well? Can comparisons of the *extents* of lapses from transcendence give us a ready-made method of going from a transcendental theory to comparative conclusions?

This can, however, hardly work. The difficulty lies in the fact that there are different features involved in identifying distance, related, among other distinctions, to (1) disparate domains of imperfection, (2) distinct dimensionalities of transgressions and (3) diverse ways of weighing different infractions. The identification of transcendence, which is what a transcendental theory does, would not yield any means of addressing these problems to arrive at a relational ranking of departures from transcendence.

In the context of the Rawlsian analysis of the just society, departures may occur in many different spaces. They can include the breaching of liberty, which, furthermore, can involve diverse violations of distinctive liberties. There can also be violations – again in possibly disparate forms – of the demands of equity in the distribution of primary goods (there can be many different departures from the demands of Difference Principle, which forms a part of Rawls's second principle). Similarly, very different and diverse transgressions can occur from the perfectly just society in other transcendental theories of justice (for example, those that would replace the Rawlsian focus on "primary goods" in the Difference Principle by concentrating respectively on "capabilities," or "resources" or "opportunities," or some other way of reformulating the allocational and distributional needs of transcendental justice).

There are also disparate ways of comparing and weighting the extent of each such discrepancy and of appraising the comparative remoteness of actual distributions from what the principles of full justice would demand. Further, we have to consider departures in procedural equity (such as infringements of fair equality of public opportunities or facilities), which figure within the domain of Rawlsian demands of justice (in the first part of his "second principle"). In moving from a transcendental theory we have to find ways and means of weighting procedural failures *against* infelicities of end-state outcomes (for example, distributions of primary goods), and if we try to submerge that issue by giving lexical priority to one concern until it is entirely met, then that theory would be of little use for most problems of practical reason involving judgments of justice.

Such comparative implications are not, of course, needed in a purely transcendental theory of justice, seen as a free standing achievement, and this is not, thus, in any way an embarrassment for the transcendental theory itself, seen as an accomplishment on its own. It is in the movement from there to any possible practical use in institutional choice or policy selection that the problem arises, but that is, of course, where the practical relevance of a theory of justice has to rest.[17]

Is a transcendental approach to justice "necessary" in order to compare social states?

What about the hypothesis that the identification of the best is *necessary*, even if not *sufficient*, to rank any two alternatives in terms of justice. In the usual sense of necessity, this would be a somewhat odd possibility. In the discipline of comparative judgments in any field, relative assessment of two alternatives tends in general to be a matter between them, without there being the necessity to beseech the help of a third – "irrelevant" – alternative (even a *transcendental* "irrelevant" alternative). Indeed, it is not at all obvious why in making the judgment that some social arrangement x is better than an alternative arrangement y, we have to invoke the identification that some quite different alternative z is the "best" or the "right" social arrangement.

There is, however, a weaker form of the hypothesis of necessity, which merely asserts that if comparative assessments can be systematically made, then that discipline must also be able to identify the very best. The claim, in this case, would be not so much that two alternatives cannot be compared in terms of justice without first knowing what the best or the perfect alternative is, but that the comparative ranking of the different alternatives must *inter alia* also be able to identify the answer to the transcendental question regarding the perfectly just society. Or, to put it in another way, if the transcendental question cannot be answered, then neither can the comparative.

But does the maximally articulated sequence of pairwise comparisons invariably lead us to the very best? The answer must, again, be "No," since (1) the ranking can be incomplete, and (2) even a complete ordering may not yield a transcendental alternative over an infinite set.

---

[17] The argument is developed more fully in Sen 2006, 2009.

It is, in fact, only with a "well-ordered" ranking (for example, a complete and transitive ordering over a finite set) that we can be sure that the set of pairwise comparisons must also identify a "best" alternative.

The practical relevance of this mathematical point is the following. A theory of justice that makes systematic room for incompleteness allows one to arrive at possibly quite strong judgments (for example, about the injustice of continuing famines in a world of prosperity, or of persistently grotesque subjugation of women, and so on), without having to find highly differentiated assessment of every political and social arrangement in comparison with every other arrangement (e.g. addressing such questions as: is a top income tax rate of 35 percent more just or less just than a top rate of 36 percent?).

I have discussed elsewhere why a systematic and disciplined theory of normative evaluation, including assessment of social justice, need not take a "totalist" form.[18] Incompleteness may be of the lasting kind for several different reasons, including unbridgeable gaps in information and judgmental unresolvability involving disparate considerations that cannot be entirely eliminated, even with full information.

For example, it may be hard to resolve the overall balance of the comparative claims of equity considerations that lie behind Rawlsian lexicographic maximin, compared with, say, sum-ranking in a gross or equity-adjusted form (through summing the indicators of individual advantages or their concave transforms). And yet, despite such durable ambiguity, we may still be able to agree readily that there is a clear social failure involved in the persistence of famines, or of endemic hunger or in exclusion from medical access. They can be very useful for the advancement of justice, even after taking note of the costs involved. Similarly, we may acknowledge the possibility that liberties of different persons may, to some extent, conflict with each other (so that any fine-tuning of the demands of equal liberty may be hard to work out), and yet strongly agree that arbitrary incarceration of accused people, without access to court procedures, would be an unjust violation of liberty that calls for urgent rectification.

Conclusion

Thus, the hiatus between the comparative approach that is central to economics and the transcendental approach common in contemporary moral philosophy works both ways. The question "what is a just society?" is neither a good *starting point* for a useful theory of justice,

---

[18] Sen 1970; 1997; 1999; 2004.

nor a plausible *end point* to it. A systematic theory of comparative justice does not need, nor does it necessarily yield, an answer to the question "what is a just society?"

I must, therefore, assert the relevance of the economists' approach to justice and injustice through the comparative route, rather than remaining confined by the political philosophers' usual preference for the transcendental approach to a theory of justice. Since I have argued elsewhere, for example in my book *On Ethics and Economics*,[19] how important it is for economists to learn from political and moral philosophers, it gives me some happiness to be able to argue that philosophers too have something to learn from economists. Benefiting from interdisciplinary understanding has to be a two-way process. There is something to give as well as something to take.

To return to the general thematic point that I have been trying to make, there is certainly a good deal to gain from exploring the interrelations between ethics, economics and law (I could have given many other examples to illustrate the point, if time permitted, distinct from the ones discussed here). However, the exercise can be more productive if each discipline is given its due and understood in an adequately capacious form, which sometimes does not happen. There is indeed much to learn from each other, but we have to take each other more seriously than we often seem to do. The fruitfulness of interdisciplinary work depends greatly on our willingness to see the full strength of each discipline.

Acknowledgements

This chapter was first presented at a conference on "Ethics, Economics, and Law," Ritsumeikan University, October 28, 2005. In preparing this talk I greatly benefited from discussions with Kaushik Basu, Akeel Bilgrami, Reiko Gotoh, Carol Rovane, Maurice Salles, Thomas Scanlon, and Kotaro Suzumura.

References

Becker, Gary 1996. *Accounting for Tastes*, Cambridge, MA: Harvard University Press.
Frisch, Ragnar 1971. "Sommerbeid mellom politikere og Okonometrikere on formuleringen av politiske preferenser," *Sosialøkonomen*, **25** (6): 5–13 (the translation is by Loav Bjerkholt, 1994. "Ragnar Frisch: The Originator of Econometrics," mimeographed).

[19] Sen 1987.

Jolls, Christine, Sunstein, Cass and Thaler, Richard 1998. "A Behavioral Approach to Law and Economics," *Stanford Law Review*, **50** (5): 1471–50.

Posner, Richard and Parisi, Francesco 1997. "Law and Economics: An Introduction," in Posner and Parisi (eds.) 1997, *Law and Economics*, vol. I, Lyme: Edward Elgar Publishing, 3–57.

Rabin, Matthew 1993. "Incorporating Fairness into Game Theory and Economics," *American Economic Review*, **83** (5): 1281–302.

Rawls, John 1971. *A Theory of Justice*, Cambridge, MA: Harvard University Press.

   1993. *Political Liberalism*, New York: Columbia University Press.

   1999. *A Theory of Justice*, revised edn., Cambridge, MA: Harvard University Press.

Sen, A. K. 1970. *Collective Choice and Social Welfare*, San Francisco: Holden-Day.

   1973. "Behaviour and the Concept of Preference," *Economica*, **40** (159): 241–59.

   1977. "Rational Fools: A Critique of the Behavioral Foundations of Economic Theory," *Philosophy and Public Affairs*, **6** (4): 317–44.

   1982. *Choice, Welfare and Measurement*, Oxford: Blackwell; republished, Cambridge, MA: Harvard University Press (1997).

   1985. "Goals, Commitment and Identity," *Journal of Law, Economics and Organization*, **1** (2): 341–55.

   1987. *On Ethics and Economics*, New York: Blackwell.

   1997. "Maximization and the Act of Choice," *Econometrica*, **65** (4): 745–79.

   1999. "The Possibility of Social Choice," *American Economic Review*, **89** (3): 349–78.

   2002. *Rationality and Freedom*, Cambridge, MA: Belknap Press of Harvard University Press.

   2004. "Incompleteness and Reasoned Choice," *Synthese*, **140** (1–2): 43–59.

   2006. "What Do We Want from a Theory of Justice?" *Journal of Philosophy*, **103** (5): 215–38.

   2009. *The Idea of Justice*, London: Allen Lane, Penguin, and Cambridge, MA: Belknap Press of Harvard University.

Smith, Adam 1976a. *The Theory of Moral Sentiments*, 6th revised edn. [1790], ed. D. D. Raphael and A. L. Macfie, Oxford: Clarendon Press; originally published 1759.

Smith, Adam 1976b. *An Inquiry into the Nature and Causes of the Wealth of Nations*, ed. R. H. Campbell and A. S. Skinner, Oxford: Clarendon Press; originally published 1776.

Suzumura, Kotaro 1983. *Rational Choice, Collective Decisions, and Social Welfare*, Cambridge University Press.

2   Neorepublicanism and Sen's economic, legal, and ethical desiderata

Philip Pettit

Amartya Sen's overview of developments in the interaction of economics, law and ethics gives us three take-home messages. Economics should not be taken to postulate a self-seeking *homo economicus*, incapable of commitment to others and even of sympathy with others. Law should not be assessed wholly on the basis of its economic payoffs but on the basis of its broader benefits in the organization of public life. And ethics should not be construed – or pursued – as the search for an ideal model of justice, without any desire to find a yardstick for the comparative appraisal of imperfect systems. These messages identify what we may describe, for short, as economic, legal and ethical desiderata on a political theory.

I have some small reservations about how Sen understands the notion of commitment, which I have outlined elsewhere (Pettit 2005). But those reservations apart, I entirely endorse the take-home messages of his chapter. What I propose to do in this brief response is to show how the neorepublican philosophy that has come to prominence in recent political thinking can fully satisfy the desiderata outlined by Sen (Pettit 1997b; Skinner 1998; Maynor 2003; Laborde and Maynor 2007). I apologize for the fact that, since I am one of those aligned with this reworked republicanism, the exercise has a somewhat self-serving aspect. But it may be Sen-serving as well as self-serving, for the notions of freedom and capability that he and Martha Nussbaum have been developing make for a very direct connection with the neorepublican approach (Pettit 2001; Pettit in press a).

Nerorepublicanism

Like the tradition on which it draws, neorepublicanism is first and foremost a theory of freedom. It focuses on the requirements of freedom in a distinctive sense of that ideal and casts other ethical requirements such as those of justice or community or welfare as secondary concerns;

they call for satisfaction in the measure in which their satisfaction serves the cause of republican freedom.

What is freedom in the preferred, republican sense? Take a given choice with alternatives, A, B and C. You are free in this sense to the extent that others exercise only reasoned control over what you choose amongst those alternatives. They exercise only the control that consists in providing reasons for acting one way or another, on a take-it-or-leave-it basis. Those who resort to either sort of measure, reasoned or unreasoned, will exercise some control over you; they will make it more probable that you behave in a designated manner than it would have been had they not been present. But only those who exercised unreasoned control will reduce your freedom in the choice on hand (Pettit 2007b).

To avoid the unreasoned control of others in a given choice is not the same as avoiding the interference of others in that choice: avoiding their active obstruction or coercion or manipulation. There are two reasons for this. Others may control you without active interference if they stand by in a monitoring position and only interfere on a need-for-interference basis. They let you go as you will, if you are inclined to act as they want, but they are prepared to take steps to block or inhibit or redirect your choice – or at least to make you regret that type of choice and avoid it in the future – if your pattern of behavior, or their pattern of preference, should change. Thus interference may be absent while control remains present. Control will remain present, indeed, even if others are so well disposed that they allow you to act on whatever happens to be your preference. To the extent that they retain the power of interference, and are ready to interfere should their disposition change, they remain your masters. You operate only within their power and you are not a free agent.

But not only may control obtain without active interference. The opposite is also true: that you may endure active interference without having to endure control. Suppose that you prefer that others exercise a certain obstruction or coercion or even manipulation in your life, say in order to cope with an addiction; you are happy to allow your spouse to lock away the whiskey or the cigars for fear of your own inclination. To the extent that you can call off this interference in your life and affairs, should you change your mind, that interference will not represent a way in which you are controlled by others. Others figure as your agents in this story, and the control will ultimately be exercised by yourself.

The neorepublican tradition takes freedom from such control – freedom as non-domination – as the central ideal in the design of social and political institutions. More particularly, it valorizes freedom as non-domination in those choices that each can fully enjoy, consistently with others enjoying them at the same time: in those choices that count as basic liberties (Pettit 2008). Freedom in this sense is a property of persons; it is a status that they enjoy to the extent that they are more or less proof against alien control by others. Intuitively, it is the property of being able to stand equal with others in a position where all can see, and all can see that it is universally seen, that the person cannot be pushed around with impunity. Attempts to push the person around will be met with resistance, or, should they succeed, the perpetrators will be subject to a sort of redress that is designed to vindicate the standing of the victim.

Should I have said that the neorepublican maximand is not freedom as non-domination as such but rather equal freedom as non-domination? If this formula is preferred, I am happy to go along with it. But for the record I think that freedom as non-domination is the sort of property such that the best way to maximize it from any less than perfect position will be to take steps towards ensuring greater equality in its enjoyment (Pettit 1997b; Lovett 2001). Let the weaker be further protected and that will increase their aggregate non-domination without necessarily reducing anybody else's. Let the stronger be further protected and two features of the move are likely to make it ineffective. First, the extra protection is unlikely to increase the non-domination of the strong as much as it would have increased the non-domination of the weaker; it may just make assurance doubly assured. And second, the extra protection is likely to give them yet a further resource for imposing on the weaker and so reducing the non-domination of the weaker.

One of the features of neorepublicanism, unlike the older tradition on which it draws, is that it has an inclusive conception of the members of any society; they include at least all those who are adult and able-minded, not just the propertied, mainstream males on which political theory has traditionally focused. How then does it suggest that the freedom of non-domination of citizens should be served in any society? By two sorts of steps, broadly conceived. First of all, the state ought to make resources available across the citizenry that are designed to guard against anyone's being dominated – dominated, not just interfered with – by other members or groups of members. And second, the state ought to impose constraints on itself that are designed to make its own interference – its interference in taxation, legislation and punishment – subject to the ultimate control of citizens. Citizens ought to be protected against the domination of non-state parties by the power of a state that is itself undominating.[1]

---

[1] There is a third requirement that I ignore here: that the undominating state also be undominated; in particular, that it be undominated by other states or by other international presences. If the state is dominated in this way then, assuming it is controlled

Guarding against private power, on republican lines, requires a wide range of interventions. One is to firm up the infrastructure of non-domination that requires, ideally, a flourishing economy, a legal order, an inclusive knowledge system, a sound health system and a sustainable environment. A second is to empower the vulnerable, providing them with the resources of basic functioning (Sen 1985; Nussbaum 1992). A third is to provide protection for the people as a whole against criminal offenders. And a fourth is to regulate the powerful agents and agencies that, regardless of the other measures in place, still manage to exercise a certain control over ordinary citizens.

There are many forms that initiatives in these areas might assume, and institutional imagination is required to ensure that a variety of possibilities are put on the table for consideration. Take, for example, the issue of what protections should be put in place to empower the more vulnerable in relationships where there is a real prospect of domination: say, domestic or workplace relations. The vulnerable might be given rights that enable them to trigger the law against certain abuses, as in the right of a worker to sue for wrongful dismissal or a woman to charge her husband with domestic violence. Or the vulnerable might be given more powers with which to counter the dominating, as when workers are allowed to strike or wives to seek separation or divorce on a no-fault basis. Or the alternatives available to the vulnerable might be improved, as when a state income is available to those workers who leave employment or there is a possibility for the victims of domestic abuse to seek refuge in homes for battered women. Or a mix of those measures might be adopted. There are a variety of different possibilities.

Let us turn now to the second issue, bearing on how the state might be made non-dominating. How might political institutions be designed so that people are guarded against the guardians themselves?

The first point to register in dealing with this question is that people are subject to certain social and political necessities that are not in themselves sources of domination. These necessities have always been acknowledged in a realistic way by the main streams of republican thought, although they are rejected in utopian strands of state-of-nature thinking. The first necessity is that we are all born into an ongoing society; the second that ours is a world in which there is no effective possibility of living out of society; and the third that every society has to organize its business centrally and coercively. These facts do not testify in themselves to any domination by others. It is not because of the

by the people, its domination will mean their domination. I address this issue in Pettit (in press b).

controlling presence of certain powers in our lives that we are forced to live in society, under a collective regime. We live, as by a natural necessity, under these constraints; they are as inescapable as gravity.

When will a government be dominating, then, and when non-dominating? Government will dominate any citizen if its initiatives are not controlled by the citizenry as a whole – the people – or if that citizen does not have an equal share in such civic or popular control. Government will be non-dominating for a citizen if its initiatives are subject to popular control, and if that citizen enjoys equality with others in the exercise of that control. Government as such is a natural necessity, on this picture. It will be undominating in relation to me, a randomly chosen citizen – it will be subject to my control in the highest feasible degree – insofar as the people as a whole control what is done, and I play an equal part in the exercise of that collective control. In a slogan, the non-dominating government will be the government that is subject to the effective and equally shared control of the people or citizenry.

This account of what is required to make government interference non-dominating supports a number of immediate implications. The first is that the non-dominating government will have to be democratic in the basic, etymological sense of the word. It will have to be a government that is subject to the *kratos* or power of the *demos* or people – as we may assume, the equally shared power of the people. But what does democracy in this basic, republican sense require? A second and third implication of the account given shed some light on that question.

The second implication is that the citizenry may exercise effective and equal control over government, and be in that sense a democratic people, even when the governing individuals or body are distinct from the people themselves. That I control what is done by someone does not require that I am that very person; and that a people controls how government acts does not require that it is the governing agency. That government is subject to effective and equal popular control does not entail, then, that it has to be exercised by the people themselves, as in Rousseau's image of the self-governing assembly. Rousseau went beyond traditional republican doctrine in giving such importance to the idea of the participatory assembly.

But the conception of non-dominating government also has a third implication, bearing on electoral rather than participatory democracy. The fact that those in government are controlled effectively and equally by the people does not entail that they are elected; nor does the fact that they are elected mean that they are popularly controlled. That certain officials are appointed by elected authorities, for example – or even that they inherit office, as in the case of the constitutional monarch – does not mean that they are uncontrolled; they may be subject to checks and balances that make them quite responsive to the people. And, on the other side, the fact that certain authorities are elected does not guarantee that they are subject to popular control. Let someone not care about being re-elected, and the fact that they came to office via election may have no controlling effect on their actions. This has always been recognized in mainstream republicanism, as when James Madison (1987), one of the founders of the American republic, warned against the problem of an "elective despotism."

I cannot go further into the measures that might be proposed at this point for ensuring that government is subject to the effective and equally shared control of the people or citizenry. I hope that what I have said is enough to communicate a sense of the neorepublican project, and that it will provide an adequate base for returning to Amartya Sen's three desiderata and asking after how far they are likely to be satisfied under the approach.

The ethical desideratum

Taking the desiderata in reverse order, let me first consider Sen's principle that an ethics ought to allow us to compare imperfect systems for their performance in respect of justice and not focus exclusively on the ideal of a perfectly just society. Sen does not mean that a normative theory ought to be able to provide a complete ordering of alternative possible systems, for he recognizes that sometimes the best orderings we can achieve are incomplete; there are some comparisons that they may not enable us to decide in a determinate way. But he does argue strongly that ethics cannot hope to retain any serious relevance if it abjures the task of ordering altogether.

Although he does not say so, this principle gives strong *prima facie* support to consequentialism rather than to non-consequentialist alternatives. According to consequentialists, the right is a maximizing function of the good, however the good is understood. What is right in any set of alternatives is that which produces the most good or the most expected good – we need not dwell on that distinction – and alternatives can be ranked in an order of rightness to the extent that their scores on goodness are determinate enough to support that ranking. I do not say that non-consequentialist approaches cannot satisfy Sen's ordering desideratum – T. M. Scanlon's (1998) contractualism does well on this count (Pettit 2006) – but I do say that consequentialism is uniquely well fitted to meet it. There is no need for special stipulations on how to adapt a consequential theory to the ranking of less than ideal alternatives. The very character of consequentialist theory ensures that it will be useful for this purpose.

The reason that neorepublicanism can meet the ordering desideratum is that the tradition on which it draws and the spirit of the thesis it advances combine, as I have argued elsewhere (Pettit 1997b), to give it a consequentialist construal. The approach is not only distinguished by the way in which it interprets the ideal of freedom but by the fact that it argues that freedom under that interpretation should be maximized by social and political institutions. Those institutions should take whatever form promises to deliver the highest level of freedom obtainable under existing and likely circumstances.

This being the case, then, neorepublicanism is guaranteed to meet Sen's desideratum on the need for normative theory to be able to rank imperfect political alternatives, not just to identify an unobtainable ideal. It may not provide a complete ranking, of course. There may be indeterminacies about how relatively important are protections against private and public domination, for example, as there may be indeterminacies on more particular matters. And those indeterminacies may disable us from ranking certain alternatives against each other. But nevertheless the spirit of the approach ought to be wholly congenial from Sen's perspective.[2]

The legal desideratum

What of the desideratum according to which law should be valued for a broad range of social benefits, not just as a coordinating device with certain economic payoffs? Neorepublicanism is bound to see law as the primary means whereby the state seeks two goals: one, to order social life with a view to guarding against private domination; and two, to constrain what the state itself may do, thereby protecting against public domination. Thus the approach is in no danger of failing to meet the legal desideratum.

The private ordering role of law appears under many different guises. Law establishes crimes and the most appropriate responses to crimes (Braithwaite and Pettit 1990; Pettit 1997a). Law characterizes the torts for which private remedy may be sought. Law sets up the conditions under which contracts are binding. And so on. On all of these

[2] In token of the real-world applicability of the approach, I might draw attention to the explicit reliance of the Spanish President, José Luís Rodríguez Zapatero, on republican principles. For a review of his performance, judged by neorepublican criteria, see Pettit 2007a.

more or less salient matters, the neorepublican criterion of maximizing freedom as non-domination will be potentially relevant. And equally it will be relevant in one less obvious aspect, connected to the definition of basic liberties. Some choices may qualify as basic liberties – that is, as choices that all can enjoy, consistently with others doing so equally – without recourse to law. But many will not. Outstandingly, for example, the freedom to hold private property can only be identified on the basis of laws that define the titles, broad or qualified, that confer ownership and the rights, wide or restricted, that ownership gives.

The private ordering role that law exercises under the neorepublican perspective already means that systems of law should be assessed by a much wider range of criteria than economic payoffs. And the public aspect of law underscores this lesson. One of the most significant roles that law plays in the republican tradition, for example, is to limit the discretion of government. It plays this role insofar as it imposes rule-of-law constraints of government. Under those constraints, government should rule by law, not by ad hoc measures. And the law by which it rules should bear on individuals by general category, not by particular name or designation; have only prospective rather than retrospective relevance; and assume a promulgated, precise form that enables people to know what is expected of them. Law should provide the means of constructing the republic in the image of an empire of laws, in the old phrase, and not of men (Harrington 1992). It should channel and constrain government interference with a view to reducing the chances of state domination.

The economic desideratum

The economic desideratum requires a political theory not to operate with a narrow, self-seeking view of individual motivation but to make room for the richer account that is provided in Sen's *oeuvre*. This desideratum becomes relevant to republican purposes in the question as to what assumptions republicanism should make in arguing for imposing this or that design on public institutions.

One design assumption that is commonly recommended in the literature, and that goes back to the eighteenth century, is the knaves principle, as it is sometimes known. This is the principle that we should design institutions so that they will be reliable, even if the people living under them turn out to be malevolent and vicious (Brennan and Buchanan 1981). The ideal constitution, in Bernard Mandeville's formulation of the idea (1731: 332), has to be one which "remains unshaken though most men should prove knaves."

Sen's economic desideratum argues, plausibly, against reliance on the knaves principle. The question that arises for our purposes, then, is whether neorepublicanism would support the knaves principle as a basis for designing the institutions of public life. I conclude with some reasons for thinking that it wouldn't.

The tradition of republican thought has always been experimental or empirical, with lessons for institutional design being drawn from historical analogies, in particular analogies from the history of the decline of the Roman republic; here the classic text is Machiavelli's (1965) *Discourses*. This fits with the consequentialist image in which I reconstruct republicanism, for if the right institutions are the best institutions for promoting freedom as non-domination, then the right institutions are those that we have empirical reason to regard as the best.

From this empirical, consequentialist perspective, it is bound to seem like mere prejudice to assert that we should design institutions on the knaves principle. The reason is that if people are not actually knaves, then it may be bad practice to design institutions as if they were; it may lead to a system in which there is less freedom as non-domination enjoyed in the society rather than more. As it happens, the empirical evidence argues that not only are people not generally knaves – not narrow self-seekers, in Sen's sense – but it is likely to do considerable harm to design institutions on the assumptions that they are.[3] Put such institutions in place and they may make knaves of quite ordinary people, reducing rather than promoting the general level of compliance with republican standards.

There are a number of now quite well-documented effects that explain this finding; most of them are intuitively plausible.

1. *Hiding of virtue.* Many spontaneous compliers are likely to be motivated by the regard and trust that their compliance earns; but that motivation is undermined if rewards or penalties are so knave-apt that people can only expect their compliance to be seen as knavishly prudent, not as virtuous.
2. *Labeling.* Labeling is notoriously effective in leading people to act according to label, and introducing knave-apt sanctions in an undiscriminating way can have the effect of labeling all relevant parties, including the naturally compliant, as potential deviants.
3. *Sanction-dependency.* Even if compliers continue to comply in the presence of knave-apt sanctions, their compliance may become sanction-dependent – it may become conditional on identifying

---

[3] For further references see Pettit 1997b and Brennan and Pettit 2004: ch. 13

suitable rewards or penalties – and they may be more likely to deviate when a suitable temptation arises.

4. *Defiance.* Compliers may feel themselves alienated, undervalued, resentful, even defiant, in face of sanctions that represent them as parties who need watching; and such feelings are quite likely to reduce their motivation to comply.

5. *Closing of ranks.* The introduction of knave-apt sanctions, in particular penalties, may cause those whom they affect to develop a lot of solidarity, so that they are unwilling to blow the whistle on one another, they close ranks around anyone under threat and they develop the habit of shifting the blame onto other individuals or groups.

6. *Adverse selection.* The salience of knave-apt sanctions, be they rewards or penalties, may mean that spontaneous compliers are no longer attracted to public office; the people attracted may be those whose motivation would not be undermined by the presence of such sanctions (Brennan 1996).

Conclusion

The three desiderata identified in Amartya Sen's discussion, then, are fully honored in the neorepublican way of thinking. Republican theory naturally focuses on the assessment of real-world systems, not just on the identification of an other-worldly regime. It holds out a view of law under which it is a device for achieving a broad range of social benefits, not just those that figure in economic analyses. And it operates with an empirically informed model of the basis on which to design institutions, spurning the theoretically motivated idea that human beings are rational, self-seeking morons.

References

Braithwaite, J. and P. Pettit 1990. *Not Just Deserts: A Republican Theory of Criminal Justice.* Oxford University Press.

Brennan, G. 1996. "Selection and the Currency of Reward," in *The Theory of Institutional Design,* ed. R.E. Goodin. Cambridge University Press, 256–76.

Brennan, G. and J. Buchanan 1981. "The Normative Purpose of Economic 'Science': Rediscovery of an Eighteenth Century Method," *International Review of Law and Economics* 1: 155–66.

Brennan, G. and P. Pettit 2004. *The Economy of Esteem: An Essay on Civil and Political Society.* Oxford University Press.

Harrington, J. 1992. *The Commonwealth of Oceana and A System of Politics.* Cambridge University Press.

Laborde, C. and J. Maynor (eds.) 2007. *Republicanism and Political Theory*. Oxford: Blackwell.
Lovett, F. N. 2001. "Domination: A Preliminary Analysis," *Monist* **84**: 98–112.
Machiavelli, N. 1965. *The Chief Works and Others*. Durham, NC: Duke University Press.
Madison, J., A. Hamilton and J. Jay 1987. *The Federalist Papers*. Harmondsworth: Penguin.
Mandeville, B. 1731. *Free Thoughts on Religion, the Church and National Happiness*. London. [Reprinted 2006, Cosimo Inc., New York.]
Maynor, J. 2003. *Republicanism in the Modern World*. Cambridge: Polity Press.
Nussbaum, M. 1992. "Human Functioning and Social Justice," *Political Theory* **20**: 202–46.
Pettit, P. 1997a. "Republican Theory and Criminal Punishment," *Utilitas* **9**: 59–79.
  1997b. *Republicanism: A Theory of Freedom and Government*. Oxford University Press.
  2001. "Capability and Freedom: A Defence of Sen," *Economics and Philosophy* **17**: 1–20.
  2005. "Construing Sen on Commitment," *Economics and Philosophy* **21**: 15–32.
  2006. "Can Contract Theory Ground Morality?" in *Moral Theories*, ed. J. Dreier. Oxford: Blackwell, 77–96.
  2007a. *Examen a Zapatero*. Madrid: Temas de Hoy.
  2007b. "Republican Liberty: Three Axioms, Four Theorems," in *Republicanism and Political Theory*, ed. C. Laborde and J. Manor. Oxford: Blackwell, 102–30.
  2008. "The Basic Liberties," in *Essays on H.L.A. Hart*, ed. M. Kramer. Oxford University Press, 201–24.
  (in press a). "Freedom in the Spirit of Sen," in *Amartya Sen: Contemporary Philosophers in Focus*, ed. C. Morris. Cambridge University Press.
  (in press b). "A Republican Law of Peoples," *European Journal of Political Theory*, special issue on Republicanism and International Relations.
Scanlon, T. M. 1998. *What We Owe to Each Other*. Cambridge, MA: Harvard University Press.
Sen, A. 1985. *Commodities and Capabilities*. Amsterdam: North-Holland.
Skinner, Q. 1998. *Liberty before Liberalism*. Cambridge University Press.

3   The Prajâpati test: response to Amartya Sen

Marcel Hénaff

I agree with Professor Amartya Sen that the new intellectual trend in legal studies developed under the label of "law and economics," by only, or mostly, referring to the narrowest version of "rational choice theory," deprives itself of a complex and comprehensive understanding of both disciplines. If law studies wish to emulate the scientific rigor that is promoted by the dominant neoclassical school of economics, then by the same token it is understandable that they would be tempted to adopt the strict utilitarian principles and methodology of "rational choice theory" in its most rigorist form.

Professor Sen made an interesting distinction between this old hardline version of the "rational choice theory" according to which everyone aims at maximizing his/her own interest and a more flexible or permissive version, such as that developed by Gary Becker, which explains how interest or concern for others can constitute an integral part of our own self-interest. Sen in his paper commented on such explanations in the following terms: "They may well love other people, but whatever their feelings are towards others is reflected in their *own* welfare, and it is their own welfare that they continue to pursue. That is, they may do nice things to others precisely because they would themselves suffer, given their concern for others, if they neglected these concerns."[1]

At this point Sen proposes an interesting counterexample originally given by the economist Ragnar Frisch. It is the story of two cakes. The narrator, a nice husband, does not ask himself which of the two cakes (there are only two) he prefers and would like to eat, but he is rather anxious to know which one his wife would choose. He decides to offer her the very cake he himself prefers. This could be a typical narrative situation in the manner of Jose Luis Borges. But as Frisch points out – and this is precisely what Professor Sen wants to emphasize – the problem lies in the difficulty or even the impossibility for rational choice theory to account for such disinterested behavior. In

[1] This volume, p. 43.

66

order to preserve the hypothesis of radically self-interested motivation, that theory must paradoxically include, as Gary Becker does, generosity toward others as a factor in the comfort of the selfish agent. For example: being generous makes it possible to avoid feelings of guilt or makes one feel better by seeing the satisfaction of others, which is the understanding of sympathy proposed by Adam Smith in his *Theory of Moral Sentiments*. Another solution would consist of presupposing that human beings are altruistic to the same extent that they are selfish. But by doing so what is lost is the foundational principle of classical economic reasoning; human behavior then becomes unpredictable. As Hirschman explained in *The Passions and the Interests* passions are erratic, whereas interests are stable. Self-interest can therefore provide the foundation for the presupposition of rational choice theory. Is there an alternative?

In order to illuminate the dilemma presented by Frisch in the story of the two cakes and to imagine a totally different option, let me present another story about food, which Professor Sen probably knows since this narrative is taken from one of the great writings of the Veda, called the *Shatapatha Brâhmana*.

Here is the story: The first human being was called Prajâpati (or Purusa in some other texts of the Veda); Prajâpati was everything at the same time: heaven and earth, air and water, and wind and fire. He was all the living beings in the universe; he was the universe itself and he also was the first human. However, he was unable to draw a distinction among the various spirits he saw in the universe and to separate demons from the gods. Therefore he offered them a feast of rich food. Some started eating, everyone for himself, with gluttony and voracity, whereas the others did something quite different and apparently strange: they took the food with their hands and presented it to each other's mouth. Prajâpati then understood that the latter were gods and were the ones that humans must admire and imitate. Let us call this the *Prajâpati test*.

This very old and admirable story might contain the answer to Frisch's dilemma about the two cakes and a possible answer to any hypothesis concerning radical human selfishness. Selfishness is not to be denied, and altruism in itself is not an answer. It only reveals or indicates a more essential relational structure or disposition among humans. Which one? If we read this story with the eyes of supporters of rational choice theory, demons are more rational and gods are stupid. The demons eat what is offered to them in the most selfish way and by doing so they maximize their satisfaction, since each one can choose the pieces of food that he prefers. Gods, on the contrary, seem irrational from two points of view. First, by offering to each other the food each one can easily access himself, they merely perform a zero-gain operation that does not increase the amount of food available. Second, they deprive themselves of the opportunity of choosing the pieces of food they might find the most desirable.

So why did the wise people who invented this story and those who passed it on for centuries find it exemplary? Anyone educated in the Christian tradition would probably interpret this legend in terms of *agape*, the Greek word for generous love or affection. But this would merely be the expression of a prejudice. There is no need to baptize the gods of the Veda to make them more acceptable. If indeed we consider their gesture more closely, we realize that it includes no such thing as charity or even altruism: (1) the gods do not try to share the food; they do not need to do so since the food is abundant; (2) for the same reasons solidarity is not an issue in this case. What are the gods doing then? And why did Prajâpati admire their gesture so much? We could – and even have to – answer that by offering food to each other *the gods want to affirm and confirm the fact that they exist for each other, and that they want to express through the food that they eat the necessity but also the pleasure of being together, of being an organic and coherent group.*

The lesson of wisdom conveyed by this tale tells us that we do not exist alone, that we are by definition interrelated and interdependent. Our own existence is at stake in the existence of others. We are by definition constituted through this relation. To be human means to recognize the fact of this foundational interconnection. This is neither a moral statement nor a religious position, nor a psychological interpretation. It means that human beings are constituted in this way, and that this is what makes them specifically human.

By behaving as they do, the gods in this story are identified as Gods, i.e. as models for humans to imitate. More decisively, it means that *we are not regulated by a pecking order* – as is presupposed by rational choice theory – but that every time we meet each other we invent or renew *the necessity of recognizing each other*. This means that as humans we exist through mutual acceptance, through an implicit convention, a *politeia*. It also means that we understand that the things of the world – such as food or other goods – are not only commodities but also a means of expressing the fact that we matter for each other. Humans are those living beings that, paradoxically, *establish conventions by nature*. Conventions do not mean explicit contracts or pacts, but the fact that rules do not belong to the realm of self-regulation but of *intentionality*. Rules in this sense are not natural, nor are they arbitrary. They are what an animal capable of *politeia* can do. At the same time, humans more than any other animals are autonomous and have a radical claim to this autonomy. They are proud of it: pride and honor are the moral sentiments that are associated with this claim. We must therefore accept the legitimacy of selfishness (this is the positive side of individualism), but at the same time we must recognize that we are constitutively connected to each other. This interconnection does not in itself imply that there is peace and love between humans. It can also lead to conflict and destruction. The very fact of recognizing each other, through the food that is reciprocally offered, instead of consuming it separately, is precisely what creates the possibility of establishing peace and avoiding confrontation (which is what keeps happening among demons in the *Brâhmana*).

Let me give another beautiful example told by Claude Lévi-Strauss at the beginning of his *Elementary Structures of Kinship*, in the chapter entitled "The Principle of Reciprocity." Lévi-Strauss's purpose is to explain the rules of exogamy, which are based on the prohibition of incest, which essentially means that the spouse must be found in a different group. Through a detailed demonstration Lévi-Strauss emphasizes the fact that this prohibition is not based on biological or moral grounds, but rather is motivated by a requirement of reciprocity. To make his point clear he proposes a very simple example, which, once again, is a story about food and social relationships. Lévi-Strauss relates an observation he made in Southern France in a very ordinary and inexpensive restaurant where various workers used to come and have lunch every day: there was only one set-price menu for everybody and a small bottle of red wine was placed by each plate. Customers very often had to sit in front of someone they did not know, although some already knew each other. However, all of them would start their lunch in the same way, by filling up the glass of the person sitting in front of them. Why such a strange behavior? This is also a zero-gain operation. What can be its benefit? The answer is the same as in the Prajâpati story: through this gesture the relationship of reciprocal recognition between the participants is expressed and celebrated. In Japan it is inconceivable to help oneself to a glass of sake, without doubt for the very same reason. We have to receive it from another guest sitting at the same table.

It is interesting to note that food or beverage is at the core of these stories. Both belong to the most basic domain of everyday life and therefore have to do with the most useful of behaviors; for this very reason they should provide excellent examples for any rational choice theory. But in the three narratives we have discussed – beginning with that of Frisch – what we see is the opposite. The reason could be the following: because food refers to a fundamental need, because eating it provides a strong satisfaction, and because producing it implies cooperation, it becomes the most significant way for humans to express the fact that they are not just surviving and satisfying their needs, but that they enjoy being together and accept that they constitute a society.

What then is really at stake here is the *constitutive reciprocity* of human beings. There is no doubt that we are selfish and that this defect is (in Vedic terms) our "demonic" side; but we also are reciprocal animals and this is the accomplishment of our rationality rather than its undermining. We also experience hierarchies and relationships of domination; these dimensions can prevail in situations of conflict or survival, but privileging these hierarchies – as rational choice theory implicitly does – amounts to nothing more than instituting violence and ignoring the fact that *we are only humans by recognizing each other*, by instituting a *politeia*, and by adopting laws that express this will to public reciprocal recognition. The theorists of "law and economics" should remember this. Their use of rational choice theory does not increase the rationality of the explanation but reduces it. If we choose to integrate altruism in the concept of selfishness, as Gary Baker proposes, then endless sophistic reversing games can be played in economic theory. This pirouette is a clear indication of the limitation – and weakness – of such an argument.

Finally, this also means that there is no either/or alternative between considering selfishness alone as constituting rational behavior and placing reciprocal recognition in the category of the reasonable. We must reject this dilemma. Rationality is also on the side of a comprehensive understanding of justice. To me this is exactly what Professor Sen has demonstrated in his capabilities approach by questioning the limitation of so-called rational choice theory, which, in its hardline version, can produce only "rational fools," to use his well-known expression.

Part II

4 The power of a democratic public

Philip Pettit

Introduction

There are three aspects to democracy, all of them important for ensuring that the *demos* or people truly have *kratos* or power over their government. First of all, the government must be able to make a credible claim to speak and act in the people's name; it must have the general acceptance of the members of the domestic polity, however tacitly this is given. That first aspect marks off a democracy from the colonial form of government that is imposed from outside a country. It enables us to speak of the people as the ultimate sovereign, the ultimate source of political authority.

That the people are sovereign in this sense, however, does not mean that government is elected under universal franchise. It requires only that should the people generally come to disapprove of a government – say, a monarchical or aristocratic government – then they are entitled to resist and reject it. The second aspect of democracy also indicts any elitist dispensation, however benign, as undemocratic. It requires that the people serve in an electoral role as well as in the role of a sovereign.

But the fact that the people serve in these two roles does not yet mean, intuitively, that the people have much control or power over government. For all that the right of resistance and election enjoin, those in government might yet behave in a more or less arbitrary, even dictatorial fashion; they might deal unjustly with ordinary citizens. As many different commentators have noted, respect for those rights is no guarantee against what James Madison (Madison *et al.* 1987) described as an elective despotism.

The third aspect of democracy guards against the possibility of arbitrary government – if you like, against a salient form of injustice – as the first two guard against the possibilities of government being colonial or elitist. It puts measures in place that are designed to ensure that whatever is done by government is done under more or less restrictive constraints that reflect commonly shared ideas in the populace; for example, ideas as to what equal respect and concern require of government. Those ideas constitute the public culture or public philosophy established in the community. The third aspect of democracy would empower the public by giving those ideas an important role in shaping how government operates.

The first aspect of democracy entails that government is in the people's name, exercised with their authorization. The second ensures that government operates with the people's warrant, being appointed on the basis of their electoral preference. The third implies that government is on the public's terms, being conducted within constraints that they impose. Not only do the people authorize and appoint their government; they also audit it for compliance with suitable constraints. They hold it effectively to account for how far it measures up to public expectations.

Government may be	non-colonial	+ non-elitist	+ non-arbitrary
in the people's name	Popular authorization		
+ by the electorate's warrant		Electoral appointment	
+ on the public's terms			Public auditing

This essay is addressed to the third aspect of democracy. I want to explore what is involved in the people's serving, not as a sovereign, and not as an electorate, but as a public that can hold government effectively to account. The essay is in two main sections. In the first I look at the idea of the public and in the second at the power that the public can exercise in monitoring and regulating government.

The idea of a public

The making of a public

We can readily imagine a populace, even a populace that lives under what is otherwise a democratic regime, that does not constitute a public. Such a populace would be apathetic about how things are done in the society as a whole or they would take an interest in those doings only to the extent that they impacted on their own private, atomized interests. They would relate to one another in the way in which the customers in a common mall or market relate. While they might generate aggregate effects through acting in a common context – this, in the way the consumers in a market might force prices to a competitive equilibrium – they would do so accidentally, as a result of each pursuing his or her own goals: say, in the market case, the goal of buying at the cheapest price available.

The members of a population constitute a public in my sense insofar as they transcend this individual closure. They talk and exchange ideas on issues of common concern, matters of political moment, and do so to some purpose and effect. They do not let their collective life and affairs evolve as under the writ of an unchallengeable divinity. They get exercised about the way things go, they share their reactions, they form different views, they argue over their differences. They do not resign themselves to the rule of government, as to a blank necessity, but treat every claim and proposal made by those in power as fair game for debate and contestation.

Importantly, the members of a public don't just do this in separate circles, insulated by impermeable membranes. The different views they form are aired in speeches, in pamphlets, in the media, so that the eddies of private debate connect up in mainstream currents. The public gathers whenever two or more get together in discussion of common affairs, and it may gather in any of a variety of forums, ranging from the workplace canteen to the city café, the street-corner harangue to the formal debate, the television interview to the printed exchange. But those forums are not disconnected from one another. The use of public media, whether on the rostrum of Roman debate (Millar 1998), in the council of the medieval republic (Waley 1988), or in the television studio of today, maintains the flow of ideas between different circles. No conversation is closed; none can fix on just the ideas maintained in the local coterie.

The fact that a public is essentially involved in such exchange and discussion may suggest that, like a debating society, it is really just an arena for the development of rival views about politics. But that would be quite misleading. The very fact that members of a public squabble over differences ensures that they accept a range of propositions as commonplaces that all endorse. Building progressively towards dissensus, as the members of a public inevitably do – such are the circumstances of politics (Waldron 1999) – they create a bedrock of agreement to provide a context and a platform for their differences. And they do this unwittingly and unavoidably, generating their commonalities as side-effects of the difference-marking enterprise.[1]

Participatory commonplaces

There are two broad sorts of commonalities that will more or less inevitably emerge in any public. The first are common assumptions about the titles that people have to participate in the ongoing exchange and to

---

[1] For other approaches to the public see Dewey 1991; Richardson 2002: ch 13.

be treated as participants proper. If people are admitted to discussion at any center of public debate, routinely enjoying the address of others and routinely getting a hearing from them, then they are recognized in effect as equal voices with equal claims to speak. The practice incorporates them in such a way that should they occasionally be silenced or ignored – or worse, should they be treated with duplicity or force – then they will be able to appeal to the requirements of the practice in order to vindicate their position. They will be able to argue that its success presupposes the satisfaction of ideals that the offending treatment breaches. In the practice that remains true to those ideals, achieving its communicative ends properly – in what Jürgen Habermas (1984; 1989) calls the ideal speech situation – no one can be denied a right to speak on an equal footing with others, a right to be given a fair hearing by those others, and associated rights not to be trampled on in various ways.

The point here is not mysterious. Suppose I play chess with you, recognizing you as a suitable opponent. Contingently on my continuing to play chess, I have to treat you in a certain way. I have to respect the rules of the game, give you an opportunity to make your moves, comply with the rules in the moves I make myself, and eschew aggressive or threatening behavior. I may refuse to treat you in that way, of course, but if I do I have to give up any pretence of playing chess. In denying you the status of a chess-player, as established within the practice, I have to abandon the purport of relating to you as one player to another.

The point made about participants in public discussion of common concerns is parallel, though, as we shall see, it is in one respect even more powerful. People may give up the pretence of engaging with certain others within the practice of such discussion. But so far as they do not give up this pretence – and they do not generally do so in an ongoing civil society – they have to recognize those others as having a certain standing and a certain set of claims on how they should be treated. Chess-players must deal with one another within the rules of chess and must renounce fraud or violence. Participants in public discourse must deal with one another within the rules of discourse – they must give one another a voice and a hearing – and, equally of course, they must renounce deception or force; if they do not, then they can be condemned in the name of ideals that they will have implicitly endorsed.

I said that the point about participants in public discourse was parallel to the point about chess-players but also more powerful. It is more powerful, because of one important disanalogy. I might play chess with you every weekend but treat you in the intervening periods in an appalling manner; you, after all, might be my chess-playing slave. But I can hardly relate to you on regular occasions as one member of the public to another, yet treat you in intervening periods as someone I can push around, exploiting the extra strength or resources or connections that I happen to enjoy.

Were I to push you around in this way, you would be unlikely to be forthright in discussion; you would naturally want to keep me sweet, out of fear of what I may do when the debate is over – a parallel lesson may even hold in the chess case. But this is a fact I am in a position to recognize. And it is a fact that is salient enough to be recognizable by all; no thinking person can fail to notice it, fail to register that others must notice it, and so on. It follows that so far as people participate with one another in public discourse, they must be assumed to eschew the resort to fraud or force, not just while discussion continues, but at other times as well. Let someone fail in such a regard and others are in a position to ask how they can be expected to treat that person as someone with whom they are to debate on an equal and open footing. We can readily imagine the incredulity with which they would raise the query.

If this line of thought is right, then whenever a public emerges, there is good reason to expect that members will recognize one another as equal voices with equal claims to speak and get a hearing. They will acknowledge one another's rights as presumptive participants in exchange. They may not always honor those rights, not living up to the ideals implicit in the practice, but they will have to be taken to countenance them and to expose themselves to rebuke in the event of not complying.

Participatory rights might be recognized as general claims, spelled out in more or less abstract principles, or they might be recognized just as a matter of case-by-case compliance and case-by-case complaint. Logicians recognize as a general truth the logical principle that the truth of a conditional, "if p, then q," together with the truth of its antecedent, "p," will ensure the truth of the consequent, "q." Ordinary people only recognize this principle – *modus ponens*, as it is called – in a more tacit fashion: they acknowledge it so far as they generally comply with its demands, and they admit the relevance of complaint should they or others fail to comply.

Participatory rights and principles will certainly attract the tacit form of acceptance, but they are also likely to be spelled out and endorsed in more abstract form. It is going to be in the interest of most members in most contexts that such principles be articulated as common commitments; this will assure each against the dangers that others might not comply. There should be no shortage of political entrepreneurs who are willing to proclaim such rights, daring anyone to raise a voice of dissent.

Before I seem to wax too enthusiastic about the participatory commonplaces that a public should be expected to endorse, I should add that in any society, alas, the public may be an exclusive club. It may cut out women, as publics did in nineteenth-century Europe, America, and Australasia, and as many still do in various countries throughout the world. Or it may cut out those who belong to minority religions or minority sects. But still, this need not be a reason for utter despondency. The historical experience has been that once a public has formed, it is difficult to guard its borders and insulate them against others. Outsiders quickly catch on to the common issues and themes addressed in the public discourse. And if they speak, however guardedly, or in however limited a context, it will require a positive effort not to give them a hearing. Short of strict surveillance by a police force or a priesthood, any genuine public is liable to be porous at the periphery. It is in the nature of publics, left on their own, to grow.

Inferential commonplaces

The second category of commonalities that will emerge in any ongoing public constitute what I call inferential commonplaces as distinct from participatory ones. Participatory commonplaces are the assumptions that all members must be taken to endorse in virtue of treating one another as fellow participants in public discourse. Inferential commonplaces are assumptions that all must be taken to endorse so far as they come to agree on what count as arguments – arguments, not necessarily persuasive arguments – and what as hopeless *non sequiturs*: things that just do not follow.

Consider the explanation offered by the Renaissance medical expert Paracelsus for why syphilis ought to be treated with a salve of mercury as well as by internal administration of the metal: "the metal mercury is the sign of the planet, Mercury, and that in turn signs the market place, and syphilis is contracted in the market place" (Hacking 1983: 71). However forceful the argument may have once seemed, no one today could take it seriously. The presupposition of the argument, that there is a medical significance in the names and roles of the planets, is utterly incredible to a contemporary audience. Rejecting that presupposition out of hand, we see no relevance whatsoever in the argument produced. There is no connection, however weak, that we can acknowledge between the premises adduced and the conclusion asserted.

This rather recherché example helps to bring out a point that often goes without notice. When we find an argument relevant in any discussion then we must give some credence to the connection it posits or presupposes between the premises and the conclusion. We may not find the argument compelling, whether because of rejecting a premise or thinking that the support the premises offer for the conclusion is outweighed by other considerations. But even if we reject an argument, marking out a point of explicit disagreement with our interlocutor, the fact of accepting its relevance means that we will have acknowledged an implicit point of agreement. The intended effect of the response may have been to focus on a difference, but the unintended side-effect will have been to mark out a common presupposition.

This may seem too clever by half. Can't we put everything up front in an argument and not allow presuppositions to sneak in and establish areas of agreement behind our backs? No, we can't, for a reason that was deftly established by Lewis Carroll in a famous discussion of deductive reasoning, published in the 1890s. Better known as the author of *Alice's Adventures in Wonderland*, he also made contributions as a logician.

In his characteristically engaging way, Carroll (1895) imagines a character, the Tortoise, who complains to his companion, Achilles, that he just cannot seem to derive anything from anything. Achilles, confident he can help, produces a standard bit of deductive reasoning on the pattern of: p; if p, then q; therefore q. Tortoise says that he just cannot see how to get to "q" from those premises but notices that he might perhaps do so if allowed a further premise that licenses the move: a premise to the effect that if the premises are true, the conclusion follows. Fine, replies Achilles exultantly, let me give you that premise and then you can make the deduction. But, alas, the Tortoise demurs again. He can't get to the conclusion "q," even from the original premises, call them "A," and the new premise, "if A, then q." Perhaps if he could just have another premise to the effect that if those enhanced premises are true, it follows that q? Fine, Achilles is delighted to concede: take it. But then hesitation strikes again and the Tortoise wonders if he doesn't need yet a further premise to the effect that if those doubly enhanced premises are true, then q. The regress opening up begins at this stage to dawn even on Achilles. Speed is not everything in argument, or anywhere else; perhaps the Tortoise is moving as fast as it is possible to go.

The lesson of Carroll's article, lost on poor Achilles, is that no matter how rich the premises adduced in an argument, nothing can be taken to follow from them except on the basis of a presupposition that itself remains unsaid. If the presupposition is spelled out as an extra premise, then the new argument will in turn depend for its force on the acceptance of a further, unarticulated presupposition. There is no possibility in argument of putting everything up front. Argument must always advance on the basis of an unavowed infrastructure of agreement (see too Wittgenstein 1958). And what is true of accepting an argument holds also for agreeing that the argument is valid and relevant, even while rejecting a premise or putting other considerations on the table.

Taking advantage of this observation, let us return now to the political domain. The observation suggests that if the members of a public succeed in maintaining dialogue and exchange, then, regardless of the cleavages that open up between them, they will inevitably build those disagreements on a body of agreed presuppositions. Let one person argue from the value of equality to the need for a universal health service, for example, and another argue from the value of quality in health provision to the need for keeping a private component in the system. Insofar as they do not reject one another's arguments as irrelevant, they will display a common presupposition to the effect that both equality of distribution and quality of service are relevant values. They will divide on the case for a universal health service only because of weighting those values differently or differing on some related matter of fact: they may differ, for example, on whether universal health provision would reduce the quality of service. But from our viewpoint, the important thing to notice is how much they agree on. They presuppose in common that the equality of health consumers and the quality of health provision both matter in the society.

Suppose by contrast with this case that one person argues for a universal health service on the grounds that this is the only way of ensuring that regardless of religious inhibition, people are subjected to whatever treatment doctors recommend. I imagine that in most contemporary societies that argument would be greeted with a blank stare. People would just not endorse the presupposition that people's religious inhibitions about the medical treatments they receive should be ignored by doctors; the argument would not wash. It would be treated as irrelevant, or even as pointing to a consideration against the very conclusion it was meant to support.

The emerging picture is that if a public gets successfully established in a society, generating a healthy, continuing process of debate, then it will do so through a dynamic, evolving convergence on common presuppositions of argument and inference. At any time there will be some members of the public, or at least of the society, who will dissent from the most basic presuppositions. There will be the rebels that others may follow in due time; there will be the zealots who refuse to accept the implications of a shared public life; and there will be those who just don't meet the standards for sharing a public life. But these figures will, of necessity, be marginal to the mainstream life. The presuppositions will carry the day amongst the vast majority of their fellows.

The presuppositions will not just pass without saying among the population; they will have to register with participants in public exchange, and presumably in a more or less explicit form. In order for people to be able to conduct themselves with assurance in exchange with others, they will need to be able to know what sort of argument is likely to go down well, and what is not. And they will need to be able to rely on others knowing this too, and on their expecting them to know it in turn. The common presuppositions of argument will have to attain the status of commonplaces, in other words, being propositions that nearly everyone admits, expects everyone to admit, expects everyone to expect everyone to admit, and so on. Only people who are party to those inferential commonplaces will know their way about in the public space of the society.

Apart from the public space of any society, of course, there will also be sub-public spaces; there will be sub-publics that are marked off by belonging to some more confined group than the public as a whole. In all likelihood, there will be a denser set of inferential commonplaces accepted within any such sub-culture than across the society as a whole. Insofar as people take part in properly public debate, however – debate that is supposed to reach across more sectarian divides – they will have to avoid invoking those more local commonplaces; they will have to know and rely on presuppositions that are endorsed on all sides.

Argument and rhetoric

The participatory and inferential commonplaces that inform a society like ours, then, will provide reasons for or against certain collective decisions that each recognizes as relevant, each recognizes as having this recognized status, and so on in the usual hierarchy. The commonplaces that play this role in a contemporary democracy may be more or less universally compelling considerations to the effect that everyone should be treated as an equal, that children should be provided with a basic education, that members should be protected against individual destitution or natural disaster, and so on. But they may also include culturally specific considerations, bearing on limits to private property, or the position of a certain religion in public life, or the need for cultural homogeneity. And they will also naturally include some considerations on how the government should be organized, how it should inform itself on various matters, and how it should conduct its business.

In speaking of these considerations as reasons, and in speaking of argument and inference and debate, as I have throughout, I may seem to have an excessively intellectual picture of the political forum (Young 2000; Viroli 2002). But for all I assume, the exchange that character-izes the public world need not take the form of abstract disputation and argument. It will materialize just as often in the sage use of a cliché, the shaft of effective irony, the construction of a deft metaphor, the invoca-tion of a vivid grievance, the deployment of a telling phrase, the resort to humor and mockery. The tropes of rhetoric may be as essential to the exchange of ideas, indeed, as any of the tools of logic; and they are likely, of course, to be much more effective. If the tools of logic are needed to show people why they should move position, the tropes of rhetoric may be necessary to get them to budge; this was the claim of both classical and Renaissance rhetoricians (Skinner 1996). Rhetorical devices serve to make a censured position feel uncomfortable, letting it be the butt of humor or abuse; and they help to give the recommended alternative a habitable or otherwise inviting cast (McGeer and Pettit 2009).

But even if public exchange is often rhetorical in character, rather than austerely intellectual, still it can proceed only on the basis of com-mon presupposition. A cliché or metaphor will be found telling and worthy of contestation only so far as it is seen as picking up a relevant aspect of things. A joke or shaft of irony will strike home only so far as everyone can be expected to see the point. However colorful and emo-tive the medium of exchange, it still comes down to a sort of debate; it is still meant to put a case for one side of an argument and against another. It can do this only if it draws on an accumulating, evolving reservoir of shared assumption, seeking to use that common ground for the support of a favored, if unshared proposal.

Connections

In concluding this account of a public and of the participatory and inferential commonplaces by which a public is characterized, I should emphasize that I am not plowing a lone or novel furrow. Classical and medieval sources recognized the impact that the views of the com-mon people could have in public life, though they generally thought of that impact coming about in public assembly and protest (Waley 1988; Hansen 1991; Millar 1998). But by the late seventeenth century, it was already clear that the views of the people could come to mat-ter, even when they were aired in diverse sites of discussion, among smaller groups of people. In the England of the 1690s and early 1700s the short-lived practice of three-year elections, together with the emer-gence of coffee-houses and other places of middle-class exchange and commerce, created a public in our contemporary sense. It made salient the fact that things that were said in relatively decentralized, dissensual exchanges could easily generate waves of common assumption – a *lingua franca* of ideas and opinions – that no public figure would dare offend (Habermas 1989; Knights 2005).

The ideas that emerged in eighteenth century England became mainstays of democratic culture in succeeding periods and in other places. They infiltrated Britain's American colonies and inspired French aficionados of contemporary Britain such as the Baron de Montesquieu; and they thereby laid the foundations for the American and French revolutions. They included ideas of individual rights – historical rights, as the British thought of them – religious tolerance, the value of personal independence, the limited authority of government, and the importance of protections like trial by jury and *habeas corpus*.

The recognition of the public and the importance of public opinion can be associated with the idea of civil society that became celebrated in the nineteenth century among thinkers as diverse as G. W. F. Hegel, Alexis de Tocqueville, and John Stuart Mill. Charles Taylor (2004) distinguishes between civil society in the Lockean sense of a pre-political people, and a more political sense of the idea that he associates with the eighteenth-century French thinker, the Baron de Montesquieu. In this more political sense, civil society exists within the polity, rather than before the polity. While it connects people on the basis of pre-political commonalities of interests, ideas, and norms, it organizes them in such a way that they naturally resist unnecessary political intrusion in their lives, and they submit the aims of the polity to continual review and discussion.

Two contemporary political philosophers have emphasized the role in the life of a public of the sorts of commonplaces I have been discussing. One is the German philosopher and social theorist Jürgen Habermas, the other the outstanding, twentieth-century exponent of American liberalism, John Rawls.

Habermas, who wrote his first book on the emergence of the public sphere (Habermas 1989), is particularly well known for insisting on the way in which participatory commonplaces become established as part of the pragmatics of communication. He sees an ideal speech situation adumbrated in every overture of a properly communicative kind, suggesting that the norms that characterize this regulative, horizontal ideal amount to nothing less than a discourse ethic; a set of principles sufficient to provide a moral framework for society (Benhabib 1990). While he does not comment as such on shared commonplaces, he argues that within the sphere of public life, the participatory principles preside over processes of communication in which bodies of opinion form at different centers and constitute a natural constraint on what government can or should try to do (Habermas 1994).

Rawls's early work was devoted to the abstract project of articulating the demands of justice (Rawls 1971). But he took to heart a variety of criticisms that, among other assaults, attacked the apparent pretension to provide a theory of justice for every place and time. Acknowledging that his starting point was provided by ideas prevalent and accepted in his own constitutional tradition, he came to present his views as an attempt to articulate the requirements of those historically situated assumptions: to work up a conception of justice from them (Rawls 1993; 2001).

I think we can see the ideas of which Rawls speaks here as a close cousin of the commonplaces that I have been discussing. While he tells no story as to why they should emerge, he certainly thinks that their emergence is inevitable, and that it is equally inevitable that they should provide bearings for the assessment of government. The thought, in his own words, is this:

[T]he political culture of a democratic society that has worked reasonably well over a considerable period of time normally contains, at least implicitly, certain fundamental ideas from which it is possible to work up a political conception of justice suitable for a constitutional regime (Rawls 2001: 34–5).[2]

Empowering the public

The question of power

We have seen that once a public sphere of discussion has emerged in society, it will become a source of two sorts of commonplace, participatory and inferential. Members of the public go very different ways as they form rival views on the direction that political policy ought to take. But out of that very divergence, a body of common assumption is born. Participatory and inferential commonplaces materialize as the inevitable side-products of the exchange. They emerge as unintended precipitates that the exercise secretes, not – or at least not in the first place – as matters that attract explicit consensus.

---

[2] The commonplaces or common reasons on which I focus may differ in some respects from the public reasons emphasized by Rawls (1999). I emphasize three points that are not made in Rawls and might even be rejected by him: first, that they are generated as a by-product of ongoing debate; second, that they are relevant to such debate, no matter at what site it occurs, private or public, informal or formal; and third, that in principle the common reasons that operate in a society, or even in the international public world, may not be reasons that carry independent moral force: we may disapprove of their having the role they are given in debate. I am grateful for a discussion on this topic with Tim Scanlon.

Can the public, so conceived, exercise control over government? Can it contribute in that sense to a democracy: a regime in which the *demos* or people have *kratos* or control? By the account given in the previous section, a public is going to be characterized by the participatory and inferential commonplaces it supports. That suggests in turn that the public will rule so far as those commonplaces rule. The public will be in power to the extent that those commonplaces constrain and channel what happens in government.

The empowering of public commonplaces

How might such shared ideas be empowered? Those in government should be required to justify the decisions they make on the basis of such ideas, perhaps by invoking constitutional or procedural constraints that are presumptively rooted in those ideas. And the justifications offered by the authorities should always be subject to challenge – potentially effective challenge – by members of the public.

What effects might we expect a successful regime of justification and challenge to have? First, it would remove from the agenda of government any policies that were clearly in conflict with received ideas, indicting them as downright unacceptable to the public. But this would naturally leave a number of different policies on the table as potential responses to any policy issue. By my characterization, after all, the relevant commonplaces are common to people who hold by different policy stances. And so we should expect a regime of justification and challenge to have a second effect, too.

The successful regime, to move to that effect, would identify and impose processes of decision-making for selecting the winner on any policy question from among the eligible candidates available. The recommended process, which might vary from issue to issue, could be a parliamentary vote, a referral to the courts, the formation of an advisory commission, the resort to a popular referendum, even perhaps the use of a lottery. In any case it would have to be a process that could be viewed as impartial and fair from a variety of perspectives; this is a minimal condition we would expect to see fulfilled and there is considerable evidence that it weighs heavily in democratic polities (Tyler *et al.* 1997).

If this is right, then the public will rule in a polity insofar as its shared ideas filter out any unacceptable policy candidates and any unacceptable procedures for resolving the issue between acceptable candidates. Government will propose, the public dispose. Or, recognizing how various proposals are likely to go down with the public, government will propose within constraints that reflect the public disposition.

How is the control envisaged here going to be imposed? Elections may help in the measure to which the authorities seek re-election, whether for themselves or their party. For such politicians will have an incentive for presenting their policies as grounded in reasons that all can accept, even if some challenge the weight given to those reasons or the empirical facts assumed in invoking them. And their opponents equally have an incentive to challenge the claims implicit in such a presentation. But elections can be a frail constraint, since the theater of politics allows each side to put an attractive spin on their policies and to mute the effect of opposition challenge in a hurly-burly of accusation and abuse (Pettit 2000a; 2000b).

In order for those in government to be held to account, and kept to the terms on which the public commissions them, it is essential that there be a number of non-electoral as well as electoral checks on government. The non-electoral devices used will be various, reflecting the influences and requirements of the reasons validated in common exchange. They are almost certain to include rule-of-law constraints on how government acts; individual-right constraints on what it does; institutional restrictions such as the separation of powers, accountability measures, and the depoliticization of certain decisions (Pettit 2004); and, perhaps most important, exposure to a power of effective invigilation and contestation on the part of ordinary people and their representatives.

Popular invigilation and contestation of government requires a public that is active in discussion, sustaining, regenerating, and developing the body of received commonplaces on what government should be doing and how government should be acting. But it also requires a public that is active in raising questions and bringing challenges against those in power. This exercise can be supported and channeled by the existence of an effective parliamentary opposition and by the appointment of statutory officers of review such as human rights commissioners and ombudsmen. But it must take root among ordinary people, if it is to have a real impact.

In a complex democracy the popular invigilation and contestation of government will almost certainly have to be promoted via nongovernmental organizations such as environmental and labor groupings, ethnic minority and feminist networks, and movements associated with consumer rights, prisoners' rights, and the like. These specialized, often passionate circles are essential if the people are to mount a sustained, effective surveillance of government. The eighteenth-century Scots writer Adam Ferguson (1767: 167) put the point well when he said that good government cannot be secured by law and constitution alone; it relies crucially on "the refractory and turbulent zeal" of an engaged people.

A democratic power

Imagine a society, then, in which received commonplaces are imposed on government by these and other measures, and the public effectively keeps the government in check. There are two grounds on which it may be said that the control envisaged is not really the sort of control that we should associate with democracy. But neither is very persuasive.

The first basis of objection may be that it is not really the people who act when contestations of the kind at which we have been gesturing are brought against government. Rather the contesting agents are going to be opposition politicians, statutory officers, and more or less specialized pressure groups. Democracy requires that the people control government, it will be said, and the people will not control government unless the people act.

This objection is premised on a fallacy. Control is not always hands-on control. It may be control that is exercised at arm's length; it may even be control that is exercised by other hands than those of the controller. With a collective entity like the people, as with a commercial corporation or a voluntary association, it is inevitable that many of the things it does are done by the hands of a few, not by the hands of the many. Democracy, as we might put it, does not entail "demopraxis"; popular control does not entail popular action.

If the agents who invigilate and contest government act with the approval and consent of the people, then they can certainly be said to act in the people's name. And those agents clearly do act with popular approval and consent, given that the people endorse the constitutional and other arrangements whereby these individuals and bodies are enabled to bring their challenges. The endorsement of the people can be inferred from the absence of objection to the freedom of speech, association, and information that the exercise presupposes, and to the arrangements whereby challenges are adjudicated in parliament, in the courts and tribunals, in the press, and at the hustings. Not only does no one actually object to those aspects of democratic life, indeed; in most contemporary democracies it would be electoral suicide to do so.

The second ground on which the control described may be said to be undemocratic is that it does not empower the right sort of state or attitude on the part of the people. Democracy is often said to empower and enact the will of the people taken collectively – whatever that is – or the preferences or judgments of the people, taken one by one. And that goes with thinking that when an agent controls a process, the control is guided by the agent's will, or preference, or judgment. But public invigilation and contestation is not guided by any such state of the popular mind. It empowers the common reasons that have currency amongst the public. That is all. And that, it may be said, is not enough; it does not give us a title to speak of the public as exercising control.

Talk of control would not be legitimate, it is true, if common reasons were empowered without awareness on the part of the people, or without their acquiescence. Suppose that another agent decided to act for the satisfaction of my preferences and this was not something I knew or wanted. Would that give me control? Well, it might be said to give control to my preferences. But it would not really give me control; it would not put me, considered as an agent, in charge. The same lesson will carry with the common reasons of the people. Were those reasons empowered without the awareness or acquiescence of the people then that would not give control to the people, considered an agent or set of agents. It would not put them in charge.

This is no problem, however, for the line taken here. The dispensation I have described puts factors in play that provide each with evidence; first, that common presuppositions can be invoked against government; second, that this is evident to each; third, that it is evident to each that this is evident to each; and so on. In short, the dispensation ensures that it will be a matter of shared awareness that common, presupposed reasons have such standing in public life (Lewis 1969). And if this empowerment is a matter of common awareness, then it is also a matter of common acquiescence. The members of democratic publics don't display any inclination to complain about the empowerment, although they are in a position where they could contest it with some hope of success.

An attractive power

The sort of control that a public has over democratic decision-making, at least in the ideal scenario, can be compared with the control that individual agents enjoy when their values are duly empowered in their decisions. Akratic agents will act intentionally insofar as they act in a rational manner on rationally formed attitudes. But they will only enjoy self-control, as we say, if the actions they take are required to conform to the values that they reflectively endorse; they must not act on attitudes that may be spontaneously formed but run counter to those values. Similarly we can say that a people will only enjoy a corresponding sort of control if the actions taken in their name by government are required to conform to the common reasons or values that they endorse in the course of arguing and even disagreeing among themselves.

When I as an individual agent monitor my attitudinal formation – say, the formation of beliefs, desires, and intentions – for its conformity to various values, I put constraints on what can emerge from that process, but I do not determine the outcome in detail. I try to ensure that whatever belief I form on any issue, it is a belief that is formed in the light of all the evidence. Or I try to ensure that whatever intention I form in some decision, it is an intention that reflects the demands of one or another person. But I do not ensure that I will form the belief that p or the intention to X. That I form that belief or intention is due to the attitude-forming process, and while I put important constraints on that process – those that reflects my values – I do not dictate what in particular it is going to produce. In view of the self-regulation I can say that I intended to form a belief or intention that was consistent with such and such values. But I cannot say that I intended to form the belief that p or the intention to X.

The situation is more or less exactly parallel with the control of the public. The electoral and non-electoral regime of popular control that we have been describing puts important constraints, reflective of publicly shared presuppositions, on what the governmental process produces. At least that is the ideal. But even in the ideal it does not determine the outcome of that process in any detail. The constraints imposed allow us to say that the public controls for what the government does, by analogy with the sense in which my evaluative self-regulation controls for what I come to believe, desire, and intend. But what the public controls for is the respect for the public commonplaces of reasoning, not for the detailed form that respectful policies assume.

There can be little doubt about the attraction of such public control of government. The public is taken to include the whole population, or at the very least the whole, more or less permanent, more or less competent adult population. Such an inclusive form of rule would ensure that everyone is treated equally, given the participatory principles that have to be endorsed in any open, public discussion. And it would ensure that everyone is treated in a manner that accords with ideas that all find so acceptable they take them for granted; they are the presuppositions or pre-judgments on which normal argument proceeds. This prospect cannot fail to appeal.

Public ideas might vary from place to place, of course, and they might evolve in various ways over time. But at no particular time and place could people seriously complain about being treated in a way that conforms to ideas that are so deeply endorsed in their own milieu. The reformers and zealots who come to reject some deep presuppositions of their society will rail at the restrictions imposed on them, of course, and at the failure of others to heed their protests and arguments. But I do not think that this should give us pause.

Reformers must concede that it is legitimate, pending the day when they cease to be outliers, for government to be forced to conform to the society's assumptions. And zealots can scarcely command a serious hearing. It is not the case that they acknowledge the claims of a public, as the reformers do, arguing that that public should question some of its presuppositions. They reject the claims of the public altogether, insisting that regardless of how far people disagree, all should still conform – all should be made to conform – to the ideas that they or their particular sect cherish.

Connections

Both Habermas and Rawls gesture at the importance of the public having the sort of control over government that I have been charting. Habermas sees the best hope for democracy in communicative connections between "the parliamentary bodies and the informal networks of the public sphere." He thinks that these processes of communication, anonymous or "subjectless," hold out the prospect for controlling political judgment and decision in a rational way. Under their influence, he says, "more or less rational opinion- and will-formation can take place" (Habermas 1994: 8).

Rawls expresses himself rather differently but to a similar, broad effect. In his earlier work he represents a well-ordered society as one that is controlled by a publicly endorsed conception of justice, but this shifts somewhat as his position develops. He comes to see his conception of justice as articulating the demands of the ideas accepted in the constitutional and cultural tradition of his own, liberal society. These ideas have the status there, he says, of public reasons: they bear on judgments about public matters; they are publicly or commonly recognized as reasons that serve in debate about such matters; and they are not tied to any sectarian doctrine: they are truly reasons of the public (Rawls 1993: 213). And so Rawls is able to recast the well-ordered society, not as a society governed by a publicly endorsed conception of justice but, more concretely, as a society where such public reasons – the building blocks of a conception of justice – rule.

Rawls thinks that public reasons will rule under a regime where the authorities are required to justify their policies in public terms, and citizens are positioned to challenge those justifications. He insists that the authorities should always deliberate and defend themselves in the currency of public reasons, prescribing that: "judges, legislators, chief executives, and other government officials, as well as candidates for public office, act from and follow the idea of public reason." And he assumes that those very public reasons will figure in the interrogation to which citizens submit the organization and behavior of government, as they debate "constitutional essentials and matters of basic justice," elaborating the public conception of justice that should rule in their lives (Rawls 1999: 55–6).

But the idea of the empowered public has other connections besides those with Habermas and Rawls. It can also be seen as a contemporary interpretation of the classical republican idea that government should always be conducted for the safety of the people and, more concretely, for the common good, the public interest. Rawls (1999: 71) himself notices the connection when he identifies the regime of pubic reasons as one member of a family of doctrines that he describes as common good conceptions of justice.

Republicans put a premium on freedom as non-domination and, recognizing that government is essential for protecting people against private domination, focus on how to ensure that it is not itself a source of public domination (Pettit 1997; Skinner 1998). Government will have to interfere in people's lives and affairs, if it is to do its job; it will have to impose taxation, coercive laws, and penal sanctions. The central idea in the tradition is that if it is forced to track the public interest when it perpetrates this interference – if in that sense its interference is non-arbitrary – then government will not be dominating; it will not have the aspect of a *dominus* or master in relation to people but rather the aspect of their servant.

The role that the common good or the public interest plays in traditional republican doctrine can be plausibly assigned to the body of public commonplaces that we have been discussing here. Those commonplaces will pick out a certain pattern of policy and process as one by which government should be constrained. That pattern represents something in the interest of people as members of the public and in their interest, moreover, by their own lights. It makes a lot of sense to equate this with the common good and to represent it as the target that republicans should want government to track.

This construal may actually be quite faithful to the idea of the common good that historical republicans took for granted. They thought of the common good as something that was good for citizens as citizens in just the manner of this idea; they did not equate it, for example, with whatever happened to lie in the overlap between people's private interests. And in the smaller, simpler societies for which they wrote, they almost certainly took it for granted that the common good was always the common good according to common lights, not the common good according to lights inaccessible to ordinary people. As in the approach taken here, their common good was not something in the name of which government could claim to be acting paternalistically – acting in people's real but unrecognized interest. The common good was assumed to be readily perceptible and, in the normal case, actually perceived.

Conclusion

There are three aspects or dimensions to democracy, as I suggested in the introduction to this paper. Government must be authorized in popular consent, it must be appointed on the basis of electoral preference, and it must be constrained by the shared expectations of a contestatory public. The third dimension of democracy is the most neglected, and I hope that this essay may help to make a case for its importance. Government has to be controlled by assumptions that pass muster across the full range of a deliberative public. That is the only protection against elective despotism, as Madison called it, and it is the only basis on which to expect that government will be a force for justice.

References

Benhabib, S. 1990. *The Communicative Ethics Controversy*. Cambridge, MA: MIT Press.

Carroll, L. 1895. "What the Tortoise Said to Achilles," *Mind*, 4: 278–80.

Dewey, J. 1991. *The Public and Its Problems*. Athens, OH: Ohio University Press.

Ferguson, A. 1767. *An Essay on the History of Civil Society*. Edinburgh: Millar and Caddel (reprinted New York: Garland, 1971).

Habermas, J. 1984, 1989. *A Theory of Communicative Action*, vols. I and II. Cambridge: Polity Press.

  1989. *The Structural Transformation of the Public Sphere*. Cambridge, MA: MIT Press.

  1994. "Three Normative Models of Democracy," *Constellations*, 1: 1–10.

Hacking, I. 1983. *Representing and Intervening: Introductory Topics in the Philosophy of Natural Science*. Cambridge University Press.

Hansen, M. H. 1991. *The Athenian Democracy in the Age of Demosthenes*. Oxford: Blackwell.

Knights, M. 2005. *Representation and Misrepresentation in Later Stuart Britain: Partisanship and Political Culture*. Oxford University Press.

Lewis, D. 1969. *Convention*. Cambridge, MA: Harvard University Press.

Madison, J., A. Hamilton and J. Jay 1987. *The Federalist Papers*. Harmondsworth: Penguin.

McGeer, V. and P. Pettit 2009. "Judgmental Stickiness, Rhetorical Therapy," in R. Bourke and R. Geuss (eds.) *Political Judgment: Essays in Honor of John Dunn*. Cambridge University Press, 48–73.

Millar, F. 1998. *The Crowd in Rome in the Late Republic*. Ann Arbor: University of Michigan Press.

Pettit, P. 1997. *Republicanism: A Theory of Freedom and Government*. Oxford University Press.

   2000a. "Democracy, Electoral and Contestatory," *Nomos*, **42**: 105–44.

   2000b. "Minority Claims under Two Conceptions of Democracy," in D. Ivison, P. Patton and W. Sanders (eds.) *Political Theory and the Rights of Indigenous Peoples*. Cambridge University Press: 199–215.

   2004. "Depoliticizing Democracy," *Ratio Juris*, **17**: 52–65.

Rawls, J. 1971. *A Theory of Justice*. Oxford University Press.

   1993. *Political Liberalism*. New York: Columbia University Press.

   1999. *The Law of Peoples*. Cambridge, MA: Harvard University Press.

   2001. *Justice as Fairness: A Restatement*. Cambridge, MA: Harvard University Press.

Richardson, H. 2002. *Democratic Autonomy*. New York: Oxford University Press.

Skinner, Q. 1996. *Reason and Rhetoric in the Philosophy of Hobbes*. Cambridge University Press.

Skinner, Q. 1998. *Liberty before Liberalism*. Cambridge University Press.

Taylor, C. 2004. *Modern Social Imaginaries*. Durham, NC: Duke University Press.

Tyler, T. R., R. J. Boeckmann, H. J. Smith and Y. Y. Huo. 1997. *Social Justice in a Diverse Society*. Boulder, CO: Westview Press.

Viroli, M. 2002. *Republicanism*. New York: Hill and Wang.

Waldron, J. 1999. *Law and Disagreement*. Oxford University Press.

Waley, D. 1988. *The Italian City-Republics*, 3rd edn. London: Longman.

Wittgenstein, L. 1958. *Philosophical Investigations*. Oxford: Blackwell.

Young, I. 2000. *Inclusion and Democracy*. Oxford University Press.

5   The challenge of gender justice

Martha C. Nussbaum

Data

Women are unequal to men, all over the world, unequal in basic opportunities and life chances of the sort that lie at the heart of the idea of social justice. Take education. In forty-three countries, male literacy rates are fifteen or more percentage points higher than the female rate; this comprises one fourth of the nations in the world. In secondary education, the gaps are even more striking. Moreover, as is generally not the case with basic literacy, these gaps are actually growing: in twenty-seven countries the secondary school enrollment of girls declined between 1985 and 1997 – and this during a time of rapid technological advancement, in which skills become ever more important as passports to economic opportunity.

Take exposure to violence. Although data are very difficult to come by, it is generally agreed that exposure to violence, both physical and sexual, at the hands of strangers, acquaintances, and intimate partners is a huge fact in female life around the world.[1] The *Human Development Report* 2000 reports that between 10 and 47 percent of women in the nine countries studied were physically assaulted by an intimate partner.[2] In the United States, intimate partner violence made up 20 percent of all non-fatal violent crime experienced by women in 2001. The National Violence Against Women Survey reports that 52 percent of surveyed women said that they were physically assaulted either as children or as adults. Eighteen percent of women had experienced rape at some time in their lives.

There are many other areas of basic opportunity we could discuss here, ranging from land rights to political participation to access to professional and managerial positions. But let me conclude this introduction by mentioning some well-known facts about the most basic life-chance of all, the chance to live. As Amartya Sen's work on "missing

[1] For a fuller statement of these data, see Nussbaum (2005b: 167–83).
[2] UNDP (2000).

94

women" shows, sex ratios in many countries indicate that large num-
bers of women the world over have died because they have received
unequal treatment – whether outright infanticide is involved, or, as
is more common, unequal nutrition and health care.[3] More recently,
with the widespread availability of amniocentesis, females don't even
get the chance to be born. The natality ratios studied by Jean Drèze
and Amartya Sen in *India: Development and Participation*[4] indicate a
huge problem of sex-selective abortion, not only in developing and poor
countries but also in some quite prosperous ones: South Korea has one
of the worst natality ratios in the world, indicative of a huge problem of
sex-selective abortion.

These are urgent practical issues, issues of basic justice. The challenge
of gender justice is in that sense a practical political challenge for governments around the world, for international agencies and agreements,
for nongovernmental organizations, and for individuals of good will.

The challenge of gender justice, however, is also a theoretical challenge. The progress of women toward full equality has been slowed by
inadequate theories of justice, and it is currently being hastened by the
correction of these theories. My chapter focuses on theories of justice in the Western tradition of liberalism, which are, I believe, strong
and still viable today, with suitable revisions. I argue that these theories contained gross structural inadequacies where women's issues are
concerned. Reforming them, therefore, has not been simply a matter
of extending to women the same protections the theories had already
given to men. It required serious and deep rethinking of the whole
structure of the theories. I suggest that this rethinking has taken place
in four stages, the last of which is just beginning. The conclusion suggests some further tasks that philosophical theorizing about justice will
need to address in the future.

My paper in that way focuses on the challenge of gender justice. I hope,
however, that it will emerge that the theoretical changes demanded by
women were really important for the adequacy of the theories as theories of human justice more generally. In that sense, women's demand for
full equality opened up problems for the whole structure of the theory
that had not been faced, and thus helped to contribute to the progress
of the modern world toward justice for all human beings.

A thread running through my entire argument will be the idea of
what I might call "de-naturing nature." One of the biggest problems
with liberal theories of justice, in their original form, was that they

---

[3] Drèze and Sen (1989: 52), and Drèze and Sen (1995: chapter 7).
[4] Drèze and Sen (2002: 257–62).

assumed a certain picture of the "nature" of men and women, repeatedly made claims about those natures, and then used such claims to support dubious theoretical propositions. The idea of nature, however, was never used in a very clear or philosophically adequate manner. When used by philosophers from Locke to Rousseau, and even by the great John Rawls (who, at least in early work, spoke easily and uncritically of "natural affections"), the term "nature" was often ambiguous. To say that a certain characteristic is "by nature" might mean (a) that it is the way things are without human or cultural intervention, or, perhaps, the way they are as a result of inherited characteristics, unaltered by culture. But of course it is extremely difficult to separate the influence of biological inheritance from that of culture, since we know that culture begins to affect young children very early, especially in the area of gender. For example, experiments show that young infants are played with differently, talked to differently, and so forth, depending on whether the adult believes it is a boy or a girl. (If they think it's a girl, they are more likely to hold "her" close and protect "her," and to characterize "her" crying as expressing "fear"; if they think it's a boy, they are more inclined to bounce "him" in the air vigorously, and to characterize "his" crying as "anger.") So, most often, when people said that some characteristic was "by nature," what they were really saying, or all they had any warrant for saying was (b) that this is the way things typically are, the way we are used to things being.

Given that people are very prone to think that the way things always have been is the way they must be, this second usage of "by nature" typically slipped into a third: to say that a characteristic exists "by nature" is to say that (c) this is the way things must be, and they cannot be any other way. Finally, since people often think that custom is good and diversions from custom are bad, and because many accept a religious picture of the world according to which things are created in the best and most proper way, people also often used "by nature" to mean (d) the way it is right and proper for things to be. Thus to call something "unnatural" was often to condemn it – even though human beings usually make whatever progress they make by tampering with "nature" in sense (a). Most people don't object to tool use, to eyeglasses, to medical interventions for disease. So calling women who sought careers "unnatural" in the pejorative sense, meaning "inappropriate and bad," should have been supported by some *extra* argument as to why this particular divergence was bad. Usually no such arguments were forthcoming. A lot of the good work done by feminist philosophers and their friends over the past century or two has been to unravel this mess and to expose the weaknesses in argument that arose from an uncritical reliance on the slippery notion of "nature." This critical examination was begun by the great John Stuart Mill, the one male liberal philosopher for whom gender justice was a central concern of his entire career, in his wonderful essay called "Nature," which ought to be read by anyone who cares about this topic.[5]

Step one: criticizing the private–public distinction[6]

Virtually all political theories in the Western liberal tradition distinguish a public realm, the realm of contract, rights, and political choice, from a so-called private realm, a realm secluded from the public realm, usually understood to be equivalent to the domain of the family. Notice that even this equivalence is quite questionable. The Western bourgeois family fits the model well, because the nuclear family, consisting of the marital couple and its children, typically lives in relative seclusion, in its own dwelling place, which is geographically separated from other dwelling places. Many styles of family life the world over do not work like this. Sometimes the home is porous, without clear boundaries. It blends seamlessly into the village. Sometimes there is a separate dwelling place, but lots of different people live there, in-laws, grandparents, and so forth. One sign of the unreflective nature of the public–private distinction was that people typically didn't even bother to ask whether it could be sensibly applied to societies of different kinds. And yet they were happy enough to assert that it had its foundations in "nature."

The public–private distinction went like this. The outer public realm is the realm where law rules. In this realm, citizens are all equal before the law, and respect for that equality is the glue that holds society together. The inner private realm is the realm of love. Its bonds are deep and natural, and they would actually be ruined by thinking of contract or law in connection with this realm.[7] Nor is equality a particularly important value in the private realm. We would expect, indeed, to find a natural hierarchy between parents and children, and, often, between men and women. There is nothing wrong with this, and even to ask questions about what rights wives and children have is to have what philosopher Bernard Williams, in a different though related context, called "one thought too many."

The public–private distinction was typically supported by an appeal to "nature" that slid conveniently from "nature" in sense (b), what is customary, to nature in sense (d), what is right and proper. The fact

[5] Mill (1998: 3–65).　[6] Essential reading here is Okin (1979).
[7] See, on this, Okin (1989).

that women typically stayed at home and men typically took charge of the political realm was magically transformed into a norm: this is the way things ought to be, and each realm is the proper realm for each.

Notice that it is a common thing in human life, when someone wants to maintain a traditional privilege, for that person to claim that thinking of rights, contract, and law would actually ruin the great relationship that exists. In my youth I was briefly a professional actress, and I recall hearing just that argument from management, when they wanted to convince us to work for no wages, in violation of the contractual conditions established by Actors' Equity, the actors' union. Management said: artists are creative people, and creativity, and the love that goes into it, will be tarnished and defiled by all this talk of contract. As the trade union deputy in my theatre company, I didn't believe that argument then, and I certainly don't believe it now. Artists work much better under contract, because a good contract protects their working conditions and their working hours, something that enhances creativity. So, when I contemplate the argument that thinking about rights, contract, and law would ruin the family and the love that exists inside it – an argument that is still made today by anti-liberal thinkers such as Michael Sandel and the late Allan Bloom – my first instinct is to ask whose power and privileges are under threat, what the people in power are so afraid of that they would not let the amicable face of law into their dwellings.

It is not difficult to answer this question. What the private–public distinction did was, first of all, to keep women out of the political realm, and to suggest that this was somehow right and proper. Men have their realm, women have theirs. Nature decrees that things be this way. (Only it turned out that the so-called women's realm was also ruled by men, because ruling the household, too, was taken to be a part of men's nature, even if the household was a naturally female realm.) Such arguments were made with deep seriousness, as if they were real arguments – even in courts of law. In 1873 Myra Bradwell, denied the right to practice law in the state of Illinois, went to court to challenge her exclusion from that part of the public realm. Since she was already practicing law, it could not be claimed that she lacked the ability or that she didn't want to do it. So the US Supreme Court reached for the old public–private distinction, backing it up with the artillery of Nature. The "natural timidity and delicacy" of the female sex, said Justice Bradley in a famous opinion, "evidently unfits it" for many of the "occupations of civil life" – including the practice of law.[8] Of course the very fact that Myra Bradwell was quite a good lawyer made this

[8] *Bradwell* v. *Illinois*, 83 US (16 Wall.) 130 (1873).

fact totally non-"evident." What could "nature" even mean in this context? If women can't do a thing – as Mill had already observed in *The Subjection of Women* – then it seems utterly useless to forbid them to do it.[9] What "nature" really meant, clearly, was deep-rooted custom, and the unwillingness of men to give up a traditional privilege.

One power claim can sometimes give way in order to protect another. The first woman permitted to take a law degree in the English-speaking world, in 1893, was an Indian woman named Cornelia Sorabji, a woman from the Parsi community who had come to Oxford in order to get credentials that would help her represent Hindu women who lived in *purdah* or seclusion from men, and who, not being able to see a lawyer, were being cheated out of their estates. The British, deeply racist and convinced that Hinduism was a beastly religion, were so impressed by the need to foil the interests of greedy Hindu men that they made this one exception to their otherwise confident assertion of the private–public distinction and the rhetoric of Nature that went with it. Racism took precedence over sexism.[10]

Back to my argument, however. The second bad thing the private–public distinction did was make it all right for women to have grossly unequal property and inheritance rights (if they had those rights at all). This inequality is still a subject of struggle today: witness the recent successful efforts of feminists, led by economic theorist Bina Agarwal, to reform the Hindu Succession Act in India so that, at long last, men and women have fully equal shares. Agarwal's research demonstrates that land ownership is the single most significant variable relevant to whether a woman experiences domestic violence. Husbands apparently treat land-owning wives better. So we are talking about a matter of wide-ranging significance.

Third, what the private–public distinction did was to shield otherwise criminal behavior from the eye of the law. Domestic violence, rape within marriage, the sexual and physical abuse of children, were all ignored as if they either did not take place or, worse still, were right and good. There were no laws against them, or, even when there were, they were never enforced. Marital rape was thought to be a contradiction in terms, since marriage was taken to convey unlimited access to the body of the wife. Many people felt the same about wife-beating and child-beating. For the law to intervene would be to compromise and taint a cherished masculine privilege. And that too was taken to be against Nature.[11]

---

[9] Mill (1988).   [10] Sorabji (2001).
[11] See MacKinnon (1989: 168–70); Nussbaum (2005a; a shortened version appears in Nussbaum 2003a).

Liberal philosophers did not all go along with this. John Stuart Mill, in the vanguard here as elsewhere, went to jail in his youth for distributing contraceptive literature in London – a key way to compromise male power in the household; much later, as a Member of Parliament, he introduced the first bill for women's suffrage. But Mill also fought on the theoretical front, struggling throughout his career for the removal of the whole baneful private–public distinction, which he considered a blot upon liberalism. For Mill, liberalism was about equal respect for each and every person. By abandoning their principles at the door of the home, liberal theorists were selling out their most cherished ideas. Mill focused particular attention on the problem of rape within marriage, and the failure of law to treat it as a criminal act. He argued that the idea that a wife has no right to refuse intercourse to her husband made her lot worse than that of a slave. Female slaves, he says, are often raped, but at least in principle the law takes this to be wrong, and society thinks that the female slave at least has the right to struggle against it. "Not so the wife: however brutal a tyrant she may unfortunately be chained to ... he can claim from her and enforce the lowest degradation of a human being, that of being made the instrument of an animal function contrary to her inclinations."[12]

Despite Mill's foresightedness and clarity, liberal political theory has still not unequivocally rejected the public–private distinction. Even the great John Rawls, who does officially reject it, nonetheless wavered until the end of his life, treating the family as a political institution, part of society's "basic structure," but also saying that it has the status of a voluntary institution, like a university or a church. If it is a voluntary institution, that means that principles of justice limit it in a more external and lesser way, although there would still be some limits. Rawls never made it fully clear what limits on the conduct of family members his theory would allow.[13] At least this much is clear: by now no major liberal thinker, Rawls included, supports any of the gross injustices that I have just chronicled. All believe that women should have fully equal political rights and property rights. All hold, as well, that crimes of violence that take place in the home are criminal and should be prosecuted by law. The residual uncertainty about how much law can interfere with the home represents a real dilemma over the value of intimate association, something addressed in the concluding section.

Despite the fact that police the world over are still lax in prosecuting crimes of violence within the family, despite the fact that marital rape

---

[12] Mill (1988: 33).
[13] See my criticism in Nussbaum (2000: chapter 4), and my review of numerous critiques in Nussbaum (2003b).

is not even counted as a crime in many countries and is counted as a lesser crime than stranger rape in about half of the states in the United States, liberal political *theory*, at least, has more or less passed beyond step one.

Step two: criticizing inadequate conceptions of equal treatment

Liberal political theory arose as an alternative to patriarchal, feudal, and monarchical theories. Its key notion is that of the equal worth and dignity of each and every human being.[14] Thus, it would seem that liberal theorists ought to understand that treating people as equals means treating them with due regard for that equal dignity. This is not necessarily the same thing as treating everyone the same. Especially in unjust societies, which all actual societies are, people occupy different starting positions, many of them constructed by a legacy of injustice. In such circumstances, treating people with due regard for their equal dignity would mean systematically removing the obstacles that tradition and power have erected against them, in such a way that their equal worth gets truly fair treatment. If I begin as a peasant and you begin as a king, and then we are treated exactly the same, I will probably continue to lag way behind you, because you begin with some huge initial advantages over me: wealth, education, superior nutrition, a sense of your worth and confidence, power over others. So true liberalism has naturally led to redistributive economic policies and to social policies favoring at least some rectification of background hierarchies, through affirmative measures designed to aid traditionally disadvantaged groups.

There is, however, a lot of debate within liberal theory about how this norm of fairness is to be achieved, and somehow or other American law emerged with a particularly bad set of concepts in this area. American legal theorists widely believed that treating people as equals required giving them similar treatment. In part this was just confusion, but in part, too, the view probably derives from Americans' extreme suspicion of affirmative measures toward equality undertaken by the state. A particularly flagrant example of this confused reasoning can be seen in one of the most famous law review articles of all time, by a distinguished federal judge: Herbert Wechsler's "Toward Neutral Principles of Constitutional Law."[15]

Wechsler begins unobjectionably, arguing that judges need criteria that are not arbitrary or capricious, "criteria that can be framed and

---

[14] See Nussbaum (1999b).   [15] Wechsler (1959).

tested as an exercise of reason and not merely as an act of willfulness or will." They should be able to articulate their reasons in public, and should not function simply as a "naked power organ." As his argument continues, however, it becomes clear that Wechsler takes the demand for principled neutrality to entail standing so far back from the experience of the parties, and the human meaning of the facts, that hierarchy and subordination cannot be seen. He turns to criticism of the famous Supreme Court case, *Brown v. Board of Education* (1954), in which the Court held that "separate but equal" schools for blacks and whites were unconstitutional. The court argued that the black schools were not truly equal because, even if treatment is really similar, the separation was associated with stigma and hierarchy, and entailed a loss of self-respect for black children. Wechsler now argues that it is inappropriate to consider the unequal experience of students in the two schools. All that they can properly consider is the facts: what the schools are like and what facilities are offered. He ends by concluding that segregation poses equal and symmetrical disadvantages to both black and whites. He mentions a case where he and an African-American colleague could not eat lunch together in a Washington restaurant, saying that the disadvantage involved was exactly the same for both. This conclusion is of course quite implausible and a sign of the more general obtuseness involved in Wechsler's claim that treating similarly was sufficient for treating as equals. The fact that Wechsler couldn't eat with the colleague was an inconvenience; for the colleague, it was a mark of stigma and inferiority.

Fortunately, the US Supreme Court reasoned differently in *Brown*, holding that similar treatment was not sufficient for the equal protection of the laws.[16] In 1967, a case arose that led to an even more striking affirmation of an anti-hierarchy conception of equal treatment and the equal protection of the laws.

In 1958, Mildred Jeter, a black woman, and Richard Loving, a white man, were married in the District of Columbia in accordance with its laws. They then returned to Virginia, their state of residence, establishing their home in Caroline County. In October of that year, a grand jury issued an indictment charging the Lovings with violating Virginia's ban on interracial marriages. After pleading guilty to the charge, they were sentenced to one year in jail; the judge suspended the sentence on condition that they leave the state for at least twenty-five years. In his opinion, he stated that:

Almighty God created the races white, black, yellow, malay and red, and he placed them on separate continents. And but for the interference with his

---

[16] *Brown v. Board of Education of Topeka*, 347 US 483 (1954).

arrangement there would be no cause for such marriages. The fact that he separated the races shows that he did not intend for the races to mix.

(Notice the appeal to nature here. At least the Virginia court reveals the theological nature of its argument.) Taking up residence in the District of Columbia, where interracial marriage was legal, the Lovings went to court challenging the constitutionality of Virginia's anti-miscegenation laws. In 1966, the Virginia Supreme Court upheld the constitutionality of the laws; the Lovings appealed to the US Supreme Court. The state's central argument was that the law does not violate Equal Protection because the two races suffer equal and symmetrical disadvantages from the prohibition. Blacks can't marry whites, and whites can't marry blacks. Thus the statutes "do not constitute an invidious discrimination based upon race." On June 12, 1967, in a unanimous decision, the US Supreme Court ruled the laws unconstitutional, arguing that they were clearly intended to uphold White Supremacy, and that there is "patently no legitimate overriding purpose independent of invidious racial discrimination which justifies this classification." The Court stated explicitly the mere fact of a law's equal and neutral application does not mean that it does not constitute "an arbitrary and invidious discrimination."[17]

What the Supreme Court had done was to interpret the idea of equal protection in keeping with the true underlying spirit of liberal theory, which is anti-feudal and anti-monarchical, wresting the theory's core away from the misleading interpretations of some legal theorists. In the two decades that followed, feminist theorists did the same thing for hierarchies of sex and gender. They argued that treating women and men similarly was not enough for genuine treatment as equals. What was relevant was to consider hierarchies of power and opportunity, and what would be required to demolish those. Thus, insurance companies that denied women pregnancy benefits, claiming that this was all right because they did the same for men – no pregnant women got benefits, and no pregnant men got benefits – were told that this was not enough: lack of insurance during pregnancy was a major barrier to women's full equality in the workplace, so genuine treating-as-equals required giving such benefits.[18]

In the important area of sexual harassment law, sexual harassment, too, was interpreted in keeping with ideas of illegitimate hierarchy and subordination, rather than in terms of similar treatment. Consider the case of Mary Carr, the first woman who worked in the General Motors

---

[17] *Loving* v. *Virginia*, 388 US 1 (1967); the summary of earlier decisions is from the Supreme Court opinion.
[18] See MacKinnon (1989: chapter 12).

Plant in Indiana, and who was subjected for years to an obscene and intimidating torrent of abuse from her male co-workers, who feared that hiring women meant fewer jobs for men.[19] At trial, management claimed that the atmosphere of bad language and malice was symmetrical on both sides: Carr herself had on occasion used some bad language to her male co-workers. The judge in the case – a Reagan appointee, and quite a conservative judge, but one who read the theoretical literature – said that the asymmetry of power between Carr and the group of men had to be considered. Her use of a four-letter word just didn't mean the same thing as their verbal abuse of her, given this asymmetry. In these ways, feminist concepts of equal treatment, brought in from the already developed law of race, corrected and enriched legal thought.

By now, the second step in reforming liberal theory has by and large been taken by theorists. In practice, there remains widespread resistance to the concept of affirmative action or compensatory discrimination, and widespread attachment to the idea that if people are treated similarly, that is all that need be done, although there is also broad if not unanimous support for all the particular decisions on race and gender that I have mentioned in this section. Theory, however, has made decisive progress.

Step three: the recognition of deformed preferences

For some liberal theorists, liberalism is all about respect for people's preferences, and the only legitimate role for the liberal state is as a kind of response-mechanism, as voters register their preferences. Preferences, in this view, are typically understood as "hard-wired," that is, given with the person and unaffected by mutable social conditions. That is why respecting preferences is seen as a way of respecting persons. No major philosopher ever said this in so many words, but Hobbes and Hume said things that could certainly be taken as going in that direction. This way of looking at the liberal state became dominant with the dominance of neoliberal welfare economics, particularly of what is called the "Chicago school." (Obviously enough, I am not fond of this name, since it conceals so much else that goes on at the University of Chicago!)

Few economic welfarists followed this line of thinking all the way. All, for example, seem to support constitutional democracy rather than

---

[19] *Mary Jane Carr* v. *Allison Gas Turbine Division, General Motors Corp.*, 32 F. 3d 1007 (7th Cir. 1994). I discuss this case, and Richard Posner's opinion in it, in Nussbaum (1995: chapter 4).

pure majoritarian democracy. In his book *Overcoming Law*, Richard Posner, the founder of the law-and-economics movement and a leading federal judge (in fact, the judge I mentioned in the Mary Carr case) frankly acknowledges that the economic welfarist needs to become non-welfarist where basic rights are at stake, following Mill rather than a pure preference-utilitarianism.[20] For example, says Posner, the preference of the majority to limit the freedom of speech should not be allowed to determine people's speech rights. Censorship of the press should not be favored just because the majority wants it. No doubt Posner is influenced by the fact that his daily job is that of interpreting the US Constitution, which does protect basic rights in this way. On the whole, however, the major economic theorists in this area were pretty uncritical of preferences, thinking of them as the basic material of social choice, and thinking it quite dangerous, or threatening, to scrutinize them or rank them in any way.

Obviously enough, however, there are many things wrong with people's preferences that might lead us to think them, or lots of them, a very bad basis for political choice. Preferences, first, are often ill-informed and contain incomplete rather than complete views of the relevant terrain. Most neoclassical welfarists admit at least this much, incorporating the idea of full information into their preference-based normative accounts. Second, preferences may be sadistic or malicious, and it seems plausible that those preferences should not count, either at all or as much as others, when we think about social choice. Some neoclassical economists have explicitly favored excluding such preferences: John Harsanyi, for example, admits that this correction involves a rather major departure from standard welfarism. Third, some preferences are distorted by lack of options: thus people's choice to perform certain occupations may reflect not a genuinely free choice, but just a capitulation to a bad set of constraints. This defect is still harder to correct within neoclassical theory, since correction would involve deciding what decent or just background conditions are, what options people ought to have. But even "Chicago school" economist Gary Becker, in his Nobel Prize address, grants that this problem is a large one in the areas of both gender and race.[21]

Finally, preferences themselves may be adaptations to a bad state of affairs: that is, people may learn actually not to want things that their situation has put out of reach. This is different from lack of options,

---

[20] Posner (1995).
[21] This paragraph and the following three summarize the argument of Nussbaum (2000: chapter 2).

since people may still long for things that they can't have. But the point made by both Jon Elster and Amartya Sen is that people often learn not to want those unattainable things. Sen focuses on cases involving gender: women brought up to think that a proper or good women won't go to school will come to think this herself, and not to have a preference for much schooling.

The problem of adaptation is the deepest of the four. It seems impossible to correct within welfarism. It pushes us in the direction of a substantive account of which freedoms and opportunities are genuinely worthwhile. In such a view, these freedoms or capabilities have intrinsic importance, not simply preference-dependent importance.

Once again, the great John Stuart Mill already understood the problem of adaptation and other deformed preferences. Mill said that men, not content with enslaving women's bodies, enslaved their minds as well, teaching them that docility, sweetness, and obedience are the marks of a good woman. Women often buy into this picture, and thus come to lack ambition for achievements that men would like them not to strive for.

In the recent era, however, Mill's insight was largely neglected. The correction of liberal theory came, this time, from two utterly different sources, not much in contact with one another. On the one hand, the work of Elster in political science and Sen in economics transformed the debate in that latter profession. Meanwhile, radical feminists, in particular Catharine MacKinnon, had already articulated the same insight in a very thoroughgoing way, holding that even the sexual desires of women often represent adaptations to a demeaning or objectifying view of women. Men want to use women like objects, so they teach them that it is sexy to dress oneself up as a sex object and allow oneself to be used. The dominant message of pornography, in particular, is that women like to be used and exploited, sometimes even abused. A message is sent to both men and women that this is sexy, and people's sexual desires are shaped by the message. Women even come to take sexual pleasure in submission and abandonment of will, sometimes even in abuse, because that is what they learn through the images of gender and sexuality that suffuse their society.

It's obvious that this correction goes deeper than the other corrections of preference that I have mentioned, in that it requires us to rethink the myth of "nature" at a deeper level. Nothing, not even sexual desire, is utterly "natural," meaning given, unaffected by social conditions. Even in this area, much is custom, and many customs are quite bad. We are just beginning to learn how a reformulated liberalism might incorporate this insight.

Step four: dealing with the problem of care

My next step is still in its early stages, and it is one with which my own recent work is particularly concerned. Part of the myth of women's "nature" is the idea that care within the family will be done all by women, out of love, and that this is somehow not work, but just part of love. There is a huge amount of care work to be done in any society: care for children, housework, care for the elderly (an increasing problem), care for people with lifelong illnesses or disabilities (an increasing problem in the light of the HIV/AIDS pandemic, and the reason why the World Health Organization has devoted particular attention to the problem of care labor). Most of this work is done by women, all over the world, and most of it is unpaid. Moreover, it is not even recognized by the market as work. And yet, it obviously exerts a huge influence on the rest of a woman's life. Even when women have equal education and equal employment opportunities, they are hobbled by the care responsibilities they disproportionately bear, and so it is difficult for them to succeed at work, or for the workplace to have fully equal respect for them.

The myth of Nature here plays a very pernicious role. Women and men are both taught from an early age that it is women's nature to care for children and elderly parents, and that what this means is that women have biological instincts that would be utterly frustrated if they didn't do these things. So imposing this work on women comes to look like a benefit to them, preventing terrible frustration. Women are strongly pressured by such pictures: if they don't really want to have children at all, or to give up their jobs to care full-time for those they do have, they are made to feel "unnatural" in the normative sense, like freaks or bad people. The appeal to Nature also helps men reason that this very arduous work is really not work at all, but just the playing out of an innate instinct, like eating or sleeping.

Obviously enough, thinking well about this problem requires giving up the public–private distinction and recognizing that what goes on in the home is economically significant work. It also requires thinking critically about preferences and recognizing the large role of social norms in creating them. But more yet is required. In my recent book *Frontiers of Justice*,[22] I argue that the tradition of liberal political theory, if it is going to come to grips with the problem of care work, will have to qualify very seriously its reliance on the image of society as the outcome of a social contract for mutual advantage.

In all the major versions of this idea of the social contract, from John Locke to John Rawls, the assumption is made that the participants in

---

[22] Nussbaum (2006).

the social contract are "free, equal, and independent," to use Locke's phrase, are "fully cooperating members of society over a complete life," to use Rawls's phrase. But this assumption is false, and it is false in a way that, I argue, seriously distorts the choice of political principles, making provision for care and due respect for care labor much less central than they ought to be.

I argue that if we reject the Lockean image of the social contract we can still retain a political theory that is in key respects basically liberal: based on the idea of the equal worth of each person, and on respect for each individual life. We may solve the problem, I think, in two related ways. One solution would be to develop a form of contractualism that departs from the Lockean idea of the social compact, but uses, instead, something like Thomas Scanlon's idea that good principles would be such that no individual could reasonably refuse them. Scanlon's contractualism, however, would have to be combined with a political account of primary goods if it were to be useful for political, not just ethical, theory, a fact Scanlon frankly acknowledges.[23] This has not yet been done, since Brian Barry's use of Scanlon for political theory (in *Justice as Impartiality*[24]) doesn't do enough to describe a politically workable account of the good. On the other hand, and this is my own solution, we could begin the other way round and start from an account of the political good, in the form of an account of certain basic entitlements or opportunities that are essential for a decently just society: what I do with my version of the capabilities approach. But then, to justify the approach, we will need to bring in something analogous to Scanlon's requirement of rational acceptability – so in fact the two views will have most of the same moving parts, though arranged in a slightly different order. I hope that the dialogue between these two approaches will become ever deeper and more subtle, so that we understand this whole area of human life better, and what adequate political principles for it would be.

Challenges for the future

I have written throughout this chapter of reforming or correcting liberal theories. But why do I want to reform liberalism, rather than supplant it? The radical feminists whom I cite as having contributed to liberalism's reform would not accept that characterization of their mission. MacKinnon, for example, thinks that liberalism is hopeless. I think, however, that she misunderstands liberalism, equating it wrongly with impoverished versions of liberalism in the legal and economic literature.

[23] In conversation, cited in Nussbaum (2006).   [24] Barry (1995).

I myself think that theories in the liberal tradition are the strongest theories of justice we have, and that we ought to try as hard as we can to reform them, before concluding that they cannot be reformed. What I take to be a fundamental insight of liberalism is the idea of the boundless and equal dignity of each person, together with the idea that respecting persons requires giving them space for freedom and choice. Those deep insights do not entail any of the mistakes I have just tried to correct, and in many ways they entail the corrections that have by now been made – as Mill saw, far in advance of his time. For gender justice, in particular, liberalism seems very badly needed. What has gone wrong in the lives of women around the world is that they have so often been taken to be the supporters or adjuncts of someone else, not individuals of worth in their own right. Being respected as an individual is perfectly compatible with having deep bonds of love and obligation to others; it does not entail the selfishness that is so often attacked under the name of "Western individualism." Liberal theory is not about selfishness, it is fundamentally about equality, respect, and freedom.

To realize liberalism at its best, in the area of gender justice, we must keep working away at the problems I have mentioned, which are certainly not all solved, particularly the last two. But there are additional challenges for the future.

First, liberal feminism needs more and better arguments against cultural relativism and in favor of at least some universal norms of human freedom and possibility. In the actual political arena, cultural relativism is enormously strong, however weak it is in theory, so the liberal theorist needs to have good arguments against it. Particularly important to the theoretical articulation of these arguments is sorting out the relationship between relativism and pluralism. It is perfectly consistent to hold that local culture is not the criterion of the good (thus rejecting relativism) while also holding that people's choices in matter of culture and religion deserve respect (thus endorsing pluralism). Policies expressing respect for religious difference and other prominent types of human self-definition can be given a liberal form. But it is important to work out what exactly that form is, and how it can be compatible with the preservation of genuinely equal entitlement for all. I believe that John Rawls's *Political Liberalism* has done a great deal to show us the way here, but there is still a lot more to be done, particularly in the area of gender and family.[25]

Second, liberal feminism needs a better account of intimate association, and the freedom of association generally, and the rights they involve, one that does not fall back on the dubious public–private

[25] Rawls (2005).

distinction or the alleged sanctity of the home. But this is difficult to do: for it is pretty easy to draw a line around the home, saying law cannot enter here. It is much more difficult to say what precise types of human conduct and association deserve protection from legal interference, *no matter where they are located*. And yet that is what we have to do.

Third, liberalism needs a more detailed and richer account of emotions, desires, and other preferences, of the influences, developmental and societal, that bear on their formation, and of the many influences, good and bad, that can be brought to bear to make preferences support a just society rather than undermining it. Both the nature of emotion and desire and the role of moral education in shaping them are unfashionable topics in political theory, despite the fact that they have been at its heart in other eras, from Plato, Aristotle, and the Stoics to Adam Smith. We know much more now about child development and about the social shaping of preferences, through work in psychology and psychoanalysis, than the Greeks and Romans did, more even than the Scottish Enlightenment did. Political philosophy has still not taken the full measure of that work. Feminist theory has made large steps in the direction of incorporating accounts of desire and emotion into political theory, but the results – for example in the illuminating work of MacKinnon and Andrea Dworkin – are not yet systematically articulated, or argued in a philosophical way. This is a project that particularly interests me.

These are large tasks. Someone might think that liberal theory cannot accomplish them. But the death knell of liberalism has been sounded prematurely before. Each of the steps of reform I have mentioned has been taken in the face of naysayers who were claiming that liberalism cannot incorporate the new insight or the new critique.

Why should liberals undertake this task, with gender justice a central theoretical concern? Because the alternative is to rest content with inadequate theories of justice, and also with inadequate perceptions and understandings of some of the most important things in human life. As Mill wrote in the final sentence of *The Subjection of Women*: not to undertake this task "leaves the species less rich, to an inappreciable degree, in all that makes life valuable to the individual human being."[26]

References

Barry, Brian 1995. *Justice as Impartiality*, New York and Oxford: Oxford University Press.

[26] Mill (1988: 109).

Drèze, Jean and Sen, Amartya 1989. *Hunger and Public Action*, Oxford: Clarendon Press.

1995. *India: Economic Development and Social Opportunity*, Oxford University Press.

2002. *India: Development and Participation*, Oxford University Press.

MacKinnon, Catharine 1989. *Toward a Feminist Theory of the State*, Cambridge, MA: Harvard University Press.

Mill, J. S. 1988. *The Subjection of Women*, edited by S. M. Okin, Indianapolis: Hackett; originally published 1869.

1998. "Nature," in J. S. Mill, *Three Essays on Religion*, Amherst, NY: Prometheus Books.

Nussbaum, Martha C. 1995. *Poetic Justice: The Literary Imagination and Public Life*, Boston, MA: Beacon Press.

1999a. "The Feminist Critique of Liberalism," in Nussbaum 1999b: 55–80.

1999b. *Sex and Social Justice*, Oxford University Press.

2000. *Women and Human Development: The Capabilities Approach*, Cambridge University Press.

2003a. "What's Privacy Got to Do with It? A Comparative Approach to the Feminist Critique," in Sibyl A. Schwarzenbach and Patricia Smith (eds.) *Women and the United States Constitution: History, Interpretation, Practice*, New York: Columbia University Press, pp. 153–75.

2003b. "Rawls and Feminism," in Freeman, Samuel (ed.) *The Cambridge Companion to Rawls*, Cambridge University Press, pp. 488–520.

2005a. "Sex Equality, Liberty, and Privacy: A Comparative Approach to the Feminist Critique," in E. Sridharan, Z. Hasan, and R. Sudarshan, (eds.) *India's Living Constitution: Ideas, Practices, Controversies* (volume from a conference on the fiftieth anniversary of the Indian Constitution), New Delhi: Permanent Black, pp. 242–83.

2005b. "Women's Bodies: Violence, Security, Capabilities," *Journal of Human Development* **6**: 167–83.

2006. *Frontiers of Justice*, Cambridge, MA: Harvard University Press.

Okin, Susan Moller 1979. *Women in Western Political Thought*, Princeton University Press.

1989. *Justice, Gender, and the Family*, New York: Basic Books.

Posner, Richard A. 1995. *Overcoming Law*, Harvard University Press; reprinted 1996.

Rawls, John 2005. *Political Liberalism*, expanded edn., New York: Columbia University Press; originally published 1993.

Sorabji, C. 2001. *India Calling: The Memories of Cornelia Sorabji, India's First Woman Barrister*, Oxford University Press; first published London: Nisbet & Co., 1935.

UNDP [United Nations Development Programme] 2000. *Human Development Report 2000*, Oxford University Press.

Wechsler, Herbert 1959. "Toward Neutral Principles of Constitutional Law," *Harvard Law Review* **73** (1): 1–35.

6   Gift, market, and social justice

Marcel Hénaff

When compared with the ubiquitous power of the market, gift-giving practices can only appear marginal. Some of them, such as ritual gift-giving, are viewed as a thing of the past and often called archaic; others, such as giving gifts to loved ones or persons that one admires or who deserve to be honored, also serve to increase the circulation of commodities, in particular during the holidays; still others, such as providing assistance to persons in need, appeal to the generosity of the public and the state or, as in the case of various support projects, are performed by philanthropic foundations. None of these practices can rival specifically industrial and commercial activities, whether what is considered is the amounts or the social effects involved. Is there a purpose beyond exoticism, then, in raising the question of gift-giving as part of a debate between economy and social justice?

The question of the gift is a fascinating one, however, no matter what its various forms may be, whether this is because it involves an exchange of goods that seems immune from the laws of commercial exchange (even if the market does get something out of it) or because it reveals an altruistic quality that transcends the supposed selfishness of the rational agent, or finally, in an even more subtle way, because the participants in commercial exchange can resort to gift-giving games in order to make business practices more effective. To sum up, two conflicting things are expected from what is generically called "gift-giving": either an alternative to the system of the market that would open a new field to social justice or, on the contrary, a contribution to the dynamism of the market itself.

When a concept that applies to practices assumed to belong to the same realm is open to such divergent arguments, there is reason to believe that its definition is imprecise or even confused and that the practices involved have not been sufficiently described and categorized. This is clearly the case with the concept of gift. It is thus likely that the three examples given above do not constitute a homogeneous class of objects. It is hard to see how the following could be placed in the same

category: (a) the festivals and gifts that chiefs offer each other in turn
in traditional societies; (b) the celebrations and presents that parents
give their children on the occasion of their birthdays; (c) the donations
contributed when catastrophes occur. These examples are significant
and may be considered to exemplify three main types of gift-giving:
(a) ceremonial gift-giving, which is always described as reciprocal;
(b) generous unilateral gift-giving; (c) mutual aid or gift-giving out of
solidarity. The first type is characterized by the obligation to reciprocate the gift that has been received, as shown by ethnographic investigations; it therefore raises the issue of reciprocity (which is certainly
much more than a mere exchange of good manners). The second type
reveals a spontaneous generosity towards the givers' loved ones, which
is viewed above all as a psychological or moral quality. The third type
is evidence of a strong social dimension of altruism toward strangers[1]
and probably comes closest to what could be called social justice. It is
precisely this question of altruism that has been of concern to theoreti-
cians since the first formulation of classical and neoclassical economic
theory: rational economic agents are by definition supposed to be self-
interested, since this is the only attitude that could make their behavior
predictable and thus calculable (see Hirschman 1974). How can generous and cooperative behaviors, then, be interpreted? Moreover, how
can they be integrated within economic theory? How can they contribute to optimizing results? It would therefore seem that types two and
three above are the only ones that are worth considering in the present
debate. As for reciprocal ceremonial gift-giving, it is often viewed as
an archaic form of trade and a still awkward form of contract; in short,
its spectacular generosity appears to conceal a form of self-interested
reciprocity.

Yet, it seems to me that this type of gift-giving is the one that has
the potential for raising the most interesting questions – but only if the
analysis of this type of gift-giving is taken from a new perspective. In
fact, this theoretical renewal was largely brought about some time ago
by M. Mauss' famous essay, *The Gift* (Mauss 1990). This is indisput-
able, and my own approach is clearly situated within the perspective
opened by this essay. Yet, it is necessary to ask new questions, to go
further, and even to change course, since Mauss, although he was able
to show how exchanges of gifts transcended economic relationships,
still concluded *The Gift* by presenting gifts as an example of a different
economy assumed to be more generous, community-oriented, and just

[1] A good example of this appears in blood donation (see Titmus 1970; see also the
stimulating commentary on this book in Arrow 1972).

(Mauss 1990: 65–83). He then proposed the concept of "gift economy." This concept seems to me to be untenable and incapable of fulfilling its purpose. Mauss remained fascinated with the fact that the ceremonial exchange had the appearance of an exchange of goods; I intend to show that it is primarily an exchange of symbols and that it constitutes above all a specific procedure of public recognition between human groups in traditional societies.

My purpose is therefore: (1) on the basis of some of the ethnographic data provided and theoretical perspectives opened by Mauss' essay, to sum up the crucial characteristics of the type of gift that he called "archaic" and that I prefer to describe as a reciprocal ceremonial gift; (2) to discuss the inspiring yet problematic use that two contemporary neoclassical economists, G. A. Akerlof and C. F. Camerer, have made of this type of gift-giving; (3) starting from the question that is raised or, more accurately, presupposed by their work – namely, that of the social bond – to return to the anthropological data in order to show that the aporias relative to reciprocity, obligation, or exchange can only be overcome through a renewal of the interpretation of ceremonial gift-giving based on the concept of recognition; (4) in conclusion, building on this new foundation, to try to explain how this procedure has been transposed in modern societies and how the demand for recognition has become a central aspect of social justice. This cannot be reduced to a static view that would involve the redistribution of goods or to claims to a new set of rights; it must be understood in a positive way – in particular following A. Sen's approach – as a dynamic offer regarding the capabilities of agents.

Traditional gift-giving: Mauss' lesson

What we owe above all to Marcel Mauss' *The Gift* (Mauss 1990) is the way it set up the problem of the ceremonial gift as a sociological issue. Mauss did so based on the ethnographic materials that were available at the beginning of the twentieth century and by relating them to testimonies found in ancient Indian, Roman, Scandinavian, and Germanic literatures. He was not the first to show interest in this phenomenon, but he was the first to systematically gather the relevant but scattered data and to bring to the fore a model according to which the gift appears as a major social fact. He even called it "a total social phenomenon" (I will return to this point). The elaboration of his own synthesis owed much to Bronislav Malinowski's *The Argonauts of the Western Pacific* (Malinowski 1961) on the great cycles of gift exchange – so-called *kula* – of the Trobriand Islands, a Melanesian archipelago. This gift exchange activity constitutes the very core of indigenous social life: weeks or even months are dedicated to preparing boats and collecting precious goods – *waigu'a* – which numerous magical ceremonies aim to protect. The most important of these goods are the bracelets that move from east to west and the necklaces that move in the opposite direction. When the boats reach an island, those initiating the *kula* leave semi-precious objects on the beach as opening gifts meant to entice *kula* partners. Those who accept these gifts – called clinching gifts – are obligated to continue the cycle; the main exchange, that of bracelets and necklaces, then starts and extends over several days. When these ceremonies are over, the boats leave with the new gifts in order to enter into another exchange on the next island. A network of privileged bonds is thus woven over the whole of the archipelago through the exchange of these precious goods; some of those goods are known and reputed to be particularly beautiful and are given proper names. However, their value is not only due to the fact that they are made of rare stones or shells but above all to the fact that they have belonged to such-and-such person; it is due to the memory of the bonds that they carry with them. They constitute a source of prestige for those who hold them but also for those who have been able to give them.

The second important example that was emphasized by Mauss was that of the agonistic exchange called potlatch among the indigenous populations of the northwest coast of North America as described by Franz Boas (1911; 1966): a chief gives a celebration for another chief in the name of his own group, dealing with the other chief both as a partner to be treated and a rival to be challenged. The importance of the gifts that are given (emblazoned copper objects, woven blankets, furs, and food) is such that, even though reciprocation is mandatory, it is deliberately made difficult. Honor and prestige are awarded to the one most capable of offering excessive gifts.

The originality of Mauss' analysis lay in that he showed that these ritual gift practices implied three inseparable obligations: to give, to accept the gifts, and to reciprocate them. The obligation to reciprocate was made particularly obvious by a third example, provided by Elsdon Best's investigation among the Maori of New Zealand. Here is what a Maori elder explained: if A has given a gift to B who has given it to C, when B receives a gift from C he must give it to A. Things are clear: the movement of reciprocity must ultimately return to its source. The spirit of the thing given, called *hau*, lies in this. Reciprocity is not merely dual; it moves through the whole line of the receivers (as in the case of the so-called generalized exchange in exogamic circuits);

what is returned is not the thing itself (as many researchers mistakenly believed), but the very gesture of giving. Why is this the case? Mauss noticed it in these various examples but did not try to provide a convincing reason.

At this point, and without engaging in a precise discussion of the analyses presented by Mauss or the authors he discussed, a few remarks can be made:

- The concept of "total social fact," i.e. a phenomenon implicating all aspects of social life (religion, kinship, politics, morals, and economics) that Mauss proposed only applies to these practices of ritual gift-giving; but this means that all those aspects are embedded within this social fact, which is the sphere of all spheres; in short, it is the dominant and unifying fact of the group's life. We should note that Mauss never applied this concept to any other social fact.

- Mauss emphasized the obligatory character of the triad, giving, receiving, and reciprocating. He gave multiple examples and noted that the alternative was between exchanges of gifts – peace – and exchanges of blows – war; but he did not provide any real reason for this.

- Even though he sometimes used inappropriate terms such as "noble trade" or "contract," Mauss took care to make it clear that this type of exchange was profoundly different from exchanges in the marketplace. He noted, following Malinowski, that *kula* partners also practiced profitable exchanges called *gimwali*, i.e. barter involving various consumer goods, but that they always did so with different partners. The goods involved in the ceremonial exchange were distinct from the consumer goods (which was also the case with ceremonial currencies). This is a crucial distinction.

- Mauss emphasized the fact that what was given through the thing given was always oneself; the self of each partner and that of the group through the partners. Is this an archaic magical feature? Or is it on the contrary a central aspect of the ceremonial gift that must be understood as a commitment of a different type from strictly contractual ones?

- Mauss called this form of exchange of goods archaic; this implied that it has now disappeared or exists only in a residual form within our modernity. We will have to see if this is true.

- Finally, Mauss' concluding remarks have remained famous in that, as I have already mentioned, he proposed to consider this type of generous and glorious exchange as a kind of counter-model to the purely self-interested and selfish exchanges involved in capitalistic economy. Is there actually an economic lesson to be drawn from the practices of this ceremonial gift?

To conclude this reminder, let us say that Mauss was able to epistemologically state the issue of the ceremonial gift but that many questions remain unanswered: thus, all the consequences of the concept of total social fact as applied to the ceremonial gift remain to be drawn: what would be its equivalent in today's world? My hypothesis is that it has been transformed or transposed and that what constitutes this fact remains for us the central question of our social life, under new forms. I will add that this question does not primarily involve an exchange of goods and as such is not an economic one. But before defining it and presenting my own answer, in order to better assess what is at stake I would like to consider the economic interpretations that have been given for ritual gift-giving and to draw from them a lesson that can illuminate any alternative interpretation.

Interpretations of the ceremonial gift within economic theory

Economic explanations of gift exchange rituals were first given by a number of anthropologists (with the notable exception of Malinowski) when the first great ethnographic investigations were conducted during the last decades of the nineteenth century and the beginning of the twentieth. These views are still commonly held by anthropologists. Franz Boas, who provided remarkable descriptions of the potlatch of the Kwakiutl (Boas 1966), insisted on presenting the goods thrown into the potlatch as a loan to be later reimbursed with considerable interest. The people involved would thus be more modern and rational than we generally think. H. Codere (1950) also supported this interpretation. Many other field researchers, most importantly P. Radin (1927), L. Pospisil (1963), and T.S. Epstein (1968), viewed gift-giving practices as either an archaic form or original variation of economic exchanges. This view is still found in many anthropological treatises and textbooks. Even authors who were open to a complex understanding of social relationships and economy, such as M. Weber (1981) and K. Polanyi (1957), have tended to identify exchanges of gifts with trade. More recently, a different trend of thought has better assessed the importance of Mauss' approach and drawn its implications (Lévi-Strauss 1969; Strathern 1971; Sahlins 1972; Gregory 1982; Weiner 1992; Godebout and Caillé 1998; Godelier 1999). This is not the proper place to discuss this rich debate, which has left its mark on the discipline of anthropology. However, it may be interesting to notice the interest that contemporary neoclassical economists have shown in traditional gift-giving. The approach has somehow been reversed: economists now expect anthropology – that of traditional gift exchange – to illuminate a question that belongs to their own discipline. Such an attempt can only prove to be stimulating, despite the epistemological and methodological difficulties involved. We can surmise that the hypotheses presented will depend on the way in which this exchange itself has been understood. I will discuss two of these hypotheses, chosen for the quality of their argument and the importance of the question that lies below them.

Wage and gift exchange according to George A. Akerlof

Akerlof[2] proposed an explanation using the logic of the gift based on a consideration of the work contract (Akerlof 1982; 1984). What is the social issue raised by the concept of work? Akerlof did not ask this question; however, both K. Marx and K. Polanyi showed, in different but concordant ways, that work is inseparable from life itself and thus from the worker. Selling one's labor amounts to willingly or unwillingly entering some part of oneself, some dimension of one's life, into the marketplace, even though one may wish to keep the two separate. This very difficulty is the source of many conflicts. Employers may consider that they are only remunerating recognized competence as well as the time and energy that were spent. Everything else is of no concern to them and in any case does not belong to them. However, workers may also invest something else into their work: a concern with quality and effectiveness; a wish for their company to succeed[3]. Employers may also be interested in systematically encouraging this attitude on the part of their workers and may wish to obtain this additional cooperation that cannot be explicitly stated in the work contract. This aspect of wage activity has not remained unnoticed by economists, who have taken some pains to integrate it into the framework of neoclassical theory. This gave rise to a variety of considerations (drawn from game theory and the prisoner's dilemma) on the advantages provided by cooperation and increased trust. In the two articles mentioned above, Akerlof has distinguished himself among the authors addressing these considerations by proposing to understand this additional provision as an exchange of gifts between employers and employees. He has proposed establishing within any work contract a distinction between two parts: the first is explicit and concerns the wage and the level of production expected; the second is implicit and concerns the employees' attitude,

[2] It is worth mentioning that G. A. Akerlof, a professor of economics at UC Berkeley, specializes in wages, employment, and inflation issues. He won the 2001 Nobel Prize for economics (along with M. Pence and J. Stiglitz).
[3] H. Leibenstein had already discussed this in a leading work (Leibenstein 1976).

i.e. their active cooperation, upon which increases in productivity depend, and therefore the way this "additional service" is remunerated. As shown by a specific case study undertaken by G. C. Homans (1954), on which Akerlof's article was based, employers express their expectations by offering a wage that is higher than the market-clearing wage. This offer, which is not subject to direct negotiation, brings about an adequate response on the part of the employees – a better cooperation that leads to increased productivity – which Akerlof proposed to understand as an exchange of gifts. He considered that in the case studied a reciprocity involving an implicit obligation is established, at least in the response. He recognized that this response remains partly contractual in nature, which is why he called it a "partial" exchange of gifts.[4] Akerlof had read Mauss' work; he even explicitly referred to *The Gift*; he was therefore aware that traditional gift-giving involved a triple obligation: giving, receiving, and returning. In this case, the obligation concerns only the return stage, since nothing forces the employers to give or the employees to accept; but once the latter have accepted the counter-gift becomes compulsory. It is in this different sense that the exchange of gifts can be said to be "partial."

Leaving aside certain technical considerations of Akerlof's demonstration, this reminder makes it possible to present a few critical questions. First, it is clear that Akerlof never intended to stray from the realm of neoclassical economic reasoning. He even explicitly stated this. This means that the framework into which he integrated the issue of the gift remained that of utilitarianism and the theory of the rational agent. Gift exchange, as understood by Akerlof, is and remains strictly instrumental: the final output is indeed an increase in productivity. The subtext is obvious: the system of the gift should not be despised; this old practice that remains imprinted in our mental structures can still prove very useful. Second, Akerlof did not consider the possibility that the exchange might be initiated by the employees and that the response would then be up to the employers. Why not? But this would probably undermine the neoclassical theses on the pre-eminence of supply. Third, Akerlof relied on a notion of reciprocity that he assumed to be self-evident and general. He used it in the same way whether he applied it to contractual agreements or gift-giving relationships; however, he was aware that the nature of the response was not the same in both cases; the obligation involved in a contractual clause is primarily a legal

[4] "Of course, the worker does not strictly give his labor as a gift to the firm; he expects a wage in return and, if not paid, will almost certainly sue in court. Likewise, the firm does not give the wage strictly as a gift. If the worker consistently fails to meet certain minimum standards, he will almost surely be dismissed" (1984: 151).

one and of a different nature from the obligation involved in responding to a generous offer, which depends on the agent's will to cooperate.
Fourth, Akerlof showed a lack of caution when using the concept of gift.
He did refer to the type of gift discussed by Mauss, which is the ritual
one, but along with many others he did not wonder whether or not this
concept belonged to a homogeneous category. In fact, in the traditional
gift-giving that Mauss discussed, the three obligations to give, receive,
and return are not only inseparable but endowed with a ritual character; the exchange takes place in a glorious and festive spirit, what is
expected from it is prestige rather than profit, and it aims above all at
creating or reinforcing bonds between the partners (and also at something else that Mauss did not perceive and that I intend to show below).
In any case, assuming a direct analogy between implicit work contract
and traditional gift, as Akerlof did, shows a misunderstanding of the
nature of the latter.

Yet there is no doubt that an exchange occurs. Its form suggests something that is familiar to anthropologists: barter, i.e. a mutually profitable
exchange of goods, based on mutual trust and following rules that are
constraining although not formalized; trust and good will are greater
within the group or with known partners than with strangers;[5] in short,
this exchange intended toward mutual profit, which aims at keeping an
equivalence, involves good will and positive feelings (this is an experience we have all had with the courteous local grocer whom we pay back
by frequently patronizing his shop; or with the considerate waitress to
whom we will give a tip, the percentage of which is often set in advance
and forms part of the wage). In this "friendly barter," all the variables
are consistent with Homans' example and better fit what Akerlof stated
from the start, i.e. that this unstated contract constituted the second
part of the written contract. We have not left the realm of the contract.
But in this case we cannot talk of an exchange of gifts, even in a partial form. We can conclude that Akerlof may have found it appealing to
refer to traditional gift-giving, but that he could do so only at the cost
of misunderstanding it and therefore providing an inaccurate analogy.
However, this attempt produced something very interesting: Akerlof,
following Homans, mentioned the fact that feelings develop between
employers and employees and among the latter; this is precisely what

---

[5] Malinowski not only highlighted the *gimwali* barter, which is performed over long distances along with the *kula* exchange of goods, but also the barter that occurs among
people who know each other well; the latter type is based on trust and involves personal partners and obligatory reciprocity, and equivalence is left to the appreciation of
each participant (1961: ch. 6)

brought him to the hypothesis of an exchange of gifts:[6] he claimed that it was trivial to recognize that we give gifts to those for whom we have feelings, but that it was a fact of nature.[7] Except for this concept of naturalness, which conceals the real issue, this intuition seems very perceptive to me, since it suggests that contracts do not in and of themselves provide improvements in the quality of the social bond between all agents; it also suggests that this emotional bond of reciprocal trust that predates, includes, and finally facilitates specifically commercial relationships must be theorized in terms of gift-giving. In the end, this social bond is akin to a stranger that economists would keep encountering on their way without knowing where he comes from and why he is walking on the same road as they are. Let us acknowledge the fact that Akerlof at least implicitly recognized his existence, even if he was not able to give him a name.

Reciprocal gift-giving and business according to Colin Camerer

Another example of the resort made to the traditional model of exchange of gifts is to be found in the work of another economist, Colin F. Camerer (1988).[8] Although he provided well-chosen references to anthropological literature, he too is considered as unequivocally belonging to the neoclassical trend. In fact, his hypotheses are formulated and his calculations based on the most widespread model in the profession, that of game theory. His argument is all the more interesting because his understanding of traditional gift-giving procedures seems to me to be quite relevant, at least to some extent. However, it remains to see whether his argument is acceptable from a broader perspective.

The introduction of game theory and in particular of the prisoner's dilemma (first formulated by A. W. Tucker in 1950) initially had a negative effect by profoundly undermining the dogma of the "invisible hand," i.e. the supposedly spontaneous harmony of individual interests. However, its positive effect has been much more interesting: neoclassical theory has been forced to specifically take into account the agents' expectations, establish their rationality in a new way, and explain that

[6] "Why should there be any portion of labor that is given as a gift to the firm or of treatment of the worker by the firm that can be considered a gift? The answer to this at once trivial and profound question is: Persons who work for an institution (a firm in that case) tend to develop sentiment for their co-workers and for that institution" (1984: 152).

[7] "For the same reason that persons (brothers, for example) share gifts as showing sentiment for each other, it is natural that persons have utility for making gifts to institutions for which they have sentiment" (ibid.).

[8] C. F. Camerer, a professor at the California Institute of Technology (Cal Tech), specializes in economic strategy and has written extensively on game theory.

the harmony conceived by Adam Smith was not a given but the product of the interplay of choices that presuppose trust between partners. This trust is constantly challenged – granted to various degrees or refused – either through the interaction between economic partners or through other types of relationships that are not directly economic but involve economic consequences.

Camerer had the interesting idea that exchanges of gifts could play a central part in establishing trust and therefore cooperation between partners; such exchanges can even make it possible to test the extent of this trust and cooperation. Camerer presented two types of examples taken from two very distant areas. The first concerns the building of long-term relationships between courtship partners; what is at stake in this case is the sincerity of the other partner and his or her wish to consider marriage and therefore the responsibility of having children and engaging his or her financial resources in the partnership. The second example concerns the decision to be made by two agents who are considering partnership in a joint enterprise of an economic type.

In the case of courtship partners, mutual affection is expressed through gifts that are typical of these relationships (such as jewelry, perfume, and clothing) and must belong to a decorative category. Camerer remarked that a gradation must be followed in these reciprocal gifts. For instance, starting the exchange with an excessive gift can generate embarrassment and dependence, whereas giving overly inexpensive gifts can indicate a wish to keep a distance. Camerer is not enough of a sociologist or ethnologist to qualify these criteria in terms of tastes related to specific cultures or social groups (the case of Japan would be highly instructive in this respect), but he accurately perceived that the strategic aspect of this giving game consists of testing the other's intentions and prompting an adequate response (i.e. temporary or long-term engagement). The second case involves gifts between current or prospective business partners: such partners build mutual trust by inviting one another to restaurants or shows and exchanging conventional gifts (such as chocolate, champagne, or whisky) at traditional occasions such as New Year. In this case also, a proportional gradation in the value of the gifts must be followed. For each partner, the way in which these gifts are modulated constitutes a clear test of the other's intentions, including of the risk of misplaced trust or denial of cooperation.

I will not discuss all the considerations that involve the diversity of the strategic options analyzed by Camerer and the calculation of their cost. Even though Camerer did not state it in these terms, he perceived quite well that the gift-giving game had a dialogic or, more precisely, agonistic character; it is an interplay of action and response. Reciprocity plays an essential part in this. Camerer also realized that these gifts were not economic in nature; according to him, their value as signs transcends their economic value. They are signals indicating levels of trust. Camerer, along with anthropologists, called them symbolic (although he did not discuss this concept). He even insisted throughout his article, and rightly so, on the fact that what mattered was not the efficient character of the gifts – otherwise they would be subject to the sole criterion of their market value; moreover, their limited practical usefulness or even utter uselessness emphasizes the fact that they primarily fulfill conventions rather than needs; this confirms their symbolic status and ensures their power as "signals," which consists of indicating the level of trust that is granted or expected.

What Camerer discussed was neither the unconditional and generous type of gift-giving that is unilateral and therefore irrelevant within a situation of reciprocity nor giving out of solidarity, which consists of helping people in need. His gift-giving game is very clearly situated within the heritage of traditional ceremonial gift exchange: it does involve the triple obligation to give, receive, and reciprocate. Camerer also noted the ritual or at least conventional character of these exchanges. This is the extent of the analogies that can be found between these and traditional ceremonial exchanges. Beyond this, they remain within the framework of a strategic relationship between partners facing a problem involving trust and cooperation, the stake of which is primarily economic. For Camerer (as for Akerlof), gift-giving relationships are enclosed within market relationships and are interesting only as the means of a strategy whose goal is to maximize efficiency through improved cooperation.

The examples analyzed by Camerer seem to me to be convincing and to match our common intuition in this area. However, several questions remain unanswered and are not even implicitly raised. First, why are these exchanges of gifts capable of generating trust and modulating its levels? Why are words not enough? What is this non-economic gesture that precedes or accompanies the economic act? Is it what is left of an ancient magic? How come well-designed contracts that include every conceivable guarantee are not enough to fulfill every expectation and generate trust? Finally, there is a more general issue that has not been raised by Camerer: how come the rational agent who is by definition presupposed to be self-interested (since this self-interestedness is what defines his rational behavior) needs to grant and inspire trust? These are the questions that we must now confront through a renewed approach to ceremonial gift-giving.

Rethinking reciprocal ceremonial gift-giving and drawing the consequences

I have presented two cases in which contemporary economists referred to the concept of gift-giving and its traditional manifestations – with an explicit reference to Mauss – in order to renew and enrich a standard argument. I remarked that in each case the arguments that have been developed only partly fulfilled the criteria of Mauss' theory of gift-giving. It should also be noted that neither Akerlof nor Camerer took the chance (as Gary Becker [1993] did) of stating hypotheses on the presence or absence of altruistic dispositions in economic agents or on the fact that they could be included, as preferences, within the very logic of selfishness. Like these authors, I will restrict the scope of my project to ceremonial gift-giving in order to question whether this might make it possible to understand the expectation of trust that is presupposed by their analyses. They understand this trust as a condition to be created for tactical reasons, whereas we should wonder why it is important for such a broader and more inclusive relationship of trust to exist prior to the emergence of strictly contractual relationships and in order to make them possible. But how can we account for this? Can the data relative to ceremonial gift-giving help us answer this question in a convincing manner?

Let us recall the variables that can be identified by ethnographers in all ceremonial gift-giving: (1) things exchanged: precious objects or beings; festive food; (2) formal procedures: recognized rituals; (3) level of communication: public; (4) caused or expected effects: (a) strong bond between partners, (b) prestige, rank; (5) type of choice: mandatory; (6) type of relationship: reciprocal; (7) attitude in the exchange: generous rivalry.[9]

Not only does the coordinated set of these variables prohibit an economic interpretation;[10] it also forces us to establish clear distinctions between (a) ceremonial gift-giving, (b) gratification gift-giving of a unilateral type, and (c) giving out of solidarity. The latter two may or may

[9] In the case of ritual gift-giving, this categorization therefore complements the general definition of the ceremonial act that has been provided by Malinowski: "I shall call an action ceremonial if it is: (1) public; (2) carried on under observance of definite formalities; (3) if it has sociological, religious or magical import, and carries with it obligations" (1961: 95).

[10] This does not mean that there is no economy; ceremonial gift-giving in no way replaces commercial exchange (whether or not it involves money); the two constitute two different spheres; it would be naive to oppose "gift-giving societies" to "market societies"; there is no such thing as a gift-giving economy that would predate a profit-seeking economy. We will soon be able to see that the dividing line is situated elsewhere.

not involve precious goods; they imply little or no ritual; they are not necessarily public; they do not aim at gaining prestige and are neither mandatory nor reciprocal. At this point the following questions must be raised: is ceremonial gift-giving, which is often called "archaic," exclusively found in traditional societies? Does anything remain for us of this type of gift-giving, beyond vestiges such as dinner invitations and protocolar gifts? Are the two other forms of gift-giving specifically modern? Are they also more moral and purer because they are valued as unconditional? But then what is the meaning of the mandatory character of traditional gift-giving? Is the imperative of reciprocity a way of subjecting gift-giving to interest, as Seneca thought 2,000 years ago (see *De Beneficiis*), and as modern authors (from La Rochefoucauld to Bourdieu and Derrida) have also stated? In short, how can the obligation to give in return for a present that has been received be justified?

This is indeed the question that fascinated Mauss: "Why is it that a present that has been received must necessarily be reciprocated?" (1990: 3). Yet Mauss did not directly pose this more obvious question: why is there an imperative to give in the first place? Mauss probably proceeded in this way because for him as for everyone else within the Western moral and religious culture, giving was always regarded as a deeply laudable gesture, whereas having to reciprocate seemed surprising or even petty (it was not expected of children or the poor). Hence the implicit consensus on this idea: moral – pure and unilateral – gift-giving is the unrecognized reason and missed aim of ritual gift-giving, which is thus regarded as "archaic." The aporias concerning gift-giving – which is assumed to be at the same time free and mandatory, generous and rewarding – are related to this confusion.

Escaping them requires a different approach. The one that I am presenting[11] avoids primarily focusing on the fact that ceremonial gift-giving is an "exchange of goods"; this is not false, but focusing on it above all else impedes understanding its essential element. We must try to ask this question in a different way and move to entirely different ground. This can be done in two stages.

First, it would be interesting to focus on ritual exchanges occurring on the occasion of a first encounter – opening gifts – as described by ancient literatures and ethnographic investigations. The approach and acceptance of others are always presented as mediated by goods that are offered and accepted by both parties. A. Strathern (1971: xii) related how the arrival of the first Australian civil servant in a village located in the high valleys of New Guinea, where it was believed that

---

[11] See also Hénaff (2002; 2004).

some dead people became cannibalistic white ghosts, caused great anxiety and called for a test: the Australian was offered some pigs and he responded by offering precious shells; the villagers concluded that they were indeed dealing with a fellow human being. The opening gifts ritual is above all a procedure of reciprocal recognition in the triple sense of identifying, accepting, and finally honoring others.

The second stage is this: faced with these facts, we may wonder whether other animal societies, in particular those closest to ours – great apes – display comparable behaviors. What has been shown by research in this field (McGrew 1992; Premack and Premack 1994), especially that conducted on chimpanzees (Goodall 1986; de Waal 1989), is that: (1) reciprocal recognition as identification is performed through sounds, smells, and above all coordinated sets of gestures; (2) recognition as acceptance takes place through postures and procedures of reciprocity (such as grooming, sharing of space) but never through objects given as tokens and kept in exchange for others that are given either immediately or later (which has nothing to do with the sharing of food or the mating rituals of certain birds, reptiles, and insects). Adam Smith sensed this quite well: "Nobody ever saw a dog make a fair and deliberate exchange of one bone for another with another dog" (1998: 21). It seems that humans alone resort to the procedure consisting of committing oneself by giving something of oneself as a token and substitute of oneself. An agent can be called a self to the extent that he vouches for himself in front of other agents. That he does this through the mediation of a thing that comes from himself, as a part of himself, is remarkable. This recalls the classical Greek and Roman procedure of the pact performed through a *sym-bolon* (derived from *ballein*, to put; *syn*, together), a piece of pottery broken in two, of which each partner would keep one half that could fit the other as witness for the future that an agreement had been made. According to this model, reciprocal gift-giving is nothing more than the originating gesture of reciprocal recognition between humans, a gesture that is found in no other living beings in that it is mediated by a thing, but a thing that comes from oneself, stands for oneself, and bears witness to the commitment that was made. This is what creates an institution and an alliance – a *politeia* – beyond a mere social self-regulation. This marks the emergence of the political animal – *zoön politikon*. Forming an alliance means bringing together the self and the strangeness of the other through an element that comes from oneself and is desirable by the other. This element brings the two sides together: there is no alliance without an Ark of the Covenant. This reciprocal recognition through the exchange of something that specifically belongs to the group (or to its representative) and is offered to the other is at the core of the exogamic relationship (the wife that is given is "the gift par excellence," according to Lévi-Strauss [1969: 552]) and illuminates the prohibition of incest, which constitutes its key. This prohibition is above all a positive imperative of reciprocity. Humanness is defined by moving outside of the "natural" group based on consanguinity, through a recognition of and alliance with the other.

Yet it would be a mistake to understand the gesture of reciprocal recognition as evidence of a natural disposition toward consensus. On the contrary, opening gifts show that recognition is offered against the background of the possibility of a conflict; many testimonies show that there is a narrow margin between acceptance and confrontation; the gift itself may be a deceit.[12] The meaning of the gift-giving procedure lies in the very possibility of a fight. This procedure must be understood as a risky bet or even a challenge: giving in order to seduce (literally *se-ducere*, to bring toward oneself) and to bind. The risk that one takes calls for the risk involved in the other's response, since the risk taken is at the same time an expression of trust: it consists of presenting the other with a token of oneself that is also a substitute for oneself. Each party both grants and demands it. This involves the structure of a game and an alternation principle analogous to that of any game between partners, or rather to that of a duel. Entering the game amounts to having to reply.[13] Among humans, the two moral feelings – alternating between active and passive – that are associated with this requirement are called honor and respect. The interplay of gift and counter-gift precisely matches the alternation of blows in a duel (in fact, the same partners involved in the exchange of gifts are also responsible for vindicatory justice in case an offense was committed). This involves neither moral choice nor altruism or charity, but only the requirement to reply that is specific to action among the living. But there is more to this: the "game" is at the same time the pact that is accepted through the goods exchanged. It can therefore be said that reciprocal ceremonial gift-giving confronts and resolves in a particularly elegant way the prisoner's dilemma (decision-making based on limited information or involving uncertainty regarding others). One bets on trust and obtains it through a response that guarantees it.

Let us remark that opening gifts make it possible to most clearly grasp the structure of reciprocal ceremonial gift-giving; however, they remain

---

[12] See Hénaff (2004).

[13] As in exchanges of greetings, this reciprocal offer of words and gestures – in which we sense that *it is mandatory to respond* – is for us the most ordinary and obvious experience of the logic of reply involved in ceremonial gift-giving; Goffman (1961) accurately sensed this in *Encounters*, without theorizing it in this way.

infrequent events. One of the major functions of rituals thus consists of stabilizing and preserving the alliance through time through agreed-upon exchanges (such as *kula* or potlatch) and all kinds of celebrations. The complex system of matrimonial alliances is the primary means of indexing this public reciprocal recognition of the reproduction of life itself and the alternation of generations.

Three concepts now need to be clarified: reciprocity, obligation, and exchange. How can the concept of reciprocity be understood as applied to the ceremonial exchange discussed in this presentation? It must be understood in its strongest sense. This presupposes the existence of different degrees of reciprocity. At least three can be distinguished: (1) according to a weak interpretation, reciprocity is conceived of as a complementariness[14] (such as that between different professions) or transitivity: a movement of alternation (also called back and forth movement) from A to B and B to A – this use of the concept of reciprocity is not relevant; (2) according to an intermediate interpretation, reciprocity is identified with mutuality. The latter presupposes a simultaneity and symmetry either of feelings (love, friendship) or of positions (as in the clauses of a contract); ordinary language often confuses mutuality and reciprocity because of the equivalence between the parties involved; (3) according to the strong interpretation, reciprocity is – and necessarily is – the response of agent B to the action of agent A, and so on. Actions are thus characterized by their successiveness and positions by their alternating dissymmetry; this does not imply any inequality between agents; on the contrary, a balance is obtained through alternation and therefore develops or is anticipated through time.[15] This type of reciprocity is explicitly situated within the realm of action, in which agents respond to each other, i.e. are not in a mere relationship of material causality but also of free causality (if we use Kant's terminology): they are responsible for their decisions and by definition accountable for them. Games between two parties (individuals or groups) provide a good model of reciprocity; hence their frequent use as metaphors of social exchanges. The case of ceremonial gift-giving seems to be the most radical one: not only is there interplay between action and reaction or address and response, but in addition reciprocity is mandatory

---

[14] This identification of reciprocity with complementariness has been criticized by A. Gouldner in an influential article (Gouldner 1960).

[15] The issue of debt-inducing gifts cannot be ignored, i. e. that of gifts to which receivers are incapable of responding, or of responding on time (which differs from the case of unilateral gifts – such as grace – which do not have to be returned); gifts become unequal when inequality has already developed elsewhere and for other reasons (see Hénaff [2002]).

and consists for each partner of committing oneself toward the other. No doubt this is the strongest mode of reciprocity.

But then what is the meaning of the obligation to respond in ceremonial gift-giving? It is neither a physical necessity to react (as in the case of living organisms responding to external stimuli) nor a truly legal obligation (which would provide for sanctions, as is the case when contracts are not abided by) or a moral requirement (in the sense that it would be immoral not to respond). At this point the metaphor of a game between two partners becomes illuminating: not to respond amounts to taking oneself out of the game, with the reservation that this "game" is a social one and that the choice one is presented with is between accepting and refusing to recognize the other, which is to say between accepting and rejecting the possibility of living together. The ceremonial gift-giving relationship is from the start a pact constitutive of a society; it is the model of a convention.

These clarifications of the concepts of reciprocity and obligation make it possible to better understand the extent to which the concept of exchange is itself prone to confusing and in the end contradictory uses.[16] In this case also, three levels can be identified: (1) exchanges that involve mere circulation, as in the case of exchanges between gases, or exchanges through reversals of positions (A turns into B and B into A); (2) the next level is marked by the intentionality of the agents; this is the exchange of goods as described by Adam Smith at the beginning of his *Inquiry*: in other words, trade, whether operated directly with goods – barter – or through a currency that serves as a shared measuring unit. The latter form has taken on such a broad extension that it has ended up as the reference for all exchanges. Once again, its legal form is the contract and therefore mutual advantage; (3) exchanges of gifts that are unrelated to level 2 and follow an entirely different model: that of exchanges of blows in a fight or of turns in a ball game; we now return to reciprocity in the strong sense: as returning gesture, response, alternating dissymmetry. Failure to understand this strong form of reciprocal exchange that involves a necessary reply (the alternative being taking oneself out of the game) leads to interpreting the reciprocity of ceremonial gift-giving as a self-interested expectation and to concluding that, in contrast, the only genuine form of gift-giving is the unilateral

---

[16] In the social sciences, the number of books and articles that have mixed up these various types of exchange without taking any precaution is so great that it would be tedious to try to list them all; this is the case with anthropologists themselves, and even more so the sociologists and philosophers who have discussed social relationships; this very frequent confusion is clear evidence that the specificity of the ceremonial exchange of gifts has not been seriously recognized.

one (whether it is an act of unilateral gratification or a gesture of mutual aid). This misunderstanding cannot be overcome by emphasizing the generous and sumptuary character of ceremonial gift-giving (as Mauss did) but only by understanding that it constitutes above all a procedure of public and reciprocal recognition between groups, a specifically human procedure, which is mediated through goods endowed with a symbolic status; it constitutes the instauration of the human community as convention, or better put, as an alliance in the strongest sense, i.e. intentionally bringing self and non-self, "us" and "them," together. Thus, what is involved in alliance is reciprocal recognition, but recognition of what? The answer could be: the honor that is at stake and the respect that is given and returned are the expression of a universally held expectation – for one's dignity to be affirmed and confirmed. This raises other crucial questions that we must now consider.

Social justice, recognition, and capabilities

Before stating my next point, I would like to return to the use Akerlof and Camerer have made of ceremonial gift-giving. I hope it is now clear that the indisputably intelligent manner in which they have isolated some of its segments and instrumentalized some of the procedures involved in it cannot fit an approach such as the one I am presenting, which, following Mauss' example but in a different way, intends to grasp this practice as a "total social fact."

The question of recognition today

One question must be raised: in contemporary developed societies, what is the expression of this public reciprocal recognition that is ensured by ritual exchanges of gifts in traditional societies? In my opinion, only one answer can be given: this public recognition is affirmed and guaranteed by law. Therefore, the modern heritage of ceremonial gift-giving will not be found at the economic level of the exchange of goods but at the institutional level of rights. Showing how this transformation has occurred, within many different societies, would pertain to historical anthropology. I will not try to develop this in detail. However, we must remember that the ceremonial exchanges discussed above concern societies whose organization is determined by units such as clans, lineages, moieties, and segments; in most of these cases, the forms of authority are identified with the statuses provided by kinship systems. For this very reason, public relationships between groups operate above all (though not only) through matrimonial alliances. Thus, as soon as an evolution develops that leads to the emergence of an authority that transcends kinship groups, individuals then appear as members of larger groups – such as cities or kingdoms – while remaining members of lineages or clans. Greek tragedies, such as Aeschylus' *Oresteia*, express this transition and the crisis that comes with it. But the new identity prevails over the old (this is the crisis presented by Sophocles' *Antigone*). But if the law states the rights and obligations of each individual as citizen, what becomes of the public reciprocity of the participants in ceremonial gift-giving? It can be said that it takes the form of the relationship that is instituted between citizens and sovereign power within what is called public space. This initiates the model of the pact that will from then on underlie every political relationship in the West. It can be claimed that, at this institutional level, the requirement of reciprocity has changed into a right to equality. Within industrialized societies, this institutional level is no longer restricted to the political and legal realms; it now also includes economic activity (which was considered in ancient times as private business – the realm of the *oikos*). The emergence of political economy during the seventeenth and especially the eighteenth century is evidence of the emergence of the economy as politics. This new space gives rise to the question of recognition and as a consequence to that of its relationship with social justice. But before dealing with it, we must notice the existence of other spaces (or other orders, to borrow Pascal's term) of recognition. I see at least two others. One of them can be defined as the space of common ways of life, of everyday work and neighborhood relationships, and of practices related to cultural, religious, sportive, and civic traditions: at this level, more direct forms of recognition (through celebrations, conversations, and civic activities) develop between groups, generating or reinforcing community bonds. Finally, there is the space of personal life, which includes that of inter-subjective relationships of love and friendship, and more generally that of ethical relationships. In this space, recognition takes the form of the respect that every human being owes to and expects from every other. In short, at least three (often overlapping) spheres of recognition can be identified: public, common, and private.

The question of social justice first arises within the first sphere (even though its repercussions on the two other spheres seem obvious). The current formulation of this question developed in a specific way at the time of the Industrial Revolution and of the considerable inequalities of income that it generated. Since the nineteenth century, it has been at the core of social movements and socialist theories. What has until now been understood as social justice involves above all income levels, wages, and working conditions (such as schedules and safety), as well as access to healthcare, scheduled rest periods, and unemployment insurance: in short, social goods that are generally considered as belonging to the area of redistribution.

Since these demands are now better met within developed countries, it seems that, in the past two decades, the most vocal claims have aimed at obtaining new forms of equality between different ethnic, cultural, religious, professional, and gender identities, as well as those involving differences in sexual orientation, handicap, and age. All these claims form the base of what is called "struggles for recognition," which are supposed to be taking over from the struggles for social justice, and even to constitute the new priority. The work of important thinkers such as Charles Taylor (1992) and Axel Honneth (1995) has been used to formulate the philosophical foundations of this debate, even though the former has mostly restricted his analysis to the issue of ethnic minorities and the latter to the general issue of inter-subjective recognition and to the forms taken by social contempt, through a re-examination and development of some of Hegel's early writings. These authors have also been criticized, by Nancy Fraser and Axel Honneth (2003) among others, for leaving aside the question of social justice in favor of that of a struggle for recognition between agencies based on their differences in identities. Fraser argues that both of these perspectives are necessary and that they must be combined with each other. This seems to be a common-sense position, but it may be that it aims to resolve a nonexistent dilemma, since accepting this dilemma amounts to assuming that the question of recognition concerns above all a certain type of new rights. Such a position seems untenable to me. The legitimacy of these demands is unquestionable, as is the fact that they are expressed through the vocabulary of recognition. What is questionable is the assumption that the space of social justice as it has been understood in the past two centuries, particularly from the perspective of economic inequality, is not as such the very space of the relationships of recognition in the strongest sense. This is the level at which this question arises and has always arisen. These new demands bring important additional variables to the struggle against inequality but do not constitute as such the emergence of a struggle for recognition. The latter is already fully present within movements for social justice. But in order to understand this, we must consider economic equality itself in a different way; it can no longer be restricted to the sole criterion of income but must take into account all the variables of human diversity.

Amartya Sen's answer

Amartya Sen's capabilities approach makes it possible to understand this and to transform the terms of the present debate. What makes his approach particularly interesting is that, without relinquishing the ground of classical economic analysis or its mathematical tools, he has been able through a very rigorous logical development to raise questions and construct arguments that make it impossible for economists to ignore the issues of social justice. Sen's first approach – building on the work of Arrow – consisted of challenging the dominant model, that of utilitarian theory. By first demonstrating the fragility of the information on which the utilitarian approach based its calculation of the collective choices using the summation of preferences – defined by commodities alone – he showed the entirely abstract character of the figure of the rational agent as well as of Pareto's optimum.

As a consequence, the concept of utility postulated as sole criterion became ineffective. However, Sen did not reject the concept of well-being, but he refused to define it as utility alone, since the latter implies an unacceptable restriction of the field of analysis. Broadening the information basis amounts to taking into account, to the broadest possible extent, the diversity of the situations and needs of the agents. This of course includes income levels and fair distribution of income, but also and above all what determines the specific social activity of agents: their political and cultural environment, social class, ethnicity, gender, level of education, health, age, and physical handicaps if any. Sen called such variables functionings; they also open possibilities of action that he defined as capabilities. In other words, the real choices of the agents (which a science worthy of its name cannot ignore without relying on fictions) are made based on multiple and specific conditions and on abilities to act that remain open within these conditions. Raising from this perspective the question of well-being – which constitutes at the same time the cornerstone and the last ground to defend of every neo-classical economist's argumentation – makes it necessary to integrate all these variables into the definition of well-being, which amounts to taking into account not only the agents' limitations but also their achievements and potentials. This also means that normative questions must be part of the description, and, as a consequence, that the requirements of social justice lie at the core of economic analysis insofar as it aims at accurately defining the nature of well-being.

This is where Sen's approach meets Rawls' *A Theory of Justice*. Sen adopted Rawls fundamental definition of "primary goods" as based on two principles; first, every person has an equal right to all basic liberties, excluding any infringement upon those of any other person; second, social and economic inequalities are only acceptable if (1) they are tied to positions that are open to all and (2) they can serve the interests of the least privileged. Without entering into a precise discussion of these two principles, let us remark that the first is consistent with the definition of negative freedom given by Berlin (1969) and expresses a requirement of non-interference; the second implies a hierarchy of priorities and a requirement of efficiency that aims at maximizing the total amount of resources available. Sen takes up the framework of this approach, which marks a radical break with the utilitarian hypothesis. In other words, the demand for well-being is referred to goods that concern the dignity of the person (which clearly shows Rawls' Kantian heritage). But Sen objected that this leaves aside the question of the concrete content of liberties as well as of the accomplishments of equality and the forms of its denial.

What is at stake for him is not only to guarantee the access of agents to primary goods but also to determine what agents are capable of doing, in short to understand how they can convert these resources into actual liberties. This is what capabilities mean. By formulating the question in this manner (for example "Equality of What?" [Sen 1992: ch. 1]) and by assigning himself this program, Sen has opened, without explicitly claiming it, a remarkable path to those who intend to raise the issue in terms of recognition, since the dichotomy that appeared to exist between distributive justice and consideration given to differences now becomes irrelevant. The specific content of differences is precisely the object of the capabilities approach, not so much in terms of demands as of affirmation.[17]

Finally, what makes Sen's work particularly convincing is the close articulation he has maintained between methodology and ethical questioning. In terms of method, what has made it possible for him to extend or go beyond Rawls' analyses has been the determination of what he has called "spaces of evaluation," i.e. the evaluation of equality based on criteria differentiated according to priorities (such as health, education, gender, and cultural traditions); all of these must then be weighted depending on the information bases. The standard method of aggregation of utility alone can no longer define global welfare. At this point the capabilities methodology – i.e. the integration of the diversity of factors into the analysis – leads to ethical questions because, as Sen stated in *Inequality Reexamined* (Sen 1992: ch. 3), it takes into account a whole set of actions and states as being important in and of themselves

---

[17] See for instance "Class, Gender, and Other Groups" (Sen 1992: ch. 8).

and not merely because they are or might be sources of utility. Ethical requirements are therefore included in the factors that must be taken into account. The moral indifference of standard theory is primarily due to the narrow character of its information base. A little science takes us away from ethics; a lot of science brings us back to it. Yet how do we know that some actions or states are important in and of themselves? Sen gives several examples of this, which show that these actions or states are tied to the feeling of self-esteem that leads for instance to placing the demand for freedom above the demand for well-being. But this also opens the way to a different view of recognition. Beyond the gaining of rights guaranteed by just institutions, and extending the capabilities through which these rights are exercised in the real world, there is always an attitude or rather an action that presupposes a value judgment implying a relationship with others. Self-esteem requires that respect be offered and esteem received. There is in this a structure of reciprocity that is essential to the ethical relationship. This form of reciprocity seems to me to constitute the very core of the question of recognition. It remains to determine the nature of what is recognized between and within agents.

Conclusion

To answer this question and to conclude I would simply like to state this: one way or another, and from a normative point of view, what is at stake in capabilities is always the dignity of the agent; better incomes, health, education, and gender equality are not ends in themselves but confirmations of each person's humanness. This is what takes this approach radically beyond the utilitarian one.[18] This is what Sen had in mind when he stated that obtaining self-esteem was tied to acquiring capabilities. For him, dignity is an ultimate horizon of legitimization, even though he did not explicitly propose this. In the same manner, it can be asked why Rawls did not include dignity among the primary goods – freedom and equality. The answer seems obvious: these two principles are precisely what guarantee dignity. From this point of view, Sen and Rawls are right not to directly ask this question: dignity as such does not belong to the realm of rights. It is what makes us demand rights, what rights aim at, and what is confirmed through their fulfillment. Rights may concern public forms of respect that are due to agents in their various (ethnic, gender, generational, professional, etc.) identities, but dignity

[18] This is why authors such as Brennan and Pettit (2004) could conceive of an *Economy of Esteem*.

as a value of humankind cannot be legislated.[19] It can therefore be said that the affirmation of dignity presupposes the achievement of social justice; but dignity is not in and of itself an achievement or a capability. It is always what is ultimately implied in primary goods and substantial rights; this constitutes the first sphere of recognition, i.e. the necessary institutional framework of the public affirmation of our dignity. Yet this affirmation becomes effective only when it is expressed within social and inter-subjective relationships through gestures of reciprocal respect. The importance of the two other spheres of recognition mentioned above now becomes more apparent: first, the common space of relationships between groups that have developed according to traditional civilities, particular cultural forms, and more generally through ways of life that imply the constant interaction of agents depending on their statuses, professions, civic responsibilities (such as civil servants, bonzes, lawyers, etc.); dignity is always what is at stake in the reciprocal acceptance of these established or inherited identities. But in addition to this formal recognition tied to legitimate social differentiations and accepted roles, another sphere exists: that of more direct interpersonal relationships, either of an intimate nature – such as love and friendship – or of a more distant character – such as those between neighbors, colleagues, and associates – or with strangers; these relationships, which follow specific expressions, are only possible and human as a result of the attitude of respect that testifies to the dignity that we recognize in the very person of others at the same time as they recognize it in us as persons. This constitutes the ethical relationship. To say that it is reciprocal does not amount to saying that it is conditional (*ex ante*: I will only respect you if you respect me) or that it aims at obtaining a compensation (*ex post*: you have respected me; I will therefore also respect you). What is at stake in this recognition that is offered from the start is the affirmation by everyone that this dignity makes us human beings in our relationship itself, and that the dignity I claim for myself is the very one that I grant anybody who appears or might appear before me. The unconditional recognition of the dignity of others is at the same time the affirmation of my own dignity. This is indeed the lesson of the ceremonial gift-giving of traditional societies, at the level of human groups. It is not primarily a demand. On the contrary, it is an offer, the very generosity of which constitutes its aspect of challenge, wager, and trust. These encounters are festive rituals because the enjoyment involved in reciprocal recognition is also the pleasure of being together. It would be

---

[19] What is at stake is indeed a human value rather than a question of the legal status of what is called "dignities," i.e. public functions held by "dignitaries."

a good thing for *homo economicus*, who has so few opportunities to laugh and celebrate, to sometimes remember this.
Translated from the French by Jean-Louis Morhange.

Bibliography

Akerlof, George A. 1982. "Labor Contract as Partial Gift Exchange," *Quarterly Journal of Economics*, **97** (4): 543–69; reprinted in Akerlof, 1984. *An Economics Theorist's Book of Tales*, Cambridge University Press, ch. 8.
    1984. "Gift Exchange and Efficiency-Wage Theory," *American Economic Review*, **74** (2): 79–83.
Arrow, Kenneth J. 1972. "Gifts and Exchanges," *Philosophy and Public Affairs*, 1: 342–62.
Bard, K. A. and Parker, S. T. (eds.) 1996. *Reaching into Thought. The Minds of the Great Apes*, Cambridge University Press.
Becker, Gary S. 1993. *The Economic Way of Looking at Behavior*, Stanford: Hoover Institution.
Belshaw, Cyril S. 1965. *Traditional Exchanges and Modern Markets*, Englewood Cliffs, NJ: Prentice-Hall.
Berlin, Isaiah 1969. *Four Essays on Liberty*, Oxford University Press.
Boas, Franz 1911. *Handbook of American Indian Languages*, vols. I and II (Smithsonian Institution Bureau of American Ethnology, Bulletin, 40), Washington, DC: Government Printing Office.
    1966. *Kwakiutl Ethnography*, ed. Helen Codere, University of Chicago Press.
    1969. *Contribution to the Ethnology of the Kwakiutl*, New York: AMS Press; originally published New York: Colombia University Press, 1925.
Brennan, Geoffrey and Pettit, Philip 2004. *The Economy of Esteem: An Essay on Civil and Political Society*, Oxford University Press.
Codere, Helen 1950. *Fighting with Property: A Study of Kwakiutl Potlatching and Warfare, 1792–1930*, New York: J. J. Augustin.
Camerer, Colin F. 1988. "Gifts as Economic Signals and Social Symbols," *American Journal of Sociology*, **94** (Supplement): 180–214.
Cheal, David 1988. *The Gift Economy*, London: Routledge.
Dumouchel, Paul 2006. "Trust as an Action," *European Journal of Sociology*, **46** (3): 417–28.
Epstein, T. S 1968. *Capitalism, Primitive and Modern: Some Aspects of Tolai Economic Growth*, East Lansing: Michigan State University Press.
Fraser, Nancy and Honneth, Axel 2003. *Redistribution Or Recognition? A Political-Philosophical Exchange*, New York: Verso.
Godbout, Jacques & Caîllé, Alain 1998. *The World of the Gift*, Ithaca, McGill-Queen, University Press.
Godelier, Maurice 1999. *The Enigma of the Gift*, University of Chicago Press.
Goffman, Ervin 1961. *Encounters: Two Studies in the Sociology of Interaction*, Indianapolis: Boss-Merill.
Goodall, Jane 1986. *The Chimpanzees of Gombe: Patterns of Behavior*, Cambridge, MA: Belknap Press of Harvard University Press.

Gouldner, Alvin W. 1960. "The Norm of Reciprocity: A Preliminary Statement," *American Sociological Review*, **25** (2): 161–78.

Gregory, Chris A. 1982. *Gifts and Commodities*, London: Academic Press.

Hénaff, Marcel 2002. *Le prix de la vérité: le don, l'argent, la philosophie*, Paris: Seuil; *The Price of Truth*, 2010 (forthcoming). Stanford University Press.

2004. "Gift Exchange, Play and Deception," in C. Gerschlager (ed.), *Deception in Markets: An Economic Analysis*, New York: Palgrave Macmillan, 323–35.

Herskovits, Melville J. 1965. *Economic Anthropology: The Economic Life of Primitive Peoples*, New York: Norton; originally published New York: Knopf, 1952.

Hirschman, Albert 1974. *The Passions and the Interests: Political Arguments for Capitalism before Its Triumph*, Princeton University Press.

Hollis, Martin 1998. *Trust within Reason*, Cambridge University Press.

Homans, G. C. 1954. "The Cash Posters: A Study of a Group of Working Girls," *American Sociological Review*, **19** (6): 724–33; reprinted in Homans 1962. *Sentiments and Activities: Essays in Social Science*, New York: Free Press of Glencoe, 75–90.

Honneth, Axel 1995. *The Struggle for Recognition: The Moral Grammar of the Social Conflict*, Cambridge: Polity Press.

Leibenstein, Harvey 1976. *Beyond Economic Man: A New Foundation of Microeconomics*, Cambridge, MA: Harvard University Press.

Lévi-Strauss, Claude 1969. *The Elementary Structures of Kinship*, Boston: Beacon Press.

Malinowski, Bronislav 1961. *The Argonauts of the Western Pacific: An Account of Native Enterprise and Adventure in the Archipelagoes of Melanesian New Guinea*, New York: E. P. Dutton & Co.; originally published in French 1924, Année Sociologique 2nd serie.T.1.

Mauss, Marcel 1990. *The Gift: The Form and Reason for Exchange in Archaic Societies*, New York: W. W. Norton; originally published Glencoe, IL: Free Press, 1954.

McGrew, W. C. 1992. *Chimpanzee Material Culture: Implication for Human Evolution*, Cambridge University Press.

McGrew, W. C., Marchant, L. F., and Nishida, T. (eds.) 1996. *Great Ape Societies*, Cambridge University Press.

Nussbaum, Martha C. and Sen, Amartya K. 1993. *The Quality of Life*, Oxford: Clarendon Press.

Osteen, Mark (ed.) 2002. *The Question of the Gift. Essays across Disciplines*, London and New York: Routledge.

Polanyi, Karl 1957. *The Great Transformation*, Boston: Beacon Press; originally published New York: Rinehart, 1944.

Pospisil, L. 1963. *Kapauku Papuan Economy*, New Haven: Dept. of Anthropology, Yale University.

Premack, D. and Premack, A. J. 1994. "Why Animals Have Neither Culture Nor History," in T. Ingold (ed.) *Companion Encyclopedia of Anthropology*, London and New York: Routledge, 350–65.

Radin, Paul 1927. *The Story of the American Indian*, New York: Boni & Liveright.

Rawls, John 1971. *A Theory of Justice*, Cambridge, MA: Harvard University Press.

Sahlins, Marshall 1972. *Stone Age Economics*, Chicago: Aldine-Atherton.

Sen, Amartya K. 1977. "Rational Fools: A Critique of the Behavioral Foundations of Economic Theory," *Philosophy and Public Affairs*, **6** (4): 317–44.

1987. *On Ethics and Economics*, Oxford: Blackwell.

1992. *Inequality Reexamined*, Cambridge, MA: Harvard University Press.

1993. *On Economic Inequality*, Oxford: Clarendon Press.

1999. *Development as Freedom*, New York: Knopf.

Simmel, Georg 1958. *Gesammelte Werke*, Berlin: Duncker and Humblot.

Smith, Adam 1998. *An Inquiry into the Nature and Causes of the Wealth of Nations [1763]*, ed. K. Sutherland, Oxford University Press.

Stanford, Craig 2001. "The Ape's Gift: Meat-Eating, Meat-Sharing, and Human Evolution," in F. de Waal (ed.) *Tree of Origin: What Primate Behavior Can Tell Us about Human Social Evolution*, Cambridge, MA: Harvard University Press, 95–117.

Strathern, Andrew 1971. *The Rope of Moka: Big-Men and Ceremonial Exchange in Mount Hagen New Guinea*, Cambridge University Press.

Taylor, Charles 1992. *Multiculturalism and "The Politics of Recognition,"* Princeton University Press.

Titmus, Richard 1970. *The Gift Relationship: From Human Blood to Social Policy*, London: Allen and Unwin.

de Waal, Frans B.M. 1989. *Peacemaking among Primates*, Cambridge, MA: Harvard University Press.

Walzer, Michael 1983. *Spheres of Justice. A Defense of Pluralism and Equality*, New York: Basic Books.

Weber, Max 1981. *General Economic History*, New Brunswick, NJ: Transaction Books; originally published c.1927.

Weiner, Annette 1992. *Inalienable Possessions: The Paradox of Keeping-While-Giving*, Berkeley: University of California Press.

Williamson, O. 1993. "Calculativeness, Trust and Economic Organization," *Journal of Law and Economics*, **36** (1): 453–86.

7   Justice and public reciprocity

Reiko Gotoh

Introduction

Is there any society where

Each individual produces different kinds of values that can be evaluated not only by the market but also by diverse social discourses or public reasoning?

And where

Every individual has access to enough resources (income, goods, services) to maintain his well-being, without losing the social basis of independence, responsibility and self-respect?

Such a society would be a "well-being society" that exemplifies the idea of going beyond the logic and ethics of the market. Its first feature is that it has plural evaluation systems other than the market price mechanism. The market's price mechanism evaluates goods and services based on universal supply and demand. It cannot allow price changes based on special privileges, and it contains no point of view from which we can ethically reflect upon its process and results. On the other hand, in a "well-being society" there are plural evaluation systems based on local relationships and public reasoning. These systems are diverse, taking place in communities, through Non Public Organization (NPO) activities or volunteer groups, and they are connected to each other in a consistent way, to the extent that resource transfers among them can be carried out publicly. The second feature is that each individual is committed "to work and to provide if possible" not by a legal obligation or by incentive devices, but by a publicly realized reciprocal relationship based on a shared rule.

To describe this society in a more concrete manner, I will examine the first major review of the Japanese public assistance system, which took place in 2003–4. The reason for this choice is that the Japanese public assistance system was established to realize "the right to well-being" based on the distribution principle, which may be described as "if you are in need receive resources." This principle is essentially different from that of the market and historically has guaranteed a comparatively high level of benefits. However, in practice, a clear logic and ethics to justify this principle is lacking. In consequence, the system on one hand has opted for restricting citizen's rights in exchange for receiving benefits, and, on the other hand, has adopted the logic of the market in evaluating what it is to be "in need" or what is the "well-being" of individuals.

This has led to a tension that became apparent in the system's first major review. Ideas concerning its reform diverged in sharply opposite directions. One was that public assistance should be transformed in conformity with the market principle that can be translated as "if you work, you receive a reward," or, if that turned out to be impossible, that support should be reduced in a significant way and wider restrictions should be imposed upon recipients. The other was that the public assistance system should maintain its distribution principle and that ways of evaluating "to be in need" or "well-being" should go beyond the logic of the market.

This is ultimately nothing but a conflict concerning conceptions of a well-being society. Can we conceive a society where all individuals are guaranteed the right to well-being without losing the social basis of independence, responsibility, and self-respect? Can we establish a logic and ethics of support systems which are essentially different from the market even under circumstances of the so-called matured market? And why should we do so?

In an attempt to answer these questions, this chapter examines first the way of evaluating what it is to be "in need," focusing on the results of research on single-mother households. This review reaches the following conclusions. (1) There are values which are indispensable to individuals in order for them to remain independent. These should be taken into account directly; however, their evaluation requires us to go beyond revealed consumption or the agent's satisfaction with their consumption level. The capability approach proposed by Amartya Sen proves very useful in this context. (2) In order to protect those values in a society characterized by a plurality of living conditions, we should redesign public assistance so as to compensate for individual shortages that derive from personal characteristics or from particular demands when they are still in an early stage, before they create insuperable difficulties.

Based on these results, I then sketch a picture of a two-layered public assistance system. The first layer consists of a reason-based system of public assistances, and the second layer consists of a general public assistance system. The first layer has the merit of implementing public assistance in relation to specific reasons that are publicly recognized. Yet there remains a problem: can public recognition cover all reasons individuals have to require assistance? Given that we inevitably depend on social categories or groups to identify these reasons, we cannot answer this question positively. Thus, the second layer, general public assistance, focuses directly on the individuals' lack of resources in terms of well-being rather than on particular publicly recognized reasons to receive help, and is proposed as complementing the reason-based system. Neither of the two levels has an absolute priority, and individuals who satisfy both must choose one or the other.

This proposal is open to the following criticisms, since the underlying principle of this two-layered public assistance, "if you are in need, you receive resources," has an asymmetrical form in the sense that it does not require any contribution in exchange for receiving support. It may be said, first, that we cannot guarantee its feasibility, its ability to implement its purpose to secure enough resources to compensate total needs, and that, furthermore, the existence of this system can have a negative effect by decreasing individuals' will to work. Second, it may be said that it does violence to the principle of fairness or equity, because no obligation corresponding to the right to well-being is imposed upon individuals who enjoy this right.

In the fifth section I respond to this criticism by introducing a conception of public reciprocity which argues that there is a correspondence between purpose and feasibility or between right and obligation in society as a whole rather than between particular individuals. This conception is essentially distinct from, and sometimes contradicts, approaches based on self-interest and aims at lessening the constraints of commitment in relation to ethical obligations or the guilty conscience often experienced by those who enjoy the advantages of the right to well-being.

Japanese public assistance: principles beyond the market, practice within the market

In this section, we take a brief look at some features of Japanese public assistance. Japan is one of the few countries which has *the right to well-being* explicitly mentioned in its constitution (Article 25, Japanese Constitution). Japanese public assistance, regulated by the "life protection law," is supposed to provide resources to all members of society who are in need. Its aim is "to secure basic well-being" and "to enhance independence." "Basic well-being" in this context means "to maintain the minimum standard of wholesome and cultured living." Its three main principles are the following:

1. Non-discrimination principle (Article 2, Life Protection Law):
   To secure the basic well-being of all individuals without any discrimination.

2. Needs-regarding principle (Article 1, 9, Life Protection Law):
   To distribute resources based not on contributions or merits but on needs.

3. Complementary principle (Article 4, Life Protection Law):
   Public assistance should be a last resort system. When providing for individuals who are in need, priority should be given to all other available means: the market, insurance, allowance or other systems.

Note first that the "needs regarding principle" requires taking account of not only common needs, but also particular needs that various individuals may have. Actually, the so-called "additional provision," to which I refer later, aims to cover particular needs derived from personal characteristics such as age, gender, pregnancy, disability, and so on, in order to assure basic well-being for all.

Second, though the non-discrimination principle and the needs-regarding principle together require no discriminative condition except "to be in need," the complementary principle opens the door to external constraints and threatens to substantially restrict the range of possible recipients. The complementary principle requires those who apply for help to exhaust all personal assets, including financial assets, labor capacities, and personal support in all other available systems before applying for public assistance. However, since in Japan there are few ways of using personal assets in order to earn sufficient income other than the market, receiving public assistance implies using up all personal assets in the market and leaving public assistance implies being able to participate in the market. One of the problems raised here is that, as the market itself is neutral and anonymous and creates no personal and social relationships, through consuming one's personal assets in the market, one tends to lose, as well, one's personal and social relationships, without which it is difficult to participate in the market again.

Third, historically, given the aim "to secure basic well-being" in a market-oriented society, a benefit level sufficient to significantly reduce the difference in average consumption level between recipients and non-recipients has been pursued. The "average consumption equilibrium method" currently adopted in Japan is a criterion that keeps that difference within a certain range. Yet it has led to heated arguments among specialists in welfare policies about how to achieve two goals explicitly stated in the system, "to secure basic well-being" and "to enhance independence" and how to relate one to the other, when "independence" is interpreted in a broad sense that includes the ability to live in society even when this ability depends on maintaining certain particular types of social relations.[1]

However, recently, a criticism has been vigorously put forward, mainly by economists, to wit: that the level of benefit in Japanese public assistance is too high to maintain individuals' motivation to be independent. The reason why this criticism at first sight seems akin to the traditional argument, but is essentially different, is that the meaning of independence on which it depends is narrow rather than broad, as it is reduced to participating in the market, and its theoretical foundation is the neoclassical economic approach to the problem of labor incentive. It is clear that it is both the traditional argument and this new criticism, as well as the fact that the number of recipients has increased since the mid-1990s, that motivated the first major review of the Japanese public assistance system since the end of the Second World War, a review which took place in August 2003.[2] This led to a proposal to introduce the "self-support promoting services" program, while cutting the allowances for the special needs of elder recipients and single-mother recipients.[3]

In the next section, I will examine the validity of this proposal by analyzing the results of research on social life conducted in 2003 in Japan that includes a comparison between single-mother household recipients and low-income single-mother non-recipient households.[4] Is it true that the level of income support provided by public assistance is too high to maintain individuals' motivation for "independence"?

Capability approach to well-being inside and outside the market

The main reasons for cutting allowances for the elderly and single mothers were explained as follows:

1. We can observe that the average consumption level of single-mother recipients is higher than that of the non-recipient low-income single

---

[1] Typically, in the case of a disability, it is usually the case that social independence only becomes possible through the support of others.

[2] The result of a committee report was published in December (Ministry of Health, Labour and Welfare [2004]).

[3] The proposal to cut the allowance for the elderly and single mothers could not find a consensus in the committee, yet in practice it has been gradually enacted since then.

[4] Committee of Research and Analysis on Social Life (2003).

mothers. Thus, it was concluded that support had reached such a high level that it went beyond the minimum necessary to maintain wholesome and cultured living.[5]

2. The actual benefit level might have an adverse effect on certain individuals, reducing their motivation to remain independent. In order to promote "individual independence" and to encourage individuals not to resort to public assistance and to keep earning their living by themselves, the level of income support should be lower than it now is.[6]

Let us examine these arguments, from the point of view of the capability approach, which focuses not on commodities or utilities, but on the possibility for an individual achieving various *functionings* (the set of possible *functionings* one has is called one's "capability"), which are indispensable for him or her to "lead the kind of lives he has reason to value."[7]

There are many situations of extreme hardship among non-recipient low-income single-mother households in Japan. They achieve a much lower level of functioning than is necessary to live decently, because of their miserable living circumstances (most are exposed to noise, sunshine, wind, rain and humidity because of leaky roofs or bad insulation); they live in extremely small dwellings (with no private bathroom, no lavatory/toilet or bathtub, or separation of kitchen and bedroom). As for enjoying a variety of food, regular meals, seasonal clothes, and participation in weekday school events, they are in a much worse situation than "recipient single-mother households." This is partially related to their low wages and difficult working conditions. They experience many difficulties, such as fewer holidays, more night shifts, more irregular job shifts, and stressful working conditions. About 80 percent of low-income single-mother households say that every month their household accounts go into the red (this is true of low-income households in general) and few possess financial assets or have access to either private life or disability insurance.

---

[5] Some may deduce a different conclusion from the same observation: that it shows that the system does not work very well, because it indicates that some persons who should receive assistance actually do not receive any. This conclusion is appropriate in that it points to the fact that the so-called "take-up" rate has been too low in Japan. I wish to thank Professor Paul Dumouchel for his remark on this point.

[6] We must note that there is a hidden assumption here: that the main reason why individuals enter into and cannot exit from public assistance is their personal lack of motivation to work and to earn by themselves, something which I will refute later on in this paper.

[7] Sen (1999b:10, 18). Note that since "reason" is interpersonal in its nature, it is expected to support public recognition. As for the details of the capability approach, see Sen (1980; 1985; 1992; 1999a; 1999b) Suzumura and Gotoh (2001: ch. 6).

On the other hand, there also are some positive aspects of single-mother low-income households when it comes to other kinds of *functionings*, especially when it comes to social relations (with friends, relatives, or neighbors) and to future-oriented activities. A higher percentage is involved in social and cultural activities like children's birthday parties, writing letters, using the internet or cellular phone, enjoying books, cinema, karaoke, or driving. About half save money (although the amount is small) occasionally. As for future plans for their children, a ratio similar to that of married low-income households plans to send their children to university or junior college.

Let us move to the single-mother recipient households. In terms of living conditions and housing, they also face a difficult situation (they do not have enough space to spread out beds for all the family). More of them than low-income single-mother non-recipients answered that they have been rejected for jobs or fired from their jobs, and more complained of the deterioration in their health or that of other members of their family. Furthermore, the ratio of those who have friends, relatives, or neighbors they can count on in hard times is significantly lower than that of low-income non-recipient single-mother households. Finally the ratio of those that are planning to send their children to university or junior college is again much lower than among low-income single-mother non-recipient households.

Meanwhile, the average expenditure (consumption level) for food-stuffs, electricity and water supplies, furniture, clothes, and shoes exceeds that of low-income single-mother non-recipient households, and general complaints about difficulties associated with work are less frequent. However the average expenditure for commodities such as Sunday clothes, formal dresses, gift exchange, the internet, outings with children, birthday parties for children, religious ceremonies (e.g. celebration of New Year), as well as education and transportation expenditures, which are related to social activities, and future planning, is much lower than that of low-income single-mother non-recipient households. Yet, the ratio of those who answer that "their quality of living is the worst" is lower than among non-recipient low-income single-mother households. Finally, the ratio of those who respond negatively to the question: "are you satisfied with your current living conditions?" is also lower.

With these results to hand, we can criticize the reasons, mentioned earlier, that were put forward to justify the reform of Japanese public assistance. First, the fact that the average consumption level of single-mother recipient households is higher for some commodities than low-income single-mother non-recipient households doesn't imply that the benefit level has gone beyond the minimum level to maintain whole-some and cultured living. This is because the low-income single-mother households, which are referred to here for comparison, cannot be said to have reached that minimum level. Moreover, even single-mother recipient households themselves cannot be said to have reached the minimum level, except for some factors which are achievable through consumption of commodities like clothes, shoes, and so on.

The latter point is related to the second criticism of the foundations of the proposal mentioned above. Can we say the actual benefit level reduces the motivation of individuals to be independent? Or can we say that a lower benefit level is a necessary or sufficient condition to keep and to promote individuals' motivation to be independent? Or does independence demand more conditions as its social bases?

To examine this problem, we should inquire into the situations recipi-ents and non-recipients are forced to face and that underlie their actual choices, focusing on the capability of recipients and not simply an index of commodities or of utility (satisfaction).[8]

As observed above, single-mother recipient households characteris-tically spend less on social activities and on investments for the future and consume more commodities commonly regarded as "necessities." For their part low-income single-mother non-recipients consume fewer commodities commonly regarded as "necessities" and spend not only more money, but also more time on social activities with children and on investments for the future, both of which are usually regarded as luxuries.

From these features, we can say that the single-mother recipients achieve a very low level of the *functioning of social activities and future planning* but a higher level of the *functioning of materially decent living* than non-recipients, while the non-recipients achieve the opposite.

Can we claim that these achievements are only the result of voluntary choices based on personal preference? In order to answer that question we need to examine the real opportunities open to recipients and non-recipients alike, that is, their capabilities, the real options from which they can actually choose.

It is clear that low-income non-recipients have less opportunity to achieve the functioning of *materially decent living* because of their low wages and unstable income, even if they would prefer to choose a

---

[8] Satisfaction seems to depend on the reference point, e.g. if the reference point is income or consumption level those who do not receive income support are inclined to say they are satisfied with their current situation, while if the reference point is more ideal, e.g. their future plan for themselves or their children or their past memories of themselves, persons are inclined to say they are dissatisfied.

slightly higher level of materially decent living than they currently have. Actually they are always threatened by the slightest market changes and are always struggling to manage their time and money.

Why then do they hesitate to seek public assistance? Here it is easy to imagine that they deeply fear losing their personal assets, which they are required to exhaust in order to qualify for public assistance. If such is the case, why do they try so hard to keep those personal assets? The answer seems to be "independence," a desire to achieve the *functioning* of social and cultural activities and future planning as well as financial managements, crisis management, life planning, and communication with others. Personal assets are viewed as the necessary social bases of their future independence.

However, one question remains. Can they maintain their "independence" forever without any income support? Can their fears and hesitations, which push back the point at which they would be ready to accept public support, prevent them from falling into ever greater poverty? Their patent shortages of opportunities to achieve the *functioning* of materially decent living may ultimately destroy the basic conditions necessary in order to keep their independence.

What about the recipient's capability? To get an adequate image of it, we must take note of the nature of the situation that recipients face. First, items like "social activities and investments for future" are not publicly recognized as "necessities" in Japan, and many recipients hesitate to spend time and money for such "luxuries" in the face of unobservable social pressure. Second, they actually have limited opportunities to work because of health problems or a lack of publicly funded childcare. Third, they have very few personal assets since they were requested to exhaust almost all of them when they applied for public assistance.

Thus, we can see that the real opportunity of recipients to achieve the *functioning of social and cultural activities* is quite restricted, even though the opportunity to achieve the *functioning of materially decent living* is larger than that of non-recipients. In addition, we can fear that recipients' tendency to invest more in "necessities" and less in social activities and future planning may hamper their ability to restore their personal assets, which are precious initial conditions of independence, as revealed by the fears and hesitations of non-recipient.

In conclusion, even if we can say that the consumption level or achieved *functionings* of a single mother are her own choices, according to her own preferences, we cannot say her capability is her choice. It is one of the merits of the capability approach to further our understanding of the objective conditions under which an individual chooses a specific bundle of consumption or *functioning* given her own preference and of the reasons why an individual develops his or her preferences.

In the next section, I want to consider a way of reforming the system that is based on the understanding that neither recipients nor non-recipients dominate one another in their capabilities, and that both of them have difficulties of their own in relation to "independence."

Idea of two-layered public assistance

In a modern society with a mature market economy and universal price mechanism, there is no doubt that the money-indexed consumption level is a key for measuring well-being without private information on an individual's conception of the good. However, it is also true that there are values that are not measurable by money, which are hardly to be met in the market and yet without which market activity could not continue to function. For example, private human support, occupational careers, medical insurance records, social networks, relations with children or volunteers, communication abilities (sociability), habitudes, friends, lovers, consolations, and so on. These are fortunes which individuals happen to have, they also are goods which individuals endeavor to obtain. They constitute external conditions that exist outside of individuals, yet they extend their roots deeply into an individual's personality.

Based on this framework, I wish to propose an idea to reform the public assistance system, a concept that I call the "two-layered public assistance system." The provisions of this system are: (1) sufficient income support to ensure a decent consumption level of necessities in the market and (2) various resources which are necessary to permit the social activities and future planning that generate, maintain, or help recover the social bases of independence.

Two-layered public assistance system

First layer: a family of reason-based public assistances Reason-based public assistance is designed to support individuals facing certain difficulties that are derived from particular characteristics which are publicly recognized as engendering hardship. Its basic conception of distribution is the needs-regarding principle, where a need is measured by the burden each particular characteristic brings in relation to actual social circumstances. For example, income shortage because of the particular demands for goods or services that come from being a single mother, or caring for sick persons, or devoting oneself to volunteer activities in a society where the market is matured but public services are less developed. Or the opportunity shortage that results from the lack of a skill in high demand, for example one related to languages or information technology, a lack that may derive from either immigration or from belonging to a minority group in a highly culturally homogeneous society.

Second layer: general public assistance system This general assistance system is designed to compensate for a shortage of resources (material or non-material) in the light of the outcome state, that is to say the capability an individual actually has, something which is determined both by the personal features of individuals, e.g. pregnancy, particular diseases or conditions, single-mothering, age, physical or mental disabilities,[9] and by the resources individuals can actually access, e.g. income, house, financial stock, having access to a care-giver, language education, job training, and so on.[10]

Concretely, one major difference between the two levels is that the complementary principle which requires exhausting one's personal assets before becoming entitled to help does not apply to the first level. However a comparatively stringent restriction on the level of earning or wealth shall be imposed. Something like the complementary principle is partially applied in the second level to the extent that personal assets are recognized as substantively contributing to an individual's capability. However, assets are not used as a means of selection that leads to refusing help to an individual. As long as a shortage in an individual's capability is recognized she is entitled to assistance.

It is also important to note that neither of the two levels has priority over the other. Once an individual is fully informed of the advantages and constraints of both systems, if it becomes clear that she satisfies both, she can choose either the first or the second layer of assistance.

Note that the layer of reason-based public assistances constitutes plural evaluation systems based on public reasoning, which includes such forms of assistance as monetary supports for existing local agencies like community-based activities, volunteer circles, or NPO/NGO

---

[9] Some characteristics may cancel one another out in terms of their effect on outcome capability, for example, a woman who is very small but pregnant may need just an average amount of food, so one characteristic cancels the other out.

[10] It is usual for individual characteristics to partially overlap in the items which are identified in reason-based public assistance systems. So in practice, to create consistency among plural reason-based assistances, priorities and weights of items must be decided by considering both the intrinsic meaning of each item and the composed influences of combined items.

activities. Meanwhile the general public assistance can be also interpreted as an evaluation system whose informational base is individual shortage of capability. These evaluations will be achieved through
public reasoning or discussions, which, as Rawls and Sen point out,
contribute to the discovery of individual needs that should be directly
taken into account and require going beyond evaluations made by the
market price mechanism.[11]

One of the advantages of the two-layered public assistance system
is that, because reason-based public assistance refers to observable
characteristics, it is more difficult for individuals to report false information in an attempt to increase their benefit. This means that the system is less vulnerable to the problem of informational manipulation.[12]
Moreover, identification of the reason for providing support promotes
public reflection on the reason why certain types of characteristics
predispose an individual to difficulties in given social and historical
circumstances.[13]

In view of the present situation in Japan, where many individuals who
struggle with difficulties and suffer from income or opportunity shortage refrain from applying for public assistance because they fear that in
consequence they will have to give up their particular type of activities
or style of existence, reason-based public assistances seem to offer an
interesting alternative.

If we nonetheless also need a more general public system, it is because
the following practical difficulties inevitably occur. First, given that the
identification of the relevant individual characteristics depends on a
political process based on people's common sense, it tends to rely on
the stereotypes that happen to be present in society. Second, it can
take a long time to achieve public recognition for some characteristics, and this time lag can be fatal to individual values. Furthermore,
there is a logical limitation to all reason-based assistance schemes. Any
reason inevitably separates qualified persons from persons unqualified
for support. No matter how many reasons are identified, we cannot
rule out the possibility that a person in need may be left without help.
This is always possible, because the reasons why one falls into need are
usually too complex to be classified into types and depend on many
personal contingencies. Finally, there may be individuals who refuse to

---

[11] Rawls (1993: 110f.); Sen (1999b: 16–17).
[12] Concerning research on targeting systems in terms of normative economics, see Sen
(1995).
[13] Thus the first-layer system allows us to address the problem of compensation for historical injustice and protection of minority interests. I owe this insight to discussions
with Professor Paul Dumouchel on multiculturalism and social justice.

be classified into certain social categories or groups in order to protect their personal identity or self-respect.

Considering these difficulties, it seems reasonable to provide a two-layer system. The interplay between the two levels enhances individuals' ability to maintain the social bases of their independence, responsibility, and self-respect as well as their desire for such goods. However, as mentioned in the introduction, some will strongly criticize this system, especially its second layer, general public assistance, from the point of views of feasibility and fairness. The remainder of this chapter investigates the logic and ethics underlying the two-layer public assistance system proposed here.

The conception of public reciprocity

Let us suppose there is an individual who is in need, appears to have the ability to work, but has no intention to do so and cannot or will not receive any personal or community-based assistance. Should we leave him in need? The second-layer public assistance system outlined above argues that even these individuals should be given help as long as they are in need. If this is so, who then will be motivated to work and provide in order for this help to even be possible? Can we say that such a system satisfies the requirement of fairness or equity?

I want to respond to this difficulty by introducing a new conception of *public reciprocity*. It rests on a logic and ethics approach that sustains the individual's will and inclination to work, that supports his or her commitment to respect an ethical obligation to work and to provide if he or she can. This logic and ethics is quite different from those approaches that resort either to considerations of self-interest, to categorical imperatives, or to legal obligations and punishments.[14]

This conception of *public reciprocity* is similar to the conception of *mutual advantage* which motivates private contracts or cooperative games, since like mutual advantage *public reciprocity* is expected to provide a ground for voluntary interactions among individuals. However, it is different from mutual advantage in that *public reciprocity* does not rule out cases where after implementing the original contract or scheme of cooperation an agent may lose some advantage while others will gain without any corresponding burden.

It is to some extent similar to the modern conception of *gift* – or a variation of it which is followed by a counter-gift sometimes in a remote

---

[14] On the conception of reciprocity and its relation to different conceptions of the gift please refer to the contributions of Professor Marcel Hénaff included in this volume.

future or a return that takes a different form; however, *public reciprocity*, like the modern gift, often exhibits unilateral transfers among individuals. Yet it is different from a gift in that individuals involved in *public reciprocity* are not limited to contexts of direct or close relationships with particular individuals in particular places.[15]

Public reciprocity of course involves an idea of reciprocity or mutuality in the usual sense, but it does not necessarily require direct symmetry between individuals or between their reward and contribution ratio.[16] In *public reciprocity*, reciprocity is realized through certain rules that are adopted through a reciprocal procedure and which in themselves represent reciprocal correspondences in society as a whole.

Let me explain this conception of public reciprocity in more detail. Typically it can be illustrated by the following quotations from John Rawls.

[T]hey are ready to propose principles and standards as fair terms of cooperation and to abide by them willingly, given the assurance that others will likewise do so" (Rawls 1993: 49).
[T]hey (the concepts of justice and fairness) share a fundamental element in common, which I shall call the concept of reciprocity (Rawls 1971b: 190) ... It is this aspect of justice for which utilitarianism ... is unable to account; but this aspect is expressed, and allowed for, even if in a misleading way, by the idea of the social contract (ibid.: 192).

The first quotation expresses the idea of *reciprocal procedure*.[17] The phrase "given the assurance that others will likewise do so" indicates a sufficient condition under which individuals have the inclination to propose fair rules and to abide by them, something which alleviates in consequence the strains of commitment to justice.[18] The other quotation tries to capture an idea of reciprocity that is present in the rules

---

[15] This definition of gift is different from the classical one, and closer to what Professor Marcel Hénaff calls "ceremonial gift," which is a form of reciprocity and not a unilateral transfer (Hénaff 2004).

[16] On this point, Lawrence Becker, the author of *Reciprocity*, seems to take a similar position, since his concept of "proportionality" goes beyond the literal meaning of the term. "The problem is what sort of reciprocation to make when we seem unable to do anything that equals either the benefits we have received or the sum total of the sacrifices that have gone into producing those benefits. Here it is important to remember that such benefits typically come to us by way of people's participation in on-going social institutions (rituals, voluntary associations, governments). What is fitting is reciprocal participation in those institutions" (Becker 1986: 113–14).

[17] For a detailed view of this conception of reciprocity in the context to Rawls, see Gutmann and Thompson (1996: 53); Gotoh (2004).

[18] "Thus the parties must weigh with care whether they will be able to stick by their commitment in all circumstances" (Rawls 1971a: 176).

themselves. Let us explicate the meaning of this idea by paraphrasing it as follows.

Definition: reciprocity-representing rule

A rule is said to *represent* reciprocity if reciprocity is realized by that rule provided that individuals accept and respect the rule. Individuals can accept and respect the rule, if, first, they can expect that reciprocity will be realized by following the rule, and, second, if they all positively value reciprocity itself.[19]

Given this idea, reciprocity based on rules can be described in the following way:

Definition: rule-based reciprocity

A rule is said to be *reciprocal* if it is realized through a reciprocal procedure and if itself it *represents* reciprocity.

Let us examine the rule of public assistance proposed earlier in the light of the following two questions. Is a law of public assistance that proposes to distribute benefits on the basis of needs rather than contribution or merit a rule such that reciprocity is realized, provided that all individuals accept and respect the rule?

There is a simple version of the rule of public assistance that says: "If you are in need, receive help"; since this has an asymmetrical form, it seems difficult to say that it represents reciprocity. However, there is also a fuller version of the rule which says: "If you can work and afford to provide, do so, if you are in need receive help and be well."

We can observe that in the full version, the first part, "If you can work and afford to provide, do so" and the second part of the rule "if you are in need, receive help and be well" are both conditional and correspond to each other. Here we can recognize two types of correspondence. First, there is a *purpose-feasibility correspondence*, that is, the second part of the rule shows the purpose of the first and the first part constitutes the condition of feasibility of the second. Note that though this *purpose-feasibility correspondence* takes the form of an individual

---

[19] The expectation that reciprocity will be realized under the rule and giving a high value to reciprocity are necessary conditions for accepting and applying this rule, even though they are not sufficient conditions. "Justice" is a candidate for another necessary condition for acceptance and respect of the rule; as Rawls says: "we can ask for the willing cooperation of everyone only if the terms of the scheme are reasonable" (ibid.: 103).

prescription of rational behavior under uncertainty ("For all As, if A can work and afford to provide, A should do so, in order to make it possible that if A falls into need, A can receive resources and be well"), the correspondence itself does not need to be revealed within one person. It is only realized within society taken as a whole ("For all As, if A can work and afford to provide, do so, in order to make it possible that if some are in need they can receive help and be well"). Indeed, under this rule, *purpose-feasibility correspondence* can be realized in a society[20]if and only if the total resources provided by workers are not less than the total resources received by those who are needy.

This means that, for each individual, the rule implies an *ethical obligation*, because, once it is accepted, anyone who can work and provide ought to do so (at least as long as the possibility that the system will be unfeasible because of the absence of her marginal contribution cannot be ruled out), regardless of her prediction considering the probability that she herself might be needy in the future. Similarly, the rule also implies *a right* for each individual since once it is accepted that anyone who is in need can receive help regardless of whether or not she might later on become able to work and to provide. Actually, there may be an individual who believes she can work throughout the whole course of her life and never need help, while there can also be an individual who recognizes that she must be needy all her life. Even so, this rule requires one to work and to provide if one can, and allows one to receive and be well if one is in need.

In addition, we should understand that the former part of the rule also stipulates "a right to work and provide" and consequently imposes an obligation on society to make "the ethical obligation to work and provide if they can" really feasible. That is to say, society should provide substantive opportunities for diverse individuals to be able to work if they can, not only in the labor market, but also in the community or public sector with the support of care services, job training, and so on. Individuals share this social obligation and realize it in society through, for example, inventing work opportunities for themselves and others, to the extent they actually can do so, on the basis of the right to well-being and the right to work they themselves have.

---

[20] When I say "a society" I mean a political body, which has common rules and economic systems taken as a whole, and which consists of diverse groups that have their own rules and systems. It can be wider than a historical nation-state and can extend beyond direct individual relationships as far as the conception of public reciprocity can reach.

Second, the rule exhibits what may be called *a right–ethical obligation correspondence*. This correspondence also need not be revealed within one person. What is required is that it be realized within society as a whole. Every individual has "a right and an ethical obligation to work and provide if he can" and every individual has "a right to receive and be well if he is needy."

Finally, following this rule, a reciprocal relationship can be realized in spite of explicit asymmetries among individual actions, distributions, or relationships between actions–distributions ratios. First, a reciprocal relationship can be realized among individuals who work and provide if they can recognize a certain form of equality between each other through focusing not on the differences in their contributions, rewards, or contributions–rewards ratio but on the similarity that they all actually work and provide. (I can expect him to work and provide, as I do, if he can expect me to work and provide, as he does; he can expect me to work and provide, as he does, if I can expect him to work and provide, as I do.) Second, a reciprocal relationship can be realized among those who are in need and receive if they can recognize there is a certain equality between each other by focusing on not their differences in needs, benefits, or needs–benefits ratios but the similarity that they are all actually needy and receive.[21] Third, a reciprocal relationship can be realized among all, both those "who work and provide" and those "who are needy and receive," inasmuch as they can expect each other to equally respect the rule and to be equally constrained by it. Let me illustrate this last point. Suppose for example that, as mentioned at the start of this section, there is an individual who only receives resources although he appears able to work. Even in this case, if others can expect that since he also respects the rule and is constrained by the rule, he will begin to work when he actually becomes able to do so, there remains a certain reciprocity through everyone's commitment to respect the rule.

To summarize, the proposed rule of public assistance is a rule such that reciprocity in the following four senses can be realized if all individuals accept and respect it:

1. *purpose–feasibility correspondence*;
2. *rights–ethical obligation correspondence*;

---

[21] Note that the individuals who are participating in the different types of reason-based public assistances have a possibility to be relating to each other in both the first and second forms of reciprocity. In either case, the point is in the shift of the conception of equality, which focus on the similarity in their diverse contributions to society through their various activities or in their diverse situations of being needy.

3. *reciprocal relationship through recognition of a certain equality in actions or in expectation of actions* among individuals who work and provide or among individuals who are needy and receive;
4. *reciprocal relationship under law* among all individuals including those "who work and provide" and those "who are needy and receive" can be realized.

In addition, as Rawls pointed out for "the difference principle," we may be able to find a right correspondence between contingencies and social activities, for example between "being able to provide resources" and the "social activity of providing resources" or between "not being able to obtain resources" and the "social activity of receiving resources."[22] Yet in this case we should notice that Rawls opposes a kind of lump-sum tax which imposes a tax on all able individuals based on the simple fact that they are able to provide resources.

Furthermore, if we focus not on the probability of a risk but on risk as a fact, no one can entirely avoid the risk of being in need; given this, we can discover a type of equality between the individual who works and provides and the individual who receives. I want to label this idea as "risk as a viewpoint," to distinguish it from an economic concern based on the calculation of individual probability.

Concluding remark

In conclusion, we can respond to the criticisms addressed to the two-layered public assistance system concerning its feasibility and fairness or equity as follows. This rule supports feasibility through the correspondence between the condition of working and providing and the purpose of providing well-being in society as a whole. This rule also guarantees a kind of fairness and equity, because, though under this law we can respect "the right to well-being" without any condition other than respecting the same right for others, we can therefore perceive a fair correspondence between "the right to well-being" and "the obligation to work and provide if possible" in society taken as a whole.

This conception of public reciprocity sustains an ethical obligation to be accepted by people in the sense that it makes it easier for them to recognize this obligation. Generally, we can reasonably say "*ought to* implies *can*," whose contraposition is "*cannot* implies that one is

[22] See Rawls (1971a: 102–3).

immune from obligation," because, for example, it is impossible for an individual who cannot work and provide to fulfill the obligation to work and to provide. Yet, we cannot reasonably assume that *"can implies ought to"* (have an obligation), without further investigations concerning the justice of the situation. Furthermore, even if we can recognize that justice is involved here, we may hesitate to say that there is an obligation, if the satisfaction of justice would impose severe hardship on individuals. Thus, in general, we cannot reasonably say that an individual "can work and provide resources" implies that he or she "ought to work and provide resources." However, if we recognize the conception of public reciprocity advanced here, can't we reasonably say that individuals have an ethical obligation to work and provide if they can?

Of course ethical obligations have no power to constrain individuals legally or to impose punishment. Similarly, the constitutional prescriptions in Japan cannot oblige individuals to work with legal punishments. Yet, they can guarantee circumstances where an individual who works and provides finds himself in a context where reciprocity is satisfied both logically and actually. The public assistance system established in a society might also serve to illustrate the meaning of "production" and of "contribution" and of the various kinds of values which exist in society and which should rightly be evaluated by going beyond the perspective of the market.

Finally, let me make a few remarks on this conception of public reciprocity itself. First, it sustains not only a conception of justice which requires individual acceptance, but also a conception of mutual advantage in the sense that it realizes a beneficial reciprocal relationship. Second, while this conception of public reciprocity is a political conception that is put forward in an attempt to resolve political issues on the basis of laws, institutions, or policies, it is also a moral conception, in the sense that it is subject to individual "acceptance" and "commitment" and includes the substantive virtue of reciprocity.

It may be true that individuals have a tendency to lose their motivation to work if they can obtain benefits without having to contribute in return. Yet, it may also be the case that individuals have a tendency to lose their motivation to work if the predictable result of their activity merely relates to themselves or to their interest. What is required in the reform of public assistance in Japan is not to cut its costs or the number of recipients but to construct plural evaluation systems, in which people can produce various kinds of values. What is required from "ethics, economics, and law" is to invent ways of evaluating that do not depend on the logic and ethics of market.

Acknowledgements

I am most grateful to Professor Amartya Sen, who has opened the splendid vistas expounded in this paper, and all those participants who gave me helpful comments on previous versions of this chapter, originally given at a conference on "Ethics, Economics, and Law" at the Ritsumeikan University, October 28, 2005. I received many insightful and clarifying comments from Professor Paul Dumouchel. Needless to say, all the remaining deficiencies of the present version are my sole responsibility. Last but not least, my gratitude goes to the financial support, through a Grant-in-Aid for Scientific Research, from the Japan Society for Promotion of Sciences.

References

Becker, L. C. 1986. *Reciprocity*, London: Routledge & Kegan Paul.

Committee of Research and Analysis on Social Life 2003. *Report on Research and Analysis on Social Life*, Tokyo: Ministry of Health, Labour and Welfare (in Japanese).

Gotoh, R. 2004. "The Possibility of Public-Provision Unit in Global Context – Towards 'Social Contract' Based on Reciprocity," mimeo.

Gutmann, A. and Thompson D. 1996. *Democracy and Disagreement*, Cambridge, Mass.: Harvard University Press.

Hénaff, M. 2004. "Gift Exchange, Play and Deception," in C. Gerschlager (ed.), *Deception in Markets: An Economic Analysis*, New York: Palgrave Macmillan.

Ministry of Health, Labour and Welfare 2004. "Report: Special Committee on Japanese Public Assistance," Tokyo: Ministry of Health, Labour and Welfare.

Rawls, J. 1971a. *A Theory of Justice*, Cambridge, MA: Harvard University Press.

1971b. "Justice as Reciprocity," in Rawls 1999, pp. 190–224.

1993. *Political Liberalism*, New York: Columbia University Press.

Sen, A. K. 1980. "Equality of What?" *The Tanner Lectures on Human Values*, vol. I, Salt Lake City: University of Utah Press; reprinted in Sen 1982. *Choice, Welfare and Measurement*, Oxford: Blackwell, pp. 353–69.

1985. *Commodities and Capabilities*, Amsterdam: North-Holland.

1992. *Inequality Reexamined*, Oxford: Clarendon Press.

1995. "The Political Economy of Targeting," in D. van de Walle and K. Nead (eds.), *Public Spending and the Poor: Theory and Evidence*, Baltimore: The Johns Hopkins University Press, pp. 5–15.

1999a. *Reason before Identity: The Romanes Lecture for 1998*, Oxford University Press.

1999b. *Development as Freedom*, New York: Alfred A. Knopf.

Suzumura, K. and Gotoh, R. 2001. *Amartya Sen: Economics and Ethics*, Tokyo: Jikkyo-Shuppan-sha (in Japanese).

8   Reasoning with preferences?

John Broome

8.1   Reasoning and requirements of rationality

Preferences lie at the heart of economic theory. Amartya Sen's work, starting with his remarkable book *Collective Choice and Social Welfare*, has taken the formal study of preferences to a new level of sophistication. Sen has exposed many of the standard presumptions of economics to careful criticism. Economists generally take it for granted that the preferences of rational people satisfy various formal conditions – transitivity is the most prominent of them. Sen has examined each of these conditions, and asked whether the preferences of a rational person must indeed satisfy them.

This paper approaches the formal properties of rational preferences from a different direction. It does not directly ask what conditions, if any, a rational person's preferences must satisfy. Instead, it asks how a rational person could bring her preferences to satisfy those conditions, whatever they may be. Suppose for example that rational preferences must be transitive; then this paper looks for a process through which a person may come to make her preferences transitive.

If there is such a process, it will be reasoning; I am looking for a process of reasoning with preferences. This investigation supports Sen's program indirectly. If some condition is genuinely required by rationality, one would expect there to be some way in which a rational person could bring herself to satisfy it. If there is no such way to satisfy it, that suggests the condition may not be required by rationality after all.

We may describe rationality by specifying what it requires. Rationality requires certain things of you. It requires you not to have contradictory beliefs or intentions, not to intend something you believe to be impossible, to believe what obviously follows from something you believe, and so on. Its requirements can be expressed using schemata such as:

> *Modus ponens.* Rationality requires of N that, if N believes p and N believes that if p then q, then N believes q.

Necessary means. Rationality requires of N that, if N intends that e, and if N believes that e will be so only if m is so, and if N believes m will be so only if she intends that m, then N intends that m.

Enkrasia. Rationality requires of N that, if N believes she ought to F, and if N believes she will F only if she intends to F, then N intends to F.

It may be questioned whether any of these formulae express genuine requirements of rationality. Their precise formulation may be inaccurate, at least. But these formulae are not the subject of this paper, and for the sake of argument I shall assume they are correct. In any case, they are only examples of requirements of rationality (or 'rational requirements', as I shall often say); rationality requires many things of you besides these. Notice that all of these particular requirements govern conditional statements. They have a 'wide scope', as I shall say. None governs a single belief or intention of yours.

Many people think that rationality makes requirements on your preferences, too. In order to have an example to work with, I shall concentrate on this familiar one:

Transitivity. Rationality requires of N that if N prefers a to b and N prefers b to c, then N prefers a to c.

This too has a wide scope. It is particularly controversial whether or not this is a genuine requirement of rationality. But in this paper I shall not engage directly in controversy about it; I shall assume that *Transitivity* expresses a genuine requirement. I shall ask how, given that it is a rational requirement, you may come to satisfy it.

By what process can you come to satisfy a particular requirement of rationality? Often, you simply find yourself satisfying it. You intend to visit Venice; you believe the only way to do so is to buy a ticket (and that you will not do so unless you intend to); and you find yourself intending to buy a ticket. You satisfy *Necessary means* in this instance. You come to do so as a result of some automatic, unconscious causal process that you do not control; it just happens. Many of your preferences satisfy *Transitivity* in a similar way. Presumably there is some evolutionary explanation of why this sort of thing happens.

Possibly an ideally rational creature would find itself satisfying all the requirements of rationality this way. But mortals fail to satisfy very many of them. However, we mortals do have a way of improving our score. We can bring ourselves to satisfy some requirements by our own activity of reasoning. Reasoning is an activity – something we do – through which we can satisfy some requirements in particular instances. For example, we can come to believe a particular consequence of what we believe by thinking the matter through.

Some unconscious processes could be called unconscious reasoning. But in this paper I am interested only in conscious processes, and I shall give the name 'reasoning' to those ones only. Unconscious processes are not activities, and I am interested in reasoning as an activity.

I am assuming rationality imposes requirements on your preferences, such as *Transitivity*. No doubt you find yourself satisfying some of those requirements through unconscious processes. But when you do not, can you bring yourself to satisfy them through reasoning? Briefly: can you reason with preferences? That is the topic of this paper.

I am interested in correct reasoning only. Various mental activities of yours might accidentally lead you to satisfy a rational requirement, and various of those activities might qualify as reasoning. But a reasoning activity that systematically leads you to satisfy a rational requirement would have to be *correct* reasoning.

Why does it matter whether you can reason with preferences? It is important in itself to understand the process of reasoning, but there is another reason too. In 'Why be rational?', Niko Kolodny argues that, for any rational requirement on you, there must be a process of reasoning through which you can bring yourself to satisfy that requirement. If he is right, and if it turned out that you cannot reason with preferences, it would follow that there are no rational requirements on preferences (Kolodny 2005).

As it happens, I am not convinced by Kolodny's arguments, for reasons I cannot set out in this paper.[1] I remain agnostic about his conclusion. For all I know, there may be requirements of rationality that you can come to satisfy only by unconscious processes that you do not control. But even so, if it should turn out that no process of reasoning could bring you to have, say, transitive preferences, that would cast some doubt on the claim that rationality requires you to have transitive preferences. We would certainly want an explanation of how there could be this requirement on you without your being able to bring yourself to satisfy it. In this way, the question of reasoning reflects back on to the question of what rationality requires.

You certainly cannot rely on unconscious processes to get all your preferences into rational order; anyone's system of preferences is too big and complex for that. This is particularly true of preferences among uncertain prospects. The axioms of expected utility theory are supposed

---

[1] See Broome (2007).

to express requirements of rationality for these preferences, and no one satisfies those axioms automatically.

Reasoning with preferences, and indeed reasoning in general, has not been much discussed. Many authors write about what rationality requires of your preferences and other mental states. Having stated some requirements, they leave it at that. They do not consider by what process you may come to satisfy their requirements. Why not? I think they must take it for granted that, once you know what the requirements of rationality are, you can bring yourself to satisfy them by reasoning. I think they must implicitly rely on a particular model of reasoning. They must think you can reason your way to satisfying a requirement by starting from the requirement itself as a premise. More exactly, their model starts from your believing some proposition such as the ones I have labelled *Modus ponens, Necessary means* or *Transitivity*, and you reason from there. These are propositions about your mental states, so your reasoning starts from a belief about your mental states. I shall call this a 'second-order belief', and I shall call this model of reasoning the 'second-order model'. It is an all-purpose model. It can be applied to reasoning with mental states of all kinds – beliefs, intentions, preferences and so   on.

But for some mental states, reasoning cannot work as the second-order model supposes. The model does not work for beliefs, for one thing. Section 8.2 explains why not. Section 8.3 describes an alternative, first-order model of reasoning, which is more successful for beliefs. It does not depend on any second-order belief about your mental states. But it is not such an all-purpose model; it is not straightforward to extend it beyond beliefs to other mental states. I shall next consider how successfully the two models can apply to preferences. Section 8.4 distinguishes a broad concept of preference from our ordinary one, as I need to do. Section 8.5 applies the second-order model to broad preferences with moderate success. Section 8.6 applies the first-order model to ordinary preferences, again with moderate success. The central issue that arises in this section is how far ordinary preferences can be distinguished from beliefs about betterness. It may turn out that what appears to be reasoning with ordinary preferences is really nothing other than theoretical reasoning about which alternatives are better than which. Section 8.7 considers whether that is so.

My main conclusion is that the second-order model of reasoning is unsuccessful for ordinary preferences, as it is for beliefs. Possibly this model may work for broad preferences. Nevertheless, we may indeed be able to reason with ordinary preferences, because the first-order model is more successful.

However, as a result of the argument in Section 8.7, I find I cannot clearly distinguish first-order reasoning with preferences from theoretical reasoning about the goodness of the alternatives. What supports reasoning of this type may be the transitivity of betterness: the fact that, if *a* is better than *b* and *b* better than *c*, then *a* is better than *c*. This is a feature of the semantics of 'better than'. It is not a coherence requirement on preferences. It will entail the coherence requirement that preferences are transitive if there is a separate requirement that you prefer, of two things, the one you believe to be better. This point gives us a new handle on a question that Amartya Sen has raised to prominence.[2] If indeed rationality requires you to have transitive preferences, that may not be because of anything internal to preferences. It may be because of a connection between preferences and the external world – specifically a connection between preferences and the relative goodness of the options. Sen's work was an important stimulus for this paper.

8.2   Second-order theoretical reasoning

I start with theoretical reasoning – reasoning with beliefs. I shall use an example in which you come to satisfy the requirement *Modus ponens*. It is a case of simple deductive reasoning, which should be paradigmatic of theoretical reasoning.

You wake up and hear rain, so you believe it is raining. Your long experience with snow has taught you that, if it is raining, the snow will melt. However, because you are still sleepy and have not yet thought about the snow, you do not yet believe the snow will melt. So you do not satisfy *Modus ponens* in this instance. You believe it is raining; you believe that if it is raining the snow will melt, but you do not believe the snow will melt. By reasoning, you can surely bring yourself to satisfy the requirement in this instance. How will your reasoning go?

This section investigates the second-order model. I shall take a generally sceptical stance towards it. I shall argue it does not work for theoretical reasoning, nor for reasoning with ordinary preferences. Given that, I shall be generous towards this model, and make concessions to help it on its way. I shall make assumptions that support it, even when I cannot fully justify them.

The second-order model supposes that your reasoning sets out from a belief in the requirement itself. So let us suppose you do actually believe the requirement *Modus ponens* in this instance. You believe rationality requires of you that: you believe the snow will melt if you believe it is

---

[2] Sen (1993).

raining and you believe that if it is raining the snow will melt. Can you get by reasoning from this belief to satisfying the requirement itself, as the second-order model supposes?

One plausible pattern of reasoning offers a clue as to how you might do so. Suppose you believe you ought to do something – buy cherries, say. You might say to yourself:

> *I ought to buy cherries,*
> *So I shall buy cherries.*

I mean the second of these sentences to express an intention of yours, rather than a belief that you will buy cherries. I shall say more about the idea of saying to yourself in Section 8.3. This is plausibly a little piece of reasoning, through which your normative belief that you ought to buy cherries brings you to form the intention of buying cherries. Normally, when you intend to do something, your intention causes you in due course to do it. So in due course you are likely to buy cherries, as a final result of your normative belief that you ought to do so.

I think that what you say to yourself here is indeed reasoning, and moreover correct reasoning. By means of reasoning on this pattern, you can bring yourself to satisfy the rational requirement *Enkrasia*: to intend to do what you believe you ought to do. I shall call it 'kratic reasoning'. In this paper I shall not argue that kratic reasoning is genuine, correct reasoning; I shall simply assume it is. I do so to smooth the way for the second-order model; it is one of my concessions to the model. In a moment, I shall show how the second-order model can made use of it.

As a second concession, I shall assume you can derive a strictly normative belief from your belief in the rational requirement. I have already assumed you believe rationality requires you to satisfy the condition that you believe the snow will melt if you believe it is raining and you believe that if it is raining the snow will melt. Now, I assume you go further and derive the belief that you ought to satisfy this condition. Questions might be asked about this step.[3] First, even though rationality requires you to satisfy this condition, does it follow that you ought to satisfy it? Suppose, for instance, very bad consequences would result from your satisfying it; ought you to satisfy it then? Second, even if it does actually follow, how can we assume you make this inference, so it is reflected in your own beliefs?

To give the second-order model a chance, I cannot avoid making this questionable assumption. If correct second-order reasoning is to

---

[3] See Broome (2005).

bring you to satisfy some condition, you need to believe you ought to satisfy it. It is not good enough for you to believe merely that rationality requires you to satisfy it. Suppose, say, you believed rationality requires you to satisfy a condition but also believed you ought not to satisfy it. In that case, correct reasoning could not possibly lead you to satisfy it. So correct reasoning needs an ought belief, not merely a belief about a rational requirement.

I give the model an ought belief, therefore. I assume you believe you ought to believe the snow will melt if you believe it is raining and you believe that if it is raining the snow will melt. That should put you in a position to go through this piece of kratic reasoning, modelled on the cherries example:

> *I ought to believe the snow will melt if I believe it is raining and I believe that if it is raining the snow will melt.*
> *So I shall believe the snow will melt if I believe it is raining and I believe that if it is raining the snow will melt.*

The second sentence is supposed to express an intention. Because the content of your premise-belief has a wide scope, you end with an intention that has a wide scope. What you intend is the conditional proposition that you believe the snow will melt if you believe it is raining and you believe that if it is raining the snow will melt.

Suppose you get as far as this. What happens next? If you are to follow the precedent of cherries, this intention would normally cause you to fulfil it. But there are two difficulties standing in the way of that result.

The first is the wide scope of your intention. Kratic reasoning could take you to a more specific intention only if you started with a more specific normative belief. To get by kratic reasoning to an intention to believe the snow will melt, you would have to start from a belief that you ought to believe the snow will melt. But you cannot acquire this specific normative belief by correct reasoning from your initial belief in the broad-scope rational requirement you are under.

To see why not, notice it may not be true that you ought to believe the snow will melt. Perhaps you ought not to believe it is raining; perhaps the rain you hear is on a recording that you set as your alarm call. If you ought not to believe it is raining, it may well not be the case that you ought to believe the snow will melt. On the other hand, we are assuming it is true that rationality requires you to believe the snow will melt if you believe it is raining and you believe that if it is raining the snow will melt. You cannot by correct reasoning derive a belief that may not be true from one that is true.

So by correct kratic reasoning you cannot arrive at an intention to believe specifically that the snow will melt. But it is that specific belief the reasoning is supposed to lead you to. That is the first difficulty.

It may not be a serious one. All your intentions are indefinite to some degree, and yet you manage to fulfil many of them. If you intend to buy cherries, you could fulfil your intention by going to the greengrocer or the supermarket, in the morning or the afternoon. Somehow your intention gets narrowed to a more specific one, say to buy cherries at the supermarket, leaving home at 12.30. This narrowing can happen without your having a normative belief that you ought to buy cherries at the supermarket, leaving home at 12.30. It certainly can happen; we do not have to worry about how. I shall assume the same thing could happen in the present case. I shall assume your wide-scope intention could be narrowed to an intention to believe the snow will melt. This is rather plausible, since you do in fact believe it is raining and that if it is raining the snow will melt. I treat it as another concession to the second-order model.

But now you meet the second difficulty. This is the fatal one. Intending to believe a particular proposition is normally ineffective; it normally does not get you to believe the proposition. (Because you probably know that, you probably cannot even form an intention to believe a particular proposition. You cannot intend something and at the same time believe the intention will be ineffective.)

There are exceptions. You may be able to acquire a belief in a particular proposition by using some external means – going regularly to church or taking a belief pill, for example. If an external means is available to you of coming to believe a particular proposition, then you may be able to intend to believe this proposition, and this intention may cause you to believe it, using the means. However, the last step – using an external means such as going regularly to church or taking a belief pill – is not a mental process. It therefore cannot form part of a process of reasoning. So the second-order model of reasoning cannot work through your using an external means.

On the other hand, you cannot come to believe a proposition by intending to believe that proposition, without using an external means. You can do some things without using an external means; raising your hand is one example. Intending to raise your hand can bring you to raise your hand without using an external means. But intending to believe a proposition cannot bring you to believe that proposition without using an external means. In his 'Deciding to believe', Bernard Williams (1973) argued this was a necessary feature of belief; I have been persuaded by an argument of Jonathan Bennett's that it is a contingent feature of our psychology.[4] But whether necessary or contingent, it is a truth. It prevents the second-order model of theoretical reasoning from working in the way I have been investigating.

That way was through kratic reasoning, by which a normative belief leads to an intention. Could the second-order model work more directly, without involving any intention? Could it be that believing rationality requires you to be in a particular mental state, or believing that you ought to be in a particular mental state, simply causes you to enter that state, without your forming an intention of doing so? Could this happen in a way that is sufficiently regular to count as reasoning?

T. M. Scanlon thinks it can happen for some states: those he calls 'judgement-sensitive attitudes'. These are 'attitudes that an ideally rational person would come to have whenever that person judged there to be sufficient reason for them ...'.[5] So, for instance, if you were ideally rational, you would come to have a belief whenever you judged there to be sufficient reason for you to have it or, as I prefer to say, whenever you judged you ought to have it.

I find Scanlon's view implausible. Your beliefs are not normally caused by any normative beliefs you might have about what you ought to believe. If you believe you ought to have some belief, that would not normally cause you to have the belief. Suppose you believe you ought to believe you are attractive, because believing you are attractive will relax you, make you more approachable and improve your life. This would not normally cause you to believe you are attractive. Normally, our beliefs are caused by evidence, not by normative beliefs about what we ought to believe.

I agree that beliefs are judgement-sensitive in a different sense. If you were ideally rational, you would come to have a belief whenever you judged there was sufficient evidence for the content of the belief. You would come to believe you are attractive when you judge there is sufficient evidence that you are attractive. Beliefs are genuinely judgement-sensitive in this sense, but it is not Scanlon's sense. Your judgement in this case is about the content of the belief, not about the belief itself. It is a first-order belief, not a second-order one.

Judgement-sensitivity in Scanlon's sense is sensitivity to a second-order normative judgement about the belief itself. A second-order judgement of this sort often accompanies a first-order one. When you judge there is sufficient evidence for some proposition, you may well also judge you have sufficient reason to believe the proposition. But

[4] Bennett (1990).   [5] Scanlon (1998: 20).

what causes you to believe the proposition, if you do, is the first-order judgement, not the second-order one. A way to test this is to look at cases where you make the second-order judgement but not the first-order one. My example of believing you are attractive is one of those. Examples like that show a second-order judgement does not normally cause you to have the belief.

In any case, even if beliefs were judgement-sensitive in Scanlon's sense, that would not directly help the second-order model of reasoning. In my example, your second-order judgement is not that you ought to have a particular belief. Instead, it has a wide scope. It is the judgement that you ought to satisfy the conditional: that you believe the snow will melt if you believe it is raining and you believe that if it is raining the snow will melt. It is particularly implausible that this judgement could cause you to enter the complex mental state described by the conditional, without kratic reasoning and without your forming an intention.

I conclude that the second-order model of reasoning fails for theoretical reasoning. It requires a sort of control over your beliefs that actually you do not have. So I come to the first-order model.

8.3   First-order theoretical reasoning

I shall stick to the same paradigmatic example of theoretical reasoning. You believe it is raining, and you believe that if it is raining the snow will melt, but you do not believe the snow will melt. So you do not satisfy the requirement *Modus ponens* in this instance. But you can bring yourself to satisfy it by saying to yourself that:

> It is raining.
> If it is raining the snow will melt.
> So the snow will melt.

Here, I have written down a sequence of sentences, which designate propositions. You do not necessarily say the sentences to yourself; you might reason in Swedish, say. But you do say to yourself the propositions that these sentences designate. You say to yourself that it is raining, and that if it is raining the snow will melt, and then you say that the snow will melt. I shall mention the point of the word 'so' at the end of this section.

You initially believe the first two of these propositions; in saying them to yourself you are expressing your beliefs. You do not initially believe the third. But when you say it to yourself, you express a belief in it. By the time you come to say it, your reasoning has brought you to believe it. By this time, you satisfy *Modus ponens*. That is how the first-order model of reasoning works.

The propositions you say to yourself constitute the contents of your beliefs. You can reason with beliefs only because they are states that have contents. Their content gives you something to reason about.

Saying something to yourself is an act. Sometimes, no doubt, you say things to yourself out loud, but more often you do it silently. In that case, I could alternatively have said you call the proposition to mind; 'saying to yourself' is just a more graphic way of describing what you do. One thing it does is bring the beliefs together, if you have not previously done that in your mind.

Your acts of saying to yourself are part of your reasoning but not the whole. Your reasoning is the causal process whereby some of your mental states cause you to acquire a new mental state. It includes a sequence of acts, and it is itself a complex activity. To be reasoning, the process must involve acts of saying to yourself. Some of your beliefs cause you to acquire a new belief, through some acts of this sort. The process ends when you acquire your new belief.

The acquisition of this belief is an act. Described one way, the acquisition is something you intend. When you embark on your reasoning, you intend to come to believe whatever is the conclusion that emerges from the reasoning. You intend that, if *p* is the proposition that emerges from the reasoning, you believe *p*. However, you do not intend to believe the specific proposition that emerges. In the example, you do not intend to believe the snow will melt. Coming to believe the snow will melt is an act like finding your glasses under the bed, after looking for them. You intend to find your glasses, and this makes it the case that your finding them under the bed is an act. But you do not intend to find them under the bed. I said in Section 8.2 that you cannot come to believe a particular proposition by intending to believe that proposition. But you can acquire a belief by means of a procedure you intend.

Since reasoning is a process that takes place among mental states, acts of saying to yourself can only form a part of it when they express mental states. In the example, in saying to yourself that it is raining, you must express a belief of yours that it is raining. When you say to yourself that the snow will melt, you must express a belief of yours that the snow will melt, and so on. In the context of belief, saying to yourself is asserting to yourself. True, you could say to yourself the sequence of sentences:

> *It is raining.*
> *If it is raining the snow will melt.*
> *So the snow will melt.*

even if you did not have the corresponding beliefs. (In this paper, I use italics in place of quotation marks.) But in doing that you would not be reasoning, because you would not be going through a process that takes place among your beliefs.

In the course of your reasoning, you do not say to yourself any propositions about your mental states; you say to yourself the propositions that constitute the contents of your mental states. In the example, you do not say to yourself that you believe it is raining, nor that you ought to believe the snow will melt. No second-order beliefs about your mental states are involved. We may say you reason *with* your beliefs. You reason *about* the content of your beliefs.

The second-order model of reasoning was supposed to set out from a belief about your beliefs. But it was blocked because there is no route of reasoning from there to actually modifying your first-order beliefs. On the other hand, the process I am now describing directly modifies your first-order beliefs, because it works on their contents. When you conclude that the snow will melt, in doing that you are directly acquiring a new belief.

This needs emphasis. There are two aspects to theoretical reasoning. One is identifying a particular conclusion-proposition on the basis of the premise-propositions. The other is your coming to believe the conclusion-proposition. It is tempting to try and divide reasoning into two stages according to these two aspects: first picking out a new proposition, then coming to believe it. But if there were these two stages, at the end of the first stage the new proposition would be parked somewhere in your consciousness, without your having any particular attitude towards it. We would have to explain how you then come to believe it. The explanation could not go through your believing you ought to believe it, nor through your intending to believe it, because, as I said earlier, neither of these attitudes will succeed in getting you to believe it. At least, they cannot have this effect through any process that can be reasoning. In any case, this explanation would leave us with the equally difficult task of explaining how you come to have one of these attitudes.

The truth is that you believe the proposition as you identify it. We cannot split reasoning into the two stages. Theoretical reasoning is imbued with belief all the way through. As I put it just now: you are reasoning with beliefs. You do not reason and then acquire a belief.

To summarize what we have learned so far from this paradigmatic example: reasoning is a process whereby some of your mental states give rise to another mental state; the mental states involved must be ones that have contents; in reasoning you say to yourself the propositions that constitute these contents, and you reason about these contents.

This cannot be a full characterization of reasoning. Not just any mental process that has these features is reasoning. For example, suppose you believe that it is raining and that if it is raining the snow willmelt. Suppose you say to yourself that it is raining and that if it is raining the snow will melt, and suppose this causes you to believe you hear trumpets. That bizarre process is probably not reasoning.

You might think that true reasoning can only be separated from bizarre processes like this by the presence of a second-order belief. In my example of genuine reasoning, you moved from believing it is raining and believing that if it is raining the snow will melt to believing the snow will melt. You might think this process is reasoning only if you have the second-order belief that rationality requires you to believe the snow will melt if you believe it is raining and you believe that if it is raining the snow will melt.

Even if this was so, it would not restore the second-order model of reasoning. The reasoning is still conducted at the first order, even if a second-order belief needs to be present in the background. But actually I think it is not so. A sophisticated reasoner may have this second-order belief, but I do not see why you need so much sophistication in order to reason. I do not see why you need to have the concept of a rational requirement, or even the concept of a belief.

It is more plausible that a different sort of background belief is needed to separate your reasoning process from others such as the bizarre one. You might need to believe that, from the proposition that it is raining and the proposition that if it is raining the snow will melt, it follows that the snow will melt. That is to say, you might need in the background, not a second-order belief about what rationality requires of your beliefs, but a belief about the inferential relations that hold among the propositions that constitute the contents of your beliefs. I do not deny that a belief such as this may be a necessary condition for you to reason. But even if it is necessary in the background, it is not itself a part of the reasoning; it does not constitute an extra premise. That is the lesson taught us by Lewis Carroll in 'What the tortoise said to Achilles' (Carroll 1895). So the first-order model of reasoning is not affected, even if this belief is necessary in the background.

My own view is that reasoning processes are computational. This is what characterizes them as reasoning and distinguishes them from bizarre ones such as the one I described. If I am right, it adds to the ways in which reasoning is an activity, since computation is something you do. You operate on the contents of your beliefs computationally. I think that, when you say to yourself the word 'so' or its equivalent in another language, it marks your computation. Computation is too big and difficult a topic to broach in this paper. I shall allow myself the assumption that theoretical reasoning is an operation on the contents of beliefs.

My snow example is paradigmatic of theoretical reasoning, in that it is an example of deductive reasoning by *modus ponens*. But it represents only a small fraction of theoretical reasoning, and it leaves a great deal to be explained. For one thing, reasoning often does not proceed in the linear fashion illustrated in the example. In the example, your reasoning sets out from some initial beliefs and concludes with a new belief. But theoretical reasoning often leads you to drop one or more of your initial beliefs, rather than acquire a new one.[6] Dropping a premise-belief will bring you to satisfy the requirement *Modus ponens* just as well as acquiring a conclusion-belief will. A fuller account of theoretical reasoning will need to explain how it can turn around and cause this backwards effect. Besides that, there are many other patterns of theoretical reasoning to be accounted for too. But none of that is for this paper. I described theoretical reasoning only in order to illustrate the two different models of reasoning. Now I turn to preferences.

8.4   Concepts of preference

I need first to distinguish two concepts of preference. This conventional definition defines a broad concept:

> *Broad preference.* N prefers a to b if and only if N is in a mental state that would typically cause N to choose a were N to have a choice between a and b only.

We call the mental state a *preference* for a over b.

This definition is broad because it allows mental states of various sorts to count as preferences. For one thing, it allows an intention to be a preference. Suppose you intend to choose biking if ever you have a choice between biking and driving only. This is a state that would typically cause you to choose biking, were you to have a choice between biking and driving only. So you prefer biking to driving according to the definition.

This definition is too broad to capture accurately our ordinary concept of a preference. Ordinarily, we make a difference between preferring one thing to another and intending to choose one thing rather than another. You might intend to choose biking – perhaps on grounds of health – though actually you prefer driving. You can intend to choose

---

[6] Gilbert Harman particularly emphasizes this point in Harman (1986).

something you do not prefer, and you can prefer something you do not intend to choose. The definition does not allow for that possibility.

According to our ordinary concept, a preference is like a desire rather than like an intention. It is a sort of comparative desire. The notion of preference may even be reducible to the notion of desire: to prefer A to B may simply be to desire A more than B. What is the difference between a desire and an intention? To specify the difference analytically is a difficult and contentious matter. Both desires and intentions are mental states that can be identified by their functional roles; the difficulty is to spell out what their different roles are. They are similar in that a desire to do something and an intention to do something are both dispositions to do that thing. But they are dispositions of different sorts. In so far as they cause you to do the thing, they do so in characteristically different ways. It is difficult to spell out their different roles in detail. For my purposes I do not need to. We naively have a good understanding of the difference between a desire and an intention, and I only need to remind you of it. The next two paragraphs do so.

Desires are more remote from action than intentions are. When you intend to do something, you are committed to doing it, but that is not necessarily so when you desire it. To a large extent, your intentions control your actions. Often they do so through processes of reasoning, specifically through instrumental reasoning in which you figure out appropriate means to ends that you intend.[7] On the other hand, in so far as your desires influence your actions, they generally do so through your intentions. To desire to do something is to be disposed to intend to do it. Since to intend to do it is itself to be disposed to do it, to desire to do something is also to be disposed to do that thing, but more remotely. A desire of yours is only one influence on your intentions. Other influences include other desires that may conflict with it, your beliefs about what you ought to do, whims that strike you, confusions that afflict you, and so on. Consequently, if you desire to do something, you may not intend to do it, and you may intend to do something without desiring to do it.

You can acquire an intention by making a decision. For example, you may one day decide to go to Venice, and you will then intend to go to Venice. But deciding to go to Venice does not make you desire to go to Venice. You cannot acquire a desire by making a decision, without using an external means. You may have an external means available of acquiring the desire to go to Venice; you might spend hours poring over glossy picture books, for example. If so, you can decide to acquire the

---

[7] Bratman (1987) is a full account of the characteristic role of intentions in controlling actions.

desire, and then acquire the desire using the means. But you cannot acquire the desire by deciding to, without using an external means. In this respect a desire is like a belief. I said it is a contingent fact of our psychology that you cannot acquire a belief by deciding to acquire it, without using an external means. I think the same is true of a desire.

According to our ordinary concept, a preference is like a desire in this respect. You cannot acquire an ordinary preference by deciding to, without using an external means. In a recent paper, Christian Piller claims that you can decide to have a particular preference, but I disagree with him about that if he is thinking of an ordinary preference.[8] His example is this:

> What if we got two pots of gold, if we preferred this saucer of mud to a pot of gold? I would certainly say 'Yes, please, can I have the saucer of mud' ... If I honestly and instantaneously say 'I want the mud, not the gold. Please!' then I do prefer the saucer of mud to the pot of gold.

If the prize of two pots of gold is awarded for having a broad preference for the saucer of mud over a pot of gold, Piller wins it fair and square. A broad preference can be acquired by decision. In this case, Piller acquires by decision the disposition to choose the saucer of mud rather than a pot of gold. This disposition is the prize-winning broad preference.

However, if the prize is awarded for having an ordinary preference for the saucer of mud rather than a pot of gold, Piller is not entitled to it. He may say 'I want the mud, not the gold. Please!', but that utterance has to be understood as a pressing request to be given the mud. I do not suggest he is dishonest in making it. However, if he really meant to assert that he wants the saucer of mud more than a pot of gold, I am sorry to say I would not believe him. His sorry tale makes it plain that gold is all he wants; he has no desire for the mud. His decision to choose the saucer of mud does not give him an ordinary preference for the mud over a pot of gold.

You can acquire some broad preferences by making a decision, because those broad preferences are intentions. Those broad preferences are not ordinary preferences. On the other hand, all ordinary preferences are broad preferences. They satisfy the definition: an ordinary preference for a over b is a mental state that typically causes you to choose a over b. But not just any mental state with this property is an ordinary preference. Evidently more conditions need to be added to the

---

[8] See Piller (2006). I have no quarrel with Piller's conclusion that there can be attitude-based reasons for a preference, even an ordinary preference. Just because you cannot choose to have an ordinary preference, it does not follow there are no attitude-based reasons for you to have it.

definition of a broad preference if we are to arrive at a correct definition of an ordinary preference.

In "Preference, deliberation and satisfaction" (Olsaretti 2006), Philip Pettit argues like me that the concept of broad preference is broader that our ordinary concept. He also thinks that more conditions must be added to the definition. He mentions conditions on the mental state's collateral connections with other mental states. The axioms of decision theory illustrate the sort of conditions he has in mind. But Pettit's objection to broad preference is different from mine. If a creature's behaviour is very chaotic, we might not be able to recognize the creature as having preferences at all. So even if it was in one particular state that met the definition of a broad preference, we might not count that state as truly a preference. That is Pettit's concern, and it is a real one. But only minimal further conditions are required for this reason. If a pigeon nearly always circles to the left, we have no difficulty in attributing to it a preference for circling to the left rather than the right, even if the rest of its behaviour is fairly chaotic. Certainly, we may have preferences that are very far from satisfying the axioms of decision theory.

To define a preference in the ordinary sense, we need to add conditions of a different sort from Pettit's. They need to distinguish a preference from an intention, and they will have to do so by specifying its functional role. As I say, this is difficult to do, and I shall not try to do it here. I hope I have said enough to separate the ordinary concept of preference from the broad one, by recalling our ordinary understanding of the difference between a preference and an intention.

8.5   Second-order reasoning for broad preferences

The central question of this paper is whether there is an activity of reasoning by means of which you can bring yourself to satisfy requirements of rationality on preferences. Now we have two concepts of preference, this question divides into two. Can you reason with broad preferences? Can you reason with narrow preferences? I shall start with broad ones.

The broad concept of preference is an artificial, theoretical one. Nevertheless, it seems to be the one most authors have had in mind when they consider rational requirements on preferences. The most popular defence of the requirement *Transitivity* is the money-pump argument, which is directed at broad preferences. Here is the argument, put briefly.[9] Suppose you prefer a to b and you prefer b to c, but

---

[9] Details of the argument are debated. The most convincing version of it appears in Rabinowicz (2000).

you do not prefer *a* to *c*. For simplicity, assume that your preferences are complete, so that, since you do not prefer *a* to *c*, either you prefer *c* to *a* or you are indifferent between *a* and *c*. Suppose you initially possess *c*. Now a dealer offers to swap *b* for your *c*, provided you pay her some small fee for making the transaction. Since you prefer *b* to *c*, you agree if the fee is small enough. Now you possess *b*. Next, this dealer offers to swap *a* for your *c*, again for a small fee. If the fee is small enough, you again agree. Finally, she offers to swap *c* for your *a*, this time without a fee. Since you either prefer *c* to *a* or are indifferent between the two, you are willing to make this transaction too. If you do make it, you end up possessing *c*, having handed over two small fees. You are back where you started, but poorer. It seems irrational to have preferences that allow you to be exploited in this way. That is the money-pump argument.

In this story, it is your dispositions to choose that allow you to be exploited. These dispositions constitute your broad preferences. Your ordinary preferences do not come into the argument. So the money-pump argument applies to broad preferences and not ordinary ones. It is an example of a class of arguments known as 'pragmatic arguments', which are supposed to demonstrate that rationality imposes various requirements on your preferences. All of them are aimed at broad preferences.

Because a broad preference can be an intention, you may be able to acquire a broad preference by making a decision. This opens the possibility that the second-order model of reasoning can work for broad preferences. That is, you may be able to reason your way from a belief in the requirement itself to satisfying the requirement. Since I have already set out the steps of the second-order model in the context of theoretical reasoning, I need only retrace them very quickly here. Suppose that, in the broad sense, you prefer biking to walking, and you prefer walking to driving, but you do not prefer biking to driving. You do not satisfy *Transitivity*. But suppose you believe in the requirement of transitivity itself in this instance: you believe rationality requires you to prefer biking to driving if you prefer biking to walking and walking to driving. (Perhaps you have been convinced by the money-pump argument.) Suppose indeed you have the normative belief that you ought to prefer biking to driving if you prefer biking to walking and walking to driving. By kratic reasoning, you might be able to form the intention of preferring biking to driving if you prefer biking to walking and walking to driving. The content of this intention is a conditional proposition, but since you actually satisfy the antecedent of the conditional – you prefer biking to walking and walking to driving – you may be able to narrow the intention down to a simple intention to prefer biking to driving. If so, you now intend to have a particular preference.

At the corresponding point in my discussion of theoretical reasoning, you had arrived at the intention to believe the snow will melt. There, I said this intention is ineffective, because intending to believe something cannot normally bring you to believe it, except by using an external means. But it seems that your intention to prefer biking to driving may be effective; it may cause you to have this preference, without your using an external means.

It is an intention to have a broad preference: to be in a mental state that would typically cause you to choose biking were you to have a choice between biking and driving only. You will have this broad preference if you intend to choose biking if ever you have a choice between biking and driving only. And that state of intention seems to be one you can put yourself into simply by deciding to choose biking if ever you have a choice between biking and driving only. So it seems your intention to prefer biking to driving may cause you to prefer biking to driving, without your using an external means. The only means you require is to make a decision. This is a mental act, and it may therefore form part of a reasoning process.

That was quick. I have apparently mapped out a complete route whereby second-order reasoning could bring you to satisfy the requirement *Transitivity*, by acquiring the preference you need in order to satisfy it. However, there are several questionable steps along the route. In Section 8.2, where I developed the second-order model of reasoning, I made questionable assumptions as concessions to the model. So I do not insist that the second-order model works for broad preferences; I simply cannot rule it out. Since broad preferences are not preferences as we ordinarily understand them, I pass quickly on to those that are.

8.6   First-order reasoning with ordinary preferences

For ordinary preferences, the second-order model can quickly be ruled out. You cannot acquire an ordinary preference by making a decision, without using an external means. This is one of the characteristics that distinguish an ordinary preference from other broad preferences. It follows that second-order reasoning will not work for ordinary preferences. The argument is the same as the one I gave for second-order theoretical reasoning.

What about first-order reasoning? First-order reasoning for preferences would be reasoning with preferences, about the contents of preferences, rather than reasoning about preferences. Is there such a thing?

The account I gave of first-order reasoning for beliefs was special to beliefs. If we are to extend it to states other than beliefs, we shall need a separate account for each state. We need one for preferences.

There is a general difficulty in the way of understanding how you can reason with states other than beliefs, operating on their contents in the way first-order reasoning requires. Beliefs have a special feature that allows you to do this sort of reasoning. When you say to yourself that it is raining, you express your mental state of belief. You also, in a different sense, express the content of that belief. You say that it is raining, which is to express the proposition that it is raining, which is the content of your belief. So you express the belief and its content together.

First-order reasoning requires this sort of double expression. It is reasoning with mental states, and you have to express those states in order to reason with them. But as well as that, reasoning is about the contents of the mental states. You need those contents before your mind, which means you have to present them to yourself, or express them to yourself. So your expression of your states also has to express the contents of those states.

But at first sight, few mental states share with beliefs the property that you can express them and their content together. Consider a desire, for example. We normally take a desire to have a content, and most philosophers take its content to be a proposition. Suppose you want to be loved. Then according to the common view, the content of your desire is the proposition that you are loved. But suppose you expressed this content by saying 'I am loved'. Then you would not be expressing the desire. If you are expressing any mental state of yours, it would have to be a belief that you are loved. You can only express this belief if you have it, and you may or may not have it, but at any rate you are not expressing a desire to be loved. So you are not putting yourself in a position to reason with your desire to be loved.

A preference is a more complicated example. We can take a preference to be a relation between two propositions, and we can take that pair of propositions to be its content. Suppose you prefer walking to driving. We can take this as a preference for the proposition that you walk over the proposition that you drive. What could you say to yourself to express this preference? Evidently neither of the propositions that constitute its content. And to say that you prefer walking to driving does not express the preference either. At best it would be expressing the belief that you have the preference, if you happen to have that belief. Consequently, it seems you cannot reason with preferences. That is the difficulty.

The difficulty arises over reasoning with all mental states apart from beliefs. But there is a way to overcome it. We can revise our notion of the content of a mental state. Philosophers commonly assume that mental states of different types can have the same content, which they take to be a proposition. So you might have a belief that you are loved, or a desire to be loved, and either state would have as its content the proposition that you are loved. Either state has the same content, but in the two different cases you stand in a different relation to the content – a believing relation in one and a desiring relation in the other. In the complicated case of a preference, you stand in a preferring relation to a pair of propositions. That is the common view.

The alternative is to take the content of a mental state to be a proposition together with a mark of some sort, which marks the type of state it is.[10] In this way the differences in mental states can be absorbed into the contents of the states. For instance, if you believe you are loved, the content of your belief is the proposition that you are loved together with a belief mark. If you desire to be loved, the content of your desire is this proposition together with a desire mark.

How do we refer to these contents? I shall explain in a moment how we do so in English. But it will be clearer if I start with an artificial language. The language must have the resources to designate marks; I shall give the name 'markers' to the linguistic items that do this job. Let the marker for belief be 'yes' and the marker for desire be 'nice'. If you believe you are loved, you might designate the content of your belief by the artificial sentence 'I am loved – yes.' If I also believe you are loved, I have a belief with the same content as yours, but I would designate it using the second person sentence 'You are loved – yes.' If you want to be loved, you might say 'I am loved – nice.' If I want you to be loved, I have a desire with the same content as yours. I might say 'You are loved – nice.'

A preference is again more complicated. If you prefer walking to driving, the content of your state is the pair of propositions that you walk and that you drive, together with a preference mark. You might designate it by the artificial sentence 'I walk – rather – I drive.'

If you say this sentence to yourself, you are expressing the preference, and you are also expressing the content of the preference. In this way, a mark gives a preference the special feature that a belief has: expressing the content of the preference is also expressing the preference itself. So, when you express the preference, you make its content available to be reasoned about. Preferences become available for reasoning with.

---

[10] Examples of this idea appear in Hare (1952) and Grice (2001).

The purpose of marks is to distinguish between different sort of mental states. One sort of state can be distinguished by the absence of a mark, provided all the others have marks. It is convenient to give beliefs this special status. So from here on, I shall drop the 'yes' marker, and take the content of a belief to be a proposition without a mark.

Marks give us the beginning of an account of first-order reasoning with mental states other than beliefs. Your reasoning will be a process in which you express your mental states to yourself using marked sentences, operate on their contents and emerge with a new mental state. But this is only the very beginning of an account. The next thing that needs to be done is to make the account realistic. If we are really to use marked sentences in our reasoning, we must have actual marked sentences in our language. Do we?

We do. Natural languages can express beliefs and their contents. They also contain devices that allow them to express many other mental states and their contents. If their contents are indeed propositions with marks, as I am assuming, some of these devices are what I called markers. English uses special constructions or special moods of verbs to serve as markers.

For example, a desire is marked by an optative construction. Robert Browning said 'Oh, to be in England now that April's there!' This optative sentence designates the proposition that Browning is in England now in April, together with the mark for desire. When Browning said to himself 'Oh, to be in England now that April's there', he expressed his desire to be in England, and also the content of his desire, understood as a proposition with a mark. Translated into my artificial language, he said 'I am in England now that April's there – nice.'

As Jonathan Dancy pointed out to me, English has a marker for preference too. The sentence 'Rather walk than drive' is the English equivalent of my artificial 'I walk – rather – I drive.' It designates the pair of propositions that you walk and that you drive, with the mark for preference.

On the face of it, this construction puts you in a position to reason with your preferences. Suppose you prefer walking to driving and biking to walking, but you do not prefer biking to driving. You do not satisfy the requirement *Transitivity*. But you may say to yourself:

> *Rather walk than drive.*
> *Rather bike than walk.*
> *So, rather bike than drive.*

When you say each of the first two sentences, you are expressing a preference you have. Saying these sentences to yourself causes you to have a new preference that you did not previously have. By the time you say the third sentence to yourself, you are also expressing this new preference. By causing you to have it, this process has brought you to satisfy *Transitivity*. Intuitively, this seems a plausible instance of reasoning with preferences.

The contents of your preferences are pairs of propositions, with marks attached. I can designate them using sentences in my artificial language. Since I am speaking of you, I shall put them in the second person. The contents are:

> You walk – rather – you drive.
> You bike – rather – you walk.
> You bike – rather – you drive.

The process I have described satisfies the description of first-order reasoning that I gave in Section 8.3. It is a process whereby some of your mental states give rise to another mental state; the mental states involved have contents; in the course of the reasoning you say to yourself the propositions that constitute these contents, and you reason about these contents. So on the face of it, this is a genuine example of first-order reasoning with preferences.

However, much more needs to be done to make that conclusion secure. For one thing, we need to generalize: are there similar processes that can bring you to satisfy other requirements on preferences? For another, can we find a criterion for correct reasoning with preferences, as opposed to incorrect reasoning? Certainly, if this is to be genuine reasoning, there must be such a distinction.

8.7   Preferences and beliefs about betterness

But I think the most difficult challenge is to demonstrate that this is really reasoning with *preferences*. When you use a sentence like 'Rather walk than drive' you may well be expressing a belief about betterness, and not a preference – in this case, the belief that walking is better than driving. The betterness in question need not be absolute betterness from the point of view of the universe. It might be betterness for you, or betterness relative to your point of view, or something else.

If your sentences express beliefs rather than preferences, the contents of the reasoning I have described would be the sequence of propositions:

> It is better that you walk than that you drive.
> It is better that you bike than that you walk.
> So it is better that you bike than that you drive

The process that proceeds by your expressing these propositions to yourself constitutes correct reasoning, because the betterness relation is transitive. If it is better that you walk than that you drive, and better that you bike than that you walk, it is better that you bike than that you drive. But this is theoretical reasoning with beliefs. It is not reasoning with preferences. Perhaps the pattern of reasoning I presented in Section 8.6 is always theoretical reasoning; perhaps it is never reasoning with preferences, as I suggested.

What is the difference between a preference and a belief about betterness? Not very much, possibly. A belief about betterness may satisfy the definition of broad preference that I gave in Section 8.4: a belief that a is better than b may be a mental state that would typically cause you to choose a were you to have a choice between a and b only. I explained that, to define preference in its ordinary sense, we would have to add conditions to this definition of broad preference. I explained that conditions are needed to separate a preference for a over b from an intention to choose a rather than b. It now emerges that we also need conditions to separate a preference for a over b from a belief that a is better than b. But these conditions will be hard to find. The functional role of a belief about betterness may not be very different from the functional role of a preference; it will be hard to separate them.

A belief about betterness does differ from a preference in one respect. It is a state that has a content that is a proposition. The contents of beliefs, being propositions, stand in logical relations to each other. The logical relations among contents induce rational requirements on beliefs. An example is the requirement *Modus ponens,* which derives from the logical relation among propositions known as 'modus ponens'. Moreover, we have reasoning processes for beliefs that allow us to follow up these logical relations, and thereby bring ourselves to satisfy some of the rational requirements on beliefs. These facts are special to beliefs, and seem to separate them from preferences.

But we commonly think there are rational requirements on preferences too, and I have been assuming so in this paper. Moreover, I am now investigating the idea that we have reasoning processes for preferences that allow us to bring ourselves to satisfy some of these requirements. If these things are true, it further reduces the functional difference between preferences and beliefs about betterness. Both are governed by rational requirements and, for both, these rational requirements can sometimes be satisfied by reasoning.

Furthermore, there is a case for thinking that the rational requirements on preferences, if they truly exist, derive from the logical relations among propositions about betterness. I take this point from

Amartya Sen.[11] Why does rationality require your preferences to be transitive? I have mentioned the money-pump argument, but here is another possible explanation. Rationality requires you to prefer *a* to *b* if and only if you believe *a* is better than *b*. And rationality requires you to believe *a* is better than *c* if you believe *a* is better than *b* and *b* is better than *c*. And this is so in turn because, as a matter of logic, if *a* is better than *b*, and *b* is better than *c*, then *a* is better than *c*. I do not insist this is the correct explanation of the *Transitivity* requirement, but it is a plausible one.

The upshot is that it is hard to distinguish the functional roles of a preference and a belief about betterness. This explains why many philosophers who are noncognitivist about value think that a belief about betterness is indeed nothing other than a preference. In so far as the two converge, I am inclined in the opposite direction: a preference may be nothing other than a belief about goodness. It may turn out that reasoning with preferences is really nothing other than reasoning with beliefs.

Acknowledgements

This paper is reprinted with amendments from *Preferences and Well-Being*, edited by Serena Olsaretti, Cambridge University Press, 2006. It has been greatly improved as a result of extremely helpful comments I received from Krister Bykvist and Serena Olsaretti. Part of it was written while I held a Leverhulme Major Research Fellowship; I thank the Leverhulme Trust for its generous support.

References

Bennett, Jonathan 1990. 'Why is belief involuntary?', *Analysis*, **50** (2): 87–107.
Bratman, Michael E. 1987. *Intention, Plans and Practical Reason*, Cambridge, MA: Harvard University Press.
Broome, John 2005. 'Does rationality give us reasons?', *Philosophical Issues*, **15** (1): 321–37.
    2007. 'Wide or narrow scope', *Mind*, **116**: 359–70.
Carroll, Lewis 1895. 'What the tortoise said to Achilles', *Mind*, **4**: 278–80.
Grice, Paul 2001. *Aspects of Reason* (with an introduction by Richard Warner), Oxford University Press.
Hare, R. M. 1952. *The Language of Morals*, Oxford University Press.
Harman, Gilbert 1986. *Change in View: Principles of Reasoning*, Cambridge, MA: MIT Press.
Kolodny, Niko 2005. 'Why be rational?', *Mind*, **114**: 509–63.

---

[11] Sen (1993).

Olsaretti, Serena (ed.) 2006. *Preferences and Well-Being* (Royal Institute of Philosophy Supplements, 81), Cambridge University Press.

Pettit, Philip 2006. 'Preference, deliberation and satisfaction', in Olsaretti (ed.), *Preferences and Well-Being*, pp. 131–54.

Piller, Christian 2006. 'Content-related and attitude-related reasons for preferences', in Olsaretti (ed.), *Preferences and Well-Being*, pp. 155–82.

Rabinowicz, Wlodek 2000. 'Money pump with foresight', in Almeida, Michael J. (ed.), *Imperceptible Harms and Benefits*, Dordrecht: Kluwer, pp. 123–54.

Scanlon, T. M. 1998. *What We Owe to Each Other*, Cambridge, MA: Harvard University Press.

Sen, Amartya 1970, *Collective Choice and Social Welfare*, San Francisco: Holden-Day.

1993, 'Internal consistency of choice', *Econometrica*, **61**: 495–521.

Williams, Bernard 1973. 'Deciding to believe', in his *Problems of the Self*, Cambridge University Press, pp. 136–51.

9 Conceptions of individual rights and freedom in welfare economics: a re-examination

Prasanta K. Pattanaik and Yongsheng Xu

9.1 Introduction

Historically, much of normative economics has been guided by welfarism, i.e. the ethical principle that the welfare evaluation of alternative social policies should be based exclusively on their effects on the utilities of the individuals concerned. Though issues relating to non-utility aspects of social policies such as individual rights, freedom, and fairness are often figured into such welfaristic evaluations, they enter the evaluation process indirectly as instruments affecting the utilities of the individuals involved. Their independent status in assessing social policies is ignored by welfarism. In recent years, however, there has been growing recognition on the part of economists that welfarism constitutes a restrictive framework for normative economics, and that non-utility information, as well as information about individual utilities, must be taken into account independently in the evaluation of social policies. For example, when a certain legislation concerning, say, security, is proposed, the effects on individuals' utilities are certainly legitimate concerns. At the same time, considerations of personal liberty and individual rights to privacy also play an important and independent role in evaluating such legislation.

Among the non-utility concerns that often figure in debates about alternative social policies, two, individual rights and freedom, stand out prominently. Thanks to the pioneering contributions of Sen (1970a; 1970b; 1985; 1987; 1988), both individual rights and freedom have received much attention from welfare economists over the last three decades or so, and several models have been constructed to incorporate them in the formal analysis in welfare economics. The purpose of this chapter is to review critically some of these models. Our focus will be on the formal formulations of the concepts of rights and freedom as such rather than the specific results derived with those formulations. In particular, we shall discuss whether these formulations are consistent with our intuition about rights and freedom. Since our review will often highlight conceptual shortcomings of some of the formal models of rights and freedom, we hasten to add that, in our opinion, these models constitute one of the most exciting recent developments in welfare economics. Their shortcomings only show that, despite the progress made so far, much more work still needs to be done to fill the analytical gaps and remove the ambiguities. This is not entirely surprising, given the complexity and richness of the concepts of individual rights and freedom.

The plan of the chapter is as follows. In Section 9.2, we discuss some of the intuitive aspects of rights and freedom, which will be useful for our analysis in subsequent sections. In Section 9.3, we classify the formal formulations of individual rights and freedom into four categories: (i) outcome-based and preference-dependent formulations; (ii) outcome-based and preference-free formulations; (iii) action-based and preference-dependent formulations; and (iv) action-based and preference-free formulations. In Section 9.4.1, we discuss the classical outcome-based and preference-dependent formulation of rights (we call it the social choice formulation) in welfare economics. Section 9.4.2 discusses the action-based and preference-free game form formulation of rights. Section 9.5 is devoted to models of individual freedom. We conclude in Section 9.6.

9.2   Individual rights and freedom: some intuitive remarks

9.2.1   Individual rights

Individual rights can take various forms. In the literature, there have been numerous attempts to classify individual rights into different categories according to alternative criteria (see, among others, Hohfeld [1923], Kanger and Kanger [1966], Feinberg [1973], Fleurbaey and van Hees [2000], and van Hees [1995]). We shall not try to give a detailed account of such classificatory principles. Instead, we shall highlight only a few of these principles, which will be helpful in our subsequent discussions.

The rights of an individual always impose obligations on other agents either explicitly or implicitly. Intuitively, these obligations may be of two distinct types. First, a right may require agents other than the right-holder not to take certain specified actions; Feinberg (1973) calls these *negative rights*. For example, an individual's right to criticize the government imposes an obligation on other agents, including the government, not to penalize the individual in certain ways for criticizing the government. Thus, this right requires other agents not to take certain actions with the intention of punishing the right-holder for doing something that he is permitted to do under the right. Sometimes, however, a negative right may simply require other agents not to take certain actions without any reference to the motivation behind those actions. Thus, the right not to be arrested without a proper warrant simply prevents the state from arresting the individual without a proper warrant irrespective of the motivation the state may have for such arrest. The distinction between the two examples of negative rights given above is important for our purpose. In the first example (the right to criticize the government), the prohibition of certain actions of the other agents is contingent on their motivation; in the second example (the right not to be arrested without a proper warrant), the prohibition of certain actions of the other agents is not linked to any motivation behind those actions.

In contrast to negative rights, we have what Feinberg (1973) calls *positive rights*. Positive rights impose on other agents the obligation to do certain specific things.[1] These obligations typically take the form of fulfilling a claim of the right-holder rather than providing her immunities as corresponding obligations under negative rights do. Thus, the right of children to have access to free elementary education imposes on the state the obligation to establish free elementary schools at a reasonable distance from children. Note that this obligation is not contingent on any specific action of the children or their parents. On the other hand, the positive right of a creditor to get the loan repaid on demand at any time after a certain stipulated period requires the debtor to repay the loan if the creditor demands such repayment at any time after the stipulated period. Sometimes the same right may have the features of positive rights and negative rights simultaneously. The right of individuals to get certain types of information from the state imposes on the state the obligation to supply the relevant information, when the individual requests it, as well as the obligation not to harass the individual for requesting the information.

Another helpful distinction, due to Feinberg (1973), is the distinction between *active rights*, which give the right-holder the power to do certain specific things, and *passive rights*, which do not give any power to the right-holder to do anything specific. The right to criticize the government is an active right, while the right not to be arrested without a proper warrant, which just offers the individual immunity against a specific invasive action of the state, is a passive right. It is important

---

[1] Note that the distinction between negative and positive rights is an intuitive distinction rather than a logical distinction: after all, the obligation to do *a* can be expressed as the obligation not to do not-*a*, and the obligation not to do *a* can be expressed as the obligation to do not-*a*.

to note that most active rights that one can think of impose on agents other than the right-holder the obligation of not taking certain invasive actions with the motive of penalizing the right-holder for doing things that the right authorizes her to do.

9.2.2   Individual freedom

In our everyday conversation, when we talk about the freedom of someone, say individual i, we typically talk about i's freedom to do/to be/not to do/not to be something, say, a. Often, our statement about i's freedom to do/to be a has explicit reference to the absence of some specific constraint or class of constraints. Thus, we may say that i is free from financial problems to pursue a career as an artist. Sometimes such explicit reference to the absence of constraints may not figure in our statement about i's freedom, but, in such cases, the absence of some constraint or class of constraints is typically understood. As MacCallum (1967: 314) writes, "Whenever the freedom of some agent or agents is in question, it is always freedom from some constraint or restriction on, interference with, or barrier to doing, not doing, becoming, or not becoming something." Let i be some agent, b be certain preventing conditions involving constraints, restrictions, interferences, or barriers, and z denote something specific that one can do/be. Following MacCallum, one can then regard freedom as a triadic relation: i is free from b to do/not to do/to be/not to be z.

In the general framework of MacCallum, one can view Berlin's (1969) famous distinction between negative freedom and positive freedom as being based on the type of constraints that one may wish to emphasize. The so-called negative freedoms of an individual focus on the absence of constraints imposed by other human agents, including the state. Thus, if i does not face any constraint imposed by other agents, including the state, that prevents him from traveling abroad, then i is said to enjoy the negative freedom to travel abroad. It is, however, possible that, while enjoying the negative freedom to travel abroad, i is not actually able to travel abroad because i does not have enough money to travel abroad. i is said to enjoy the positive freedom to travel abroad if and only if there are no constraints, whether or not imposed by other agents, that prevent i from traveling abroad.[2] As we shall see later,

---

[2] While the basic idea underlying Berlin's (1969) distinction between positive freedom and negative freedom is reasonably clear, there can be considerable ambiguity about whether a particular constraint is imposed by other agents. Suppose the government deliberately chooses fiscal and monetary policies that are known to generate unemployment, and individual i and thousands of other people become unemployed

welfare economists have tended to conceive an individual's freedom as the freedom to choose an outcome from the set of all outcomes feasible for her, where the notion of feasibility of an outcome takes into account all possible constraints including those imposed by other agents. In that sense, welfare economists seem to have concentrated on positive freedom in their analysis.

9.2.3   Individual rights and freedom: a contrast and comparison

There is considerable similarity between our everyday language relating to active individual rights and that relating to freedom. We talk about an individual's freedom to do, be ... x, just as we talk about an individual's right to do, be ... x. There are, of course, important differences between rights and freedom. An individual's right implies obligations on the part of other agents to do or not to do certain things, but an individual's freedom does not necessarily imply any such obligations of others. Thus, the freedom that warlords often enjoy in strife-torn areas to kill people does not imply any moral, social, or legal obligation of anybody else not to interfere with such killings; freedom need not have any basis in morality, law, or social conventions. Rights and freedom are distinct in this respect. It is, therefore, possible that an individual may have very few rights but much freedom. On the other hand, it is also possible that an individual may have extensive rights but very little positive freedom.[3]

9.3   Formulations of individual rights and freedom: a classificatory scheme

At the cost of some oversimplification, one can think of two alternative principles for classifying the various formulations of individual rights and freedom that we find in the literature. First, we have the distinction between outcome-based (OB) formulations and action-based (AB) formulations. Second, we have the distinction between preference-dependent (PD) formulations and preference-free (PF) formulations.

Consider first the distinction between OB and AB formulations. In the OB approach to the rights of an individual, the focus is on the social states that should or should not emerge as the social outcome in

---

as a consequence. In that case, how should one view the constraint imposed on i by his lack of income? We would be inclined to view it as a constraint imposed by the government.

[3] It would not be difficult to come up with real-life examples of societies with such combinations of individual freedom and rights.

a given situation, given the rights under consideration. In contrast, in the AB approach to an individual's rights, the focus is on the action that the individual may or may not take and the actions that others must or must not take vis-à-vis the individual. The distinction between OB and AB approaches, however, should not be drawn in too sharp a fashion: the possible social outcomes do figure in AB formulations (see Section 4.1), and it is possible to transform certain AB formulations to corresponding OB formulations in a fairly straightforward fashion.[4] One can make a similar distinction between OB and AB formulations in the context of freedom. In OB formulations of individual freedom, an individual's freedom is reflected in the set of all mutually exclusive feasible outcomes available to the individual. Thus, the OB formulation of freedom visualizes an individual's freedom as being reflected in the set of outcomes from which the individual can choose any outcome that she likes. In contrast, the AB approach to freedom recognizes that often the individual may be in a position to choose one out of several actions but may not be in a position to choose an outcome since the outcome may be determined by the actions chosen by other agents as well as by the primary individual, i.e. the individual whose freedom is under consideration. Again, the distinction between OB and AB approaches to freedom should not be taken to imply that the outcomes are considered irrelevant in the AB approach. The outcomes do matter in the AB approach. Nevertheless, when outcomes for the primary individual can be affected by the actions of other individuals, it is no longer possible to conceive the primary individual's freedom in terms of her ability to choose any one of several available outcomes. Instead, one has to consider the entire structure of actions and resulting outcomes to capture the opportunities available to an individual.

In some formulations of individual rights and freedom, the notion of preferences over the outcomes plays an important role. We shall call these formulations preference-dependent (PD) formulations. On the other hand, we also have formulations of individual rights and freedom where preferences over outcomes do not play any role whatsoever. We call these preference-free (PF) formulations.

Combining the two classificatory principles that we have considered above, we can, in principle, think of four different types of formulations of individual rights or freedom, namely, OB-PD, OB-PF, AB-PD, and AB-PF. Historically, however, the discussion of individual rights in the theory of social choice and welfare seems to have been dominated

---

[4] See, for example, Gärdenfors (1981), whose outcome-based formulation of rights represents basically the same intuition as the AB formulation of Nozick (1974), Sugden (1985a), and Gaertner, Pattanaik, and Suzumura (1992) among others.

Table 9.1. *Formulations of individual rights*

	PD	PF
OB	Sen (1970a; 1970b)	Gärdenfors (1981)
AB		Nozick (1974), Sugden (1985a)
		Gaertner, Pattanaik, and Suzumura (1992)

Table 9.2. *Formulations of freedom*

	PD	PF
OB	Jones and Sugden (1982), Sen (1988)	Jones and Sugden (1982)
	Foster (1992)	Pattanaik and Xu (1990)
AB		

by the OB-PD and AB-PF approaches. Similarly, much of the discussion of individual freedom in the theory of social choice and welfare seems to have centered around OB-PD and OB-PF formulations. In the two tables above, we give examples of contributions in some of these categories in the context of individual rights as well individual freedom.

Some of the cells in the two tables are blank, indicating that we do not have any existing formulation in the relevant categories. We shall argue later that some of these categories may be useful in capturing certain aspects of rights and freedom.

9.4   Formulations of individual rights

9.4.1   *OB formulations of individual rights*

The original formulation of outcome-based and preference-dependent (OB-PD) models of individual rights is due to Sen (1970a; 1970b; 1992). Sen (1970a; 1970b) has articulated the notion of individual rights in a framework that used the notion of social preference or social ranking over social outcomes as a primitive concept. Sen (1992) uses a somewhat different framework, where social choice rather than social preference is the primitive concept. The intuitive contents of both the formal frameworks are the same, but, for our exposition of Sen's basic ideas, we shall find it more convenient to use the language of social choice. We shall refer to Sen's (1992) articulation of the idea of individual rights in terms of social choice as the social choice formulation of individual rights.[5]

Sen (1992) starts with the notion of a social decision rule, which, for every profile of individual preference orderings over social outcomes and every non-empty set, A, of (mutually exclusive) possible social outcomes, specifies exactly one non-empty subset of A. Given the profile of individual preferences and a set, A, of possible outcomes, the non-empty subset, B, of A, specified by the social decision rule is to be interpreted as the choice set or the set of socially chosen alternatives in the following sense: given the preference profile, the alternative finally chosen by the society from A should lie in B and it does not ethically matter which of the alternatives in B the society finally chooses. Sen (1992) then introduces a formulation of individual rights, which articulates a necessary condition for an individual to have a right. According to Sen, an individual, i, has a right only if there exist at least two distinct social outcomes, x and y, such that

if i strictly prefers x to y, then the society must not choose y from any set of feasible social outcomes that contains both x and y (i.e., given i's strict preference for x over y, y must not be socially chosen when x is feasible), and, similarly, if i strictly prefers y to x, then the society must not choose x from any set of feasible social outcomes that contains both x and y.... (1)

When i, x, and y are such that ($y \neq x$) and (1) holds, we say that i is *globally decisive over* (x, y).[6] Thus, for an individual to have a right in the sense of Sen, she must be globally decisive over some pair of social outcomes. The intended interpretation of x and y is that they differ only with respect to some aspects of social outcomes that relate to the "private domain" of i. Thus, intuitively, Sen's articulation of an individual's rights proceeds through two steps. First, a social state is viewed as consisting of two groups of features. The first group consists of features that relate to the private domain of some individual or other. The second group comprises all features that are taken to be in the "public domain." Secondly, in Sen's formulation, an individual's right is visualized as a constraint on the social choice of outcomes insofar as, if an individual i has a right in Sen's sense, he must be globally decisive over some pair of social outcomes; the interpretation of these two social outcomes being that they differ only with respect to some feature that

---

[5] Note that the substantive content of what we say below about the social choice formulation of individual rights applies also to Sen's (1970a; 1970b) formulation in terms of social preference.

[6] The qualification "globally" is intended to indicate that (1) applies to all sets of social outcomes containing both x and y. Later we introduce the notion of local decisiveness over a pair of social outcomes.

comes within i's private domain. Sen formulates his necessary condition for i to have a right in a very weak fashion by requiring that i be globally decisive over at least one pair of social outcomes. However, it seems consistent with Sen's intuition to strengthen the condition for i to have a right by requiring that i be globally decisive over all (x, y) such that x and y differ only with respect to some matter in the private domain of i.

To illustrate the social choice formulation of individual rights, we consider the following example, which is due to Sen (1970a; 1970b). Consider a society consisting of two individuals, 1 and 2. There is a single copy of a certain book. The book can be read by just one individual or can be read by no one. There are three possible social states (for simplicity, we assume that all other features of social states are fixed):

$(r, nr) = $ (1 reads the book, 2 does not read the book);

$(nr, r) = $ (1 does not read the book, 2 reads the book);

and

$(nr, nr) = $ (1 does not read the book, 2 does not read the book).

For any given individual, reading or not reading the book is assumed to be a matter in the private domain of that individual. The social states (r, nr) and (nr, nr) differ only with respect to 1's private feature insofar as 1 reads the book in (r, nr) and does not read the book in (nr, nr), while 2 does not read the book in either of these two social outcomes. Similarly, the social states (nr, r) and (nr, nr) differ only with respect to 2's private features. Suppose each individual has a right to read or not read the book. Then, consistent with Sen's intuition, 1 will be globally decisive over (r, nr) and (nr, nr). Similarly, 2 must be globally decisive over $((nr, r),(nr, nr))$. Suppose further that we have the following preferences of the two individuals. 1 ranks (nr, r) highest, (r, nr) next, and (nr, nr) lowest ("it's really an excellent book and I would like to see 2 read it, and it would be a huge waste if no one reads it"), while 2 ranks (nr, nr) highest, (nr, r) next, and (r, nr) lowest ("it's a terrible book, and no one should read it, but, if someone has to read it, it'd better be me"). Now suppose all the three social outcomes are feasible. Then given the above preferences, and given the right, as Sen visualizes it, of each individual to read or not to read the book, a society respecting the rights of the two individuals must reject both (nr, nr) and (nr, r) and therefore choose only (r, nr).

To assess the intuitive basis of this OB-PD formulation, it may be helpful to consider first the interpretation of the notion of a group decision rule as defined earlier. One possible interpretation of a group decision rule can be in terms of the choices that a social planner would make from different sets of social outcomes. We shall call this interpretation Interpretation I of a group decision rule. A second interpretation (call it Interpretation II) can be in terms of a (partly) decentralized decision-making process where the social planner or the government takes decisions regarding the public features of the social state and the individuals choose their respective private features in a decentralized fashion. Whether the individuals take their decisions before or after the government takes its decisions regarding the public features can be an important consideration for some purposes but is not crucial for us here. So, for the purpose of Interpretation II of a group decision rule, we shall make the (restrictive) assumption that the individuals choose their respective private features after the government chooses the public features and they have full information about the choices made by the government.

It seems to us that the social choice formulation of individual rights was heavily influenced by Interpretation I of a group decision rule. Consider again the example of reading the book, which has played such a prominent role in the earlier literature on rights in social choice theory. Assume that $\{(r, nr),(nr, r),(nr, nr)\}$ is the set of possible outcomes. Since there is only one book which only one individual can read and it is possible for either individual to read the book, the problem of the society's choice from this set of feasible outcomes can hardly be visualized in terms of the individuals' autonomous and decentralized decision-making with respect to reading or not reading the book. It is, in fact, a classical allocation problem, where a social planner has to assign a single indivisible unit of a commodity, to exactly one of several persons.

However, the very interpretation of a group decision rule as the choices to be made by a social planner or ethical observer from alternative sets of outcomes, given the individual preferences, seems to run counter to the intuitive core of a wide class of individual rights. This is particularly true of individual rights to do or be whatever they like in their "private" lives, such as the right of an individual to practice the religion of her choice, to be a vegetarian or a non-vegetarian, to read or not to read a particular book, to choose the color or style of her dress, to maintain a political diary, and so on (these are precisely the rights that received so much attention in the early discussion of individual rights in social choice theory). This is also true of many other rights that do not invoke the notion of the private life of an individual, such as the right to criticize the government, to form or join a trade union, to vote, and to move freely in one's country. It is difficult to think of any of these rights outside the framework of autonomous and decentralized decision-making by individuals with respect to certain features of the social state.

The difficulties with the social choice formulation of individual rights, however, goes beyond any specific interpretation of a group decision rule. Irrespective of how we interpret a group decision rule, the social choice formulation turns out to be inconsistent with our intuition about the rights referred to in the preceding paragraph. Gaertner, Pattanaik, and Suzumura (1992) illustrate this inconsistency with the help of a simple example. In Gaertner, Pattanaik, and Suzumura's example, we have two individuals, 1 and 2. Each individual has two shirts – white (w) and blue (b), and each individual enjoys the right to choose the color of his own shirt. All features of a social state, other than the two individuals' shirts, are assumed to be fixed. Thus, we have four feasible social states: $((w, b)$ (i.e. 1 wears white and 2 wears blue), (b, w) (i.e. 1 wears blue and 2 wears white), (w, w), and (b, b)). Since 2 enjoys the right to choose the color of his shirt, 2 needs to be globally decisive over $((w, w),(w, b))$ or $((b, w),(b, b))$ under the social choice formulation of rights. Suppose 2 is globally decisive over $((w, w),(w, b))$. Assume that the two individuals simultaneously choose their respective shirts; and that each individual is "completely ignorant" of the other individual's preferences over the four social states.[7] Let the two individuals' preferences be as follows:

1	2
(w, w)	(w, b)
(b, b)	(b, w)
(w, b)	(w, w)
(b, w)	(b, b)

Given complete ignorance about each other's preferences, suppose the two individuals behave in the "maximin" fashion. Then each will choose a white shirt. This will lead to the social choice of the outcome (w, w), but, given that 2 prefers (w, b) to (w, w), the choice of (w, w) will violate 2's global decisiveness over $((w, b),(w, w))$. Similarly, if 2 happens to be globally decisive over $((b, w),(b, b))$, with suitably chosen preferences one can show that the free and decentralized choice of shirts by the two individuals will violate 2's global decisiveness over $((b, w),(b, b))$. However, if the two individuals freely choose their respective shirts, then, no matter what social outcome results from such free choice, one can hardly claim that anybody's right to choose his shirt is violated. Thus, our intuition about the right to choose one's shirt turns out to be inconsistent with the social choice formulation of that right.

---

[7] We use the term "complete ignorance" to indicate the absence of any probabilistic belief about the other person's preferences.

To see the intuitive origin of the difficulty that the social choice formulation of rights faces in the Gaertner-Pattanaik-Suzumura example, consider what happens when we weaken the necessary condition, as stipulated by the social choice formulation, for an individual to have a right. Suppose we say that an individual, i, has a right only if there exist at least two distinct social alternatives, x and y such that

if i prefers x to y, then, given the two-element set, $\{x, y\}$, of feasible alternatives, the society must reject y; and if i prefers y to x, then, given the two-element set, $\{x, y\}$, of feasible alternatives, the society must reject x.... (2)

As before, x and y are to be interpreted as differing only with respect to private features of i. When we have i, x, and y such that $x \neq y$ and (2) holds, we shall say that i is locally decisive[8] over (x, y). (2) is clearly weaker than (1). Under this weaker formulation of individual rights, local decisiveness, rather than global decisiveness, over some pair of social outcomes becomes a necessary condition for an individual to have a right.

Irrespective of how we interpret a group decision rule, this weaker version of the social choice formulation turns out to be consistent with our intuition about the right to choose one's shirt.[9] Thus, in the Gaertner-Pattanaik-Suzumura example, suppose 2 is locally decisive over $((w, w),(w, b))$. Note that, if the set of feasible social alternatives is anything other than $\{(w, w),(w, b)\}$, then local decisiveness of 2 over $((w, w),(w, b))$ does not impose any restriction on social choice from the set of feasible outcomes. Let the set of feasible social outcomes be $\{(w, w),(w, b)\}$ so that, if 1 chooses his shirt at all, he can only choose a white shirt while 2 has two options, white and blue. Suppose 2 prefers (w, w) to (w, b). Then 2's local decisiveness over $((w, w),(w, b))$ would require $\{(w, w)\}$ to be the choice set corresponding to $\{(w, w),(w, b)\}$. It is easy to see that this does not conflict with our intuitive notion of 2's right to choose his own shirt. Suppose, consistent with our intuition about this right, 2 is left free to choose his own shirt. Given that 2 prefers (w, w) to (w, b), if 2 knows that 1 has no option but to wear a white shirt[10] then 2 will choose a white shirt. Then the social outcome to emerge from such free choice will be (w, w), exactly the outcome required by 2's local decisiveness over $((w, w),(w, b))$.

If the social choice formulation of individual rights in terms of global decisiveness conflicts with our intuition about many rights, but the weaker formulation in terms of local decisiveness does not, then the

---

[8] The term "locally" is used to indicate that the restriction postulated by (2) is applicable only to the two-element set $\{x, y\}$.

[9] Cf. Pattanaik (1996a). Note the caveat in footnote 10.

[10] In the absence of this knowledge assumption, even the formulation of individual rights in terms of local decisiveness can run into problems.

question naturally arises about the nature of the difference between global decisiveness and local decisiveness that can account for this. The intuitive difference seems to lie in a "condition of social rationality" implicit in the social choice formulation. Consider the following condition.

Let x and y be any two social outcomes. If, given the two element set, $\{x, y\}$, of feasible social outcomes, the society chooses x and rejects y, then, given any set of feasible outcomes that contains both x and y, the society must reject y. .... (3)

(3) is a weaker version of Sen's (1986) well-known Condition α, which is often considered a rather weak condition of rationality that social choices should satisfy. It can be easily seen that, though, in general, global decisiveness of an individual over a pair of social outcomes, (x, y), implies but is not implied by her local decisiveness over (x, y), the local decisiveness of an individual over (x, y) and rationality condition (3), together, imply her global decisiveness over (x, y). Thus, the social choice formulation retains some trace of the condition of social rationality stipulated by (3), while the weaker formulation in terms of local decisiveness does not incorporate any condition of social rationality. This constitutes an important difference between the two formulations. It is the modicum of social rationality embedded in the social choice formulation of individual rights that generates the difficulties the formulation faced in the Gaertner-Pattanaik-Suzumura example. That this weak trace of social rationality should come into conflict with our intuition about a large class of rights, the essence of which lies in the power of the individuals to choose separately and autonomously one of several available actions, does not come entirely as a surprise. However attractive conditions of social rationality may be as restrictions on the choices to be made by a social planner, it is not an integral part of our notion of individual rights. Further, there is no reason to expect that, in a higgledy-piggledy world where the realized social outcome is determined, at least partly, by decentralized decision-making of several individuals, the individuals will actually make their choices in such a way that the resultant social outcomes in different situations will obey any condition of social rationality. Indeed, we have several examples elsewhere in the literature (see, for example, Sugden [1985b] and Dasgupta, Kumar, and Pattanaik [2000]) where the social outcomes emerging from such autonomous individual decisions end up by violating some of the most primitive conditions of social rationality, though the individuals in these examples make their choices in a perfectly plausible fashion.

In fact, the problem may be even deeper. Not only is our intuition about a large class of rights inconsistent with the minimal trace of social rationality that is implicit in the social choice formulation of individual rights, but such intuition is also, in some ways, at odds with the very attempt to model the social decision process in terms of the formal notion of a group decision rule. Recall that the group decision rule is a function, which, for every profile of individual orderings and every non-empty set of social alternatives, specifies exactly one non-empty subset (the choice set) of that set. Thus, if the preference profile and the set of possible social outcomes remain the same, there should not be any change in the choice set under this definition. However, even this seemingly innocuous "uniformity" requirement may not be satisfied in the context of the rights that we have discussed earlier. Consider again the example of the choice of shirts where each individual freely chooses for himself one of two shirts. We have seen that, when the two individuals follow the "maximin" principle in complete ignorance of each other's preferences, the social outcome that materializes is (w, w). Suppose, other things remaining the same in the example, the two individuals' behavioral rules change so that both of them now choose their shirts according to the "maxi-max" rule. Then the social outcome will be (w, b), and our intuition tells us that this change in the choice set is exactly as it should be in a society that respects the two individuals' right to choose their respective shirts. Yet, the notion of a group decision rule will find it difficult to accommodate this change in the society's choice, given that there has been no change in the set of feasible social outcomes and the profile of individual orderings over the social outcomes.[11]

To sum up the discussion in this section, it seems to us that the traditional apparatus of social choice theory, with its emphasis on social rationality of some form or other and with its basic notion of a functional relation between the profile of individual preferences over social outcomes and the social choice(s) from any given set of possible social outcomes, does not provide a convenient framework for articulating our intuition about a very broad range of individual rights.

9.4.2   AB formulations of individual rights

The most conspicuous example of action-based and preference-free (AB-PF) models of rights is the game form formulation due to Nozick

[11] Cf. Pattanaik (1996b). It would be interesting to see whether an extended social choice framework where an extended group decision rule is defined on the basis of the set of social alternatives, the profile of individual preference orderings, and individuals' behavior will be able to accommodate the notion of individual rights in particular and the idea of an autonomous and decentralized decision-making process in general. We leave this for another occasion.

(1974), Gärdenfors (1981), Sugden (1985a), and Gaertner, Pattanaik, and Suzumura (1992), among others. The formulation can take many alternative, though closely related, forms, depending on whether one chooses to use strategic game forms, extensive game forms, or effectivity functions. For our purpose, it will be enough to consider the formulation in terms of extensive game forms. A rights structure here is visualized as an extensive game form where, at every information set I, the set of actions, $A(I)$, available to the player, $j(I)$, who takes the decision at I, is partitioned into two sets, $\overline{A}(I)$ and $\underline{A}(I)$, $\overline{A}(I)$ being interpreted as the set of all actions which are *permissible* for $j(I)$ and $\underline{A}(I)$ being interpreted as the set of all actions which are *impermissible* for $j(I)$ at I. It is this notion of permissibility and impermissibility of actions which constitutes the intuitively crucial component of the formulation. Thus, the right of individual i to practice the religion of her choice can be represented by an extensive game form where, at some information set I such that $j(I) = i$, i's permissible actions are simply the actions of practicing religion g_1 or religion g_2 or ... For all individuals $k \neq i$ and for all information sets I such that $j(I) = k$, $\overline{A}(I)$ does not include k's action of penalizing/discriminating against/... i because of the religion practiced by i. Given this structure, one can then define a permissible strategy of a player as a strategy that does not involve any impermissible action at any information set belonging to that player and an impermissible strategy of a player as a strategy that involves an impermissible action at some information set belonging to that player.[12]

The mathematical notion of a game form has no reference whatsoever to the individuals' preferences and motivations, etc. The game form approach to individual rights, therefore, seems to suggest that, to articulate what it means to say that someone has a right, it is not at all necessary to refer to preferences and motives. One of the issues that we discuss in some detail is whether it is really possible to articulate our intuition about rights in a framework that explicitly excludes all reference to preferences and motivations. We also discuss a second issue. A rights structure is an institution, which serves as a decision-making mechanism (at least for some aspects of the social state) and through which decisions are taken at different points of time with possibly different preference profiles for the individuals in the society. At any given point of time when decisions are to be taken through the institution represented by the game form, the preferences of the players are given.

[12] Later we shall consider another formal structure where the permissibility/impermissibility of a strategy is introduced as a primitive notion instead of being defined in terms of permissibility/impermissibility of actions. In some ways, this alternative structure provides extra analytical flexibility.

Given these preferences and given the game form, we have a game, and after this game is played, the outcomes are determined. How do we determine whether some rights have been violated in a particular play of the game? Note that this question is different from the question of how, given the preferences of the individuals, the individuals will exercise their rights, i.e. how the game defined by the game form and the given preferences, will actually be played. The question under consideration is not concerned with predicting how the game will be played or what sort of outcome will emerge from the game. Instead, it raises the conceptual issue of how one determines whether someone's rights have been violated once the game has been played somehow. It seems to us that a reasonably articulated conception of rights should be able to answer this question. The proponents of the game form formulation do seem to have an implicit answer to this question. It seems to be implicitly assumed that no one's rights are violated in a particular play of the game if and only if no player has used any impermissible strategy (see, for example, Deb [2004]). We raise some doubts about this implicit assumption.

Can one really represent individual rights in terms of a game form, together with a specification of permissible and impermissible actions and strategies, without any reference to the motives behind the actions of individuals? We believe that the answer to this question depends on the specific right under consideration and also on the specific aspect of a right that one may choose to emphasize.

It seems to us, insofar as the game form approach does not take into account the players' motives, it can run into serious problems in capturing the substance of a wide range of rights. To elaborate on this, we consider the following example. Consider the right of an individual, i, to practice the religion of his choice. It permits i to practice any one of several religions. At the same time, as we ordinarily understand the right to practice the religion of one's choice, it also grants i immunity from certain types of invasive actions by other agents by making those actions impermissible. Thus, in most modern societies, this right makes it impermissible for i's employer to penalize i for practicing a particular religion. i's right to practice the religion of his choice would lose much of its significance if he chooses to be a Muslim and is then fired by his employer, k, simply because he (i) chooses to be a Muslim. The right does not stipulate that k cannot fire i at all; what it really stipulates is that k must not fire i because of i's religion. A formulation of this right will fail to reflect this intuition unless it refers, directly or indirectly, to the motivation and preferences underlying k's firing of i.[13] A point that

---

[13] Van Hees (1996) discusses some aspects of a similar issue.

we would like to make here is that the problem is not confined to isolated instances of rights. The problem arises practically with all active rights (see Section 9.2 above) which grant the holder of the right certain types of immunity. As we explained above, all active rights of i, while granting i the option of doing/being a or b or ..., also simultaneously entail an obligation of all other agents not to punish/penalize/harm i for doing/being a or b or ... Therefore, a formulation, which does not have any reference to motives behind actions and which relies exclusively on the specification of permissibility or impermissibility of physical actions, will have difficulty in capturing a vital part of the intuition underlying these rights.

What happens if we "refine" the notion of an action? For example, what happens if, in our example above, we describe the action not simply as firing a worker but as firing a worker because of his religion or firing a worker because of his laziness, etc.? One can then say that the action of firing a worker because of his religion is impermissible under the worker's right to practice his religion while firing him for his laziness is permissible. If we refine the notion of an action in this fashion and specify which of these refined versions of actions are permissible in the game form and which of them are not, we would, of course, avoid the intuitive problem that we have discussed earlier. It should, however, be noted that the problem is solved only by building the motives into the description of actions and, hence, into the description of the game form itself.

One possible way of handling the problem in the framework of extensive game forms without building motivations into the description of actions may be to introduce the notion of permissibility/impermissibility of strategies directly rather than defining it in terms of permissibility/impermissibility of the actions available at the different information sets. In this modified framework, we no longer have, for any information set I, the partition of the set of feasible actions, $A(I)$, into $\overline{A}(I)$ and $\underline{A}(I)$. Instead, for each player i, the set, S_i, of all physically feasible strategies is now directly partitioned into the set, $\overline{S}_i$, of all permissible feasible strategies and the set, $\underline{S}_i$, of all feasible but impermissible strategies. This can now allow us to introduce certain nuances that could not be introduced when we first classified the actions at each information set into permissible and impermissible actions and then defined a permissible or impermissible strategy in terms of the permissibility of the actions involved in the strategy. Consider again the right to practice a religion of one's choice. Suppose individual 1, an employee of individual 2, can choose to practice either Hinduism (H) or Islam (IS). After 1 has chosen his religion and knowing what religion 1 has chosen, 2 can decide to fire 1 (F) from the job or not to fire 1 (NF). Then 2 has four feasible strategies: a(irrespective of whether 1 chooses H or IS, I shall choose F); b(irrespective of whether 1 chooses H or IS, I shall choose NF); c(if 1 chooses H, then I shall choose F, and, if 1 chooses IS, then I shall choose NF); and d(if 1 chooses H, then I shall choose NF, and, if 1 chooses IS, then I shall choose F). One way of capturing 1's right to practice the religion of his choice would be to specify {H, IS} as the set of permissible strategies of 1, {a, b} as the set of permissible strategies of 2, and {c, d} as the set of impermissible strategies of 2. It can be argued that making the strategies c and d impermissible for 2 captures the notion that 1's right does not permit 2 to fire 1 either for being a Hindu or for being a Muslim. In some ways, this is true. Other things being the same, if 2 uses strategy c, so that 2 would fire 1 when 1 practices H but not when 1 practices IS, then there is reasonable ground for saying that 2's motive is to penalize 1 for being a Hindu; and similarly in the case of d.[14] While this is true, what we are really doing here is to infer the motive of 2 in firing 1 if 1 becomes a Hindu (resp. a Muslim) by considering what 2 would have done if, other things remaining the same, 1 had become a Muslim (resp. a Hindu). The motives of 2 then remain very much a part of the intuition underlying our specification of 2's permissible strategies, even though it may not be visible in the formal structure.

We have so far argued that, for modeling, in terms of game forms, many active rights of an individual, it may be necessary to bring in the motives of other agents directly or indirectly into our formal model. This, however, is not necessarily true of all active rights. Consider one of our earlier examples that is about an active positive right and in which person A owes person B \$50. At a particular point of time, B can choose one of the two actions: to demand repayment and not to demand repayment. If B does not demand repayment, then A has the option of repaying or not repaying the loan. The right, however, requires that, if B demands repayment, then A must repay the loan; A's not repaying the loan when B demands repayment is simply not consistent with B's right no matter what may be the motives or reasons behind such non-repayment. B's right in this example is an active positive right, and, while it imposes a certain obligation on A, contingent on B's demanding a repayment of the loan, the obligation under consideration is in no way linked to the presence or absence of any specific motivation on A's part.

---

[14] Note that this nuance cannot be captured if we follow the procedure of specifying permissible and impermissible actions for each information set in the game and then define the permissibility of a strategy in terms of the permissibility of the actions involved in the strategy.

The above two examples should make it clear that no categorical answer can be given to the question of whether a right can be represented simply by a game form without bringing in, explicitly or implicitly, the players' motives. Depending on the specific right, the answer can go either way.

Consider now the issue, in the game form formulation, of identifying the situations where there are violations of individual rights. Can this be done without referring to the preferences of the individual(s) whose rights are under consideration? In the game form formulation of rights, it is obvious that, to predict the social outcome that will materialize from the exercise of rights, one needs to know, besides the game form representing the rights, the preferences of the individuals as well as the rules of behaviour that the individuals follow (reflected in some notion of an equilibrium of a game). We are not, however, concerned with this obvious relevance of individual preferences for predicting how the rights will be exercised and what social outcomes will arise from the exercise of the rights. Instead, we are concerned with the problem of assessing whether or not someone's rights have been violated given that the players have chosen their strategies somehow and a social outcome has emerged. Since the game form framework conceives the rights structure in terms of the permissibility and impermissibility of strategies, there seems to be a tendency to identify violation of rights with the adoption of impermissible strategies by some players. It is not obvious that this is always consistent with our intuition. We illustrate the difficulty with an example.

Consider an otherwise orthodox society where laws have just been introduced giving women the right to go out of home unescorted. Consider two individuals – a woman (W) and her husband (H). The woman has two possible actions available to her: w ("go out of home unescorted") and w' ("do not go out of home unescorted"). If W chooses not to go out of home unescorted, then status quo prevails and H does not have to take any decision. On the other hand, if W chooses to go out of home unescorted, then H knows this, and, knowing this, H has to choose from one of two actions: h ("punish W for going out of home unescorted") and h' ("do not punish W for going out of home unescorted"). Given the rights structure, it is permissible for W to go out of home unescorted (w) as well as not to go out of home unescorted (w'). However, if W goes out unescorted, then punishing W for going out unescorted (h) is not a permissible action for H: given that W chooses to go out unescorted, the only permissible action for H is not to punish W for going out unescorted (h'). The very simple extensive game form that represents the right here is given in Figure 9.1, where: (1) d_1 and d_2

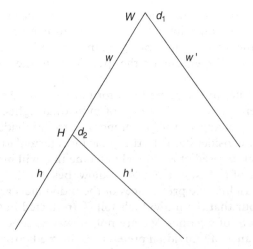

Figure 9.1 Decision tree of "right to go out of home unescorted" game

denote the two decision nodes; (2) both W and W' are permissible for W; and (3) h', but not h, is permissible for H.

We now bring in the preferences by attaching payoffs to the terminal nodes. Suppose the payoffs are as in Figure 9.2 (for each terminal node, the first number denotes the payoff of H and the second number denotes the payoff of W).

Given the payoffs, it is natural to assume that w will adopt the strategy of not going out unescorted (w) and H will adopt the impermissible strategy of taking action h if at all he finds himself at the single decision node that belongs to him. Given these choices of strategies, H will never reach his decision node, d_2, and the game will end with payoffs (100, 100). While H has adopted an impermissible strategy, it is not obvious to us that, from an intuitive point of view, there has been any actual violation of W's rights. The reason is this. Imagine a different game derived from the game in Figure 9.2 by "chopping off" the branch h' and the corresponding terminal node, i.e., by assuming that h' is simply not available to H at the information set $\{d_2\}$. W would still choose the strategy (w') in this game. Thus, the actual path through which the terminal node would be reached when this game is played is exactly the same as the actual path through which the terminal node is reached when W and H play the game in Figure 9.2. At the risk of emphasizing the obvious, we would like to clarify the following point. We are *not* saying that if an information set I is not actually reached as a consequence of the strategies adopted by the players, then the permissibility

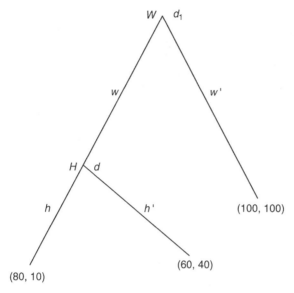

Figure 9.2 Decision tree of "right to go out of home unescorted" with payoffs

or impermissibility of the action at I specified by the strategy of the player, who takes the decision at I, is irrelevant for the purpose of judging whether someone's rights have been violated. It will be intuitively unreasonable to say that. To see this, consider Figure 9.3, where the game tree is the same as in Figure 9.2 but the payoffs are different.

In this case, it is reasonable to assume that W will use strategy (w') and H will adopt the strategy (h). However, in that case, we feel that W's right is violated. This is because, if it could be guaranteed that H would never adopt (h) or, equivalently, if the branch corresponding to the action h is chopped off the game tree, then W would like to adopt (w) and the path followed by the actual play of this changed game will be different from the path followed by the actual play of game in Figure 9.3. Intuitively, in the game in Figure 9.3, W adopts w' because she justifiably fears that, if she adopts the strategy w, then H will punish her by taking action h at $\{d_2\}$ and she will be worse off as compared to the situation where she adopts the strategy (w'). In contrast, in the game in Figure 9.2, W will adopt w' irrespective of whether h is available to H at $\{d_2\}$. Suppose, given the strategies $((w'), (h))$ adopted by the players in the game in Figure 9.2, W wants to complain to the court that her right has been actually violated. Then she will have to say something like the following: "Your Honour, I am a very orthodox woman.

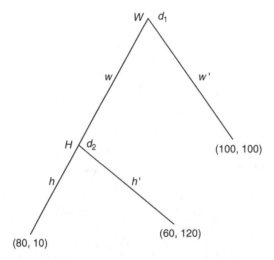

Figure 9.3 Decision tree of "right to go out of home unescorted" with modified payoffs

Even if it was not possible for my husband to punish me for going out of home unescorted, I would still not like to go out unescorted by any long shot. However, I know that my husband has decided to punish me if I go out unescorted. So my husband has really violated my rights and something should be done about that." Does this argument sound intuitively plausible and will any court entertain this petition? We do not think so.

Yet, we do feel uncomfortable about the husband's use of an impermissible strategy. We believe that there is no inherent intuitive incompatibility between this sense of discomfort and our feeling that the adoption of the strategies $((w'),(h))$ in the game in Figure 9.3 does not violate W's right. To see this, we need to recall that the extensive game form in Figure 9.1 represents an institutional framework through which decisions will be taken in many different situations with different preferences of the players. The preferences depicted in Figure 9.2 represent one such situation. In this specific situation, there may not be any actual violation of W's rights. Nevertheless, we also sense that there is a potential for a violation of W's rights if W's preferences change, so that, though the institution remains the same, the game becomes the game in Figure 9.3. It is this potential violation of W's right, which makes us uncomfortable about the equilibrium pair of strategies $((w'),(h))$ in the game in Figure 9.2. At the same time, for reasons that we have explained above, it seems to us intuitively implausible to claim that the equilibrium pair of strategies $((w'),(h))$ for the game in Figure 9.2 involves any actual violation of W's rights. We feel that it may be useful to distinguish between two distinct problems in the game form approach. The first is the problem of specifying what it means to say that an individual enjoys a particular right. The second is the problem of identifying whether that right of the individual has been violated, given information about the strategies that the players have actually adopted in that situation. Even if we ignore the relevance of individual preferences and motives in tackling the first problem, we may have to invoke the individual preferences in tackling the second problem.

Suppose we have a game form formulation of a rights structure and a particular profile of preference orderings. Further, suppose we have an actual play of the game that results from the game form and the preference profile. How do we decide whether anybody's rights have been violated by this actual play of the game? At this stage, we do not have any tight and comprehensive answer to this question. Nevertheless, in light of examples such as the one in Figure 9.2, it seems to us that the criterion for deciding whether somebody's rights have been violated needs to be more complex than the simple criterion of whether anybody has used an impermissible strategy.

9.5   Formulations of freedom

Much of the recent literature on freedom in welfare economics conceives the freedom of an individual as the opportunity to choose from the set of all outcomes available to her. Thus, if the outcome for a competitive consumer is thought of as a consumption bundle, then the consumer's freedom is seen to be the opportunity of choosing any of the consumption bundles in her budget set. Similarly, in the capability approach to the standard of living, due to Amartya Sen (1985, 1987),[15] the freedom of an individual is the opportunity to choose any one of the "functioning" bundles available to her.[16] In general, the conception of freedom developed by welfare economists has been predominantly outcome-based, and the main concern of the analysis has been to rank different sets of feasible outcomes in terms of the freedom that they offer to an agent.[17]

[15] See also Nussbaum (1988).
[16] "Functionings" are the "doings" and "beings" that people value. Being well nourished, being protected from the elements, and interaction with friends and family are just a few examples of what Sen (1985, 1987) calls functionings.
[17] In this respect, the analysis of freedom in welfare economics differs significantly from the corresponding analysis of individual rights, where the focus has been on the

While the analysis of individual rights has been increasingly in terms of strategies and actions, the analysis of freedom has remained outcome-based from the beginning. This sharp contrast in modeling strategies is rather surprising since, in many ways, the two concepts have considerable similarities. In particular, in both cases, we talk about the individual's actions (her freedom or right to do/be ... x) rather than outcomes.

Of course, sometimes the outcome may depend exclusively on the action of the individual under consideration. In such cases, it does not matter whether we think in terms of an individual's freedom to do x or the individual's freedom to choose the outcome o_x that follows when the individual does x. However the modeling of freedom in terms of the opportunity to choose an outcome can run into problems when the outcome depends on other people's actions as well as the action of the individual whose freedom is under consideration. Often no single agent, by himself, is able to control the final outcome; instead, the final outcome is determined by the strategies adopted by several individuals interacting with each other. An important case where such strategic interaction is absent is the classic case of perfect competition with a very large number of consumers and producers. Given the competitive equilibrium prices, the budget set of each consumer is defined, and a consumer can choose any consumption bundle in his budget set. Since the number of consumers is large, a consumer can choose any bundle in his budget set without affecting the equilibrium prices. Assuming that alternative consumption bundles constitute the outcomes for a consumer, we can think of each consumer as choosing an outcome from the set of outcomes available to him. Outside the realm of a classical perfectly competitive economy, however, one can think of numerous examples of strategic interaction where no direct and tight connection may exist between an agent's action or strategy and the final outcome that he may get. An ill-paid worker has the freedom to join a strike, but whether, in the process, he will lose his job or get a pay rise, may depend on how many other ill-paid workers in the same firm join the strike. Despite anti-discrimination laws, the supervisors in a firm may

incompatibility of individual rights and Pareto efficiency and there is practically no discussion of how to rank alternative situations in terms of the "amounts" of rights that they offer to an individual.

The exercise of ranking different situations in terms of the amount of freedom that an individual enjoys in each of them has followed two distinct directions: some models (see, for example, Jones and Sugden [1982] and Pattanaik and Xu [1990]) explore the problem without introducing preferences, while some other models (see Jones and Sugden [1982], Sen [1988; 1992], and Foster [1992], among others) give preferences a crucial role.

Table 9.3. *A Game form*

		2		
		a'	b'	c'
1	a	x	y	z
	b	x'	y'	z'
	c	y'	x	x

be racially discriminating against immigrant workers, and an individual immigrant worker may have the freedom to report the matter to appropriate authorities, but the final outcome of such complaint may depend on whether other immigrant workers will come forward to give evidence, whether the officer conducting the investigation takes the complaint seriously or starts with the presumption that it is yet another case of whining by foreigners, and so on.

How does one represent the freedom of agents in such cases, where the agent cannot be reasonably thought of as choosing an outcome though he certainly has choices with respect to the actions? One can take the position that, in such cases, freedom should be simply modeled as the opportunity to choose one of several actions, and one should not worry about the outcomes. Such a position seems to have serious limitations. An individual may have a large number of alternative actions available to her, but, if the outcome remains the same no matter what action she takes, then one can hardly consider her to be enjoying much freedom. Ultimately, we value the freedom to choose actions because we hope to influence the final outcomes through such choices.

In the presence of strategic interdependence, there does not seem to be any obvious way of translating the freedom to choose one of several actions into opportunities in terms of outcomes. Here we consider two possible routes; each has its own limitations as well as intuitive plausibility. As in the case of rights, here also game forms and games seem to be the most obvious conceptual tools for capturing the strategic interactions of individuals. Consider a situation where we have two individuals, 1 and 2; individual 1 can choose any one of three strategies, a, b, and c; and 2 can choose any one of three strategies, a', b', and c'. The structure of strategies and outcomes is given by the game form in Table 9.3.

Given this game form, we consider several distinct formulations (to be called formulations A, A', and B, respectively) of the freedom enjoyed by an individual, say individual 1.

Formulation A: 1 can choose any of the strategies a, b, and c, and the set of all possible outcomes is $\{x, y, z, x', y', z'\}$. If 1 chooses a, then the final outcome must lie in the set $\{x, y, z\}$, though what exactly the outcome will be will depend on what strategy 2 decides to adopt. One way of looking at this will be as follows: by choosing a, 1 really chooses an uncertain prospect; represented by the set $\{x, y, z\}$, where the final outcome will be either x or y or z. Similarly, the choice of b by 1 gives him an uncertain prospect represented by the set $\{x', y', z'\}$, and the choice of c gives 1 an uncertain prospect represented by $\{y', x\}$. 1's freedom to choose any of the strategies, a, b, and c can then be viewed as his freedom to choose any of the elements of the class $\{\{x, y, z\}, \{x', y', z'\}, \{y', x\}\}$, where each of these elements is suitably interpreted as an uncertain prospect.

Formulation A is closely related to the notion of an α-effectivity function[18] that has been used to represent the power that a player enjoys in a game form. The power of 1 here is really the power to restrict the final outcome to lie in any one of the following sets: (1) $\{x, y, z\}$; (2) $\{x', y', z'\}$; and (3) $\{y', x\}$. The freedom of choice, with respect to the outcomes, that 1 enjoys here is the freedom to choose one of these three sets as the set where the final outcome will lie. In a sense, formulation A seems to capture certain aspects of positive freedom.

Formulation A': 1 can choose any of the strategies a, b, and c. With respect to 2's choice of a', if 1 chooses a, then the final outcome is x; if 1 chooses b, then the final outcome is x'; and if 1 chooses c, then the final outcome is y'. In other words, with respect to 2's choice of a', 1 is left with an opportunity set $\{x, x', y'\}$ in which 1 can choose any of the outcomes in his opportunity set. Similarly, with respect to 2's choice of b', 1 is left with an opportunity set $\{x, y, y'\}$, and with respect to 2's choice of c', 1's opportunity set is $\{x, z, z'\}$. Depending on 2's choice of an action, 1 will have exactly one element of the set $\{\{x, x', y'\}, \{x, y, y'\}, \{x, z, z'\}\}$, where each of these elements is suitably interpreted as an opportunity set.[19] Formulation A' seems to have certain features of negative freedom.[20] The opportunity that 1 enjoys in the game form is to choose an outcome from an opportunity set that is determined by 2's action: given 2's choice of a', 1 can choose either x or x', or y'; given 2's choice of b', 1 can choose either x or y or y'; and, finally, given 2's choice of c', 1 can choose either x or z or z'.

---

[18] See, for example, Moulin (1983).

[19] Note that, we are not saying that player 1 can observe player 2's moves before choosing his strategies. What we are doing here is to visualize opportunities available to player 1 *if* player 2 is to adopt a particular strategy.

[20] The formulation is, to some extent, in the spirit of Oppenheim's (1961; 2004) conception of negative freedom.

Table 9.4. *Game Forms 4.1 and 4.2 showing a limitation of interpretation A*

2

		a'	b'	c'
	a	x	y	z
1	b	x	y	z
	c	x	y	z

Game Form 4.1

2

		a'	b'	c'
	a	x	y	z
1	b	y	z	x
	c	z	x	y

Game Form 4.2

Formulations A and A' have their limitations. Consider formulation A, and Game Forms 4.1 and 4.2. Formulation A will not be able to discriminate between 1's degrees of freedom in these two game forms, since, under each of the two game forms, the only uncertain prospect available to 1 is $\{x, y, z\}$.

Nevertheless, it seems intuitively plausible to say that Game Form 4.2 gives 1 greater influence over outcomes than Game Form 4.1. In Game Form 4.1, given a strategy of 2, what 1 chooses to do does not matter at all so far as the outcome is concerned. In contrast, 1's strategy does matter for the final outcome in Game Form 4.2. In equating 1's freedom in Game Form 4.2 with 1's freedom in Game Form 4.1, Formulation A overlooks a difference that seems to be relevant if 1's freedom is to take into account 1's ability to influence the final outcome.

Similarly, Formulation A also cannot discriminate between 1's freedom in Game Form 5.1 below and 1's freedom in Game Form 5.2.

In each case, Formulation A will translate 1's freedom to choose between strategies a and b to 1's freedom to choose between two uncertain prospects, $\{x, y\}$ and $\{x, z\}$. In doing so, Formulation A overlooks a difference between the two game forms, which may be relevant in comparing the two situations in terms of 1's freedom. For example, if we know that 1 strictly prefers x to y (this information is, of course, extraneous to the two game forms) we may feel that 1 has greater freedom in Game Form 5.1 than in Game Form 5.2.

Table 9.5. *Game Forms 5.1 and 5.2 showing a limitation of interpretation A*

		2				
		d_1	d_2	d_3	d_4	d_5
1	a	x	x	x	x	y
	b	x	x	x	x	z

Game Form 5.1

		2				
		d_1	d_2	d_3	d_4	d_5
1	a	x	y	y	y	y
	b	x	x	x	x	z

Game Form 5.2

Note that Formulations A and A' are ways of identifying an individual's opportunity to influence the outcome rather than a way of *evaluating* such opportunity. It is, therefore, possible to combine each of these two formulations with a preference-based approach to evaluating freedom as well as with a preference-free approach to such evaluation. In identifying an individual's control over the outcome, Formulations A and A' both rely exclusively on the information contained in the relevant game form and do not take into account the players' preferences at all. In contrast, the next formulations that we discuss make use of information about the players' preferences as well as the game form.

Formulation B: Suppose we have a game, that is, a game form together with the players' preferences. Let the game form be as in Table 9.3. Let G denote the game defined by this game form and the given preferences of the two players. Assume that we have some plausible notion of equilibrium and that (a, b') constitutes the unique equilibrium of the game G (presently, we shall comment on the case where there is no equilibrium and the case of multiple equilibria). Since (a, b') is the only equilibrium, 1 knows that 2 will play b' and he himself will ultimately play a. At the same time, 1 knows that he has the option of playing b or c. Since 2 is going to play b', 1 knows that: (i) by choosing a, he can get the outcome y; (ii) by choosing b, he can get the outcome y'; and (iii) by choosing c, he can get the outcome x. Thus, though he knows that he is going to choose a and get the outcome y, he also knows that he could get y' or x if he so wanted. 1's freedom can then be viewed as the freedom to choose an outcome from the set $\{y, y', x\}$.

Suppose we have two equilibria, (a, b') and (c, c'). Then all that 1 knows is that 2 will play either b' or c'. Then 1 knows that: (i) if he (i.e. individual 1) plays a, the outcome will be either y or z; (ii) if he plays b, then the outcome will be either y' or z'; and (iii) if he plays c, then the outcome will be x. Thus, in terms of outcomes, 1's opportunity set can be identified as the class $\{\{y, z\}, \{y', z'\}, \{x\}\}$, $\{y, z\}$ representing an uncertain prospect where the outcome may be either y or z, and similarly for $\{y', z'\}$ and $\{x\}$ (note that $\{x\}$ is a degenerate uncertain prospect where x is the only possible outcome). Finally, we note that Formulation B fails to identify an opportunity set in terms of outcomes if the game G does not have an equilibrium. This is clearly a limitation of the formulation.

9.6   Concluding remarks

In this chapter, we have critically reviewed several formal formulations of the notions of rights and freedom in welfare economics. In particular, we have considered: (i) the classical social choice formulation of individual rights due to Sen (1970a; 1970b; 1992); (ii) the game form formulation of individual rights due to Nozick (1974), Sugden (1985a), and Gaertner, Pattanaik, and Suzumura (1992), among others; (iii) the model of individual freedom in terms of the opportunity set of outcomes (see, for example, Jones and Sugden [1982], Sen [1988], and Pattanaik and Xu [1990]); and (iv) possible formulations of freedom in terms of game forms and games. Our focus has been on the conceptual and intuitive bases of these formal frameworks rather than on the specific results that have been derived, using them. Our main conclusions can be summed up as follows.

Like several other writers (see, for example, Sugden [1985a] and Gaertner, Pattanaik, and Suzumura [1992]), we believe that the classical social choice formulation, which constitutes the pioneering formulation of individual rights in welfare economics, conflicts in many ways with our basic intuition about a wide range of rights. The source of the trouble lies in: (i) the implicit use of certain conditions of social rationality; and, more fundamentally, (ii) the rigid functional relation, postulated by the theory of social choice, between the profiles of individual preferences and the outcomes "chosen" by the society. The game form formulation of rights has the advantage of being closer to our everyday use of the language about individual rights, but advocates of the game form approach (see, for example, Gaertner, Pattanaik, and Suzumura [1992] and Pattanaik [1996a, b]) do not seem to have appreciated sufficiently: (i) the need for bringing in the motives of individuals when we seek to model a very large class of rights (the class of "active rights," to use the terminology of Feinberg [1973]); and (ii) the need for ascertaining the individuals' preferences so as to determine whether the rights of a given individual have been violated in a specific play of the game that results when we combine the relevant game form with the preferences of the individuals. The outcome-based notion of freedom (i.e. the notion of freedom as being reflected in the set of feasible outcomes, any one of which the agent can choose at will) runs into trouble if the outcome for an individual is influenced by the actions of agents other than that individual. Such situations seem to be numerous and important in real life. While one can think of freedom as the freedom to adopt one of several feasible strategies, to evaluate to what extent such freedom is valuable to the agent, one needs to link the freedom to choose one of several strategies to the agent's ability to influence the outcome through his choice of strategies. The literature does not have any intuitively compelling way of modeling such influence. In Section 9.5 we considered a few alternative ways of establishing this link, but as we pointed out there, each of them has its own intuitive limitations. The overall conclusion that seems to emerge is that, while, over the last four decades or so, much progress has been made in the formal modeling of individual rights and freedom in welfare economics, there still remain many analytical gaps that need to be resolved.

The formulations of individual rights and freedom, rather than the specific purposes for which these formulations have been used in welfare economics, have been our main concern in this chapter. We would, however, like to conclude with a brief observation on these purposes. Possible conflicts between individual rights and the Pareto efficiency of social outcomes constitute the central theme pursued in contributions on individual rights in welfare economics. In contrast, the emphasis of the contributions on freedom in welfare economics has been on comparisons of the "amounts" of freedom that an individual enjoys in different situations. It seems to us that, given the intuitive links between the two concepts, the issues explored with reference to one of these concepts can also be fruitfully pursued in the context of the other concept. For example, it will be interesting to see how one may compare the amounts of rights that an individual enjoys in different societies, and how individual freedom may be incompatible with Pareto optimality of social outcomes.

Acknowledgements

For numerous helpful discussions and comments, we are grateful to A. Baujard, K. Basu, R. Deb, W. Gaertner, the late S. Kanger, V. Merlin,

H. S. Richardson, M. Salles, A. K. Sen, R. Sugden, K. Suzumura, and M. van Hees. We are, however, responsible for all errors that remain.

References

Berlin, I. 1969. *Four Essays on Liberty*. Oxford University Press.
Dasgupta, I., S. Kumar, and P. K. Pattanaik 2000. "Consistent Choice and Falsifiability of the Maximization Hypothesis," in R. Pollin (ed.), *Capitalism, Socialism and Radical Political Economy: Essays in Honour of Howard J. Sherman*, Cheltenham: Edward Elgar, pp. 136–53.
Deb, R. 2004. "Rights as Alternative Game Forms," *Social Choice and Welfare*, **22** (1): 83–111.
Dowding, K. and M. van Hees 2007. "Counterfactual Success and Negative Freedom," *Economics and Philosophy*, **23**: 141–62.
Feinberg, J. 1973. *Social Philosophy*, Englewood Cliffs, NJ: Prentice-Hall.
Fleurbaey, M. and M. van Hees 2000. "On Rights in Game Forms," *Synthese*, **123** (3): 295–326.
Foster, J. 1992. "Notes on Effective Freedom," mimeo, Vanderbilt University.
Gaertner, W., P. K. Pattanaik, and K. Suzumura 1992. "Individual Rights Revisited," *Economica*, **59**: 161–77.
Gärdenfors, P. 1981. "Rights, Games and Social Choice," *Nous*, **15** (3): 341–56.
Hohfeld, W. 1923. *Fundamental Legal Conceptions as Applied in Judicial Reasoning and Other Legal Essays*, ed. W. Cook, New Haven: Yale University Press.
Jones, P. and R. Sugden, 1982. "Evaluating Choice," *International Review of Law and Economics*, **2** (1): 47–65.
Kanger, S. and H. Kanger 1966. "Rights and Parliamentarism," *Theoria*, **32**: 85–115.
MacCallum, G. C. 1967. "Negative and Positive Freedom," *Philosophical Review*, **76** (3): 312–34.
Moulin, H. 1983. *The Strategy of Social Choice*, New York: North Holland.
Nozick, R. 1974, *Anarchy, State and Utopia*, New York: Basic Books.
Nussbaum, M. 1988. "Nature, Function and Capability: Aristotle on Political Distribution," *Oxford Studies in Ancient Philosophy*, supplementary volume **I:** 145–84.
Oppenheim, F. E. 1961. *Dimensions of Freedom: An Analysis*, Oxford: Blackwell.
    2004. "Social Freedom: Definition, Measurability, Valuation," *Social Choice and Welfare*, **22** (1): 175–85.
Pattanaik, P. K. 1996a. "The Liberal Paradox: Some Interpretations When Rights are Represented as Game Forms," *Analyse & Kritik*, **18**: 38–53.
    1996b. "On Modeling Individual Rights: Some Conceptual Issues," in K. J. Arrow, A. Sen, and K. Suzumura (eds.), *Social Choice Re-examined*, London: Macmillan Press Ltd., pp. 100–28.
Pattanaik, P. K. and Y. Xu 1990. "On Ranking Opportunity Sets in Terms of Freedom of Choice," *Recherches Economiques de Louvain*, **54** (3–4): 383–90.

Sen, A. K. 1970a. "The Impossibility of a Paretian Liberal," *Journal of Political Economy*, **78** (1): 152–7.

1970b. *Collective Choice and Social Welfare*, San Francisco: Holden Day.

1985. *Commodities and Capabilities*, Amsterdam: North-Holland.

1986. "Social Choice Theory," in K. Arrow and M. Intriligator (eds.), *Handbook of Mathematical Economics*, vol. III. Amsterdam: North-Holland, pp. 1073–181.

1987. *The Standard of Living* (edited by Geoffrey Hawthorn, with contributions by John Muellbauer, Ravi Kanbur, Keith Hart and Bernard Williams), Cambridge University Press.

1988. "Freedom of Choice: Concept and Content," *European Economic Review*, **32** (2–3): 269–94.

1992. "Minimal Liberty," *Economica*, **59**: 139–59.

2002. *Rationality and Freedom*. Cambridge, MA.: Harvard University Press.

Sugden, R. 1985a. "Liberty, Preference, and Choice," *Economics and Philosophy*, **1**: 213–29.

1985b. "Why Be Consistent?," *Economica*, **52**: 167–84.

van Hees, M. 1996. "Individual Rights and Legal Validity," *Analyse & Kritik*, **18**: 81–95.

1995. *Rights and Decisions*, Dordrecht: Kluwer Academic Publishers.

2000. *Legal Reductionism and Freedom*, Dordrecht: Kluwer Academic Publishers.

Part III

10 On applying synthetic indices of multidimensional well-being: health and income inequalities in France, Germany, Italy, and the United Kingdom

Andrea Brandolini

Introduction

The multidimensional view of human well-being has had a growing influence on research on inequality and poverty. This development owes much to the conceptualization of the 'capability approach' by Sen (1985; 1987), but the shift has not been confined to academic circles and has extended to policy-oriented analysis. Since 1990 the United Nations Development Programme has challenged the primacy of GDP per capita as the measure of progress by proposing the Human Development Index (HDI), which combines income with life expectancy and educational achievement (e.g. UNDP 2005). The *World Development Report 2000/2001: Attacking Poverty* opened with the statement that: 'This report accepts the now traditional view of poverty ... as encompassing not only material deprivation (measured by an appropriate concept of income or consumption), but also low achievements in education and health ... This report also broadens the notion of poverty to include vulnerability and exposure to risk – and voicelessness and powerlessness' (World Bank 2001: 15). The European Commission has long favoured the concept of social exclusion since 'more clearly than the concept of poverty, understood far too often as referring exclusively to income, it also states out the multidimensional nature of the mechanisms whereby individuals and groups are excluded from taking part in the social exchanges' (Commission of the European Communities 1992: 8).[1] The multifaceted nature of social development is implicit in the set of indicators agreed by the European Union (EU) at Laeken in December 2001 to monitor the performance of member countries: the

---

[1] Accordingly, Eurostat defined social exclusion as 'the link between low income, activity status and a number of indicators which relate to means, perceptions and satisfaction of the groups under study with respect to their standard of living and quality of life' (Mejer 2000: 1).

indicators cover regional cohesion, joblessness, school dropouts, literacy, life expectancy and health status besides income poverty and inequality (see Atkinson 2002; Atkinson *et al.* 2002).

These are only a few significant examples of the shift to a multidimensional view of human well-being in recent years. The intuitive appeal of this view can explain its popularity but offers little guidance on its practical implementation, whether for statistical analysis or policy design. The central problem is how to translate intuition into measurement. The lack of a certain durable good or housing amenity need not be a sign of material deprivation, for it may depend on personal preferences or social habits – hence the attempt of separating 'lack because one does not want' from 'lack because one cannot afford' (see, for instance, Guio 2005). 'Meeting friends or relatives less than once a month or never' – an indicator used by Eurostat (2000) following on a tradition going back to Townsend (1979) – may denote weak social ties, but also the preference for quietness of somebody living a hectic working life or the passion for web-exchanges of a blogger. These two examples only serve to illustrate the difficulties in defining non-monetary indicators, but many are the conceptual and empirical questions that arise in a multidimensional context: the identification of the relevant dimensions of well-being, the construction of the corresponding indicators and the understanding of their own metric, the methods to handle the different dimensions, the weighting of the selected indicators.

In this chapter, I concentrate on a specific issue in multidimensional measurement: the requirements and the implications of using synthetic multivariate indices of inequality and poverty. The complexity of the problems suggests that empirical measurement in multiple domains needs to be grounded in a theory of multidimensional well-being. Here, I take the perspective of the capability approach, which has the distinctive merit, as noted by Robeyns, to stress 'to a far greater extent [than other approaches] the need to integrate theory and practice, and to pay due attention to the philosophical foundations' (2006: 371).[2] After outlining alternative approaches to studying multidimensionality (see 'Strategies to study multiple dimensions'), I review the arguments for and against using synthetic measures of the distribution of well-being and explore their analytical structure (see 'Pros and cons of using synthetic measures of the distribution of well-being'). I then investigate these issues empirically by taking a specific case study: the distribution of income and health among the adult population in the four largest

[2] The operationalization of the capability approach is examined by Brandolini and D'Alessio (1998), Alkire (2002) and Kuklys (2005), among others. Empirical applications are surveyed by Robeyns (2006).

EU countries (see 'Income and health inequalities in France, Germany, Italy, and the United Kingdom'). Household incomes are distributed differently within each country: Germany shows the lowest inequality and poverty, France comes next, Italy and the United Kingdom are much higher up in the ranking. However, considering people's health together with their income changes the picture; in many cases, it leads to the reversal of the conclusion about the German ranking. The main lessons, outlined in the last section, are that broadening the informational basis to include non-monetary variables, such as health status, may affect our knowledge of inequalities, but proper attention has to be paid to the underlying methodological choices.

Strategies to study multiple dimensions

The alternative strategies to deal with the multiple dimensions of well-being basically differ for the extent of manipulation of raw data: the heavier the structure we impose on data, the nearer we get to a complete cardinal measure of well-being. A broad classification of possible strategies is given in Figure 10.1, where the main distinctions relate to

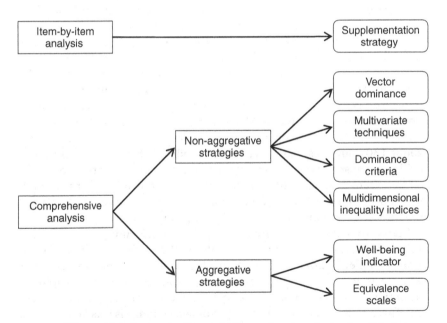

Figure 10.1 Strategies for multidimensional analysis of well-being
Source: Brandolini and D'Alessio (1998: Table 3).

whether the functionings are investigated singly or comprehensively, and whether multidimensionality is retained or collapsed into a synthetic well-being indicator at the personal level.

Indicators of standard of living can simply be considered in conjunction with the information on the distribution of income, or other indicators of monetary resources. This is the *supplementation strategy* followed by Sen in his analyses of gender discrimination in the allocation of food within Indian families (Sen 1985: Appendix B) and of mortality figures as indicators of social inequality and racial disparity (1998). Another recent example is the study by Fahey, Whelan and Maître (2005) on the relationship between income inequalities and quality of life in the enlarged European Union. No attempt is made to reduce complexity, and the constituents of well-being are examined one by one. Attention is directed not only to their univariate features, but also the pattern of cross-correlation: the latter may reveal whether income poverty compounds with other deprivations, or is instead associated with better achievements in other domains. The advantage of this strategy rests on its simplicity: it imposes little structure on the phenomena under examination and its measurement requirements are less demanding. The disadvantage, especially in the presence of a rich information set about people's standard of living, is the lack of synthesis and the difficulty of drawing a well-defined unitary picture.

The task of the alternative *comprehensive non-aggregative strategies* is to make comparisons on the basis of the entire vector of functionings. Analyses based on strict *vector dominance* impose few restrictions on the data, but their information may be limited, especially when the set of indicators is large. For instance, examining some basic average functionings (GNP per capita, death rate, life expectancy, number of inhabitants per medical doctor, illiteracy rate, consumption of calories) for about 130 countries, Gaertner (1993) reported that vector dominance held in at most a quarter of the comparisons between any two countries chosen from politically or economically homogeneous groups, though it held in roughly 90 percent of the comparisons between a country in the richest group and one in the poorest group.

Standard *multivariate statistical techniques* (e.g. Kendall 1975; Sharma 1996) may help in managing the multiple dimensions of the problem. For example, Schokkaert and Van Ootegem (1990) employed factor analysis to identify the functionings of a group of Belgian unemployed from their answers to a number of qualitative questions. They were very careful stress that their application of factor analysis was 'a mere data reduction technique', which did not guarantee that the list of functionings was complete, nor did it provide any indication about the relative valuation of the functionings; in particular, the estimated weights represented only the importance of each factor (functioning) in explaining the pattern of responses to the 46 survey questions, not their importance in the valuation function (see pp. 439–40). Factor analysis was similarly used by Nolan and Whelan (1996a; 1996b) in their study of deprivation in Ireland.

An alternative route is to specify *dominance criteria* which extend the notion of Lorenz dominance to multivariate distributions, along the lines of the seminal papers by Kolm (1977) and Atkinson and Bourguignon (1982). Dominance conditions for multidimensional poverty comparisons are developed by Bourguignon and Chakravarty (2002) and Duclos, Sahn and Younger (2006). The applications discussed by Atkinson and Bourguignon (1987), Atkinson (1992) and Jenkins and Lambert (1993) relate to the comparison of income distributions when family needs differ. By adopting the standard practice of transforming income by means of an equivalence scale one is specifying *how much* a family type is more needy than another. By contrast, dominance criteria only needs to *rank* family types in terms of needs, and may easily allow for some disagreement about the ranking itself. The cost of this weaker informational requirement is that the ordering tends to be incomplete. In order to achieve complete ordering, one needs to specify a *multidimensional index* of inequality or poverty, which associates a real number to each multivariate distribution. Research in this area is rapidly growing.[3]

The last and most structured strategy in applying the capability approach is to pursue a fully *aggregative strategy* and to construct a summary composite indicator of well-being to which standard univariate techniques can be applied. This approach was advocated by Maasoumi (1986), who used information theory to specify functional forms for the well-being aggregator (see Bourguignon 1999 for a critique and an alternative formulation). Single aggregate measure can be derived also using multivariate techniques, such as principal components (Maasoumi and Nickelsburg 1988) and cluster analysis (Hirschberg *et al.* 1991), or methods developed in efficiency analysis (Lovell *et al.* 1994; Deutsch and Silber 2005; Ramos and Silber 2005). Alternatively, the summary indicator can be expressed in monetary units, rather than in some 'well-being unit', by estimating 'functioning-equivalent income', that is income adjusted for differences in functionings (Kuklys 2005: chapter 5; Lelli 2005). In

---

[3] See Bradburd and Ross (1988), Fluckiger and Silber (1994), Tsui (1995; 1999), List (1999), Gajdos and Weymark (2005) and the surveys by Maasoumi (1999), Weymark (2006) and Lugo (2007) for inequality; Tsui (2002), Atkinson (2003), Bourguignon and Chakravarty (2003) and the survey by Bibi (2005a) for poverty.

many contexts, the estimation of functioning equivalence scales might reveal a powerful and appealing alternative. The monetization of differences in achieved functionings should not, however, conceal that well-being is a combination of valuable states of life, nor should it lead to the conclusion that an appropriate money transfer can compensate for every disadvantage.

As for a multidimensional index, the outcome of an aggregative strategy is a complete ordering. Conceptually, there is, however, an important difference. The aggregative strategy requires to that we specify a well-being indicator which summarizes all functionings for each person: inequality or deprivation are then evaluated in a unidimensional space. The multidimensional index does not entail the aggregation of functionings at the individual level and therefore avoids specifying a functional form for the well-being indicator. In practice, such an indicator may be *implicitly* defined when the index is additively separable across persons, as for the inequality measures proposed by Tsui (1995; 1999); but it should be borne in mind that 'the function U [that enters into the additive social evaluation function] is a utility function that the social evaluator uses to aggregate any individual's allocation of the q attributes into a summary statistic. The function U need not coincide with any individual's actual utility function' (Weymark 2006: 314). The difference between the two approaches emerges in the analysis of deprivation: whereas a multidimensional poverty index implies a separate threshold for each functioning, a fully aggregative strategy sets a single threshold in the space of the well-being indicator.

Pros and cons of using synthetic measures of the distribution of well-being

As just seen, a crucial decision in studying a multidimensional concept of well-being is whether to collapse all information into one number, or to keep separate the different dimensions of well-being. Both options have their own merits (see also Micklewright 2001). On the one hand, a loss of information and a sensitivity to arbitrary choices are inherent in the process of aggregation. As Sen puts it, 'the passion for aggregation makes good sense in many contexts, but it can be futile or pointless in others ... When we hear of variety, we need not invariably reach for our aggregator' (1987: 33). In the same vein, Erikson (1993: 75) expressed a strong reservation about constructing a 'simple ordered indicator of level of living', Schokkaert and Van Ootegem (1990) avoided aggregating the functionings identified with factor analysis and Nolan and Whelan (1996a; 1996b) used factor analysis solely to merge elementary components into three separate indicators of deprivation termed 'basic-lifestyle', 'secondary lifestyle' and 'housing'. On the other hand, a single number is very effective in summarizing complex problems in a simple and comprehensible way for the general public. This communicational advantage is important, as a single complete ranking is more likely to capture newspaper headlines – and people's imagination – than a comparison of multidimensional scorecards and a complex reasoning on the relations among multiple indicators. This 'eye-catching property', so labelled by Streeten (1994), has been crucial for the HDI to successfully challenge per capita income as the sole measure of development.

The HDI is a good case in point to illustrate the problems with complete aggregation. The HDI measures the average achievement in human developments in a country by taking a simple arithmetic mean of three indicators: the logarithm of GDP per capita (Y), life expectancy at birth (L) and education. The indicator for education is itself a composite index combining adult literacy (A), with a two-third weight, and gross enrolment in primary, secondary and tertiary school (G), with a one-third weight. Income is taken in logarithms 'in order to reflect diminishing returns to transforming income into human capabilities' (Anand and Sen 1994: 10). All four elementary indices are normalized by taking the proportional country's achievement over a prefixed scale. More formally, for country i, it is

$$\text{HDI}_i = \frac{1}{3}\left(\frac{L_i - \underline{L}}{\overline{L} - \underline{L}}\right) + \frac{1}{3}\left[\frac{2}{3}\left(\frac{A_i - \underline{A}}{\overline{A} - \underline{A}}\right) + \frac{1}{3}\left(\frac{G_i - \underline{G}}{\overline{G} - \underline{G}}\right)\right] + \frac{1}{3}\left(\frac{\ln Y_i - \ln \underline{Y}}{\ln \overline{Y} - \ln \underline{Y}}\right), \quad (1)$$

where the upper and lower bars indicate the maximum and minimum values, respectively. It is clear that HDI varies between 0 and 1. If we replace the prefixed minima and maxima and simplify, we obtain the following expression:

$$\text{HDI}_i = 0.0056 L_i + 0.0022 A_i + 0.0011 G_i + 0.0556 \ln Y_i - 0.3951. \quad (2)$$

The iso-HDI contours in the bivariate space spanned by GDP per capita (in current purchasing power parity [PPP] US dollars) and life expectancy at birth (in years) are plotted in Figure 10.2. These curves are drawn taking a value for the education index of 0.94 (the value of Japan), and all countries shown have values comprised between 0.93 and 0.96. Data are drawn from UNDP (2005: 219–22, Table 1) and refer to 2002–3. Two comments are in order. First, a similar value of the HDI may correspond to different situations. Argentina and Hungary, for instance, achieve virtually the same level of human development (0.863

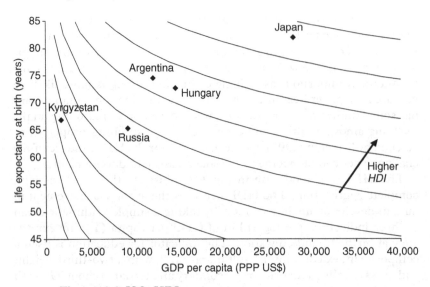

Figure 10.2 ISO–HDI contours
Source: Author's elaboration on data drawn from UNDP (2005: 219–22, Table 1). All countries shown in the figure have similar values on the education index, between 0.93 and 0.96.

and 0.862, respectively), but Argentineans are expected to live 1.8 years longer than Hungarians, even if their average per capita income is 17 percent lower. Had life expectancy been valued more than GDP per capita, say 3:1 rather than 1:1, then the Argentinean HDI would have surpassed the Hungarian (0.867 vs. 0.856). This example shows the importance of weighting, but it also highlights the loss of valuable information in identifying the areas needing policy action. Second, an expression like (2) sets a very definite rate of substitution between the different constituents of well-being. For a given value of the education index, the HDI is unchanged if life expectancy *falls* by one year at the same time as the other human capabilities that can be achieved with income *rise* by about 0.1 units, that is as GDP per capita *rises* by almost a tenth ($\Delta \ln Y = -(0.0056/0.0556) \Delta L \cong -0.1\Delta L$). According to this substitution rate, the richer a country, the higher the implicit value of extending human life: an additional year is equivalent, in HDI terms, to a reduction of per capita income by 2,658 US dollars in Japan but only 166 US dollars in Kyrgyzstan. This difference reflects the fact that income is a proxy for human capabilities that are not captured by education and life expectancy, and that at higher income levels more income is necessary to achieve these capabilities as a result of the assumption of diminishing returns. However, we might question the hypothesis that the marginal rate of substitution between life expectancy and income rises with income. The issue is not only which functional form but also whether a definite rate of substitution between the various constituents of well-being should be imposed.

It should be noted that constructing a synthetic indicator at the country level, like the HDI, is conceptually different from combining elementary indicators at the personal level, in spite of the similarities of the aggregation procedure. It is one thing to integrate multiple indicators to gauge a person's well-being, quite another to measure mean well-being in a country by taking the average of mean achievements in each dimension, regardless of how these achievements combine at the personal level. In their discussion of EU social indicators, Atkinson *et al.* (2002: 72–3) suggest that aggregation is worth pursuing at the individual level, but should be avoided at the country level, on the grounds that 'the whole thrust of the European social agenda is to emphasize the multidimensionality of social disadvantage. Politically, the process will not encourage Member States to learn from each other if attention is focused on a single rank order'. The focus of this chapter is on aggregation at the individual level. With this in mind, in the rest of this section I further examine the two issues just exposed with the HDI example: the role of the weighting structure and the functional form of the synthetic indicator.

Weighting structure

The simplest multivariate index of living standard can be written as

$$S_i = \sum_j w_j x_{ij}, \tag{3}$$

where x_{ij} is non-negative and represents the level of the jth attribute (functioning), $j = 1, \ldots, \mathcal{J}$, enjoyed by the ith person (family), $i = 1, \ldots, n$, and w_j is the corresponding weight, equal across persons. Expression (3) would become an index of deprivation if x_{ij} measured hardship. Weights are normalized to sum to unity.

Weights determine the extent to which distinct functionings contribute to well-being, and diverse weighting structures reflect different views. As suggested by Sen (1987: 30; see also Foster and Sen 1997: 205), one way to account for this difference is to specify 'ranges' of weights rather than a single set of weights, although this approach is likely to lead to a partial ordering. The practical relevance of the issue depends on the tension among different functionings: if their achievements were strongly correlated, the structure of relative weights would be less important.

The first possibility is to treat all attributes equally. *Equal weighting* may result either from an 'agnostic' attitude and a wish to reduce interference to a minimum, or from the lack of information about some kind of 'consensus' view. For instance, Mayer and Jencks (1989: 96) opted for equal weighting, after remarking that: 'ideally, we would have liked to weight [the] ten hardships according to their relative importance in the eyes of legislators and the general public, but we have no reliable basis for doing this'. (In fact, there may be disagreement among the legislators and the general public, let alone within the general public itself.) Equal weighting has the obvious drawbacks of not discriminating among constituents that are reputed to play different roles, and of double counting whenever the informational content of two distinct attributes partly overlaps.

A second route is 'to let the data speak for themselves'. With a *frequency-based weighting*, the weights are computed as some function of the relative frequencies of the attributes. For instance, several authors seem to agree with Desai and Shah (1988) and Cerioli and Zani (1990) that the smaller the proportion of people with a certain deprivation, the higher the weight that deprivation should be assigned, on the grounds that a hardship shared by a few is more important than one shared by many. However, this criterion may lead to a questionable and unbalanced structure of weights. As observed by Brandolini and D'Alessio (1998: 39), in 1995 the proportion of Italians with low achievement in health and in education were estimated at 19.5 and 8.6 percent, respectively. With these proportions, education insufficiency would be valued more than health insufficiency: a tenth more according to Desai and Shah's formula; over a half more according to Cerioli and Zani's. Whether education should be given a weight so much higher than health is certainly a matter of disagreement. An alternative procedure is to use the output of *multivariate techniques*, such as factor analysis (Nolan and Whelan 1996a; 1996b), principal components (Maasoumi and Nickelsburg 1988) or cluster analysis (Hirschberg *et al.* 1991), but we should be cautious of entrusting a mathematical algorithm with a fundamentally normative task. The same observation applies to methods developed in efficiency analysis (Lovell *et al.* 1994; Cherchye *et al.* 2004; Deutsch and Silber 2005; Ramos and Silber 2005).[4]

---

[4] Cherchye *et al.* (2004) use production frontier techniques to aggregate the EU social indicators into a synthetic indicator where weights are variable and such as to maximise the value of the indicator in each country: 'the endogenously defined weights can be interpreted as implicitly revealed policy priorities' (p. 948). There are two

A third alternative is to use *market prices* as weights. When x_{ij} denotes the quantity purchased by the ith family of the jth commodity and the weight w_j equals the market price p_j of the same commodity, the index S_i coincides with the family's total expenditure. Sugden (1993) and Srinivasan (1994) argued that the availability of such 'operational metric for weighting commodities' makes traditional real-income comparison in practice superior to the capability approach. However, market prices do not exist for functionings; even if they did, they would be inappropriate for well-being comparisons, a task for which they have not been devised, as stressed by Foster and Sen (1997).

Functional form of the synthetic indicator

A single measure of inequality or poverty in multiple domains can be obtained either by specifying a well-being function and then computing a standard univariate index, or by directly defining a multidimensional index. In the first approach, it is natural to relax the hypothesis of additive separability used in (3), because it rules out the possibility that attributes are other than perfect substitutes. As suggested by Maasoumi (1986), a straightforward generalization of S_i is offered by the class of functions showing constant elasticity of substitution (CES)

$$S_{\beta i} = \begin{cases} \left[\sum_j w_j x_{ij}^{-\beta} \right]^{-1/\beta} & \beta \neq 0 \\ \prod_j x_{ij}^{w_j} & \beta = 0 \end{cases},$$ (4)

where the weights sum to unity and β is a parameter governing the degree of substitution between the attributes: they are perfect complements as β goes to infinity and perfect substitutes for $\beta = -1$. The second approach is to derive multivariate indices of inequality and poverty that satisfy some desirable properties and can be applied directly to the vectors of attributes. I consider here two of these indices, one for inequality proposed by Tsui (1995) and one for deprivation derived by Bourguignon and Chakravarty (2003).

Tsui (1995) follows the approach pioneered by Kolm (1969) and Atkinson (1970) and identifies inequality with the social welfare loss

objections to this weighting procedure. First, many factors beyond the control of policy makers could lead to different outcomes from those aimed at, and the deduced national priorities could differ from those that motivated policy action. Second, the judgemental relativism implicit in country-specific weights is inherently at variance with a joint assessment process: weights might perhaps be chosen to vary within some range, but they should still be common to all nations.

(see Sen 1978 and 1992 for a critique of ethical inequality indices). After restricting the class of social evaluation functions to be continuous, strictly increasing, anonymous, strictly quasi-concave, separable and scale invariant, he derives the following two multidimensional (relative) inequality indices:

$$I_1 = 1 - \left[\frac{1}{n} \sum_i \prod_j \left(\frac{x_{ij}}{\mu_j} \right)^{r_j} \right]^{1/\Sigma_k r_k} \tag{5a}$$

$$I_2 = 1 - \prod_i \left[\prod_j \left(\frac{x_{ij}}{\mu_j} \right)^{r_j/\Sigma_k r_k} \right]^{1/n} \tag{5b}$$

where μ_j is the mean of attribute j over all persons and parameters r_j's must satisfy certain restrictions. The separability condition implies that the attributes can be aggregated for every person i into an indicator of well-being $S_i = \prod_j x_{ij}^{w_j}$, where $w_j = r_j/\Sigma_k r_k$ can be seen as a normalized weight on attribute j. By replacing $(1-\varepsilon)$ for $\Sigma_k r_k$, (5a) and (5b) can be rewritten as

$$I = \begin{cases} 1 - \left[\frac{1}{n} \sum_i \left(\frac{S_i}{S} \right)^{1-\varepsilon} \right]^{1/(1-\varepsilon)} & \varepsilon \neq 1 \\ 1 - \prod_i \left(\frac{S_i}{S} \right)^{1/n} & \varepsilon = 1 \end{cases} \tag{6}$$

where $S = \prod_j \mu_j^{w_j}$ is the 'representative' well-being of the society, that is the well-being of a person showing the mean achievement for each attribute. The restrictions on r_j transfer to w_j and ε; in the bivariate case, it is sufficient that $\varepsilon > 0$ and $0 < w_1 = 1 - w_2 < 1$.

This reformulation has three advantages. First, it shows the close link of the Tsui multivariate index with the Atkinson univariate index applied to the S_i's, from which it differs only for the replacement of *mean* well-being with *representative* well-being. This is indeed the appropriate normalization since 'maximizing social welfare under the constraint of fixed total resources of attributes ... requires to give to each individual the average available quantity of attributes' (Bourguignon 1999: 478). This observation exposes the conceptual diversity between using a multidimensional index and applying a univariate index to an indicator of multidimensional well-being. (Of course, the two indices coincide in the univariate case.) Second, expression (6) brings out the role of

ε, i.e. $\Sigma_k r_k$ in the original formulation, as the parameter that governs the degree of concavity, and hence of inequality aversion, of the social evaluation function. In the univariate income space, the range of economically sensible values for ε can be restricted on the basis of considerations on the preference for redistribution. A similar analysis has not been conducted in the multivariate space of well-being, but 'there is not necessarily any reason to change our views about the value of [ε] simply because we have moved to a higher dimensionality' (Atkinson 2003: 59). In the empirical analysis in the next section, I take ε to vary between 0.3 and 3, the same interval identified by Atkinson and Brandolini (2004) in the analysis of income inequality. This range includes the values used by Lugo (2007) in her application to Argentinean data. Third, expression (6) shows that the Tsui index allows for different weightings of the attributes (through the w_j's), but makes no allowance for a variation in the degree of substitution between the attributes: the Cobb-Douglas functional form of the underlying well-being indicator implies that the elasticity of substitution between two attributes is uniformly equal to unity. In the bivariate case, a straightforward generalization is represented by the index derived by Bourguignon (1999) by assuming a CES functional form for the indicator of well-being, which has the Tsui index as a special case (see Lugo 2007).

Allowing for different patterns of substitution among well-being constituents is an explicit aim of Bourguignon and Chakravarty (2003). They characterize several families of multidimensional poverty indices that differ in the way in which the Pigou-Dalton transfer principle is generalized to the multidimensional framework. I consider here the case where the transfer principle is supposed to hold for all attributes. A possible specification, in the bivariate case, is

$$P = \frac{1}{n} \sum_i \left\{ w_1 \left[\max\left(1 - \frac{x_{i1}}{z_1}, 0\right) \right]^\theta + w_2 \left[\max\left(1 - \frac{x_{i2}}{z_2}, 0\right) \right]^\theta \right\}^{\frac{\alpha}{\theta}}, \qquad (7)$$

where $\theta \geq 1$ and $\alpha > 0$, and z_j is the poverty threshold for attribute j.[5] This measure has isopoverty contours of the type shown in Figure 10.3, which are convex to the origin in the orthant where a person is poor relative to both attributes, i.e. $x_{ij} < z_j$ for $j = 1, 2$, and vertical or horizontal in the orthants where a person is poor relative to one attribute only. If θ tends to infinity, the substitutability between the two attributes tends

---

[5] This family of indices may be generalised to any number of attributes, but only at the cost of assuming the same elasticity of substitution between each pair of them (Bourguignon and Chakravarty 2003: 40).

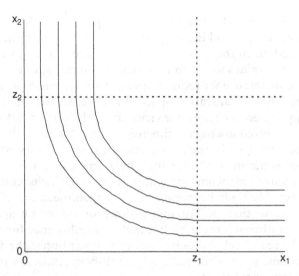

Figure 10.3 Isopoverty contours for the Bourguignon–Chakravarty
multidimensional poverty index

to 0 and the isopoverty contours become right angles: the poverty level
associated to a person who is poor in both dimensions is determined by
the attribute which is farthest away from its poverty line. At the other
extreme, if $\theta = \alpha = 1$ the two attributes are perfect substitutes and the
convex part of the isopoverty contours becomes a straight line. If an
attribute is redistributed from a poor person to another less poor person so as to increase the correlation of the two attributes in the population, the index P is non-increasing for $0 < \alpha < \theta$ and non-decreasing for
$\alpha > \theta$. In other words, the higher α relative to θ, the more the two
attributes are substitutes. Thus, the extent of deprivation as measured by
(7) depends on the interaction of three types of parameters: the degree
of concavity, α, that was already present in the univariate case, and the
weights, w_js, and the shape of the contours governed by θ, which are new
in the multidimensional case (see the insightful discussion by Atkinson
2003). In their empirical example on Brazilian data, Bourguignon and
Chakravarty (2003) consider five values for α (0, 1, 2, 3, 5) and three
values for θ (1, 2, 5); in an application to data for Egypt and Tunisia, Bibi
(2005b) takes two values for α (3, 15) and three values for θ (2, 4, ∞).
   Atkinson (2003: 60) observes that the empirical literature on multidimensional deprivation has largely concentrated on counting deprivations, rather than taking a weighted mean of shortfalls from the
poverty line as in the Bourguignon and Chakravarty index, and puts

the emphasis on the weight given to multiple deprivations. For bivariate distributions, he proposes the following deprivation indicator

$$D = 2^{-\kappa}(H_1 + H_2) + (1 - 2^{1-\kappa})H_{1,2},\qquad(8)$$

where H_j, with $j = 1,2$, is the proportion of persons deprived on the jth dimension, $H_{1,2}$ is the proportion of those deprived on both dimensions and κ varies from 0 to infinity. (Expression (8) differs from Atkinson's original formula for dividing through by 2κ.) When κ equals 0, the indicator counts all people with at least one deprivation $(D = H_1 + H_2 - H_{1,2})$, regardless of the number of failures. As κ rises, the weight on multiple deprivations increases: for $\kappa = 1$ those with two deprivations are counted twice and D gives the simple mean of the head count rates in the two dimensions; as κ goes to infinity, D tends to coincide with the proportion of people deprived on both dimensions $H_{1,2}$.

Income and health inequalities in France, Germany, Italy, and the United Kingdom

In order to illustrate the importance in empirical analysis of the methodological problems discussed so far, I examine the distribution of multidimensional well-being among the adult population of the four largest EU countries: France, Germany, Italy, and the United Kingdom. I assume that a person's well-being can be represented by two functionings: health status and command over resources.

Data sources and definitions

Data are drawn from the European Community Household Panel (ECHP), a multidimensional longitudinal household survey sponsored by Eurostat in the 1990s and discontinued in 2001. The ECHP aimed at collecting information on personal income and living standards in the EU by means of standardized national annual surveys elaborated under the coordination of Eurostat. I ignore the longitudinal nature of the database and focus on the last wave conducted in 2001. The sample includes all persons aged 16 or more, since no information on health status is collected for younger persons. Each observation is weighted by the cross-sectional weight (variable PG002).

The first functioning is the person's perception of her health condition. Indicators of self-perceived health are widely used but are not without problems because 'it is often hard to know exactly what they mean' (Wilkinson 1996: 55). For instance, it is unclear whether respondents have in mind an absolute notion or rather one adjusted for age or other factors. On the other hand, according to Currie and Madrian, 'several studies suggest that self-reported measures are good indicators of health in the sense that they are highly correlated with medically determined health status' (1999: 3315). As being in good health is a fundamental constituent of human well-being, I choose to use this indicator, despite its ambiguities. Health status is measured on a scale from 1 (very good) to 5 (very bad) and is based on the respondent's self-perception at the time of the interview (variable PH001). The variable is recoded so that 1 corresponds to the worst status and 5 to the best. All persons who declared their health to be bad or very bad (i.e. recoded values 1 or 2) are classified as health-poor.

The second functioning is represented by command over resources, as measured by income. Having an income is not itself a functioning, but many functionings, like being well-nourished or having a decent home, depend crucially on it. This is a sufficient reason for including income. As observed by Anand and Sen, 'in an indirect way – both as a proxy and as a causal antecedent – the income of a person can tell us a good deal about her ability to do things that she has reason to value. As a crucial means to a number of important ends, income has, thus, much significance even in the accounting of human development' (2000: 100). Consistently with this interpretation and the assumption made in the construction of the HDI, it may be reasonable to take some concave transformation of the income variable in order to capture diminishing returns in the conversion of income into human capabilities. Hence, I consider two alternative formulations, one using income and the other using its logarithmic transformation. However, the logarithm of income cannot be used as such with scale invariant measures of inequality, such as those discussed above: a change in the unit of account, as a result, for example, of a change in the currency unit or in the base year of a purchasing power parity index, would affect measured inequality even where no alteration had occurred in the underlying distribution of command over resources.[6] A way to obviate this problem is to apply the normalization used in the HDI and to take $dly = (\ln y_i - \ln y_-)/(\ln y_+ - \ln y_-)$ as the measure of command over resources, where y_i, y_- and y_+ are the income of person i and the pre-set minimum and maximum incomes (common to all countries), respectively. This measure is clearly unaffected by a proportional change in all incomes like that implied by a change in the unit of account. In the

---

[6] I owe this observation to Tony Atkinson. Note that the situation would be different with translation invariant inequality measures such as the absolute Kolm index.

estimation discussed below, all incomes are expressed in purchasing power standards and zy_- is chosen equal to 1, so that $\ln y_- = 0$. As dly collapses to $\ln y_i/\ln y_+$, there is no need to specify the value of the maximum income y_+ because $1/\ln y_+$ enters as a proportional factor, and any relative index of inequality is independent of its value.

With regard to the poverty line, the different economic conditions, welfare states and social structures of the four countries suggest that a relative standard is better suited than an absolute one to capture the minimum necessary level of economic resources. A person is hence defined as income-poor if her household's equivalent income is below 60% of the median of the distribution of equivalent incomes among adult persons in each country;[7] for consistency, the logarithm of this value (divided by the logarithm of y_+) is taken to be the threshold when the logarithmic transformation is used. Note that the scale invariance of the chosen inequality and poverty indices together with the assumptions made on y_-, y_+ and the poverty line imply that the results from using the logarithm of income coincide with those based on dly (henceforth, log-income). This coincidence would disappear under different assumptions.

Total household income is the sum of all monetary incomes received by household members, net of income taxes and social security contributions, in the year preceding the interview (variable HI100), divided by the purchasing power parity index provided in the ECHP database (variable PPP00). This total is adjusted for household composition (including children) with the modified OECD equivalence scale (variable HD005) and then attributed to each adult household member.

Inequality

As regards the degree of inequality of the household income distribution, the ranking of the four largest EU countries is well known: Germany shows the least unequal distribution, followed by France, while Italy and the United Kingdom exhibit far higher levels of inequality (Brandolini and Smeeding 2006). The same ranking obtains for the adult population: the Gini index goes from 26 percent in Germany and 27 percent in France to 29 and 31 percent in Italy and the United Kingdom, respectively (Table 10.1). Taking the logarithmic transformation, income concentration appears to be much lower, as predictable, and Italy and the United Kingdom reverse their relative positions. The

[7] This definition follows the methodology used by Eurostat except for considering only the adult population.

Table 10.1. *Health and income distribution statistics (percentage values)*

Country	Gini index			Head count poverty rate					Correlation coefficient	
	Income	Log-income	Health	Income	Health	Health and income	Health or income	Health and income	Health and log-income
France	27.2	3.0	12.4	15.2	8.0	2.0	21.2	0.11	0.11
Germany	25.8	2.7	15.5	11.2	19.0	3.1	27.1	0.07	0.08
Italy	29.1	3.5	13.5	19.5	11.5	2.7	28.3	0.04	0.03
United Kingdom	30.6	3.3	13.1	17.4	9.5	2.9	24.0	0.13	0.16

Source: Author's elaboration on ECHP data, Wave 8.

evidence is rather different for the health distribution: the highest Gini index is found in Germany (16 percent) and the lowest in France (12 percent), with Italy and the United Kingdom in intermediate position (over 13 percent). This diverse picture of income and health inequalities gives rise to mixed results when the two dimensions are considered jointly.

The values of the Tsui multidimensional index of inequality are plotted in Figure 10.4. The six panels corresponds to the two definitions of income (log-income on the left, income on the right) and to three values of the parameter ε representing inequality aversion (0.3, 1 and 3, from the top to the bottom). In each panel, the values on the horizontal axis represent the weight w given to income, moving right from 0 to 1, or to health, moving leftwards from 1 to 0; in the two end points, all weight is given to one attribute and the value of the index coincides with that of the Atkinson (univariate) index. When the logarithm of income is taken, the consideration of people's health leads to a rather consistent picture: multidimensional inequality is higher in Germany than in the other three countries, unless very little weight is put on the health indicator. Differences between France, Italy and the United Kingdom are small, except for high levels of inequality aversion (ε = 3): in such a case Italy is the country with the lowest inequality. The pattern is completely different when income, and not its logarithm, is considered, provided that sufficient weight is put on income ($w \geq 0.2$): Germany now exhibits the least unequal distribution of well-being, while the United Kingdom and, immediately next, Italy show the most unequal distributions for ε ≤ 1, and France for ε > 1.

The pattern of health and income inequalities in the four largest EU countries is complex. Contrary to the income-based evidence, Germany appears to be the most unequal country when well-being is represented by health status and the logarithm of income; this result tends to reverse when command over resources is measured by income. Attention has to be paid to the assumptions made in the calculation, but the greatest differences relate to the use of income or its logarithmic transform and to the degree of inequality aversion; these alternative choices are not specific to multidimensional analysis and equally arise in the univariate context. The weighting of the two attributes, the only factor that reflects here the multiple dimensions, plays a relatively minor role, except when it is very unbalanced. As noted above, the degree of substitution, the other factor specific to multidimensionality, is assumed away, since the Tsui index has by virtue of its construction a unitary elasticity of substitution.

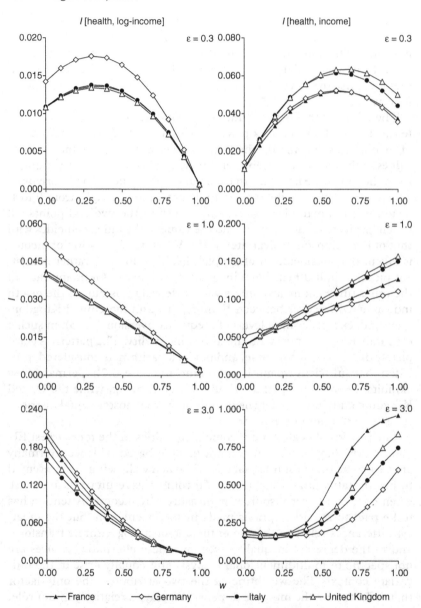

Figure 10.4 TSUI multidimensional inequality index
Source: Author's elaboration on ECHP data, Wave 8. Moving right on horizontal axis amounts to gradually shifting the weight from health only ($w = 0$) to log-income or income only ($w = 1$).

Poverty

The pattern of deprivation is similar to that of inequality in both the health and the income domains (Table 10.1).[8] The income head count poverty rate ranges from 11 percent in Germany to 20 percent in Italy; the health poverty rate varies between 8 percent in France and 19 percent in Germany. A first way to assess the extent of multivariate deprivation is to apply Atkinson's counting approach. The curves in Figure 10.5 trace the indicator D in the four countries for different values of κ. The proportion of people who are poor in at least one dimension (κ = 0) ranges from 21 percent in France to 28 percent in Italy. This proportion gradually decreases as κ rises, and converges to

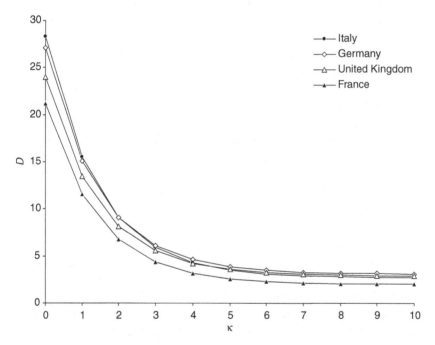

Figure 10.5 Atkinson multidimensional deprivation indicator
Source: Author's elaboration on ECHP data, Wave 8.

[8] The identification of the poor in the income space is unaffected by the logarithmic transformation because of the assumption that the threshold for log-income coincides with the logarithm of the threshold for income. However, the transformation makes a difference in the estimates of the Bourguignon and Chakravarty index, which is a function of the proportional shortfall of the variable from the respective poverty line.

the proportion of persons who are poor in both dimensions ($\kappa = 10$): 2 percent in France and around 3 percent in the other three countries. The curve for France lies uniformly below that for the United Kingdom, which in turn lies uniformly below that for Germany; as these curves do not cross, the ranking of the three countries does not depend on the weight assigned to the occurrence of multiple deprivations. The curve for Italy starts higher than the others, then crosses that for Germany at $\kappa = 2$ and that for the United Kingdom at $\kappa = 4.5$. Thus, Italy fares badly when the focus is on the proportion of deprived people but is better positioned when the attention is shifted to those who are deprived on both functionings. This result may reflect the low correlation of the health and income indicators (Table 10.1).

The Bourguignon and Chakravarty index tends to replicate this pattern, but there are notable exceptions. Assume, for the moment, that the two functionings are equally weighted and that the poverty threshold for the health status is set at 3 (deprivation occurs when the variable is strictly lower than this threshold). Figure 10.6 reports the results of the estimation for the two definitions of income (log-income on the left, income on the right), three values of the parameters α which represents poverty aversion (0.5, 1 and 5, from the top to the bottom), and six values of the parameter θ that governs the degree of substitution between the two functionings (1.1, 2, 5, 10, 100 and 500; along the horizontal axis in logarithmic scale). As θ rises, the two functionings become less and less substitutable, and the individual poverty indicator tends to reflect the worst-performing dimension. When α is below or equal to 1, the income definition is relatively unimportant: multidimensional deprivation is higher in Germany, followed by Italy, and then the United Kingdom and France (Germany and Italy appear to differ only when income is taken in logarithms). For $\alpha = 5$, i.e. for higher aversion to poverty, there is a clear deterioration of the relative position of France. Germany fares unequivocally better than Italy, regardless of the value of θ, using income, but the opposite is true taking log-income. Despite the differences, the conclusion based on the index P is qualitatively similar to that based on the counting approach, provided that poverty aversion is not high: deprivation is highest in Germany and lowest in France. This ranking changes, however, when poverty aversion is high.

How is this conclusion affected by the weighting of the two functionings? This is shown in Figure 10.7, which is like Figure 10.6 except for replacing the weights for the substitution parameter θ (assumed equal to 2) on the horizontal axis. When all weight is assigned to one functioning, at either extreme of the horizontal axis, the index P becomes

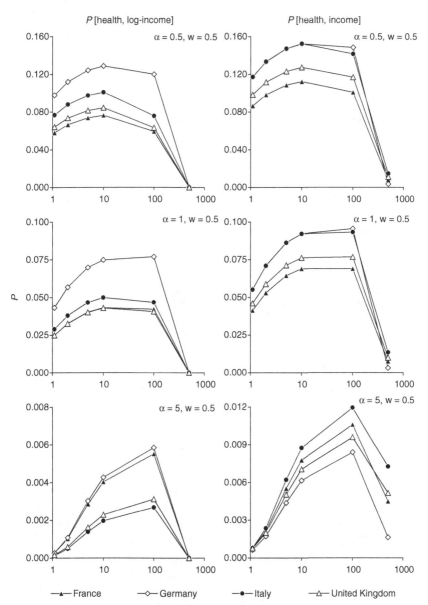

Figure 10.6 Bourguignon–Chakravarty multidimensional poverty index – I
Source: Author's elaboration on ECHP data, Wave 8. Logarithmic scale for the horizontal axis reporting the values of θ.

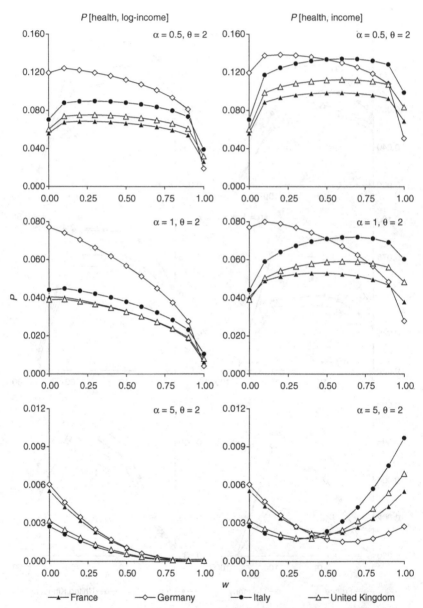

Figure 10.7 Bourguignon–Chakravarty multidimensional poverty index – II

Source: Author's elaboration on ECHP data, Wave 8. Moving right on horizontal axis amounts to gradually shifting the weight from health only ($w=0$) to log-income or income only ($w=1$).

the univariate poverty index proposed by Foster, Greer and Thorbecke (1984). When command over resources is measured by log-income (panels on the left), the ranking is as described before, with Germany showing more health ($w = 0$) and multidimensional ($0 < w < 1$) deprivation than the other three countries; the relative position of Germany improves only for income poverty ($w = 1$). The picture is somewhat more intricate when income, rather than log-income, is the variable under consideration (panels on the right). Consider Germany and Italy: when no weight is given to income ($w = 0$), Germany looks worse than Italy; as the weight is shifted from health to income, the gap between the two countries narrows and disappears for w around 0.5; as w further rises towards 1, Italy becomes increasingly more deprived than Germany. In the case where poverty aversion is high ($\alpha = 5$), there is a full reversal of the ranking of all four countries according to whether w is below or above 0.5. This example shows that weighting can matter: as the relative importance of the two functionings reflects a value judgement, it does not seem advisable to assign its determination to some mathematical or statistical algorithm, however cleverly justified.

A final point concerns the definition of the health poverty threshold. The criterion to identify the poor with those persons with (recoded) score equal to 1 or 2 is consistent with setting the threshold at any number between 2 and 3. This choice does not matter for the Atkinson indicator, but has a bearing on the Bourguignon and Chakravarty index: with the threshold equal to 3 used above, the possible values of the relative shortfalls are 1/3 and 2/3; with a threshold set at $2 + \xi$, with ξ small, they are approximately 0 and 1/2 (more precisely, $\xi/(2+\xi)$ and $(1+\xi)/(2+\xi)$). It is obvious from the inspection of (7) that the contribution of health to deprivation would be rather different had we chosen this second value. For instance, setting the threshold at 2.01 and using income, the value of P for $\theta = \alpha = 2$ would be 53 percent lower for Germany (0.0110 instead of 0.0232) and 31 percent lower for France (0.0134 instead of 0.0195); in general, this change would reverse the relative position of the two countries. Agreement on the identification of persons with a poor health status does not lead to an unambiguous definition of the poverty threshold and is consistent with rather different values of the index P. This is a rather serious shortcoming, since the problem arises for any discrete variable – unfortunately the large majority of non-monetary indicators. Note, however, that the problem relates to the characteristics of the indicator, not to the choice of a multidimensional evaluative space.

Conclusions

The multidimensional view of well-being is receiving growing attention, both in academic research and policy-oriented analysis, but the nuances of multidimensional empirical analysis are not yet fully understood. The impression is that multidimensional analysis is sometimes reduced to bunching together a number of indicators of living standard through some multivariate technique. But neglecting the role of underlying assumptions may be extremely misleading. It is of the utmost importance to develop a close link between analytical characterization and practical application of measurement tools.

In this chapter, I have addressed this question by examining two specific aspects of synthetic multidimensional indices of poverty and inequality: their functional form and their weighting structure. I have shown how using a multidimensional index is conceptually different from applying a univariate index to an indicator of multidimensional well-being, although they both end up providing a single number. The latter approach is somewhat more demanding as it implies the specification of a well-being indicator which summarizes all functionings at the individual level. In view of the empirical application, I have studied in some detail the characteristics of three multidimensional indices, one suggested by Tsui for inequality, and two proposed by Bourguignon and Chakravarty and by Atkinson for poverty. The indices proposed by Tsui and by Bourguignon and Chakravarty are axiomatically derived, while that proposed by Atkinson is a simple generalization of the practice of counting the occurrence of deprivation in multiple dimensions, which is frequently followed in empirical research. I have used these three indices to study the distribution of well-being in the four largest countries of the EU, by taking well-being to be represented by two functionings: 'command over resources' and 'health status'. Close attention has been paid to alternative measurement hypotheses: the indicator for command over resources (income vs. log-income); the relative weights of the two functionings; the values of the inequality and poverty aversion parameters; the degree of substitution between functionings; the weight assigned to multiple deprivations; the poverty threshold for the health status.

Two conclusions can be drawn. First, empirical findings confirm that measurement assumptions may considerably influence the results. This is hardly surprising, but it reinforces the obvious recommendation to carry out thorough sensitivity analyses. Yet, the difficulties of multidimensional measurement should not be overstated. The choice of the degree of poverty or inequality aversion, or the proper definition of an indicator such as command over resources, which have been extensively discussed in this chapter, would also arise in the univariate context. The problems that are new to the multivariate case are the weighting structure of the functionings and their degree of substitutability. Both these aspects are not technical hitches but the expression of implicit value judgements. Far from being a weakness of multidimensional approaches, the investigation of alternative assumptions is necessary to allow for the presence of different views in the society. This is a sufficient reason for not devolving the resolution of these measurement problems to some statistical algorithm. In this way, synthetic indices can provide valuable insights if used 'more as a dominance instrument than a strictly cardinal rule of comparison', as suggested by Bourguignon (1999: 483).

Second, the results from the analysis of well-being, as proxied by income and health, in France, Germany, Italy and the United Kingdom show that broadening the evaluative space to include people's perception of their own health modifies the picture drawn on the basis of income alone. Germany is the country with the lowest income poverty and inequality, but it appears to have the most unequal distribution of well-being for the majority of parameter configurations studied in this chapter. The least unequal distribution of well-being is found in France, although this is no longer true when the degree of poverty and inequality aversion in the social evaluation function is high. There is a distinct informative value in adopting a multidimensional perspective.

Acknowledgements

This chapter is a revised version of a paper presented at the conference on 'Ethics, Economics and Law: Against Injustice', held at the Ritsumeikan University in Kyoto, 28–30 October 2005; it draws extensively on earlier joint work with Giovanni D'Alessio. I greatly benefited from valuable comments by Sabine Alkire, Prasanta Pattanaik and other participants in the Kyoto conference as well as from the insightful remarks by Tony Atkinson on an earlier draft of the chapter. The views expressed here are solely those of the author and do not necessarily reflect those of the Bank of Italy.

References

Alkire, S. 2002. *Valuing Freedoms: Sen's Capability Approach and Poverty Reduction*, Oxford University Press.
Anand, S., and A. K. Sen 1994. 'Human Development Index: Methodology and Measurement'. United Nations Development Programme, Human

Development Report Office, Occasional Paper No. 12, July, New York: UNDP.

Anand, S., and A. K. Sen 2000, "The Income Component of the Human Development Index," *Journal of Human Development*, 1: 83–106.

Atkinson, A. B. 1970. 'On the Measurement of Inequality', *Journal of Economic Theory*, 2: 244–63.

1992. 'Measuring Poverty and Differences in Family Composition', *Economica*, 59: 1–16.

2002. 'Social Inclusion and the European Union', *Journal of Common Market Studies*, 40: 625–43.

2003. 'Multidimensional Deprivation: Contrasting Social Welfare and Counting Approaches', *Journal of Economic Inequality*, 1: 51–65.

Atkinson, A.B. and F. Bourguignon 1982. 'The Comparison of Multi-Dimensioned Distributions of Economic Status', *Review of Economic Studies*, 49: 183–201.

1987. 'Income Distribution and Differences in Needs', in Feiwel, G.R. (ed.), *Arrow and the Foundations of the Theory of Economic Policy*, Basingstoke: Macmillan, pp. 350–70.

Atkinson, A.B. and A. Brandolini 2004. 'Global World Inequality: Absolute, Relative or Intermediate?', paper presented at the 28th General Conference of the International Association for Research in Income and Wealth, Cork, Ireland, 22–28 August.

Atkinson, T., B. Cantillon, E. Marlier and B. Nolan 2002. *Social Indicators: The EU and Social Inclusion*, Oxford University Press.

Bibi, S. 2005a. 'Measuring Poverty in a Multidimensional Perspective: A Review of Literature', PEP Working Paper No. 2005–07, November, Quebec, Canada: Poverty and Economic Policy.

2005b. 'Multidimensional Poverty: A Comparison between Egypt and Tunisia', paper presented at the international conference on 'The Many Dimensions of Poverty', Brasilia, Brazil, 29–31 August. French version: Bibi, S., and A.-R. El Lahga (2008), 'Comparaisons ordinales robustes de la pauvreté multidimensionnelle: Afrique du Sud et Égypte', *Revue d'économie du développement*, 22: 5–36.

Bourguignon, F. 1999. 'Comment on "Multidimensioned Approaches to Welfare Analysis" by E. Maasoumi', in Silber, J. (ed.), *Handbook of Income Inequality Measurement*, Boston: Kluwer, pp. 477–84.

Bourguignon, F. and S.R. Chakravarty 2002. 'Multi-Dimensional Poverty Orderings', DELTA Working Paper No. 22, April, Paris: Départment et laboratoire d'économie théoretique et appliquée, ENS.

2003. 'The Measurement of Multidimensional Poverty', *Journal of Economic Inequality*, 1: 25–49.

Bradburd, R.M. and D.R. Ross 1988. 'A General Measure of Multidimensional Inequality', *Oxford Bulletin of Economics and Statistics*, 50: 429–33.

Brandolini, A. and G. D'Alessio 1998. 'Measuring Well-Being in the Functioning Space' (mimeo). Rome: Bank of Italy. Reproduced in Chiappero Martinetti, E. (ed.) (2009), *Debating Global Society: Reach and Limits of the Capability Approach*, Milan: Feltrelini Editore.

Brandolini, A. and T. M. Smeeding 2006. 'Inequality: International Evidence', in Durlauf, S. N., and L. E. Blume (eds.), *The New Palgrave Dictionary of Economics*, Basingstoke: Palgrave Macmillan, pp. 273–82.

Cerioli, A. and S. Zani 1990. 'A Fuzzy Approach to the Measurement of Poverty', in Dagum, C., and M. Zenga (eds.), *Income and Wealth Distribution, Inequality and Poverty*, Berlin: Springer-Verlag, pp. 272–84.

Cherchye, L., W. Moesen and T. Van Puyenbroeck 2004. 'Legitimately Diverse, yet Comparable: On Synthesizing Social Inclusion Performance in the EU', *Journal of Common Market Studies*, 42: 919–55.

Commission of the European Communities 1992. *Toward a Europe of Solidarity: Intensifying the Fight against Social Exclusion, Fostering Integration*. COM (92) 542, Brussels: European Commission.

Currie, J. and B. C. Madrian 1999. 'Health, Health Insurance and the Labor Market', in Ashenfelter, O. C., and D. Card (eds.), *Handbook of Labor Economics*, vol. III, part 3, Amsterdam: Elsevier, pp. 3309–416.

Desai, M. and A. Shah 1988. 'An Econometric Approach to the Measurement of Poverty', *Oxford Economic Papers*, 40: 505–22.

Deutsch, J. and J. Silber 2005. 'Measuring Multidimensional Poverty: An Empirical Comparison of Various Approaches', *Review of Income and Wealth*, 51: 145–74.

Duclos, J.-Y., D. E. Sahn and S. D. Younger 2006. 'Robust Multidimensional Poverty Comparisons', *Economic Journal*, 116: 943–68.

Erikson, R. 1993. 'Description of Inequality: The Swedish Approach to Welfare Research', in Nussbaum, M., and A. K. Sen (eds.), *The Quality of Life*, Oxford: Clarendon Press, pp. 66–83.

Eurostat 2000. *European Social Statistics. Income Poverty and Social Exclusion*, Luxembourg: Office for Official Publications of the European Communities.

Fahey, T., C. T. Whelan and B. Maître 2005. *First European Quality of Life Survey: Income inequalities and deprivation*, European Foundation for the Improvement of Living and Working Conditions, Luxembourg: Office for Official Publications of the European Communities.

Fluckiger, Y. and J. Silber 1994. 'The Gini Index and the Measurement of Multidimensional Inequality', *Oxford Bulletin of Economics and Statistics*, 56: 225–8.

Foster, J. E., J. Greer and E. Thorbecke 1984. 'A Class of Decomposable Poverty Measures', *Econometrica*, 52: 761–6.

Foster, J. E. and A. K. Sen 1997. '*On Economic Inequality* after a Quarter Century', in Sen, A. K., *On Economic Inequality*, expanded edn with a substantial annexe by J. E. Foster and A. K. Sen, Oxford: Clarendon Press, pp. 107–219.

Gaertner, W. 1993. 'Commentary to: "Amartya Sen: Capability and Well-Being"', in Nussbaum, M. and A. K. Sen (eds.), *The Quality of Life*, Oxford: Clarendon Press, pp. 62–6.

Gajdos, T. and J. A. Weymark 2005. 'Multidimensional generalized Gini indices', *Economic Theory*, 26: 471–96.

Guio, A.-C. 2005. 'Material Deprivation in the EU', *Statistics in Focus*, Population and Social Conditions, 21/2005, Luxembourg: Eurostat.

250   Against Injustice

Hirschberg, J.G., E. Maasoumi and D.J. Slottje 1991. 'Cluster Analysis for Measuring Welfare and Quality of Life Across Countries', *Journal of Econometrics*, **50**: 131–50.

Jenkins, S.P. and P.J. Lambert 1993. 'Ranking Income Distributions When Needs Differ', *Review of Income and Wealth*, **39**: 337–56.

Kendall, M. 1975. *Multivariate Analysis*, London: Griffin.

Kolm, S.-C. 1969. 'The Optimal Production of Social Justice', in Margolis, J. and H. Guitton (eds.), *Public Economics. An Analysis of Public Production and Consumption and Their Relations to the Private Sectors*, London: Macmillan, pp. 145–200.

1977. 'Multidimensional Egalitarianisms', *Quarterly Journal of Economics*, **91**: 1–13.

Kuklys, W. 2005. *Amartya Sen's Capability Approach*, Berlin: Springer.

Lelli, S. 2005. 'Using Functionings to Estimate Equivalence Scales', *Review of Income and Wealth*, **51**: 255–84.

List, C. 1999. 'Multidimensional Inequality Measurement: A Proposal', Nuffield College Working Paper in Economics, November, Oxford: Nuffield College.

Lovell, C.A.K., S. Richardson, P. Travers and L. Wood 1994. 'Resources and Functionings: A New View of Inequality in Australia', in Eichhorn, W. (ed.), *Models and Measurement of Welfare and Inequality*, Heidelberg: Springer-Verlag, pp. 787–807.

Lugo, M.A. 2007. 'Comparing Multidimensional Indices of Inequality: Methods and Application', in Bishop, J. and Y. Amiel (eds.), *Inequality and Poverty – Papers from the Society for the Study of Economic Inequality's Inaugural Meeting. Research on Economic Inequality*, Amsterdam: Elsevier JAI, vol. XIV, pp. 213–36.

Maasoumi, E. 1986. 'The Measurement and Decomposition of Multi-Dimensional Inequality', *Econometrica*, **54**: 991–7.

1999. 'Multidimensioned Approaches to Welfare Analysis', in Silber, J. (ed.), *Handbook of Income Inequality Measurement*, Boston: Kluwer, pp. 437–77.

Maasoumi, E. and G. Nickelsburg 1988. 'Multivariate Measures of Well-Being and an Analysis of Inequality in the Michigan Data', *Journal of Business & Economic Statistics*, **6**: 327–34.

Mayer, S.E. and C. Jencks 1989. 'Poverty and the Distribution of Material Hardship', *Journal of Human Resources*, **21**: 88–113.

Mejer, L. 2000. 'Social Exclusion in the EU Member States', *Statistics in Focus*, Population and Social Conditions, Theme 3, No. 1, Luxembourg: Eurostat

Micklewright, J. 2001. 'Should the UK Government Measure Poverty and Social Exclusion with a Composite Index?', in Centre for Analysis of Social Exclusion, *Indicators of Progress: A Discussion of Approaches to Monitor the Government's Strategy to Tackle Poverty and Social Exclusion*, CASE Report No. 13, London School of Economics, pp. 45–50.

Nolan, B. and C.T. Whelan 1996a. *Resources, Deprivation, and Poverty*, Oxford: Clarendon Press.

1996b. 'The Relationship between Income and Deprivation: A Dynamic Perspective', *Revue économique*, **3**: 709–17.

Ramos, X. and J. Silber 2005. 'On the Application of Efficiency Analysis to the Study of the Dimensions of Human Development', *Review of Income and Wealth*, **51**: 285–309.

Robeyns, I. 2006. 'The Capability Approach in Practice', *Journal of Political Philosophy*, **14**: 351–76.

Schokkaert, E. and L. Van Ootegem 1990. 'Sen's Concept of the Living Standard Applied to the Belgian Unemployed', *Recherches Economiques de Louvain*, **56**: 429–50.

Sen, A.K. 1978. 'Ethical Measurement of Inequality: Some Difficulties', in Krelle, W. and A.F. Shorrocks (eds.), *Personal Income Distribution*, Amsterdam: North–Holland, pp. 81–94.

1985. *Commodities and Capabilities*, Amsterdam: North Holland.

1987. *The Standard of Living*, with contributions by J. Muellbauer, R. Kanbur, K. Hart and B. Williams. Ed. G. Hawthorn, Cambridge University Press.

1992. *Inequality Reexamined*. Oxford: Clarendon Press.

1998. 'Mortality as an Indicator of Economic Success and Failure', *Economic Journal*, **108**: 1–25.

Sharma, S. 1996. *Applied Multivariate Techniques*, New York: Wiley.

Srinivasan, T.N. 1994. 'Human Development: A New Paradigm or Reinvention of the Wheel?', *American Economic Review Papers and Proceedings*, **84**: 238–43.

Streeten, P. 1994. 'Human Development: Means and Ends', *American Economic Review Papers and Proceedings*, **84**: 232–37.

Sugden, R. 1993. 'Welfare, Resources, and Capabilities: A Review of *Inequality Reexamined* by Amartya Sen', *Journal of Economic Literature*, **31**: 1947–62.

Townsend, P. 1979. *Poverty in the United Kingdom: A Survey of Household Resources and Standards of Living*, Harmondsworth: Penguin.

Tsui, K.-Y. 1995. 'Multidimensional Generalizations of the Relative and Absolute Inequality Indices: The Atkinson–Kolm–Sen Approach', *Journal of Economic Theory*, **67**: 251–65.

1999. 'Multidimensional Inequality and Multidimensional Generalized Entropy Measures: An Axiomatic Derivation', *Social Choice and Welfare*, **16**: 145–57.

2002. 'Multidimensional Poverty Indices', *Social Choice and Welfare*, **19**: 69–93.

UNDP (United Nations Development Programme) 2005. *Human Development Report 2005, International Cooperation at a Crossroads: Aid, Trade and Security in an Unequal World*, New York and Oxford: United Nations Development Programme and Oxford University Press.

Weymark, J.A. 2006. 'The normative approach to the measurement of multidimensional inequality', in Farina, F. and E. Savaglio (eds.), *Inequality and Economic Integration*, London: Routledge, pp. 303–28.

Wilkinson, R.G. 1996. *Unhealthy Societies. The Afflictions of Inequality*, London: Routledge.

World Bank 2001. *World Development Report 2000/2001: Attacking Poverty*, New York and Oxford: Oxford University Press.

11 Assessing children's capabilities: operationalizing metrics for evaluating music programs with poor children in Brazilian primary schools

Flavio Comim

Introduction

Evaluating the impact of educational changes on children's capabilities can be done in a diversity of ways. Indeed, there is no unique way of using the CA (capability approach) for normative purposes. One possible route is to define a methodology based on the most striking characteristics of the approach and then to create different categories of assessment from the particular features of the targeted programs. When the CA is used as an informational space for normative valuations we have the approach at its best. This means that the approach is incomplete by necessity (in the sense that it depends on the use of particular substantive theories) and it is not used beyond its conceptual limits.

Among the most important features of the approach, as defined by Sen (1985; 1992; 1999) and Nussbaum (2000), may be mentioned:

- objective nature of functionings and capabilities, avoiding the use of subjective metrics and the problem of adaptive preferences;
- multidimensional assessment of capability-laden normative exercises, exploring the differential impact of actions and state-of-affairs on individuals' well-being and agency;
- emphasis on autonomy as a characteristic of individuals' advantage-point, providing a distinct perspective on how people are able to shape their well-being;
- comparable results, based on the principle of *multiple realisability* (Nussbaum, 2000: 77).

When addressing the issue of children's capabilities the importance of temporal dimensions in constituting the characterization of the autonomy and well-being of individuals must be noted. The same capability has different autonomy-values if belonging to different moments in time. There are discount factors that could be applied to justify the importance of early-capabilities in comparison to late-capabilities.

Thus, if an individual misses the opportunity of developing her cognitive abilities at a certain stage in her life, it might well be too late in the future. Choices are usually time-dependent and each person's *evolving story*, as Nussbaum (1990: 94) puts it, influences her or his choices. People as human beings should adapt their choices to the particular temporal circumstances of their lives.

The usual assessment dilemma for researchers and practitioners of choosing normative categories from a pre-defined list of basic capabilities, as advocated by Nussbaum (1999; 2000), or emphasizing the processes of constitution of 'public reasoning', as argued by Sen (1999; 2005), does not have to be self-excluding, as acknowledged by both authors. Here, the justification and choice of particular capabilities might be open to several arguments related to the general importance of attributes considered essential for human life. However, the intrinsic difficulties of identification and selection of assessment categories can be assisted by the objectives of the program. Evaluating an educational action is simpler, to a larger extent, than fully characterizing the well-being (and agency) of individuals. When classifying individuals in poor vs. non-poor or health-deprived vs. healthy categories there are usually no universal guidelines apart from very basic standards (like illiteracy, mortality rates or hunger). On the other hand, when assessing social programs, the choice and justification of capability spaces will depend on the objectives of the program. This circumstance provides an analytical framework that can guide the organization of different informational spaces and the identification and choice of spaces.

The measurement of capabilities remains one illusive challenge ahead of the operationalization of the CA. In particular, the translation of normative categories into operational metrics has not yet been fully explored in the capability space. This chapter provides an attempt in this direction. More specifically, it presents an empirical assessment of a social program that targeted periphery schools in poor parts of Brazil. The social program consisted of several initiatives for introducing music teaching and music activities to poor children. With the introduction of substantive theories of children's cognitive development, the capability approach was used to systematize a variety of human development dimensions. Different metrics were built to assess the impact of the program on children's capabilities. The multidimensional, objective and counter-factual nature of capabilities are represented in this methodology.

The chapter is divided into four parts. The first part briefly introduces the program called 'Music in Schools' funded by the Italian Telecom (TIM) in Brazil. The second part presents the methodology used. The third part discusses the main results. Finally, the paper concludes with lessons learned for assessing social programs based on the CA.

TIM Music in Schools

The project 'TIM Música nas Escolas' is part of Italia Telecom's Corporate Social Responsibility Agenda in Brazil. It targets very poor students living in deprived neighbourhoods and attending primary schools in the outskirts of big Brazilian cities: Belém, Salvador, Recife, São Paulo, Rio de Janeiro and Porto Alegre. The project was assessed during its second year of implementation. Its general aim is to promote students' interest in music through (i) musical workshops and (ii) music lessons. The project tries to introduce music (learning how to play an instrument and how to use music in different activities) into the daily lives of thousands of students in Brazil. By doing so the project allows the children access to a different model of learning and social inter-action. Thus, the project provides a wider scope for communitarian inclusion and promotion of social autonomy to its participants. Its specific aims are:

- to promote the artistic development of students
- to foster their pedagogic development
- to encourage the development of the social autonomy of students, promoting the development of community ties

The project was structured around different degrees of coverage, cor-responding to different target-groups and distinct particular objectives and outcomes: (i) the promotion of an alternative model of teaching and learning (and social action) through music was shaped through a discourse of social inclusion. Activities were conceived in association with parents and local communities, allowing them a shared ownership with the institutional space provided by the school. As a result, a wide range of concerns was voiced and schools started addressing topics that were relevant to all the community; (ii) themes of musical culture were introduced to children, stimulating values of belonging and self-respect (usually very scarce among deprived children); (iii) aesthetic experi-ences were provided to children outside school hours, enriching their lives and allowing them opportunities for expressing their feeling and emotions; (iv) youth groups were organized through musical activities. Different implementation strategies were carried out according to the different objectives of the project.

It is important to remark that the project did not consist in foster-ing music appreciation among children. Respecting the wide variety of

Table 11.1. *Different target groups*

	Belém	Porto Alegre	Recife	Rio de Janeiro	Salvador	São Paulo	Total
'Ambassadors of Peace'	30	30	30	60	30	120	300 students
Children at Workshops ('oficinas')	3 schools 840 students	3 schools 840 students	6 schools 1,680 students	5 schools 2,500 students	7 schools 1,680 students	10 schools 5,000 students	34 schools 12,540 students
Nucleus	90 students	180 students	180 students	0	180 students	536 students	1,166 students

personal and regional tastes for music, it involved the teaching and use of many different kinds of music. Whereas the main focus of the group of students called 'ambassadors' was on how to play musical instruments, the focus of 'Nucleus' was on using music for games and plays. General workshops were activities for the 'oficinas' involving a mixture of both activities described above.

Students were divided into three groups according to the activities in which they participated, namely the group of (i) workshops; (ii) 'Nucleus'; and (iii) 'Ambassadors of Peace', as can be seen in Table 11.1.

Workshops were carried out every two months involving the entire school. They consisted of musical activities designed to include children of all ages and groups. There was no sense of affiliation attached to these activities. Participants in 'Nucleus' were meeting almost every week. They were divided into two sets: radio and games. Children within this group were trained to promote peace and non-violence through musical games during class breaks. Finally, the last group, called 'Ambassadors of Peace', was made up of children who received formal musical training and who received financial assistance from the project. They were named 'Ambassadors of Peace' because as part of their activities they had not only music training but also classes in citizenship. They were taught to be citizens and leaders in promoting an environment of non-violence and harmony within their schools and at home.

In assessing a social investment with many different targeted groups, one question deserves special attention. If different individuals do quite different things, shouldn't they be evaluated differently? The clear answer is: no. One of the main purposes of the evaluation is comparability among different social actions. It is only through comparability that it is possible to provide specific information about the usefulness of different instruments, providing better tools for the management of the social investment. Common standards, related to the main objectives of the program and to its most important characteristics, are essential in conceptualizing assessment exercises as part of practical management strategies.

Methodology

Music is commonly valued for its recreational or hedonic aspects. However, there is evidence provided by child psychologists and neuroscientists (see for instance, Hallam, Price and Katsarou (2002), Pecore (2000) and Rauscher (2003)) that music has an important instrumental value in the promotion of children's human development. Music is universal among cultures: all individuals have the capability of being musical, as they are capable of having a fulfilling life. Music can be seen as a set of practices, concepts and perceptions that are based on particular social constructions and interactions that are intrinsic to communities of individuals. This means that the meaning of music can alternate according to the different social contexts in which it takes place.

Perret (2004) argues that the manner in which a person sings or plays an instrument is the *fingerprint* (defining element) of her personality. It is unique, and it reveals a richness of unconscious information. The fingerprint reveals the internal rhythm of the brain, organs, mood changes and biochemistry or simply the way in which we are physically built. Cross (2001) emphasizes that the factors that grant efficiency to music in promoting children's cognitive development and socialization cannot ensure the multiple forms and functions that music has during adult age. The meaning of a music activity for an individual will depend on her personal history and narratives affecting the general system of meanings in the culture where she lives. As pointed out by Cross (2001: 36)

Music, like language, cannot be wholly private; it is a property of communities, not individuals. And these different levels at which music may be efficacious must be integrated in any understanding of its foundations. Music's very existence is best evidenced in interaction. If music is of importance in human development, evolution and life, then an attempt to render commensurable our understanding of music as interaction with our understanding of music's biological foundations is crucial in coming to terms with what Henry Plotkin ... calls 'the most complicated thing in the universe – the collective of human brains and their psychological processes that make up human culture'.

This argument was raised by Blacking (1969), who argued that the main function of music is to improve the quality of individual experience and of human relations, allowing better structures and conceptions about the patterns of human interaction. Therefore, the value of music as such is inseparable from its value as part of human experience. In this sense, musical education is a progressive reconstruction of the experience of relationships among individuals – but on a different basis.

The pattern of interaction between children and music teachers is defined by children's ability to follow and reply to temporal regularities in movement and voicing; being able to start their own set of temporal and regular sets of voice and movement. This ability is crucial to the development of human capabilities of communication and meaning. Furthermore, the identification and following of a standardized time, in association with others, facilitates harmony among affective states and interaction among children.

Wallace (1961) shows how psychic unity among groups – crucial for the dynamics of interaction at schools – is based not on the sharing of motivational structures but on the existence of common cognitive orientations. Therefore, cognition and internalization of common values represent a 'behaviour structure' presented by individuals. This is an important result because it illustrates how the assessment of a social program involving music teaching should take into account not only simply individual hedonic values but also social impacts determined by the effect of music on how children relate to each other. Taken as a whole, the evidence described above can be helpful in explaining why some dimensions are more basic than others for assessing the impact of music, in the context provided by 'Music in Schools', on children's human development.

Selecting informational spaces

This emphasis on musical social praxis suggests a selection of assessment dimensions related to individual and social musical impacts. These different dimensions interact. They are context specific. Yet, it is important to note that there is indivisibility between sound and movement that characterizes music throughout cultures and times. Music, seen as a body activity, produces not only a cognitive but also an affective impact on human development. Based on the evidence provided by the literature on the impact of music on children, briefly described above, it is possible to argue that when assessing children's well-being, the main informational spaces for evaluating the impact of music on their development are:

a. Temporal reasoning
   Following the model developed by Rauscher (2003), we can argue that children's temporal reasoning is very sensitive to musical experiences, given that knowledge produced by music needs the

development of temporal sequences of brain activities. These temporal processes are daily used by children in tasks that need the combination of elements in a sequential manner, ordering objects in a specific order to represent certain situations.

b. Spatial reasoning

Music, seen as an activity, strengthens cognitive development of special representations of basic mental structures. In its simplest form, music is a meeting of links between rhythmic standards. Spatial reasoning entails keeping certain messages and transforming others. It is a precondition for more advanced cerebral functions, such as those involved in structural organization, memory and mathematics.

c. Emotional development and expression

Music represents an association of different forms of expression. The musical experience entails the development of capabilities related to affection and emotions (happiness, sadness, etc.). This capability stimulates different ways of thinking and knowing – crucial for individuals' capabilities of coordinating their emotions. In their turn, these emotions influence individuals' predisposition to engage in structured relations (which is very noticeable in schools in the problem of lack of discipline and order during classes).

d. Social development

Music provides a standard of communication to individuals and a style of human interaction. This is particularly relevant to children and teenagers, who usually present difficulties in using other forms of communication. Consequently, music can provide an important element in shaping the social identity of individuals and in defining their social development. Having said that, it is important to note that a negative aspect might be manifested in relation to the phenomenon of 'groupishness' (seen through hostility towards those outside the group), when strong identities are forged among members of the group. However, the multiplicity of meanings that can be associated with music can be helpful in restructuring new social relations.

These dimensions provide the informational basis to the impact assessment of 'Music in Schools'. This does not mean that other dimensions are not important. The list of possible impacts of musical experience on children's development is considerable. There is evidence that music (i) improves the exploratory competence of individuals, (ii) gives intellectual satisfaction, (iii) helps in structural organization and social inclusion, (iv) fosters confidence, (v) helps with decision-making, (vi) strengthens scientific and artistic abilities, (vii) stimulates children's attention, (viii) improves children's concentration in class, (ix) develops children's linguistic ability and (x) reduces the involvement of children with drugs. However, it must be emphasized that the dimensions presented and discussed above are more basic, in the particular sense that they can be considered 'structuring': they are fundamental not only for the cognitive development of children but also for their socialization. They can shape their sense of autonomy. So, they are more basic in a capability sense. This was confirmed in interviews held with teachers and headmasters of the participating schools.

A particular list of variables based on these informational spaces was elaborated based on interviews with local coordinators and project officers. This list characterizes a set of qualitative evidences that could be used as a starting point for the assessment of the program.

Surveys and variables

The methodology developed was inspired by CA. It emphasized the use of substantive theories of children's development (e.g. Goswami 1998 and Greene and Hogan 2005) to assist the definition of informational spaces and variables considered appropriate for this social program (TIM Music in Schools). Appropriateness was judged according to the objectives and characteristics of the program. It comprised a combination of qualitative and quantitative empirical evidence in the characterization of children's development. Interviews were originally conducted with school headteachers, program officers and local coordinators. After that, surveys were formulated to address the issues raised at a grass-root level from a capability perspective (assisted by substantive theories of children's development). These surveys were (i) with children participating in the musical workshops, (ii) with children participating in the Nucleus activities, (iii) with children of the group 'Ambassadors of Peace'. Children who never participated in activities of the 'TIM Music in Schools' program were also interviewed, in each participating school, and served as control groups. The objective was to compare the performance between different groups, assessing how different degrees of exposure to music (controlling also for social background) can be related to important dimensions of children's development such as cognition, socialization and emotions.

All surveys had the same basic structure that consisted of:

• identification of children
• assessment of social and emotional links with music
• assessment of temporal-spatial reasoning
• phonographic reaction
• behavioural reaction.

Table 11.2. *Elkoshi's classification (2002)*

Categories	Numeric grade
Category 0 (zero)	0
Category A (Association)	1
Category P (Pictogram)	2
Category F (Formal answer)	4
Category G (Growth)	8

The phonographic reaction of children represents their cognitive reaction to sounds and serves to infer their ability for expression and exploratory competence. To assess the phonographic reaction, the 'Elkoshi classification' (2002) was chosen, associating different categories to a numerical scale. By doing so, this classification provides a scale in which we can assess children's cognitive reaction to music. Two pilot surveys were tried with tunes from Rossini's *William Tell*, considered very easy by the children and Tchaikovsky's *Swan Lake*, considered very boring by the children. Finally, the music of Riverdance was chosen for its musical sequence and better acceptance among the children.

The statistical analysis was based on a subgroup identification of relative frequencies, on an investigation of correlation matrixes and on a comparison of relative quality of children's performances according to control characteristics, such as gender, age, musical taste, etc. These variables were related to each general assessment category, namely: (i) temporal reasoning, (ii) spatial reasoning and (iii) phonographic reasoning. For the subgroup 'Ambassadors of Peace', a more complete analysis was carried out, with emphasis on the elements: (i) understanding of the project, (ii) social and individual impact, (iii) trust, (iv) critical reasoning and (v) emotional impact.

When aggregated, the main categories related to the general assessment (variables (i) to (iii)) gave rise to the 'General Index of Impact (GII)', three-dimensional, used to make comparisons among different control groups. This exercise allowed the development of an *evaluative benchmark* for the program, establishing a reference for the assessment of the program. The GII was elaborated after the use of substantive theories indicated the role of music in the formation of children's cognitive development and after the first round of consultation with stakeholders. The choice of dimensions was tailor-made to the objectives of 'Music in Schools' and should not be mechanically extrapolated to similar programs.

The three main dimensions related to cognitive and social development can be seen as capabilities (as opposed to being seen as functionings, as is usually the case in many capability studies) because of the following characteristics:

- objective nature: measures based on cognitive development are neither directly related (as a necessity) to the level of resources employed in social investments nor to subjective appreciations of the projects;
- multidimensional feature: the measures presented are all meant to be parts of a general description of the state of children. They are very different from summary measures that try to capture all effects of certain actions or activities. As such, they are all parts of different accounts that can be given;
- counterfactual nature: measures of cognitive and social development are simple inferences from unobservable entities.[1] Moreover, they are an intertemporal condition for future development of functionings. In this sense, spatial cognitive development is a capability because it defines a set of future possibilities of learning mathematics (functioning). Similarly, temporal cognitive development is a capability in the sense that it provides a set of future possibilities for children's literacy;
- autonomy and agency: more importantly, perhaps, the individual and social aspects related to the chosen dimensions define a set of possibilities of emotional and social understanding for children, allowing them different paths of constitution of their autonomy and identity.

In what follows the main results will be presented and analysed. Outcomes will be disaggregated according to the objectives of the program and the different target groups.

Main results

After the identification of different informational spaces and choice of variables to be used in the different surveys, the next step of the methodology consisted in the articulation of qualitative and quantitative information. For the sake of clarity, the main categories of analysis were

---

[1] The less philosophically inclined reader might feel uncomfortable with the apparent paradox of measuring 'unobservable' entities. For this reason, it is important to distinguish here between what one wishes to measure and what instrument one could use to measure it. The most common example that fits this description is the use of IQ tests to measure intelligence, which is unobservable. In our case, the chosen measures of cognitive and social development are counterfactual in the sense that they refer to 'opportunities' and might provide an indication of future 'factualities'.

presented and disaggregated into five groups, namely: (i) qualitative analysis, (ii) quantitative analysis – general results, (iii) quantitative analysis – results by cities, (iv) quantitative analysis – disaggregated by schools and (v) quantitative analysis – results of 'Ambassadors of Peace'. Here, for sake of brevity, results are reported for (i)–(iii). This progressive disaggregation provided specific information about the impact of different actions implemented at different levels. This knowledge can assist local coordinators with useful and practical information. This assessment strategy aims to produce specific information for a better management of social programs. By doing so, it reveals an important added value of evaluative strategies, namely, the provision of concrete information for a better organization and management of social initiatives.

Qualitative analysis

Subjective information about children's performance and managerial features of the project 'TIM Music in Schools' was collected through the realization of focal group discussions with local coordinators, headteachers, teachers, parents and project officers. Together they constitute an active network of participants better characterized as social capital. During all meetings the high degree of conviction and belief expressed by all agents (in the above groups) on the positive impact of the program on the lives of the participating children was remarkable. For the sake of clarity it is possible to systematize the qualitative outreach of the program within ten categories, in decreasing order of frequency:

1. Behaviour: almost all teachers, headteachers and project officers reported change in the children's behaviour during the project. Within a context of multiple levels of deprivation characterized by chronic poverty in the periphery of large Brazilian cities, the project has improved children's concentration and attention during classes.
2. Self-esteem: the tough reality of poor families, often dysfunctional, imposes a situation in which children's development is not seen as a priority. As argued by officers, the project makes the children feel special (given the level of attention dedicated to them) and consequently improves their self-esteem. This improvement in their self-esteem could be the beginning of new attitudes. For instance, children belonging to households where hygiene is not a priority may show better attitudes towards having cleaner clothes or even comb their hair differently. Moreover, self-esteem can be translated in a positive attitude towards the future ('I can'), which can be translated into new initiatives among them. Finally, the self-esteem of

whole families can be improved, with parents expressing pride in seeing their children as part of the project (in particular in the case of 'Ambassadors of Peace').

3. Personal objectives: to many children their involvement with music opened new perspectives to their lives. The simple idea of 'having objectives in life' was foreign to many of them. For instance, in Belém, at the Maria Luíza Pinto Amaral school, the deputy head spoke about the case of a child called 'Luana' (an Ambassador of Peace). According to her: 'She was a lost child, inattentive, looking for a north. Today, she has objectives in life.' Indeed, the immiserizing reality lived by children does affect their vision of their future. The project has inspired in those participating children a dream to become someone different. In the midst of high levels of material, moral and educational deprivation experienced by children attending public schools in Brazil, the deprivation of basic capabilities is an aggression that children assimilate by generating further expressions of violence. The project brought to children a new set of information, a new benchmark to their lives, stimulating their dreams and helping with the formation of objectives.

4. Musical knowledge: access to musical knowledge is usually restricted to the very few in Brazil, being limited by the low purchasing power of most families. The project brought knowledge and general culture about music to very deprived students, raising their awareness of musical activities. This was very significant, taking into account the fact that children have not many options for leisure in the periphery of large Brazilian cities.

5. Curiosity and interest: the project has raised the curiosity and interest of children, breaking with the high level of apathy and idleness that pervades the lives of poor children in Brazil. An educational system that does not stimulate the students promotes an attitude of acceptance and resignation towards life that results in general lack of interest. According to teachers, as a result of the project, many children started expressing some interest in music and other activities at school.

6. Socialization: a new attitude of friendship was observed among participating children, who started sharing objects and food. This attitude was at odds with the general rule of disrespect, where children take objects and food, instead of sharing them. A progressive change was also noted in the way that participating children started greeting their colleagues.

7. Female empowerment: it is common to find a less participative culture among deprived female children, mirroring a macho environment

prevalent in many public schools. With the project, a new attitude toward equality was introduced, empowering female children who assumed important tasks in the constitution of the different target groups.

8. Reduction in violence: the only behavioural model that pervades the reality of many public schools in Brazil is that of violence. The social history of many children is reduced to an institutional and emotional vacuum, where abusive relations flourish. With the workshops and Nucleus activities a new benchmark of behaviour was introduced to the children. During brief time frames (of a couple of months), workshops were conducive to lower levels of violence in the schools (these levels were resumed after summer breaks). The 'becoming' of children into a being with self-determination through violence stops being the only show in town, as music lessons and activities are able to provide a new relationship of respect among teachers and colleagues.

9. Happiness: to many officers, the workshops brought happiness to children. In particular, the Nucleus promoted a revival of games during breaks at schools. It was then noted that children are happier when they are playing. This observation is at odds with the tough reality of breaks in public schools in Brazil, when children are not seen playing but fighting with each other.

10. Critical thought and citizenship: the project introduced many new concepts of citizenship to children (peace, tolerance, etc.), stimulating new values and critical thought. These concepts were worked on with the children during the workshops and other meetings. To a certain extent, the project has sown the seed of democracy and public participation among deprived children.

Overall, the qualitative assessment produced by focal-group discussions was highly positive, suggesting multidimensional impacts from those educational actions. It must be noted that most of the above-mentioned elements are difficult to measure, but this should not lead to them being ignored; quite the opposite. Most participants were emphatic in arguing that TIM's contribution to the lives of the children in those communities 'was priceless'.

Quantitative analysis – general results

Two rounds of surveys were applied to more than 7,000 students during 2005 in six Brazilian cities, resulting in more than 12,000 valid questionnaires for the two rounds. The surveys were organized with the purpose of assessing the intertemporal impact of the program, allowing a

Table 11.3. *General results, round 1*

Cognitive dimensions	Non-participants	Participants	Nucleus
Temporal	2.44	2.44	2.52
Spatial	1.82	1.88	2.06
Behavioural	1.09	1.17	1.31
Standardized GII	0.60	0.60	0.67

cross-section comparison followed by 'before-and-after' analyses. The large majority of students (82.4%) were between 10 and 14 years old; 76% of the children were in the project for 6 months, with only a small part (5%) being in the project over 2 years. This happens as a result of the high turnover of students in the schools. Seven types of music dominate (70%) the musical preferences (pagode, funk, black, rock, brega, rap and hip-hop – in order of preference) of children. The emotional attachment to music was suggested by the surveys, showing that for 38.7% of children, their preferred song was also the favourite of a member of their close family (mother, father or siblings); for 30.8% it was that of their close friends; and for 8.9% that of their classmates. The large majority of children reported listening to music every day (75.7%); 22.8% listen to music when dancing, whereas 22.5% listen to music doing their chores and 20.3% listen to music doing nothing. Only a small group listens to music while studying (6.6%) or playing (4%). These descriptive statistics illustrate how diverse were the contexts in which the program was implemented. Music teaching and other musical activities were organized around children's preferences. The complex role of music, related to its importance for social interaction and multifaceted use, offered an interesting challenge for the assessment exercise.

The distribution of results followed a normal distribution. Among all variables, the one that discriminated most was the phonographic reaction, revealing children's cognitive competence and ability of expression. The main differences between participants and non-participants were not pronounced in most dimensions. However, as we moved towards other categories (such as 'Nucleus' or 'Ambassadors of Peace') where the commitment and exposure to music had more density, more meaningful differences were found, as portrayed below, based on the results of the first round of surveys.

The scores were built in absolute scales, and were standardized in a (0–1) scale in order to provide a basis of comparison among subgroups. The methodology adopted suggests that part of children's social and

Table 11.4. *Gender impacts*

Cognitive dimensions	Boys	Girls
Temporal	1.7	1.8
Spatial	1.7	1.7
Phonographic	0.7	0.7
GII	4.4	4.4
Percentage cleaning the house	9.7	35.0
Percentage doing nothing	28.1	12.8

emotional development is based on the development of their cognitive competences. A 'sensitive-to-gender' analysis shows great homogeneity between boys and girls in terms of impact assessment. Some important differences remain related to how they allocate their time. For instance, when asked what they do when listening to music, the majority of girls replied 'cleaning the house' whereas the boys replied 'doing nothing'.

The second round of surveys stressed the importance of behavioural elements in defining children's capabilities. Once again the results were standardized in a (0–1) scale, signalling a low impact if nearer to '0' and a high impact if closer to '1'. With this procedure, the outcomes were reduced to a common denominator, allowing a better comparison between different scales and giving more intuitive meaning to the results. The new GII was calculated indicating that there was a higher impact only in 'Nucleus' in comparison to other groups (confirming the main result from the first round of surveys). In the second round of surveys a question about 'happiness' was introduced to measure the degree of children's satisfaction with their lives. The evidence suggested that non-participating children were more unhappy by a very narrow margin (8.57 to 8.62) than those participating. In this case, the subjective metric was not very illuminating. A discouraging correlation was found in this survey, namely, the existence of a negative relation (statistically significant) between the level of trust between children and their respective ages and school years. This means that as children get older, they trust their classmates less. It is within this context that it was found that the number of classmates that a participating child trusts increases with her involvement with music. To the non-participating children their average number of friends is 1.98, followed by the number (2.19) of friends of those who attend musical workshops and those of 'Nucleus' (2.49). This means that children participating in 'Nucleus' activities trust their colleagues 26 percent more in comparison to those children who do not have any involvement with the program. This is a non-trivial impact of 'Music in Schools' and strong evidence that participation in the project is linked to value formation.

Can we say that these results are strictly related to the impact of music on children's human development? Certainly not. In the operation of the program, many other social activities were implemented in order to complement the music teaching and music activities taking place at school. However, the important point here is that these complementary activities were all structured around a program whose main objective is to take music to deprived children. The promotion of different values, such as those of non-violence and cooperation, was an intrinsic part of a strategy articulated around music activities. Music, for this matter, was important not only for its constitutive (e.g. cognitive value) but also for its instrumental (e.g. motivational) value. Within this context, it is useful to remark that we are not here providing any scientific evidence about the cognitive impact of music on children's development (we are employing here the evidence already available in the specialized literature) but rather using the CA to provide an impact assessment of 'Music in Schools'. By doing so, we are avoiding analyses of economic impact or opinion polls, so commonly used in Brazil and in other parts of the world, to evaluate the performance of social investment.

Quantitative analysis – results by cities

It is natural and convenient to use 'cities' as the main unit of analysis, because the main logistics of 'Music in Schools' are defined at city level, with coordinators and program officers operating at this level. Whereas the first survey explored information such as the composition of sample according to gender, years of schooling, age, format of participation, favourite songs, links between affection and musicality and activities and music, the second survey emphasized behavioural changes. The picture of the results by cities confirmed by the second survey is shown in Figure 11.1.

The overall impact of the program was assessed for all participating cities, indicating sensitive areas in two cities, namely, Salvador and Recife. In these cities, there was no meaningful impact of workshop activities and marginal results for the Nucleus. This was an important result of the assessment, suggesting that action needs to be taken in these two cities. The figures provided by a comparative exercise, where results are expressed in relation to the performance of non-participating children, highlight the negative performance of these two cities, indicating where successes and failures might lie.

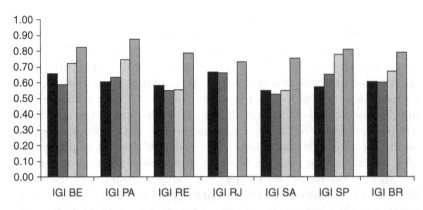

■ Non-participants   ■ Children at Workshops   ▢ Nucleus   ■ Ambassadors of Peace

Figure 11.1 GII for cities and Brazil

Table 11.5. *Percentage variation of GII for cities in comparison with non-participating children*

	Workshops	Nucleus	Ambassadors
GII Belém	−10.05	10.85	26.61
GII Porto Alegre	5.32	23.58	45.01
GII Recife	−5.71	−5.14	34.74
GII Rio de Janeiro	−0.50	N	10.07
GII Salvador	−3.93	0.10	37.74
GII São Paulo	13.95	35.28	40.87
GII Brazil			**31.15**

It is important to note that these results (expressed in terms of GII) are multidimensionally decomposable into the three main informational spaces, as discussed above. It is also possible to disaggregate the results according to subgroups (by age, gender, etc.). This was done, but the richness of results cannot be reported here because of lack of space. It should be noted, however, that information provided can help a better targeting of programs, assessing the distributive impact of social investments.

'Triangles of impact' were built to demonstrate visually and intuitively the impact of the program on different dimensions of children's human development. These triangles were produced for each school participating in the program, but for sake of brevity only the city results are presented here. To a certain extent, presenting the results in geo-metric formats seems to be a natural result of working with multidimensionality. By doing so, one would consequently use criteria of *dominance* to assess the relative performance of subgroups.

A brief inspection by cities of how the GII is distributed between its different components allows an immediate comparison among cities and subgroups. These triangles were calculated taking into account three layers of information, namely: (i) dimensions, (ii) subgroups (workshop participants, non-participants, 'Nucleus' and 'Ambassadors') and (iii) geographic scale. A fourth dimension can be introduced when dynamic comparisons ('before-and-after' analysis) are carried out.

It is interesting to see how different informational spaces can be used in this sort of normative exercise. For instance, it can be noted that 'Ambassadors of Peace' are on average older than other participants. In our sample, 63.4% were between 12 and 15 years. When asked, 97.3% of Ambassadors did not hesitate to agree that the project was positive to their lives. Within this group, 21.8% believe that the project is import-ant because they are learning something, in comparison to 17.9% who believe that the project is important because they are learning music. Leaving the world of subjective metrics, we tried to map objectively their cognitive development and reactions to counterfactual situations that they face in their daily lives, as a way of assessing their capabil-ities. The triangles reproduced in Figure 11.2 emphasize this object-ive nature of capabilities. However, it is also important to note that by selecting these three dimensions (considered more constitutive by the substantive theories that inform this assessment exercise), we are excluding others. There is also a trade-off between focus and extension of indicators that it is difficult to avoid. By no means should this be read as a dismissal of other (quantitative or qualitative) information, but as a result of a normative decision that is necessary for organizing the main results of the assessment.

Comparing the overall elements, it is possible to conclude that the program 'TIM Music in Schools' has successfully enhanced the human capabilities of children in very poor areas of Brazil. The results are far from being homogeneous, but it seems the case that higher levels of investment in musical teaching are conducive to a higher expansion of children's capabilities. This can be seen from the relative perform-ance of the four subgroups. The group 'Ambassadors of Peace' is the one that has a deeper contact with music and presents a high level of objectively measured capabilities (Ambassadors' GII *dominates* all other GIIs).

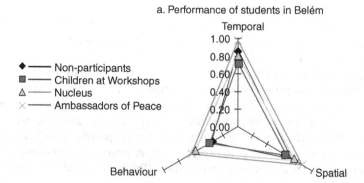

a. Performance of students in Belém

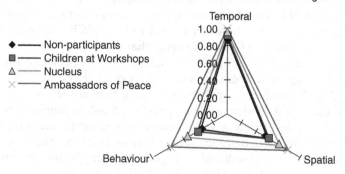

b. Performance of students in Porto Alegre

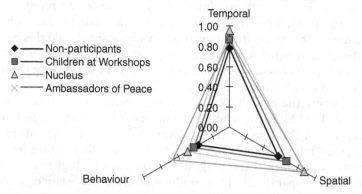

c. Performance of students in São Paulo

Figure 11.2 Triangles of impact

d. Performance of students in Rio De Janeiro

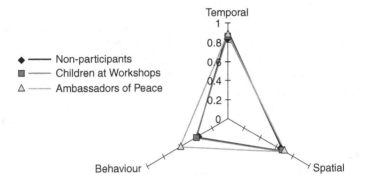

e. Performance of students in Recife

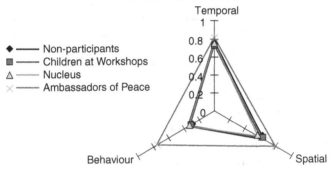

f. Performance of students in Salvador

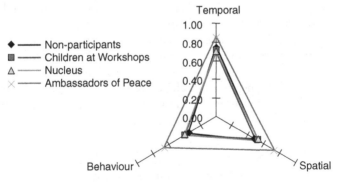

Figure 11.2 *(Cont.)*

Conclusion: a capability perspective on assessing social programs

The relative and absolute dimensions of capabilities were compared in the assessment of the project. Beyond the general normative conclusion that the project is 'capability-enhancing', there is a deeper challenge that was faced in this assessment concerning the provision of concrete information for management purposes. The different units to be chosen will depend on the objectives of the programs as well as on its managerial structure. In the case of 'TIM Music in Schools', emphasis was placed at the city level, given that all coordinators and officers were working with mandates of operating within their particular cities. But information was also produced at a school level (not reported here for reasons of space). A very high level of disaggregation is important for establishing accountability relations between supporters (e.g. Italia Telecom), providers and target groups. Strategies of CRS (Corporate Social Responsibility) are often implemented for publicity reasons, without monitoring or assessment. The same happens quite often at government level in developing countries. Assessment in order to improve (in terms of efficiency and distributive impact) the programs is certainly a need in developing countries.

Evaluating children's capabilities is at the centre of a large variety of social initiatives that are taking place in schools. Schools provide an institutional space of transformation ('of becoming') in which children are shaped according to the values and norms of particular societies. Without entering in the old debate of 'nurture vs. nature', it should be evident that society's influences are felt by children: nurture plays a role that could be stronger or weaker.

An evaluation of social programs can do more than simply 'fine tuning' administrative agendas and target groups; it can define new priorities and opportunities for exploring capabilities that were not achieved during the course of the programs. In the particular program assessed here a list of 10 suggestions was detailed in a report prepared for Italia Telecom (they are not elaborated here through lack of space). It might be interesting to mention for illustrative purposes four of these suggestions:

- Reorganization of musical workshops, suggesting a reduction in the number of children participating per meeting. Facilities are not good in many schools, and functionality could be improved by working with fewer children every time. Qualitative empirical evidence showed how self-esteem and attention are important to the development of the human capabilities of these children. Moreover, very young children have a short concentration span and cannot cope with conceptual explanations. Acknowledging this *intrinsic diversity* among children as human beings can improve the capability impact of the program.

- Strengthen the network of officers, who could learn from each other, sharing operational information and generating synergies. They usually work in isolation but are very eager to exchange their ideas with their colleagues. Somehow their potentialities remain unexplored as a result of geographic constraints. They could be empowered by the creation of a formal network among them, defined in order to promote *public discussion* in schools and the communities where they live.

- Bottom-up strategy, allowing schools to have the driving seat in the planning of their local activities. It is important to observe that not only children, but also teachers and heads are subject to multiple deprivations in these poor communities where the schools are. Thus, a way of empowering them would be through a better structure of priorities in which they would have the possibility of defining activities in a more decentralized way. This could be conducive to an institutionalization of democratic spaces at school level, where a 'culture of moral virtues' could be discussed, as suggested by a program officer.

- Creation of a 'social helpline' for families, because many children are pushed into labor, given their conditions of abject poverty. The project cannot take care of all families around all participating schools, but could provide support to children and teenagers when they feel under pressure to work or to consume drugs. The key here is to explore synergies between schools and families in taking care of children. For instance, a considerable percentage of parents are illiterate in these very poor areas in Salvador and Recife and see no point in supporting their children in finishing primary school. Social support might be needed to provide information and public understanding in a decentralized way.

To conclude, this chapter has argued that it is possible to measure capabilities (rather than simply functionings) according to their main features, namely, objectivity, multidimensional, counterfactuality and autonomy. The informational spaces selected and the resulting variables chosen were translated into specific questions (assisted by a participatory exercise) in several surveys that were carried out in six Brazilian cities during 2005. The results were analysed and presented to Italia Telecom, which was able to critically understand the program, acknowledging its main merits and potentialities. CRS needs assessment (and not only that, but government action, too). The choice of approaches can be greatly assisted by the discussion proposed by Nussbaum and Sen. Operational metrics can be defined, and apparently innocent activities, such as listening to and learning music, can prove to have a decisive effect on the development of children's capabilities.

References

Blacking, John 1969. 'Songs, Dances, Mines and Symbolism of Venda Girl's Initiation Schools, parts 1–4', *African Studies*, 28: 1–4.

Cross, I. 2001. 'Music, Cognition, Culture and Evolution', *Annals of the New York Academy of Sciences*, 930: 28–42.

Elkoshi, R. 2002. 'An Investigation into Children's Responses through Drawing to Short Musical Fragments and Complete Compositions', *Music Education Research*, 4 (2), 199–211.

Goswami, U. 1998. *Cognition in Children*, Hove: Psychology Press.

Greene, S. and Hogan, D. (eds.) 2005. *Researching Children's Experience: Approaches and Methods*, London: Sage Publications.

Hallam, S., Price, J. and Katsarou, G. 2002. 'The Effects of Background Music on Primary School Pupils' Task Performance', *Educational Studies*, 28 (2): 111–22.

Nussbaum, Martha 1990. *Love's Knowledge: Essays on Philosophy and Literature*, Oxford University Press.

1999. *Sex and Social Justice*, New York: Oxford University Press.

2000. *Women and Human Development*, Cambridge University Press.

Pecore, J. 2000. 'Bridging Contexts, Transforming Music: The Case of Elementary School Teacher Chihara Yoshio', *Ethnomusicology*, 44 (1): 120–36.

Perret, Daniel. 2004. *Roots of Musicality: Music Therapy and Personal Development*, London: Jessica Kingsley.

Rauscher, F. 2003. 'Can Music Instruction Affect Children's Cognitive Development?', *ERIC Digest*, EDS-PO-03-12, September.

Sen, Amartya 1985. *Commodities and Capabilities*, Amsterdam: Elsevier.

1992. *Inequality Reexamined*, Oxford University Press.

1999. *Development as Freedom*, Oxford University Press.

2005. 'Human Rights and Capabilities', *Journal of Human Development*, 6 (2): 151–66.

Wallace, A.F. 1961. *Culture and Personality*, New York: Random House.

12 The search for socially sustainable development: conceptual and methodological issues

Jean-Luc Dubois

Introduction

Interest in the concept of 'socially sustainable development' proceeds from two different lines of thought which became important in the 1990s. The first of these focuses on the idea of sustainable development, and the second on the issue of reducing poverty.

The idea of 'sustainable development' was widely publicized by the 1992 Earth Summit, held in Rio de Janeiro. It is derived from the Brundtland report, 'Our Common Future', published a few years earlier. Development is said to be sustainable when it meets the needs of the present without compromising the ability of future generations to meet their own needs (WCED 1987).

This implies that the process of development will improve the well-being of people now alive, while maintaining a sufficient level of resources – especially non-renewable resources, whether natural, social or human – to permit future generations to enjoy at least an equivalent standard of living. This issue is now viewed as a serious matter by many governments and civil agencies. It demands that we take into account not only the objectives and outcome of development, but also address the method and process by which development is achieved.

Several key decisions taken during the Earth Summit, including the launching of Agenda 21, recommend the implementation of measures to protect the environment at the regional, national and local levels. Agenda 21 also encourages the development of multidisciplinary research to analyze the interactions between the various dimensions of sustainable development. There was general agreement that economic, social and ecological dimensions be given priority. The French government, backed by UNESCO and the EU Commission, suggested adding the cultural dimension. Others also refer to the political dimension. However, adding new dimensions increases the complexity of the analysis and, to some extent, weakens the conclusions that can be drawn.

Following the Summit, UNDP, which in 1990 had already introduced the concept of 'human development' in reference to Sen's capability approach, began speaking about 'sustainable human development'. Human development is intended to improve people's ability to live a life that they think is worth living, and Sen's work relating capability to sustainability supports the notion of development intended to promote the capabilities of people alive now without compromising the capabilities of future generations (Sen 2000). This shift from the 'ability of future generations', as expressed in Brundtland's report, to the 'capabilities of future generations', as suggested by Sen, provided a framework for the yearly Human Development Report at the world level and the National Human Development Report at the country level (UNDP 2005). However, this raises two major issues related to social justice: the distribution of capabilities within a given generation and the transmission of capabilities from one generation to the next. Research has to be pursued on these issues, which address the question of sustainability in social terms.

The second line of reflection is related to reducing poverty. The 1990s Decade for Development was mainly devoted to this objective. Moreover, at the 2002 Johannesburg Summit, poverty reduction was officially recognized as the social dimension of sustainable development.

We do not share this view and even think that this may have been a mistake. Social sustainability – which expresses the social dimension of sustainable development – cannot be simply reduced to poverty reduction, even if in this case poverty were to include not only its usual monetary aspects (levels of income and consumption), but also living standards and conditions, the quality of life, the ownership of assets and capabilities. Social sustainability surely implies considering a much wider range of issues, such as social exclusion, the rise in vulnerability, inequitable distribution and transmission of capabilities. All these issues have a major impact on social cohesion, and their consequences may be more serious than those related to poverty.

Social exclusion can be viewed as an extreme form of absolute poverty, in which access to goods, services and relationship is denied. Any increase in inequality hampers the reduction of poverty. The feeling of vulnerability is related to a decrease in capability and an increase in the awareness of inequality. Finally, the transmission of capability may be jeopardized by factors such as HIV/AIDS or various forms of discrimination. All these factors cause more damage to the social fabric than poverty itself, with the exception of poverty traps. They weaken social bonds and introduce a risk of internal conflict and irreversible social consequences. It is via these factors that the real issue of long-term social sustainability arises, and they must also be considered as key components of the social dimension of development, in addition to poverty (Dubois and Mahieu 2002).

For these reasons, this chapter focuses on the social dimension of sustainable development. This involves providing a clear definition of what socially sustainable development is and identifying the relevant conditions for social sustainability. These conditions are related to the issues of exclusion, vulnerability, inequality and so forth as observed in the field, and are not only based on the usual poverty indicators. They promote the emergence of specific precautionary principles that could make development agencies rethink their strategies in order to ensure social sustainability.

Naturally, poverty reduction remains a key dimension of this process, especially when dealing with the constitution of assets (in relation to 'poverty of potentiality'), but it is now seen to be related to the fight against social exclusion (in relation with 'poverty of access' to goods and services) and vulnerability (in relation to 'poverty of capability'). Moreover, equity and social justice, within one generation and between generations, are also addressed by considering the 'inequality of capability' (Sen 1982).

Within this framework, the concept of social sustainability raises a set of new conceptual and methodological issues. On the conceptual side, the characteristics of the economic agent and the ethical foundations underlying economic reasoning will have to be re-examined. On the methodological side, field observations of people's socioeconomic situations and their ethical choices may help in compiling social precautionary principles to guide public action, NGO projects and policy design.

We will therefore first try to relate sustainable development to the capability approach to construct the concept of socially sustainable development. We will then go on to review the conceptual and methodological implications of this relationship.

Sustainable development and the capability approach

As was said earlier, the idea of a 'socially sustainable development' results from combining two preoccupations, i.e. sustainable development and reducing poverty. Their convergence is brought about through the capability approach. In the first case, it is the equitable distribution of capability from one generation to the next which is important; and in the second, it is the definition of poverty in terms of capability privation which counts.

From sustainable development to social sustainability

Development can be said to be sustainable when it satisfies the needs of the present generation without compromising the ability of future generations to satisfy their needs. This definition gives a universal picture of development that considers its long-term effects on people everywhere. This is quite a novel approach and contrasts with the development policies of the past 20 years, which consisted mainly in stabilization and adjustment policies and usually focused on short-term economic and financial equilibrium.

Sustainable development involves several interacting dimensions – for instance, economic, social and ecological – and this implies that each dimension must be sustainable. Sustainability is usually described as 'weak' when substitutes can replace any resources destroyed: for instance, if a polluted lake can be replaced by artificial pools, or if the victims of inequitable policy measures are provided with financial compensation. It is described as 'strong' if no replacement is possible, because the production factors are complementary and no substitute can be envisaged. This may be the case, for instance, if pollution must be limited or a human cost avoided.

Economical sustainability is expressed by the idea of self-maintaining growth. It is based on a series of macroeconomic principles related to balancing the budget, current account balance, inflation control, and so on, and basic investment rules, such as budgetary allocations, investment sector rates, capital ratio, productivity levels, consumption/saving ratios, and so on. These are intended to optimize growth without saddling future generations with excessive debt.

Ecological sustainability focuses on reducing pollution, protecting non-renewable resources, energy savings and handing natural resources to future generations. In this context, basic principles have been compiled on the basis of the concepts of weak and strong sustainability and precautionary principles. A series of management rules, such as the Hartwick rule, according to which any resource which has been destroyed must be replaced, and property rights, clean development processes, renewable resource ratios and so forth translate these principles into practically applicable concepts.

Social sustainability has not been investigated as much as the other dimensions of sustainability. The fact that it is now being taken into account in economic analyses may lead to a radical change in how we think about growth and development. It implies that future generations should inherit at least as many resources, in terms of capital or various potentialities, as the current generation. This means that the social dimension of sustainable development raises the issue of how to transmit sufficient assets and potentialities from one generation to the next. As well as physical and financial capital, these assets include human capital (including education and health), social capital (based on social interactions), rights, values, and so on, as well as the capacity to use all these potentialities in an appropriate way. Within this framework, we still have to identify and establish the key conditions, i.e. principles, standards and rules, which will ensure social sustainability.

Various aspects have to be taken into account when considering the three interrelated dimensions. First, economic and social linkage can be used to tackle the social consequences of macroeconomic policies in terms of the poverty, vulnerability and inequality various groups are facing. Second, the interconnection between the ecological and social dimensions raises the issue of trade-off between reducing poverty, on one hand, and protecting the environment, on the other. Third, we must consider the social nexus itself, which deals with access to and accumulation of human and social resources, as well as with the links between poverty, vulnerability and inequality for various groups of people.

Within this framework, the major issue is that current public policies – whether economic, social or ecological – may generate functional problems, such as poverty traps, exclusion, conflicts, etc., that jeopardize the potential benefits (in terms of access to social services), the assets and potentialities (among them human and social capital) and the capability to improve well-being for the present and future generations (Ballet, Dubois and Mahieu 2005).

An example of such issues is provided by the recent experience of a group of villages in southern Morocco in relation to a local NGO, Development and Migrations. By operating a generator, each village had four hours of electricity per day. The village council then decided, after obtaining general agreement, which public spaces should be lit and what the poorest and richest households would have to pay based on their per capita income. As a result, the richest families were indirectly subsidizing the poorer ones. Social life and the resulting relationships were sustained by means of meetings, discussions and consensus decisions.

It was such a success that the national electricity supplier, ONE, agreed to invest in electricity supply lines, transformers and equipment to connect these villages to the national grid, thus providing electricity for 24 hours a day at a much lower rate. However, each household would now have to pay ONE directly for their electricity, at a price based on the national marginal cost.

This led to a real improvement in the electricity supply, which was now permanently available, instead of being restricted to four hours per day, and at a much lower cost per hour. But this individualistic approach resulted in societal loss. As a result payment on a household basis public spaces are no longer lit. This will call for a new village initiative and the introduction of local council taxes. Moreover, even though the overall price per hour is much lower, some of the poorest families have difficulty in paying now that the rich no longer subsidize the poor.

Finally, ONE's individual-household-based approach to the supply of electricity has reduced the capability of the poorest households, who can no longer afford the minimum electricity supply they require. Simultaneously it has increased the capability of the richest, who can consume more electricity than before at a lower cost. Permanent access to electricity looks like a beneficial change in terms of reducing poverty. In fact, it has increased the inequality of capability between households, and the vulnerability of the poor, with a risk of social exclusion of the poorest and, therefore, of jeopardizing social cohesion. Such a situation can be corrected only by setting up a new redistributive system, by means of taxes or subsidies at the village level, or a new, more socially-oriented national pricing scheme.

Similar situations may arise in other domains such as health and education, where inappropriate policy measures can also generate social exclusion, increased vulnerability and inequality generating feelings of injustice and disruption of social bonds and of cohesiveness. Economists group all these issues under the generic term of 'social externalities'. These externalities can lead to dramatic and irreversible consequences, such as forced migration, suicide and social conflicts leading to civil war or genocide. At the very least, they demand that the human costs giving rise to social tension be avoided or compensation provided.

This example from Morocco shows that a social analysis of the likely impact of development policy or measures must be carried out before they are implemented and a wider view of the social situation must be taken into account.

Socially sustainable development: relating
capability and sustainability

By defining sustainable development as development that promotes the capabilities of the present generation without compromising those of future generations, Sen (2000) introduces a link between capability and sustainability and implicitly addresses the issue of the intergenerational equity of capability.

According to the capability approach, converting resources, commodities and assets into adequate functionings, 'beings' and 'doings', is intended to improve the well-being of a person, taking into account his or her specific characteristics and the social context of opportunities and constraints in which he/she lives: a person's capability results in the combination of various functionings (Sen 1987). Moreover, improving a person's capability to do and be what he/she wishes, such as receiving an education, getting a job or participating in social life, increases his/her freedom to decide what he/she values.

Within this framework, it is easy to establish the link between poverty and vulnerability. Any lack of capability reduces the capacity for well-being and can, therefore, be viewed as a situation of absolute poverty (Sen 1999), whereas vulnerability corresponds to the probability of experiencing a loss of well-being when confronted by a dramatic event or an economic shock (Dubois and Rousseau 2008). Increasing the assets and potentialities of individuals, and improving their capacity to convert resources into adequate functionings reduces their vulnerability.

The issue remains the inequality of capability among individuals within a generation, which is a key factor increasing the risk of social dysfunction and political blockage (Sen 1982; 1997). This risk increases further when capabilities are transmitted from one generation to the next, especially if this is not done fairly (Dubois 2006).

In this context, socially sustainable development could be defined as 'development that guarantees the improvement of well-being capability for all, by means of the equitable distribution of capabilities within the current generation on the one hand, and the equitable transmission of these capabilities to future generations, on the other hand' (Ballet, Dubois and Mahieu 2005: 9).

There are instances of non-sustainability attributable to the non-equitable transmission of capabilities in several countries. For instance, the present conflict in Côte d'Ivoire can be explained by intergenerational unfairness of access to farmland. In Mauritania, the danger arises from the unequal accumulation of assets and potentialities by various ethnic groups. In Southern Africa, HIV/AIDS has had a disastrous effect on food security, because sick parents are not able to teach their children to farm, and children have to leave school earlier to earn money to pay for their parents' healthcare (Dubois 2003). In France, examples can also easily be found of the ineffectiveness of the education system in transmitting appropriate capabilities to immigrants' children. The November 2005 riots of these young people in the suburbs of many large towns and cities indicate that in some case the limits of tolerance have been reached (Dubois 2006).

Socially sustainable development is therefore expected to protect social potentialities, to improve people's capabilities and to facilitate equitable transfers from one generation to the next. This implies addressing the factors that prevent the creation of potentiality (such as poverty traps), the promotion of capability (for example, social exclusion and vulnerability) and a just transfer between generations (inequity).

Searching for social sustainability

The issue is therefore to see how to ensure social sustainability, i.e. long-term sustainability in social terms. As a first step, one has to consider a few important prerequisites before trying to identify sustainability conditions.

The first prerequisite consists of distinguishing between different types of social issues. Some are related to social sectors, such as education, health, employment, and so on, whereas others concern the structure of society, through social links and interactions. When the distinction is not clearly made, ambiguity and confusion occur between these two visions of social development, i.e. more precisely between social and societal development. 'Sustainable social development' involves the social sectors and, for instance, how to ensure education and human development in the long-term. In contrast, 'socially sustainable development' focuses on the effects of education on social behaviour and on the quality of relationships with other people, as well as on self-esteem, respect and dignity. This approach confers a key role on individuals embedded in social networks, the structure of their capabilities and, through the issue of intra- and intergenerational justice, their responsibility towards present and future generations. For these reasons, the issues of social exclusion, inequality and vulnerability become fundamental, as does access to social services, primary goods and culture, i.e. more precisely the recognition of people's identity.

The second prerequisite deals with the interaction between the various components of sustainable development. The capability approach is useful here, because it can address the interrelations between various capabilities within an individual's capability structure (Ballet, Dubois and Mahieu 2007). Some policies intended to reduce poverty by improving one component of well-being, for example education, health or employment, force the capability structure to adjust. If the need for adjustment becomes too great, some capabilities may be unable to adapt and will be destroyed, leading to a destabilization of the structure and increasing the individual's vulnerability. On the other hand, strengthening some particular capabilities can also result in new inequalities between people. These are, of course, common consequences, however, they need to be addressed in time and reflected upon because of the social externalities that they generate.

Social sustainability may also conflict with other dimensions of sustainability, like economic or ecological sustainability. We know that growth policies, even when sustainable in economic terms, can generate negative social consequences, such as inequality, social exclusion, challenges to identity, social fractures, etc., which weaken social cohesion and jeopardize the development process. Some phenomena may take place in relation to ecological sustainability. For instance, failure to correctly take into account cultural values may produce negative externalities affecting the ecological or economic sustainability. More generally, the conditions of social sustainability interact with the sustainability conditions of the other dimensions. Therefore, to be consistent with the general objective of sustainability, policies will have to address all kinds of social externalities, considering the impact of economic and ecological decisions on the social dimension, as well as the effect of measures on the social dimension itself (reducing poverty, for instance).

The third prerequisite concerns the justice of the distribution of capabilities within a generation and their transmission from one generation to the next. Social sustainability requires that development result in an improvement of well-being within a generation of all the complementary aspects of standards of living, living conditions, quality of life, capability, and so on, without forgetting intra-generational justice. An unequal distribution of capabilities within a given generation increases the risk of social dysfunction and blockage. This can happen when policy measures intended to reduce poverty, such as labour-intensive work, micro-finance projects or educational programs, target specific groups of people (refugees, women, etc.) and generate inequalities and economic insecurity for other groups.

This issue may be exacerbated when considering the intergenerational transmission of capabilities. To ensure the well-being of future generations their access to various goods and services (private, public, primary), capital assets (physical, human, social) and potentiality (rights, knowledge, values), converted into capabilities, at a level at least equivalent to that enjoyed by previous generations, must be secure. However, this may be rendered impossible for two reasons. First, inequality in distribution of such endowments within one given generation is usually exacerbated in subsequent generations, unless redistributive measures ensure equitable access to services, the accumulation of assets and the transmission of capabilities. Second, the younger generation may inherit from the previous generation a heavy burden, such as having to pay off public debt or fund retirement pensions for their parents.

Social sustainability therefore requires that people's capability of well-being be improved, through equitable distribution and transmission within and between generations. Appropriate conditions to ensure this improvement will have to be found. They are based on the three previous prerequisites, dealing with the issues of reducing poverty and vulnerability in an equitable manner.

We need appropriate indicators to characterize these issues in particular socioeconomic contexts so as to be able to assess the social sustainability of development projects, or of policy measures envisaged by a country. These indicators have to be chosen according to their relevance, their sensitivity to the phenomenon under study, and the facility with which they can be applied. They set up the statistical limits (such as poverty lines, coefficient of vulnerability or aversion to inequality) required to identify thresholds and norms. Within a particular socioeconomic context, they provide the basis for defining the precautionary principles that would express the core conditions of social sustainability.

A first set of indicators focuses on describing various forms of poverty, e.g. monetary, standard of living, accessibility to goods and services (as a measure of social exclusion), assets and potentiality (rights, values), capability, and so forth. A second set is related to the assessment of inequality issues such as, for instance, gender inequalities, regional inequalities, inequality in capabilities and so on. Other indicators measure poverty traps, vulnerability, social tensions within society, and so forth.

More sophisticated and analytical indicators – such as aversion to inequality, the coefficient of vulnerability, poverty traps, and so on – may result from econometric analysis expressing the interrelations between growth, poverty and inequality (by estimating the corresponding elasticities). Other important relationships have to be addressed, such as the relations between vulnerability, risk and capability, for instance, or those between gender inequalities, vulnerability and poverty transmission, or between inequality, social cohesion and conflicts, and so on.

However, monitoring all these indicators on a regular basis raises a key question: to what extent would it be possible to devise a synthetic indicator to express the level of social sustainability or unsustainability for a given project or a country? Answering this question requires research into modelling of social sustainability and the identification of relevant conditions.

Conceptual and methodological implications

The idea of socially sustainable development raises various conceptual and methodological concerns, which address the definition of the economic agent, the ethical foundations of social sustainability and the determination of precautionary principles that could be used as societal safeguards.

From the economic agent to the responsible person

In mainstream economics, the 'individual' is usually the subject of analysis. He is considered to be autonomous, rational in his choices and assumed to be trying to maximize his utility subject to various constraints. However, as a result of social interactions, individuals can also behave in an altruistic way, integrating the utility of others into their own utility function and gaining benefit from this, even in a dilemma situation (Becker 1974).

Sen and Nussbaum go further by considering the concepts of 'agent' and 'agency'. They introduce the capacity of acting and of choosing the aim of the action. Such capacity may be used for economic objectives, like improving well-being, but also for any action relating to other people, for example promoting social justice or community participation. Such a view introduces the possibility of behaving in a way different from the conventional maximization of one's own utility and introduces the possibility of involving personal responsibility into the choice of actions affecting others.

In fact, the agent, as encountered in daily life, is embedded in a series of social networks and institutions such as the family, community, district, municipality and country. This is not only the result of the individual's personal choice, as described by Becker (1974), but also of the fact that, within these networks that provide security, a person cannot live without fulfilling a series of social obligations that confer a set of rights based on reciprocity (Mahieu 1989). Everyone who belongs to a community has to fulfil obligations, which are usually expressed as demands on time and resources made by the community, in order to benefit from the rights that it provides. Taking this set of rights and obligations into account in the personal decision process implies that the agent is not only rational, but also responsible.

This is why some authors speak of the reasonable 'subject' (Misrahi 2003) as someone involved in his/her social network and therefore responsible for both his/her current actions affecting others (i.e. ex-post responsibility), and what other people will experience in the future (i.e. prospective or ex-ante responsibility). Touraine (2005), by considering the 'personal subject', also introduces the notion of cultural links with others and the importance of identity, respect and dignity.

The idea of socially sustainable development takes into account the fact that people are involved in social relationships, stressing their freedom as well as their dependency; that they are facing the future with either hope or despair and feel responsible for their children and, via them, for future generations. All these issues imply a need to review the rules and values that are assumed to guide people in making choices with economic consequences. This is why human beings cannot be reduced to the search for the optimal satisfaction of basic needs.

The concept of a 'person' makes it possible to take such issues into account and enables us to consider a wider range of responsibilities based on responsibility towards the present generation (Levinas 1983), as well as towards future generations (Jonas 1984). By definition, a person is able to imagine the situation of the other, to imagine being the other person, and more generally to sublimate his/her own attitude towards others by extending his/her limits (Mounier 1961; Ricoeur 1995). Phenomenological and existentialist philosophies have set out to explain these personal life experiences and transcendental behaviour.

In the economic literature, the 'individual' is still usually viewed as a rational entity, isolated from the human community, while the 'person' gives importance to others and thinks in terms of unity and a common future. The person transcends him/herself by a creative life based on respect and empathy for others, which leads to commitment. In this framework, the person's freedom also implies satisfying his/her own needs but with a view to sharing and not wasting common goods and increasing the development of creative capabilities. All this contributes to widening the level of 'personhood' (Giovanola 2005), by understanding the link between freedom and responsibility.

In this way, the concept of a person provides the widest vision of a human being in charge of his/her decisions, focusing not only on him/herself, but also on others and more and more nowadays also on nature. In Japan, the Kyoto school, including the philosopher Watsuji (1949) and currently the 'public philosophy' approach (Yamawaki, Kobayashi and Ikemoto 2006), has already gone some way in this direction.

Theoretically, reference to the person's capability through his/her agency opens many analytical possibilities (Sen 1999). One can list the set of capabilities attributed to a person (Alkire 2002) and consider the 'capability for affiliation' as essential (Nussbaum 2000; 2006). The capability approach could also look at responsibility by including specific capabilities, i.e. the capabilities of feeling responsible both ex ante (like responsible parents) and ex post for his or her act (in a consequentialist view).

Dealing with social sustainability implies relating this normative definition of the person to the characteristics of his/her effective behaviour as observed in the field. This requires, in practical terms, field investigations with appropriate questionnaires to collect information about these characteristics, people's relationships, the actions that they value and to which they are ready to commit themselves.

Ethical foundations: a positive ethics approach

The observation of what people value, of the way they combine various values to produce objectives and to justify their action, can be referred to as 'positive ethics'. In fact, moral philosophy deals with the issue of personal values and usually provides convictions and rules about what one should do or not do. Ethics, in contrast, focuses mainly on the debates that arise from moral experiences to define and set up these rules. In a way, ethics can be said to be more spontaneous and to apply to specific cases, whereas moral rules are defined with a more universal objective and may also result from external decisions.

Ethics as a discipline can be divided into normative ethics and positive ethics (Ballet and Bazin 2006). Normative ethics are intended to set up a system of moral rules to guide action or to give meaning to life, whereas positive ethics observe how people behave in ethical terms with the objective of analyzing and identifying the empirical rules that account for this behaviour or action. This approach helps us to understand how people deal with dilemmas and moral situations in practical terms in everyday life and is very useful in designing and developing projects or policies.

Within this framework, two important philosophical traditions should be considered. The first approach refers to the mainstream ethics of the 'good life', which originates in Aristotle and was developed by thinkers like Hume, Bentham and Mill, converging on the aim of achieving the greatest happiness for the greatest number of people. The focus is on 'the Good', i.e. what is good for a person or group of persons. This leads to hedonistic, utilitarian and consequentialist approaches, where priority is given to freedom, property, satisfaction and utility. In these approaches, responsibility is addressed by considering the actions that directly affect others. It is an ex-post responsibility, i.e. a responsibility that is a consequence of the freedom to act.

The second approach relates to 'the Just', i.e. to a universal law, which is the expression of traditional rules, religious beliefs or legal norms that already exist. Kant's (1785) principle 'do not do anything that could harm anyone else' is an expression of this way of thinking. Priority is given to a person's intention and the obligations that he or she must satisfy. According to this approach, responsibility exists before the freedom to act. It is an ex-ante or prospective responsibility that results from the obligations of the person towards his/her community or social network. Freedoms and rights result from the satisfaction of these obligations. Both Levinas (1983), who focuses on the 'other', and Jonas (1984), who refers to future generations, consider that responsibility towards other people has priority over freedom.

The 'ethics of responsibility' tries to combine these two traditions by addressing the interaction between freedom and responsibility at the personal level and through specific action (Ricoeur 1995). For instance, in the case of emergency situations, after a dramatic event when people are confronted by vulnerability and distress, then responsibility towards others becomes the first priority. It is a situation where the 'ethics of care' prevails as part of the ethics of responsibility. In practical terms, the ethics of responsibility can be translated into a series of key questions that express how people react when faced with dilemmas between freedom and responsibility. It then becomes important to find out which ethical rules a person will actually refer to when deciding what to do.

Obtaining answers to such questions would provide the basis of the ethical foundations that underlie economic reasoning. This is required by the framework of socially sustainable development, which deals with responsibility towards future generations in terms of well-being and capability distribution.

Referring to positive ethics, rather than to normative ethics, as is usually the case, is the best way to understand how the people behave in real life and to identify the practical principles to which they refer. Positive ethics, which are based on the observation of how people adjust the moral norms of their community to their own egotistic preferences, provides some answers. Since people making decisions are often surrounded by various sets of values originating from tradition, religion, Western influence and personally constructed beliefs, a positive ethics approach may help us to understand the conflicting rules that the person faces when taking economic decisions. People consider these values to be fundamental and are frustrated when they cannot base their actions on them. This frustration may be forcefully expressed in conflicts that may jeopardize a development project or policy.

In practice, when confronted by various problems, people usually draw on several ethical systems to devise their own rules for decision-making.

This depends on how they see their own responsibilities. Taking this situation into account would help to improve the design of development projects and policies by tailoring and fine-tuning them to different social contexts.

Addressing ethical values within the development process widens the concept of social development and relates it to its cultural dimension. In this way, positive ethics provides a way to understand the choices of people, their aspirations and behaviour and the social dynamics within society. The work done by Weber (1930) on the religious values that permitted the emergence of capitalism is a good example of this approach.

Positive ethics does not preach any form of abstract goodness but considers the relativity of the moral choices made by people. These moral choices can be observed through field investigations and can be used to evaluate shifts in values resulting from conflicts faced during the development process. This requires observing and measuring not only economic behaviour but also the values underlying it. It implies designing appropriate field surveys of how people behave, asking them about the reasons of their choices, the values behind these choices, and so forth. 'Positive ethics surveys', for instance, would be appropriate tools to observe the relativity of the moral choices people make and the empirical moral rules that explain their behaviour and actions. In fact, such surveys would be quite similar to the tools recently used to measure agency in several countries (Alkire and Chirkov 2006).

The setting up of social precautionary principles

Investigations may reveal both people's characteristics and socio-economic situation, on the one hand, and their choices, the ethical rules that they follow, on the other. Combining various types of information makes it possible to identify and produce indicators that reflect the quantitative thresholds and qualitative limits accepted by people within their current set of values. This approach makes it possible to devise precautionary principles for development operations, on the basis of what has been observed.

These principles are required to prevent undesirable irreversible consequences of projects and public policies, and to avoid socially unsustainable situations. They can be used (ex ante) to design appropriate development strategies or to mitigate (ex post) the effects of external shocks. In philosophical terms, they draw their legitimacy from the ethics of responsibility. Moreover, they rehabilitate ethics in day-to-day life. By protecting human resources and potentialities, by facilitating the transfer of capabilities from one generation to the next, they play a key role in institutionalizing social sustainability.

A standard approach is usually used in drawing up such principles. First, the respective roles of the various agents involved in the decision-making process have to be examined. Second, the social consequences of various risks for people's capability structure and their agency role have to be assessed, taking into account the uncertainty of social risks. Third, alternative scenarios can be devised through ethical discussion among the stakeholders, by considering how capability and responsibility are distributed. And finally, a redistributive process has to be established, by the stakeholders themselves, to provide either compensation or rewards for the negative or positive social externalities that may arise.

A concrete example can be given by going back to the villages of southern Morocco mentioned earlier. It helps to explain the role of social safeguards that adequate precautionary principles can provide when they are based on local traditions.

To improve the standard of living, village leaders suggested using external investment to launch new income-generating activities. They chose a form of eco-tourism in which the inhabitants of the villages would host tourists. However, to maintain and protect the current social dynamics, debates with the local population were set up, examining how to proceed when implementing this type of development project. A pragmatic approach was used, based on in-depth knowledge of the villages concerned. Through a series of meetings and debates within village councils, three guiding principles slowly emerged.

First, any decision concerning the village has to be reached by consensus, through public meetings and debates. This rule can be viewed, in philosophical terms, as related to Habermas's 'ethics of discussion' (1991), i.e. it is the group itself which sets up, after discussion, the ethical rules that will guide its decision in the future.

Second, the tradition of hospitality, which is considered to be a major feature of Moroccan culture, should be respected. This implies that visiting tourists will be hosted in the best houses, even if this may benefit the richest families more than the poorest and therefore increase inequality.

Third, to avoid excessive inequality of income and assets, which could destabilize the village's social cohesion, a redistribution mechanism was adopted in order to boost the opportunities and capabilities of the poorest families. Part of the surplus generated by the visiting tourists will be allocated to the poorest families in order to improve their houses and provide for their children's education.

These are three simple rules involving 'discussion', 'hospitality' and 'sharing'. In fact, they are the expression of local precautionary principles that have emerged from debates within the villages. They emerge from the common values shared by the people and play the role of social safeguards vis-à-vis the development process.

Alternative scenarios would have been either to let the market govern the decision-making role, based solely on economic efficiency, or to allow the external investors to impose their preferred solution. In both cases, the risk of negative externalities on the villages' social cohesion would increase, people becoming frustrated by a process they do not control and which gives rise to inequity. This example differs from and complements the previous one given for the same region. It highlights the capability of people to provide, through their agency, a shared solution, expressed by precautionary principles, with the aim of reducing the risk of social dysfunction.

Conclusion

The concept of sustainable development includes the idea that what is done now should not endanger the capability of future generation to have a quality of life at least equivalent to that presently enjoyed. Socially sustainable development, which addresses the social dimension of this concept, focuses on the dynamic aspects of sustainable development and insists on the fact that it should be a form of 'development that guarantees the improvement of well-being capability for all, through an equitable distribution of capabilities within the current generation on the one hand, and the equitable transmission of these capabilities to future generations, on the other hand' (Ballet, Dubois and Mahieu 2005: 9).

This is a process which is normally related to growth, since growth produces the goods and services required to improve people's capabilities by conversion into functioning. However, the social consequences of growth, like all economic or ecological externalities, need to be controlled in order to ensure that human development remains sustainable. The objective is to make appropriate decisions that avoid generating social dysfunction that would jeopardize the development process. Such an attitude requires a feeling of responsibility towards the others, i.e. a prospective responsibility that emerges before any decision has been reached. In fact, it introduces the ethics of responsibility into persons' everyday life.

In practical terms, when designing development strategies, this approach requires specific social analysis before implementing any project or policy measure. Through these social analyses, current policies will be scrutinized to make sure that the main objective of reducing poverty is not achieved at the expense of social sustainability, as it was in the case of the supply of electricity to Moroccan villages. This implies making sure that people have equitable access to goods and services, to the various assets and potentialities and equitable distribution of capability both at the intra- and intergenerational levels.

These analyses rest on the idea of field investigations, including household surveys, panel surveys and investigations, which provide information about people's capability set, their socioeconomic situations and their behaviour in terms of ethical choices. This makes it possible to identify the thresholds, limits and norms that would help determine, by means of appropriate indicators, the social precautionary principles which can be used as safeguard to ensure social sustainability.

However, research based on empirical studies on all these issues has still to be conducted in various contexts to make it possible to determine synthetic indicators able to evaluate the social sustainability of development projects and national policies.

Acknowledgements

This chapter is based on a presentation given at the international conference in Kyoto on 'Ethics, Economics and Law: Against Injustice', Ritsumeikan University, 28–30 October 2005. The author wishes to thank Professor François-Régis Mahieu of the University of Versailles for his support and advice on an earlier version of this paper, Dr Nadia Bentaleb, Director of Migrations and Development, an international NGO based in Marseilles, for the field experiment in Morocco, and Ms Monica Gosh for the final editing of this paper.

References

Alkire, S. 2002. *Valuing Freedoms: Sen's Capability Approach and Poverty Reduction*, New York: Oxford University Press.
Alkire, S. and Chirkov, V. 2006. 'Measuring Agency: Testing a New Indicator in Kerala', paper presented at 'Freedom and Justice', Human Development and Capability Association conference, 29 August–1 September 2006, Groningen, the Netherlands.
Aristotle 1980. *The Nicomachean Ethics*, translated with an introduction by David Ross, Oxford University Press.
Ballet, J. and Bazin, D. (eds.) 2006. *Positive Ethics in Economics, Praxiology: The International Annual of Practical Philosophy and Methodology*, vol. XIV, London: Transaction Publishers.

Ballet, J., Dubois, J.-L. and Mahieu, F.-R. 2005. *L'Autre Développement, le développement socialement soutenable*, Paris: L'Harmattan.

2007. 'Responsibility for Each Other's Freedom: Agency as the Source of Collective Capability', *Journal of Human Development*, **8** (7): 185–201.

Becker, G. 1974. 'A Theory of Social Interaction', *Journal of Political Economy*, **82** (6): 1062–96.

Dubois, J.-L. 2003. 'Food Security, Vulnerability and Social Sustainability', *Cahiers de l'IFAS*, **3**: 15–21.

2006. 'Approche par les capabilités et développement durable: La transmission intergénérationnelle des capabilités', in V. Reboud (ed.), *Amartya Sen: un économiste du développement?*, Paris: AFD, pp. 199–212.

Dubois, J.-L. and Mahieu, F.-R. 2002. 'La dimension sociale du développement durable: lutte contre la pauvreté ou durabilité sociale?', in J.-Y. Martin (ed.), *Développement durable? Doctrines, pratiques, évaluations*, Paris: IRD, pp. 73–94.

Dubois, J.-L. and Rousseau, S. 2008. 'Reinforcing Households' Capabilities as a Way to Reduce Vulnerability and Prevent Poverty in Equitable Terms', in F. Comim, M. Qizilbash and S. Alkire (eds.), *The Capability Approach: Concepts, Measures and Applications*, Cambridge University Press, pp. 421–36.

Giovanola, B. 2005. 'Personhood and Human Richness: Good and Happiness in the Capability Approach and Beyond', *Review of Social Economy*, **63** (2): 249–67.

Habermas, J. 1991. *De l'éthique de la discussion*, trans. Mark Hunyadi, Paris: Éditions du Cerf, 1992.

Jonas, H. 1984. *The Imperative of Responsibility: In Search of an Ethics for the Technological Age*, University of Chicago Press.

Kant, I. 1785. *Foundations of the Metaphysics of Morals*, trans. L. W. Beck, University of Chicago Press, 1950.

Levinas, E. 1983. *Time and the Other*, trans. Richard A. Cohen, Pittsburgh: Duquesne University Press, 1987.

Mahieu, F.-R. 1989. *Fondements de la crise économique en Afrique*, Paris: L'Harmattan.

Misrahi, R. 2003. *Le sujet et son désir*, Paris: Pleins Feux.

Mounier, E. 1961. *Oeuvres d'Emmanuel Mounier*, vols. I–IV, Paris: Éditions du Seuil.

Nussbaum, M. C. 2000. *Women and Human Development: The Capabilities Approach*, Cambridge University Press.

2006. *Frontiers of Justice: Disability, Identity, Species Membership*, Cambridge, MA: Belknap Press of Harvard University Press.

Ricoeur, P. 1995. *Le Juste*, Paris: Esprit.

Sen, A. K. 1982. 'Equality of What?', in *Choice, Welfare and Measurement*, Oxford: Blackwell; Cambridge, MA: Harvard University Press, pp. 353–69.

1987. *Commodities and Capabilities*, Oxford University Press.

1997. *On Economic Inequality*, expanded edn with a substantial annex by J. E. Foster and A. Sen, Oxford: Clarendon Press.

1999. *Development as Freedom*, Oxford University Press.

2000. 'The Ends and Means of Sustainability', keynote address at the international conference on 'Transition to Sustainability', 15 May 2000, Tokyo.

Touraine, A. 2005. *Un nouveau paradigme: Pour comprendre le monde d'aujourd'hui*, Paris: Fayard.

UNDP (United Nations Development Programme) 2005. *Fifteen Years of Human Development Reports: 1990–2004*, CD-ROM, New York: UNDP.

Watsuji, T. 1949. *Rinrigaku*, trans. Yamamoto Seisaku and Robert E. Carter as *Watsuji Tetsurō's Rinrigak*, with an introduction and interpretive essay by Robert E. Carter, Albany: State University of New York Press, 1996.

WCED (World Commission on Environment and Development) 1987. *Our Common Future*, Oxford University Press.

Weber, M. 1930. *The Protestant Ethic and the Spirit of Capitalism*, London: Allen and Unwin.

Yamawaki, N., Kobayashi, M. and Ikemoto, Y. 2006. 'Public Philosophy and Capability Approach for Sustainable Development: Towards a New Formulation', paper presented at 'Freedom and Justice', Human Development and Capability Association conference, 29 August–1 September 2006, Groningen, the Netherlands.

Part IV

13 Response

Amartya Sen

Introduction

I have been asked to write a "response" to the essays in this volume, and, like an obedient boy, I will do what I have been told. And yet my thoughts on reading these wonderful articles are entirely predictable, to wit, admiration and huge appreciation. I have enjoyed, and benefitted from, reading these extremely interesting contributions on subjects that are of very great interest to me. The main thing for me to say, therefore, is "thank you," particularly since the editors and the authors have also very kindly linked their contributions, in one way or another, to my writings and have said some very generous things. Even when there are differences, the authors have expressed their disagreements in extremely gentle ways.

In fact, the whole process of intellectual events and encounters that has resulted in this volume, led by the vision of the incomparable Reiko Gotoh, has been both highly enjoyable and thoroughly stimulating. We met at the great Ritsumeikan University in the fall of 2005, spoke and heard each other, encountered good arguments and debates, and enjoyed the delights of Japan (and Kyoto in particular), and then left all the hard work of getting this volume together in the gentle hands of Reiko Gotoh (in collaboration with Paul Dumouchel). Not only has Reiko led the designing of the conference (and of this volume), but also her own highly productive approach to justice and reciprocity, which she has developed over the years (and which she presented in her own contribution to the conference in Ritsumeikan), has played a guiding part in the planning of these well-structured intellectual engagements. My gratitude for this process, culminating in this fine volume of philosophical contributions, is naturally boundless, and so is my admiration for the academic leadership that has gone into this highly constructive engagement.

Against injustice

To make my task manageable, I must restrict my focus to a few issues only, and consequently only to a few of the papers in this collection. I should, however, make clear that I have learned a great deal from many of the essays I shall not comment on, and my silence on them does not indicate my non-involvement with them, or any lack of appreciation of the significant contributions they make. I have read with much interest and benefit the analyses of empirical issues in Part III (by Andrea Brandolini, Flavio Comim, and Jean-Luc Dubois), but I will resist the temptation to join those discussions in this particular note. I decided that it would be easier to communicate some thoughts on the essays that deal primarily with theory than those that are mainly empirically oriented. The latter contributions demand a balancing of highly specialized – and circumstantially contingent – considerations along with general and generic concerns, and they are certainly much harder to engage with in a short note. I have, therefore, concentrated on the essays in Parts I and II of this volume – and then again, on only a few among the large number of issues they cover.

I begin, however, not with any essay in Parts I, II or III, but with the "Introduction" by Reiko Gotoh and Paul Dumouchel which precedes those essays. Gotoh and Dumouchel have done a wonderful job of motivating the discussion of a wide range of issues that connect ethics, economics, and law, and also of introducing the essays included in this collection. I am personally very fortunate that they have paid particular attention to what I have tried to do in these fields. I should, however, also point out that their commentary is also significantly constructive, in the way good commentaries almost invariably are, and also that many of the ideas for which they give me credit are the result of their own inquiry in the context of explicating some thoughts I have struggled to present in my writings.

One of the most important issues to have been clarified – and emphasized – in the introductory remarks of Gotoh and Dumouchel is the way the motivation of my investigation of justice is solidly based on the idea of *injustice* rather than the identification of a *just* society. I know of no society today, or any that seems about to emerge, that could be seen as being really "just." But the recognition that all societies actually encountered are unjust in one way or another does not make them in any sense alike. Injustice may come in many different ways (from the violation of personal liberties to the continuation of remediable poverty and deprivation) and the extent of nastiness may also vary – often quite dramatically. Gotoh and Dumouchel have deeply explored the big difference that is brought about if the theory of justice proceeds from the idea of identifiable injustice rather than from the characterization of a "just society" (as in mainstream theories of justice, including that of John Rawls). They point out, for example, that the much-used concept of "optimization" (or getting to the very best), so often invoked in welfare economics, may have no necessary anchorage – indeed no delineated role – in an injustice-centered theory of justice.

There is a huge difference between (1) hankering after "*the* optimum" (accepted by all "reasonable" people to be better than or at least as good as every other possibility) and (2) trying to identify manifestly unjust situations that can be feasibly bettered. I do believe that a theory of justice as practical reason has to be mainly concerned with the latter exercise, and I am grateful to Gotoh and Dumouchel for bringing out this point forcefully.

I have tried to explore the far-reaching implications of this distinction in my essay here, and also in an article, published in 2006, called "What Do We Want from a Theory of Justice?"[1] The problem is not merely that the identification of a perfectly just society is neither necessary nor sufficient for comparing and ranking feasible alternatives against each other. Nor only that a perfectly just society even when identified cannot possibly be reached or even closely approached in the contemporary world through any combination of policies and initiatives. There is the further problem that a substantiated agreement on the nature of a perfectly just society may not even emerge through any process that can claim to satisfy the exacting demands of "justice as fairness" (whether or not seen in Rawls's own terms, that is through the deliberative device of "the original position"). Reasonable people, under any device of ensuring fairness, may continue to disagree – and *plausibly* disagree – on the nature and the exact demands of the perfectly just society. And yet this will not preclude an agreement that major improvements can be made in reducing injustice through eliminating remediable outrages, such as needless hunger and starvation, removable illiteracy, correctable insecurity, or the prevalence of torture. The "transcendental" approach lands us quite unnecessarily in the remote exercise of looking for a black cat in a dark room that may or may not be there at all.

Gotoh and Dumouchel specifically focus on the nature of "patent injustice." Even though I had used that expression in my own work, they bring out with much greater force the specific relevance of the "patentness" of some injustice. The clarity that is associated with an

---

[1] Sen (2006).

alternative being "patently unjust" is certainly related in one way or another with the identification of another feasible alternative that, it can be easily agreed, dominates the first alternative, in comparative terms. An agreement on dominance (in the sense that all the contending criteria suggest the same ranking) may not always emerge, but when it does, then we do not have to get all steamed up about the relative importance of the potentially competitive criteria.

Gotoh and Dumouchel develop their points illuminatingly, and I would like to emphasize that in the context of this investigation they also bring out the central role of *comparative*, rather than *superlative*, assessments. This relates foundationally to the dichotomy between the "transcendental" approach of much of mainstream contemporary political philosophy (including the Rawlsian theory of justice) and the "comparative" approach to justice which I have been trying to explore.

Reciprocity, freedom and neorepublicanism

I go on now to the essays in Part I of this collection. It is easy for me to comment on Marcel Hénaff's contribution in his commentary on my essay. I agree with his line of analysis and accept the importance of the points he makes. Among other things, I like his focus on motivational features underlying our choices: his "Prajâpati test" illustrates the connection very well. His emphasis on "the *constitutive reciprocity* of human beings" is, undoubtedly, a very ambitious diagnosis of the forces that govern human motivation in general, but that daring hypothesis does have considerable plausibility (supported, I would argue, by the far-reaching relevance of reciprocity in public affairs as is brought out forcefully in Reiko Gotoh's essay in this volume, "Justice and Public Reciprocity"). Hénaff also presents a good discussion of the relation between the idea of justice and that of rationality – a connection, incidentally, that has received much attention recently in trying to make sense of the results of experimental games, such as "the ultimatum game," in which actually observed human behaviour is seen as being powerfully influenced by the players' sense of justice which go well beyond the narrow limits of so-called rational choice theory. As Marcel Hénaff points out, "rationality is also on the side of a comprehensive understanding of justice."

Philip Pettit's commentary on my own essay in this volume discusses with much clarity some of the conditions that need to be satisfied by theories of justice, as they emerge from what I discuss (in the process of my attempt to identify some failures of the mainstream approaches in this area). Based on this line of reasoning, he identifies something like "economic, legal, and ethical desiderata" for the adequacy of legal, political, and ethical thinking in this area, which he sees as emerging from my paper (I believe Pettit is entirely correct in this diagnosis). He goes on to establish that "the neorepublican political theory," as developed by Pettit and Quentin Skinner and others, "can fully satisfy the desiderata outlined by Sen."[2] I think he is right to make this claim also, and the demonstration he presents is both illuminating and persuasive. We do not have any significant difference on this particular issue.[3]

The question that remains is whether these specific requirements, which are not met (as discussed in my essay) by many of the mainstream theories of normative political philosophy and jurisprudence, are meant to constitute a *full* list of requirements that normative political philosophy and jurisprudence must satisfy. I have to confess that I thought of those requirements as no more than just a list of some characteristics that the particular theories I tried to criticize fail to satisfy (rather than as a full specification of comprehensive "desiderata"). It is indeed interesting that neorepublican theory does not fail where these other theories crumble, but this does not of course indicate that I must immediately sign up on the dotted line and become a card-carrying neorepublican.

Indeed, our disagreements lie elsewhere, in particular in the understanding of the nature of freedom and liberty. This is not the occasion to launch into a full-scale discussion of where we disagree. But since Philip Pettit has very helpfully discussed some issues that seem to him to make the neorepublican view of freedom the uniquely appropriate understanding of that elusive concept, I should make a few remarks on why I think freedom has other features and other connotations that are also important aspects of freedom, which the neorepublican view does not capture. My point is not that the neorepublican understanding of freedom is unimportant or irrelevant (not at all), but that it is a partial view, which captures some important aspects of freedom while missing out on others.

I have tried, in my work, to point to the inescapable heterogeneity within our understanding of the rich notion of human freedom.[4] I have also discussed why taking note of this heterogeneity is important for an

---

[2] Pettit, 1997; Skinner, 1998.
[3] Pettit points out, however, that he has "some small reservations about how Sen understands the notion of commitment." We have, in fact, discussed and argued about this point elsewhere (see Peter and Schmid, 2007), and I shall not go into this and related questions in this note.
[4] See particularly my Kenneth Arrow Lectures, included in Sen 2002: essays 20 ("Opportunities and Freedoms"), 21 ("Processes, Liberties and Rights"), and 22 ("Freedom and the Evaluation of Opportunity").

adequate understanding of freedom and through that, for the pursuit
of the idea of justice. The multifaceted view of freedom does not, of
course, preclude the case for our concentrating on some specific aspect
of freedom, in particular exercises such as the actual opportunities that
a person has (reflected, for example, in "capabilities") in extending the
reasoning behind Rawls's concentration on "primary goods." There
are other cases in which the neorepublican focus on the ultimate "control" may be just right.

So the neorepublican concentration on who can ultimately determine
what would emerge is both (1) *important* on its own as an illuminating exploration of one aspect of freedom, and (2) *inadequate* when it is
seen as the only aspect of freedom with which we need be concerned.
Since I do not have to convince Pettit on the first, I concentrate here
on the second part of that dual proposition. Consider the issue of religious freedom. Emperor Akbar, the Mughal emperor of India, insisted
on the religious freedom of everyone to pursue his or her own religious practice. His great grandson, Emperor Aurangzeb, did not offer
this opportunity to all and placed actual barriers, often through taxes
on non-Muslims, to the religious practice of people who did not share
his religious priorities. The people who enjoyed the liberty of religious
practice under Akbar had, I would argue, more freedom in an important sense than those who did not have that liberty under Aurangzeb.

However, it is obvious that neither Akbar's nor Aurangzeb's subjects
had freedom in the *neorepublican* sense. The non-Muslim Indians did not
control Akbar's decisions any more than they controlled Aurangzeb's.
My point is not that this is not a significant issue: it certainly is that. I
would vastly prefer that religious freedom be guaranteed through legal
provisions and enforceable rights, rather than being dependent on, as
in the case of Akbar, the tolerance and vision of a powerful emperor,
and I believe I have written fairly extensively on the need for guaranteed provisions. Nevertheless, I would also claim that the far-reaching
concept of freedom is not concerned *only* with that issue alone. Akbar's
non-Muslim subjects enjoyed religious freedom in an important sense
that Aurangzeb's non-Muslim subjects did not. The relevance of each
of these two concepts of freedom (and there are still others) deserves
recognition.[5] But neither precludes the relevance of the other.[6]

[5] See Sen (2002), especially essay 20.
[6] A theory of justice has to go, in fact, well beyond what we can get even by *combining*
substantive opportunities (such as capabilities) with the neorepublican concentration
on ultimate control. To illustrate, we cannot ignore the relevance of the freedoms
involved in "fair processes," as characterized, for example, in one part of the second
principle in the Rawlsian system of justice, which is concerned with making sure that

The aspect of freedom as substantive opportunity is particularly important in a world in which we cannot exercise control over everything that influences the choices and possibilities we actually enjoy. We may have to rely, to a great extent, on the police for law and order and for the freedom to go around without being bumped off, depend on public health authorities for freedom from preventable epidemics, and be thoroughly dependent on the airline pilot for the freedom to survive the flights we take (rather than trying to snatch the control of the aircraft with our own hands). What opportunities we *actually have*, through a cluster of social mechanisms, do make a difference to our being free to lead the kind of life we want and value.

Philip Pettit makes significant references to the importance of democratic control in this essay, and goes much more into related arguments in his second essay, "The power of a democratic public," in Part II of this volume. This emphasis is just right, and indeed important for neorepublican theory (there is certainly a strong connection there). And yet even with a fully operating democracy, no individual is free, as an individual, to control the entirety of the public circumstances that would affect individual lives. We may as a collectivity "control" what decisions a democracy would take (at least members of the majority are part of the group with effective leverage), but that is still not the same thing as each individual's having control over his or her life and liberties. Collective control is very important, but it is not the same thing as individual liberty.

Neorepublican theory presents an important perspective on freedom, which enriches and consolidates one aspect of that complex idea. It would be a great pity if the neorepublican theorists were to go on from that constructive contribution, to insist on denying the relevance of any concept of freedom other than their own (important as their own concept is). Freedom as an idea has a quintessential and inescapable heterogeneity within its capacious body.

Gift, reciprocity and dignity

I will not comment on Philip Pettit's interesting second paper in Part II (to which I made a passing reference above), since I have fairly

public opportunities are open to all (without anyone being excluded or handicapped on grounds of, say, race or ethnicity or caste or religion). Similarly, a theory of human rights cannot concentrate exclusively on capabilities, or only on controls, or only on particular demands of fair processes (on this see Sen 2004). It is very important to understand the inescapably heterogeneous features of what we can plausibly understand as freedom.

extensively engaged with the ideas in his other essay. Nor will I comment on Martha Nussbaum's critical assessment of the challenge of gender justice. I am largely in agreement with her insightful analyses and conclusions, and feel particularly happy that she has pointed constructively to additional issues, which have not received adequate attention at all, and on which "we must keep working away."

Nor will I comment particularly on Reiko Gotoh's essay on justice and reciprocity, to which I have already referred earlier on in this rejoinder, except to note that her analysis of public reciprocity, linked to policy making, connects closely with the epistemic investigation of gift relations (in contrast with market relations) in Marcel Hénaff's essay on "Gift, market and social justice." Indeed, Hénaff's analysis helps to clarify how Reiko Gotoh can plausibly expect to draw on reciprocity in making public policy recommendations. I appreciate the ideas and arguments presented by both of them, and their relevance for theories of justice in general, and for the use of the idea of capabilities in particular.

Hénaff ends with the very interesting claim that "from a normative point of view, what is at stake in capabilities is always the *dignity* of the agent." He points, importantly, to the need to recognize that "higher incomes, health, education, and gender equality are not ends in themselves but the confirmations of each person's humanness." While the diagnosis of the "instrumental" nature of material advantages is in line with the already established reasoning in the literature on capabilities, Hénaff goes further in making his strong interpretational claim on behalf of the reach of the idea of dignity. There can be, plausibly enough, arguments on this specific identification, but I have no doubt at all that the on-going work on capabilities – a field of work in which I am now only a very minor player – would benefit greatly from taking note of the line of reasoning presented by Marcel Hénaff.

Rights and intuitions

The essay by Prasanta Pattanaik and Yongsheng Xu is a very substantial – and most impressive – critical survey and evaluation of the conception of individual rights and freedom in welfare economics. It would be impossible to do justice to the paper in a brief note like this, especially given the broad coverage of their paper and the number of different issues on which they remark. I learned a great deal from this essay by Pattanaik and Xu, as I have done from their previous works. However, I do have, as it happens, some disagreement as well. While some of these differences have already been considered in earlier exchanges,[7] I would, nevertheless, make a few clarificatory observations here that, *inter alia*, will touch on some of our differences.

First, and this is an old disagreement, I do not think that in the social choice approach, the argument that person i's choice should be decisive for *some* differences in the so-called private domain of person i – other things the same – can be extended to cover *all* cases in which the difference is only in the private domain of i. The move from the existential quantifier to the universal one is indeed a big jump. And that jump is not, as they claim, "consistent with Sen's intuition" (p. 195). The specific circumstances of a case behind person i's choice in his own domain are surely relevant for the immunity that we may seek for that particular choice.

My original discussion of the issue in 1970 was not adequately clear on this point and could have left some ambiguities on this subject, but I have tried to clarify them in later writings. The *existence* of a case in which there is a very strong argument, based on liberty, for a person to end up getting what he wants in his own personal domain (like the right of a Sikh to wear a turban no matter what others want him to do), does not automatically entail that the person should have an unlimited right to do whatever he likes in his personal choices. Being free to wear, or not wear, a turban (other things being the same) may be socially important under these circumstances, but that does not entail that the same person should be completely free to wear a Nazi uniform – other things the same – in a gathering of holocaust survivors. There is more to discuss other than the automatic and immediate translation from the existential to the universal that Pattanaik and Xu seem to recommend. The existence of one such protected choice, depending on the case, may indeed be socially persuasive in a way that privileging all choices of an apparently personal nature may not be.[8]

Second, Pattanaik and Xu's evident sympathy for the *action-oriented* way of understanding issues of liberty is so strong, that even when they are trying to illustrate an *outcome-oriented* understanding of rights, they do this in terms of actions rather than outcomes, for example when they

---

[7] Particularly in Gaertner, Pattanaik and Suzumura (1992) and Sen (1992).

[8] Further, there may well be a case for drawing a line when person i makes her choices on purely other-regarding grounds ("whatever annoys her most"). Not drawing that line can be seen as a factor behind the so-called Gibbard paradox, see Gibbard (1974). Such cases can arise easily enough, once the universal quantifier replaces the existential quantifier. But with the existential quantifier, we do not allow, for analytical reasons that are easily checked, much room for doggedly other-regarding choices in one's personal domain.

say: "the very interpretation of a group decision rule as the choices to be made by a social planner or ethical observer from alternative sets of outcomes, given the individual preferences, seems to run counter to the intuitive core of a wide class of individual rights" (p. 196). The outcome-oriented view does not line up some grand "social planner" to undertake some unilaterally irresistible action, but judges the success or failure of an outcome-oriented right through the working of the multitude of institutions and social mechanisms through which the fulfillment of the sought-after outcome does – or does not – come about.

In thinking, for example, about the outcome-oriented right of a non-smoker not to end up inhaling a lot of cigarette smoke through the smoking of others, we have to see the actual effectiveness of various alternative laws and requirements (e.g. "not to smoke when others object," "not to smoke when others are present," "not to smoke at a public place where others could choose, otherwise, to be present," and so on). The focus is on what outcomes emerge, in terms of which this particular right is formulated (I would say very plausibly so), rather than telling some all-powerful "social planner" to undertake some predetermined action.[9]

Third, there may be some problem in Pattanaik and Xu's interpretation that "possible conflicts between individual rights and the Pareto efficiency of social outcomes constitute the central theme pursued in contributions on individual rights in welfare economics" (p. 216). The possible conflict between the Pareto principle and a plausible understanding of some liberty is, I think, interesting to bring out, and I did write a paper published in 1970 on the possibility of that conflict under one interpretation of individual rights.[10] For this it was not necessary to presume that all rights and liberties must be characterized in those terms. Nor has that assumption been made in the rather large literature my paper generated, and the further contributions were concerned mostly with the conflict between Pareto and liberty – extending, disputing, or making proposals to ameliorate the conflict. If some rights can take this form and thereby be in conflict with the Pareto principle, then that is adequate for the purpose of the exercise; there is no claim here that all rights must take this form.

And welfare economics, surely, has other concerns as well, some of which are best specified in outcome-oriented terms and others in other ways. That is not only true of the writings of the classic leader of thought in this field, to wit John Stuart Mill, it is even true of my own

---

[9] I did try to discuss this distinction in Sen (1992).
[10] See Sen (1970).

little writings – other than those concerned specifically with the conflict between the Pareto principle and some plausible formulation of rights – making use of a broad welfare-economic approach.[11]

Despite these disagreements, the Pattanaik–Xu contribution is, I think, a hugely important critical survey from which the reader, like me, will benefit. If there is one issue that I would like Pattanaik and Xu to engage with more, it is the status of *intuitions* in their evaluations of different formulations. We do certainly benefit from examining whether some formulations "are consistent with our intuition about rights and freedom" (p. 187). That is a good question to ask, but what if they are not consistent? Must all reasoning that underlies that particular formulation be, then, abandoned whenever it runs into conflict with our pre-existing intuitions about rights and freedoms?

The disciplines of moral and political philosophy have long histories of subjecting antecedent intuitions to critical scrutiny, rather than taking a quintessentially "intuitionist" approach. In undertaking such critical scrutiny, conflicts of various kinds often play an important role in generating further arguments. Even social choice theory has used this technique of re-examination on the basis of identification of inconsistency with other concerns and formulations (for example in checking whether binariness is a desirable characteristic of social choice functions, or for that matter of an individual choice function). Pattanaik and Xu's analyses bring us closer to such further examination, but we have to proceed further at some stage or other. It is important to remember that while intuitions typically are good starting points, they need not be convincing end points.

The meaning of "preference"

Finally, I comment briefly on John Broome's paper, "Reasoning with Preferences." I think this is an extremely important inquiry, and one that John Broome is ideally suited to undertake given his past work. Since Broome identifies my own position very well ("there is a case for thinking that the rational requirements on preferences, if they truly exist, derive from logical relations among propositions about betterness"), he would understand why I am particularly interested in the investigation with which his paper is concerned. Even though one of the conclusions to emerge from Broome's analysis is, plausibly enough, "that it is hard to distinguish the functional roles of a preference and a belief about goodness," there is a difference between the two in that

---

[11] See, for example, Sen (1999); (2002); and (2006).

"contents of beliefs" are "propositions," which "stand in logical relations to each other" (as Broome points out). I am delighted that John Broome is pursuing the implications of these distinctions in a definitive way.

On a different matter, I am not sure to what extent Broome and I disagree – indeed *still* disagree – about the under-characterized nature of what a preference is meant to be. One sense of a preference is certainly, as Broome suspects, "nothing other than a belief about goodness." But there are other senses, for example the binary relation that represents the actual choices of a person (if the choices have enough internal correspondence to allow such a binary characterization). Some economists have made use of another sense, with perhaps less justification, to wit, that preference is the binary relation over alternatives judged in terms of the person's self-interest. There are other senses still.

Even though Broome seems to proceed as if there is some agreed sense of what we understand by "preference," there are in fact several different senses – all of which are in use – that compete with each other as the right interpretation of the term "preference." These senses are not unrelated to each other, but they are not the same. The term has some problems of ambiguity in common with other multiple-meaning terms, such as being "mad": that can mean *insane*, but also, especially in American usage, *angry*, which is a distinct sense, even though the two meanings are not independent of each other – being almost insane with anger is an idea that links the two. Because of this plurality of meanings, it is perfectly possible for us to follow an apparently nonsensical statement like: "I am mad that she goes on saying, quite falsely, that I am mad." Similarly: "I can easily see that you do prefer this, but if you take the trouble of thinking about it carefully, this is not what you do prefer."

There is, I would argue, no unique sense of the term "preference," defined by uniform usage, and some clarification is needed on that front too, along with the kind of substantive and serious epistemic and analytical analysis in which John Broome engages with such rigor and reach. "Reasoning with preferences" has to shoot out some of these interpretational ambiguities even as it pursues the really interesting substantive issues with which John Broome's highly illuminating paper is integrally concerned.

I end this note by thanking again the editors and the authors who have made this book as interesting as it has turned out to be. We are intellectually richer because of the imaginative initiative of Reiko Gotoh and her colleagues at the Ritsumeikan University.

References

Gaertner, Wulf, Pattanaik, Prasanta K. and Suzumura, Kotaro 1992. "Individual Rights Revisited," *Economica*, **59**: 161–77.

Gibbard, A. 1974. "A Pareto-consistent Libertarian Claim," *Journal of Economic Theory*, 7: 388–410.

Peter, F. and Schmid, H. B., eds. 2007. *Rationality and Commitment*, Oxford University Press.

Pettit, P. 1997. *Republicanism: A Theory of Freedom and Government*, Oxford University Press.

Sen, A. K. 1970. "The Impossibility of a Paretian Liberal," *Journal of Political Economy*, **78**: 152–7.

1992. "Minimal Liberty," *Economica*, **59**: 139–59.

1999. *Development as Freedom*, New York: Knopf.

2002. *Rationality and Freedom*, Cambridge, MA: Harvard University Press.

2004. "Elements of a Theory of Human Rights," *Philosophy and Public Affairs*, **32**: 315–56.

2006. "What Do We Want from a Theory of Justice?" *Journal of Philosophy*, **103**: 215–38.

Skinner, Q. 1998. *Liberty before Liberalism*, Cambridge University Press.

Index

AB (action-based) formulations,
    191–2
  of individual rights, 200–9
abortion, *see* sex-selective abortion
Achilles and the Tortoise, 79, 173
active rights, 189
actors (theatre), and contracts, 98
'additional provision', 143
adverse selection, 64
'against injustice', meaning of phrase, 1
Agarwal, Bina, 99
Agenda 21., 275
aggregative strategy (for
    multidimensional study), 225–6
Akerlof, George A., 118–21
alternative economics, Sen's perspective
    on, 11–16
'ambassadors of peace' *(TIM Música nas
    Escolas* project), 255
Anand, S., 236
Argonauts of the Western Pacific (Bronislav
    Malinowski), 114
argument, public discourse, 81–2
Arrow, Kenneth, 4–5
Atkinson, A. B., 225, 231, 234, 236

Barry, Brian, 108
Basic Capability Condition, 14
basic capability, definitions, 12
Becker, Gary, 40, 42, 66, 105, 285
behaviour, of children during TIM
    project, 262
Bennett, Jonathan, 168–9
Berlin, I., 134, 190
Best, Elsdon, 115–16
Blacking, John, 256–7
Bloom, Allan, 98
Boas, Franz, 115, 117
Bourguignon, F., 225, 233
Bradley, Justice, 98–9
Bradwell, Myra, 98–9
Brandolini, A., 230

Brazil, *see TIM Música nas Escolas*
    project
Broome, John, 307–8
Brown v. Board of Education (1954), 102
Browning, Robert, 182

Camerer, Colin F., 121–3
capabilities approach
  ceremonial gift-giving, 133–5
capability approach, 11, 25, 30, 141, 221,
    see also capabilities approach
  and freedom, 209
  and sustainable development, 32–3,
    276, 277, 281, 286–7
  assessing children, 32, 252, 259, 267
  assessing social programmes, 272–4
  compared to market prices as weights,
    231
  constructing a summary composite
    indicator of well-being, 222, 225–6
  to well-being society, 144–9
capability, definitions, 12
Carr, Mary, 103–4, 105
Carroll, Lewis, 79, 173
ceremonial exchange, 24–5
ceremonial gift-giving
  Akerlof on gift exchange, 118–21
  capabilities approach, 133–5
  definitions, 113
  interpretations within economic
    theory, 117–18
  Marcel Mauss on, 114–17
  public reciprocal recognition today,
    130–2
  rethinking of, 124–30
Cerioli, A., 230
Chakravarty, S. R., 225, 233
Chicago school, 104
children, *see also TIM Música nas Escolas*
    project
  capability approach assessment of, 32,
    252–3, 259, 267